The Social Shaping of Information Superhighways

Herbert Kubicek is Professor of Applied Computer Science, Head of Telecommunications Research Group, University of Bremen, Member of the Enquete-Committee »The Future of the Media in the Economy and the Society. Germany's Path into the Information Society« of the German Federal Parliament.

William H. Dutton is Professor of Political Science, Annenberg School of Communications, University of Southern California, Los Angeles, and a former Director of the major UK research programme on the social and economic implications of information and communications technologies PICT.

Robin Williams is Director of the Social Science Research Programme, University of Edinburgh, Vice-Chairman of the Committee »Social Shaping of Technology« within the European COST-Programme and Head of an European research consortium on social learning in multimedia.

Herbert Kubicek, William H. Dutton,
Robin Williams (editors)

The Social Shaping of Information Superhighways

European and American Roads
to the Information Society

Campus Verlag · Frankfurt/New York
St. Martin's Press · New York

First published in the United States of America in 1997
Printed in Germany
   ISBN 0-312-16569-2

Library of Congress Cataloging-in-Publication Data

The social shaping of information superhighways: European and American roads to the
information society / Herbert Kubicek. William H. Dutton. Robin Williams (editors).
   p. cm.
   „Originated at an international conference entitled 'The social Shaping
of Information Higways: Comparing the NII and the EU Action
Plan' that was held in October, 1995 in Bremen. Germany" -- Pref.
   Includes Bibliographical references.
   ISBN 0-312-16569-2 (cloth)
   1. Telematics -- Europe -- Social aspects. 2. Telematics -- United States -- Social aspects.
   3. Information superhighway -- Social aspects. I. Kubicek, Herbert 1946 -,
   II. Dutton, William H., 1947- III. Williams, Robin, Dr.
   TK5105.6. S63 1997
   306. 4'6 -- dc21

Gefördert von der Volkswagen-Stiftung und der Europäischen Kommission.

Die Deutsche Bibliothek – CIP-Einheitsaufnahme

The Social Shaping of Information Superhighways: European and American Roads
to the Information Society / Herbert Kubicek; William H. Dutton; Robin Williams (eds.) –
Frankfurt/Main: Campus Verlag; New York: St. Martin's Press, 1997
   ISBN 3-593-35739-9 (Campus Verlag)
   ISBN 0-312-16569-2 (St. Martin's Press)
NE: Kubicek, H. [Hrsg.]

Preface

Cross-national approaches to the information infrastructures of the twenty-first century - information superhighways - provide a vital perspective on the ways in which social factors shape technological change in one of the most dynamic areas of contemporary policy and practice. This book seeks to illuminate the social basis of the information superhighway by comparing approaches of the United States and the European Union.

The chapters originated at an international conference entitled 'The Social Shaping of Information Highways: Comparing the NII and the EU Action Plan' that was held in October 1995 in Bremen, Germany. This conference emerged as an activity of COST/A4, a European network of social scientists interested in the social shaping of technology. With support by COST (co-operation on of scientific and technical research and the European Commission (DG XIII) and a grant by the Volkswagen Foundation it was possible to bring together more than 30 acknowledged experts from the academia, administrations and industry of eight countries. A selected set of the conference papers are published here. All have been substantially revised and up-dated for this volume.

We thank the Commission, our colleagues in COST/A4, and the Volkswagen Foundation as well as the contributors to the conference and to this volume for their support. We are especially grateful to Dr. Maggie Tierney at the University of Edinburgh and Ulrich Horst, Anette Harasimowitsch and Anne Bausch at the University of Bremen for helping us to make this collection of papers more accessible to an international audience concerned about how national and regional cultures, politics, and societies will find expression in the emerging infrastructure of the new information societies.

Herbert Kubicek   William H. Dutton   Robin Williams

Contents

1. The Social Shaping of Information Superhighways: An Introduction

Herbert Kubicek and William H. Dutton

The Information Superhighway

Information and communication technologies (ICTs) have raised high expectations since the earliest days of the computer. There was a computer revolution, a microelectronics revolution, a telematics revolution — in literature and in policy documents — expected to change economies, cultures, and society as a whole.

In the early 1970s, futurists saw ICTs as one basis for a shift from an industrial to a post-industrial, or information society (Bell 1973). It was compared to earlier change from agricultural to industrial societies in the most developed nations of the world. Yet as late as the 1980s, when networks were available, at least from a technical standpoint, to connect every factory, office and home, the public's interest in participating in this revolution was limited. Nor were major companies ready to invest in emerging technologies outside of the business sector. Even in this sector, investments were focused on basic voice and data communication networks.

For the most part, these revolutionary expectations failed to capture the public's imagination. The social and economic implications of computing and telecommunications also failed to interest the media or become an issue in election campaigns. Despite the promise of economic growth and jobs, the topic was considered to be a technical issue for the experts that was impossible to communicate to a broader public.

This conventional wisdom changed in the aftermath of the 1992 elections. Governor Bill Clinton and Senator Al Gore ran a successful presidential campaign, that featured support for the development of a new telecommunication infrastructure — an information superhighway. Al Gore had championed the development of a high-capacity computer network in the US Senate with some success (Gore 1991). But as Vice President, in December 1993, he was able to stand before the National Press Club to explain what he meant by a new information infrastructure to a far broader audience. He said: "Today, commerce rolls not just on asphalt highways but along information highways" (Gore 1993:19). The Vice President had succeeded in introducing a metaphor that would be picked up all over the world.

European governments reacted to the enthusiasm surrounding the ISH in the US by picking up the issues of modernizing telecommunication infrastructures and introducing their own programmes and metaphors. For the most part, they were reluctant to adopt the highway metaphor. The European Commission, for example, preferred to speak of approaches to the Information Society. Representatives of the German government preferred Multimedia. By the late-1990s, American politicians and futurists also began searching for new terms to hold the public's attention. Yet the idea of an ISH was important to all.

This chapter sketches the career of this metaphor of the Information Superhighway and puts it into the context of technological and economic developments in Europe and North America. It also reviews some of the key technical and policy issues tied to the ISH both to provide a background to the chapters that follow and to illustrate the role of social and cultural factors in shaping technology and policy.

The final shape of the world's information infrastructures as well as their dominant uses will depend on social factors, including the economic and cultural foundations of the ISH. This theme runs through all the following chapters which go deeper into particular aspects of ISH developments in particular nations and regions. General issues of the social shaping of technology are taken up again in the last section of this book, which looks at theoretical perspectives on the Social Shaping of Technology (SST) and the ISH in particular.

The Power of a Metaphor

Computer and telecommunications policy involves so many interconnected legal, economic, and technical details that it seldom generates media attention, nor does it interest the public. In Europe, for instance, plans to create trans-European ICT networks in the 1980s, which in many respects were forerunners of the information superhighway concept, created relatively little popular awareness (Mackintosh 1986; Mansell 1993). In the UK, the Government nominated Kenneth Baker as Minister for Industry and Information Technology in 1979 and made 1982 the Year of Information Technology, launching a public awareness campaign, but with few lasting effects (Baker 1982). In contrast, the Clinton Administration's promotion of their information superhighway vision stimulated a tremendous amount of press coverage — thousands of articles and stories — and broad public interest.

One reason for this impact is the metaphor itself. The 'information superhighway' evoked a powerful image, which crystallized many issues surrounding telecommunications infrastructures into a simple concept that could be readily understood by non-specialists. The popularizing effect was reinforced by the subsequent growth in worldwide popularity of the Internet, which gave the mass media a tangible peg on which to hang stories about what the superhighway means in practice.

Nevertheless, the metaphor leaves many asking for a more precise definition. Yet the success of this term, is due in part to its ambiguity, which allows each group to draw its own interpretation (Dutton et al. 1994, p. 5, Helmers, Hoffmann and Canzler 1995, Kleinsteuber 1996).

Leitbild-Dialogues

In the early stages of developing support for new technologies, proponents must communicate the potential of their ideas, well before anyone can actually know or demonstrate the outcome. Social science research on technology speaks of Leitbild-dialogues. A Leitbild is a German word for a vision or a paradigm, such as the paper less office, the automated shop floor, the factory of the future, or self-generating energy. It must be general in order to attract the interest of a variety of actors and mobilize the resources necessary to work out detailed plans and products (Dierkes, Hoffmann, and Marz 1992).

Given such abstract beginnings, it is not arbitrary which interpretations are offered and which are eventually picked up by politicians and the media. Definitions of a concept evolve over time through a social process that creates a shared definition. The frequent repetition and use of the concept allows it to become well-known and, finally, self-evident, or 'natural'.

Evolving definitions can direct activities in technological development, the design of pilot projects, and the creation of an appropriate legal and regulatory environment. For example, it makes a huge difference if the ISH becomes defined as the modernization of cable, satellite, or telephone systems, as opposed to the next generation of the Internet. Therefore it is important for major stakeholders, including the public, to know what interpretations are emerging from discussions and perhaps to add their own views on how the ISH should be defined.

Origins of the Metaphor

The creation of the term 'information superhighway' is attributed to U.S. Vice President Al Gore, who used it to describe what is officially called the National Information Infrastructure (NII).[1] In December 1993, Al Gore explained to the press what in his view the NII has in common with a highway system:

> One helpful way is to think of the National Information Infrastructure as a network of highways much like the Interstates begun in the 1950s. These are highways carrying information rather than people or goods. And I'm not talking about just one eight-lane turnpike. I mean a collection of Interstates and feeder roads made up of different materials in the same ways that roads can be concrete or macadam — or gravel. Some highways will be made up of fiber optics. Others will be built of coaxial or wireless. But — a key point — they must be and will be two way roads.[2]

The Vice President argued that these highways needed to support 'wide loads' — in terms of their speed or bandwidth — and be seamlessly interconnected. Television programs and other motion video require far more bits of information to convey than do plain old telephone conversations and all forms of text, voice, data, and video communications should be accom-

---

1 The metaphor of an information highway was used in discussions of interactive cable television systems in the late 1960s (see Dutton, Blumler, and Kraemer 1987: 3-26; as well as Chapter 8 in this book).
2 For the full text of this speech, see http://www.hpcc.gov./white-house/gore.nii.html

modated by an ISH that can transport them from anywhere to anywhere — in both directions.

This vision of a universal infrastructure that will permit anyone to get information from anywhere at any time, unless an individual user chooses to prohibit access, embodies a commitment to individual freedom and choice that makes the ISH attractive to many public interest groups. Until the 1990s, computer networks were used mainly by university researchers and major companies. The general public had access to telephone and broadcasting networks, including cable and satellite TV in many locales. However, most cable and broadcast satellite systems were built to distribute television programming in one direction to many people. The telephone network offers two-way communication, but it is optimized for carrying ordinary voice conversations between individuals. Computer networks like the Internet provide the potential for the same network to support one-to-one, one-to-many, and many-to-many systems for communicating any kind of information.

The Social Basis for the Highway Analogy

The almost uniformly positive adoption of the highway metaphor in the US is anchored in the particular history and meaning of America's Interstate Highway System. As the National Geographic Society (1994: 6, quoted by Klein-steuber 1996: 24) put it:

> Nothing speaks America like The Road — symbol of freedom and the pioneer spirit, celebration of democracy and individuality. Long before the automobile, Americans were obsessed with what lay beyond the horizon, placed trails across the landscape, built railroad tracks through the Western wilderness. When the motorcar rolled onto the scene, they embraced it as a pleasure machine that freed them to discover the country on their own steam.

The Interstate Highway System was built in the 1950s as one of few major national projects in the US in which federal and state governments as well as private business cooperated in pursuing the same goal. At that time, there were regional highways, with different shapes and signs. The Interstate introduced standardization of a network of these local highway networks. Justified originally as an infrastructure of value to the nation's defense, Americans have routinely experienced its usefulness in their day-to-day lives.

Considering the general scepticism Americans have shown towards big federal projects, the Interstate is an exceptional case in which federal action was widely appreciated. Senator Gore's father was one of the leading figures in the Interstate Highway Project, when he was a US Senator. Decades later, Senator Al Gore, Jr. could stand on his father's shoulders to propose his own plan for a national information infrastructure. In stark contrast, one of the leading figures in the establishment of the German Autobahn was Adolf Hitler, a legacy that makes the metaphor of an ISH not just less positive, but politically sensitive in the context of Germany.

The success of this metaphor in the US setting and elsewhere is also due to many parallels between the Internet, for example, and a highway system. For example, one technical feature of the Internet is a reliance on packet-switching instead of circuit-switching. If real highways followed the principle of circuit switching, once a driver began a journey, a whole lane up to the final destination would be kept free for this car, much as a railroad train relies on one track that is switched to its destination. In contrast, with packet-switching, the information to be transmitted is disassembled into packets of a certain size. These packets are sent into the network where they may take different routes until they reach their destination, at which they are reassembled. Data packets are less analogous to trains than to cars traveling driving on every lane of a multi-lane highway system, that take individual routes, but unload their passengers at the final destination at which they are reassembled.

While other data communication networks are built according to proprietary technical standards and optimized for certain applications, the Internet, which is a network of networks, allows for more universality. Just as there are no separate highways for trucks, busses, slow cars, and fast cars, there is only one Internet protocol, called the Transmission Control Protocol/Internet Protocol (TCP/IP), governing all kinds of traffic. The use of this standard minimizes dependence on the physical transmission medium (copper, fiber optic, wireless), the type of application or service provided, and the operating systems of the computers that are connected over the network.

Electronic mail (e-mail) and the World Wide Web are examples of 'enhanced services' that can be provided over the Internet. The functionality and control of these services resides in the user's software. The network is confined to routing the packets of data, irrespective of their content.

This concept of anything-anywhere-anytime feeds a common misunderstanding that the Internet is chaotic and unregulated. To the contrary, the Internet, in order to provide for optimum flexibility in transportation, imposes a rigid management of standard technical protocols and routing systems, including the addresses of Internet Providers. That said, this technical regulation, not content regulation - is completely independent of the application area and the content of the communication, permitting it to retain its democratic connotations.

One objection to the highway analogy is the reliance of the highway system on public funding as opposed to private investment. The ISH would generate less support if perceived as a big public works project. Therefore, the ISH is expected to be far too expensive to depend on public funds, and private telephone companies as well as other would be providers do not wish to encourage public ownership or regulation.

Nevertheless, for most of its existence, the Internet has been heavily subsidized by government funding. Internet access is paid for by users, according to different tariff structures. However, public funding has continued to be the mainstay of the Internet. Public-private forms of financing the backbone of this network of networks began to emerge only since the mid-1990s.

Many other parallels can be drawn between information superhighways and highways, but not all are positive. For example, the US Interstate contributed to the demise of the railroads, to urban sprawl, and to the explosion of automobile traffic, which has polluted the air and resulted in thousands of fatalities. While electronic communication will have unintended consequences also, for example with regard to privacy or industrial relations, ISH proponents have been quick to argue that electronic highways can substitute for travel and mitigate many undesirable consequences of our dependence on transportation of people, goods, and services.

Information Infrastructure Initiatives in the United States[3]

Strong leadership from the White House was one reason for the positive reaction to the NII in the United States. Not only did the President and Vice
President provide a vision of the social and economic importance of new telecommunication infrastructures, but they also supported this vision by creating
a policy agenda to move it forward. Within only a few months after the inau-
guration, President Bill Clinton and Vice President Al Gore set up a high-
level Information Infrastructure Task Force (IITF), chaired by the Secretary
of Commerce, the late Ronald H. Brown, to coordinate the Federal Govern-
ment´s activities, and an Advisory Council to involve the private sector more
directly in this process. In September 1993, the IITF presented the vision
statement for the NII-initiative, the *Agenda for Action* (IITF 1993).

In this *Agenda for Action*, the IITF defined the NII in a very broad sense
to include, not only the software, hardware, and physical facilities required
for a 'seamless, interactive, user-driven network', but also the information,
applications, people, and policies, such as with respect to standards and security, that would be integral components of this system. The Administration
promised to promote and support full development of each of these components, and not only in the realm of national telecommunications policy and
regulation. More broadly, it noted that the Federal government:

> ... will assist industry, labor, academia, and state and local governments in
> developing information resources and applications needed to maximize the
> potential of those underlying facilities....(and) will help educate and train
> our people so that they are prepared not only to contribute to the further
> growth of the NII, but also to understand and enjoy fully the services and
> capabilities that it will make available (IITF 1993: 6).

The Administration's ambitions were guided by a broad set of objectives,
which included the promotion of:

- private investment
- innovation in the underlying technologies and their applications
- security of information
- technical reliability

---

3 For comprehensive overviews of the US NII-Initiative, see Drake (1995) and Kahin and
   Wilson (1996).

- access to this network at affordable prices — 'universal service'
- access to government information
- privacy of personal information about users
- protection of intellectual property rights (IITF 1993: 6).

The government promised to work with other levels of government and with other nations to accomplish these objectives. Given this broad range of tasks, the IITF created an elaborate management structure to coordinate the work of numerous committees in which representatives of almost all relevant departments and governmental organizations were represented.

One year after the publication of the vision statement, the IITF was able to present a progress report that demonstrated the broad involvement of many governmental agencies (IITF 1994*a*). The Committee on Applications and Technology, hosted by the National Institute of Standards and Technology (NIST), published two related reports in that year (IITF 1994*b*, 1994*c*), covering a wide range of applications in such areas as manufacturing, electronic commerce, health care, education, environmental monitoring, libraries, public service delivery, transportation, emergency management, the arts, humanities, and public safety.

To involve the private sector the Administration convened a United States Advisory Council on The National Information Infrastructure, consisting of 25 members with nominations solicited by a variety of constituencies and interested parties. The Council was chaired by the President of National Public Radio and the Chairman of Silicon Graphics, and included representatives from different relevant industries, state governments, and trade unions. The Council presented a series of reports that stressed the broad societal goal of access for everybody, presenting statistics and successful cases from the areas of schools and libraries, and recommending concrete measures for connecting public institutions (Advisory Council 1995, 1996a, 1996b).

The *Agenda for Action* promised to devise ways to solicit public comment, ensure that all views are heard, and that all documents are made available as soon as possible. In line with this, the National Telecommunications and Information Administration (NTIA) created a site in the World Wide Web containing relevant documents and a virtual NII Library. There were inquiries, public hearings, and other activities aimed at involving the public, such as NetDays that encouraged individuals to volunteer to help wire the public schools for Internet access (see chapters 10 and 13).

Reactions in Europe

European governments and the European Commission were surprised by the enthusiastic responses to NII initiatives. Many had championed similar visions and programmes for trans-European networks during the seventies and eighties that generated comparatively little public enthusiasm.

There were variations in public reactions across the sixteen member states of the European Union, but nowhere in Europe did the public become as engaged as in the US. A sense of the European reaction can be gained from a focus on the European Commission and two countries that provide contrasting examples: the United Kingdom and Germany.[4]

The European Commission

The European Commission's (1993) White Paper on *Growth, Competitiveness and Employment* stressed the importance of transnational networks for railroads, energy, and telecommunications as important factors for the common market, and for the global competitiveness of European enterprises. The paper emphasized the significance of a coherent information infrastructure for the development of new markets and jobs within the emerging information society. Based on the White Paper, the European Council asked a group of high-level experts from industry under the leadership of Commissioner Martin Bangemann, a former minister of economics in the government of the Federal Republic of Germany and head of the Free Democratic Party (FDP), to report on the subject of the information society and to suggest immediate measures for the EU — a type of European agenda for action. This report with the title *Europe and the Global Information Society: Recommendations to the European Council*, which became known as the 'Bangemann Report', was presented to the Council at its meeting in Korfu (Bangemann Group 1994).

The Bangemann Report stressed the need for community action in order to keep and make European enterprises competitive in global markets. The report recommended the full liberalization of all telecommunications, and related

---

4 Bekkers, Koop and Nouwt (1996) provide an overview of developments in the Netherlands, while Graham (1996), Riis (1996), and Vedel (1996) discuss developments in the United Kingdom, Denmark, and France, respectively.

markets, and suggested ten areas for pilot applications in order to demonstrate the benefits of the information society to business, and the public at large (see Chapter 3).

Following this report, the Commission published its own action plan, which recommended actions in the following areas: regulatory, and legal frameworks; the promotion of networks, services, and applications; societal, and cultural aspects; and a variety of promotion activities (European Commission 1994). Suggestions for telecommunication policy and regulatory reforms were the most concrete recommendations, calling for moves to create a more competitive environment, such as by relaxing restrictions on media ownership, creating standards, supporting interconnection and interoperability across Europe, harmonizing tariffs, protecting intellectual property rights, ensuring personal privacy, and guarding the security of networks, and services.

The plan capitalized some ongoing activities of the Commission, but also added new ones. Representatives of the Commission, such as Martin Bangemann, stressed that their decision not to adopt the notion of the 'information superhighway' was deliberate (see Chapter 3). They chose instead to pursue the development of a European Information Society. As Commissioner Bangemann put it at a conference in London:

> ... the 'information superhighway' metaphor was deliberately avoided because it indicates only the infrastructure, which is just one part of the whole system ... and maybe not the most important one ... The notion of a European information society comes closer than the information superhighway metaphor in reflecting the Commission´s belief that the political and social consequences of using modern ICTs go far beyond just economic or technical reforms. These innovations are changing societies as a whole ... the way in which we live, learn, and work (Bangemann 1995).

Commission documents since the Bangemann Report have been written often with a narrower, more technical definition. For example, in speaking of the 'introduction of the information society,' the 'construction of an information society,' or that 'the information society shall be used to make information accessible', it suggests that the concept is being used as a substitute for a technical definition of an information infrastructure. Moreover, the information society is not described in detail, except for references to the importance of ICTs, information markets, and the information sector as a source of employment.

In contrast, in many US NII documents, the concept of an information infrastructure is claimed to be much more than the telecommunications infrastructure. But if President Clinton had campaigned for an 'information society,' it would have inevitably raised the specter of Lyndon Johnson's Great Society, or other liberal visions of government programs that have been avoided by nearly all American politicians of the nineties.

Within the European Commission, Martin Bangeman continued to lead the promotion of activities as Commissioner for Industrial Affairs, Information Technology and Telecommunications, with his cabinet, and the corresponding departments (Directorate General) DG III and DG XIII. However, various departments responsible for competition, for regional development and cohesion, and for labour, among others, launched their own initiatives.

In order to promote public awareness, the Commission created the Information Society Project Office (ISPO) as a 'one-stop-shop' for all kinds of information related to the Information Society.[5] In addition, the Commission set up an 'Information Society Forum' in July 1995. As a 'think-tank' for the Commission, its aim was 'to offer representatives from a wide variety of different groups an opportunity to contribute to an open discussion about the social aspects of the information society'.[6]

The Forum contains 124 members, proposed by the member state governments, and is chaired by leading figures in telecommunications, broadcasting, and consumer affairs. Working groups were set up on such topics as: impacts on the economy and employment; social and democratic values in electronic communities; electronic service delivery in the public sector; changes in education, training, and learning; cultural implications and the future of the media; and sustainable development.

The Forum presented its first annual report with the title *Networks for People and their Communities*. (Forum Information Society 1996) In addition, Commissioner Padraig Flynn, responsible for employment and social affairs, nominated a Group of High-Level Experts for Social and Societal Aspects of the Information Society, mainly from academia, who submitted

---

5   ISPO Information Package and www server (http://www.ispo.cec.be).
6   Quoted from "Information Society Forum: The Current State of Play". In: IT Magazine, News Review, No. 18, Oct./Nov. 1995, p. 2.

their interim report on *A European Information Society for All* in January 1996 (European Commission 1996*a*). In July 1996, the corresponding Directorate General, DG V, submitted a draft for a Greenbook addressing two of the topics of this report, employment and social cohesion (European Commission 1996*b*).

In a review of the original Action Plan, written two years before, the European Commission (1996*c*) emphasized four areas of particular priority: 1) improving the economic environment for the application of ICTs, 2) supporting investment in the future, such as in research and education, announcing an action plan 'learning in the information society', 3) putting people first, such as improving citizen access to services and protecting consumer interests, and 4) meeting the global challenge, such as to pursuing negotiations at the World Trade Organization (WTO), that include the developing nations in the information society.

These new priorities have been integrated into a Rolling Action Plan, which is essentially a list, that is continually updated, of all important measures required to further 'implement the information society'. The first version mentioned more than one hundred actions!

The United Kingdom

Differences of opinion exist about the effectiveness of the UK's approach to 'information superhighway' and 'information society' policies, which principally revolve around the most appropriate role for government.[7] One strongly-held critical perception is that too much time, energy, and resources had been devoted in the 1980s and early 1990s to a relatively narrow range of regulatory issues, such as the timing of BT's entry into entertainment provision in the UK, when there is so much more at stake in the development of new telecommunication infrastructures. A contrasting view is that the Conservative government, which had been in power since 1979, had achieved a similar outcome to that sought by the NII and EU information society programmes, albeit by a more piecemeal strategy based on regulated competition.

---

7   UK policy developments and differing evaluations of their effectiveness are examined in
    more detail in Dutton, Blumler *et al.* (1994: 18-22).

In the 1970s, the main technological vision in the UK had been built around the image of the 'micro chip' and Silicon Valley in California. This technology was emphasized in a BBC Television programme 'When the Chips are Down' in 1978 that triggered a widespread debate on employment and other implications of the microelectronics revolution. The momentum created by the 'micro-chip' debate was an important factor for the Government giving a high priority to policies promoting IT production, such as sponsoring an IT awareness campaign in 1982, and funding many IT applications, technology development, and research initiatives, including the Programme on Information and Communication Technologies (PICT), which sought to conduct research on the long-term social and economic implications of ICTs.

However, the Conservatives' general policy, particularly since the government of Margaret Thatcher, was to move away from public-led to market-led development of ICTs as well as other technologies and industries (CCTA 1994). This was the dominant force which motivated a series of policy decisions that reshaped the UK telecommunications environment, for example, by privatizing BT and introducing competition into many areas of telecommunications provision. The two-wired model of network connections into the home was encouraged by preventing BT and other PTOs from competing directly with cable TV suppliers in the carrying of entertainment services, which gave an investment incentive to the cable companies that helped their networks to expand in the mid-1990s and created competing infrastructures for the provision of telephone as well as video services.[8] Supporters of the government's ICT policies point to a survey (Harrison 1994) which found that the UK's overall telecommunications infrastructure compared favourably with those of other leading industrialized countries.

This perspective has been challenged. For instance, the degree to which regulatory controls on their own can facilitate user innovation is questioned by those who argue that determined UK leadership in encouraging telecommunications competition has not been reflected in practical innovations — particularly in public services where Britain lagged behind countries like the

---

8 Key reports which supported these decisions on telecommunications policy included ITAP (1982) and DTI (1988). A 1991 Government White Paper (DTI 1991) maintained the entertainment restrictions on PTOs until 2001, with the possibility of review in 1998.

USA (Mansell 1996). The cross-party House of Commons Trade and Industry Select Committee (1994) claimed that the entertainment restrictions on PTOs could damage Britain's international competitiveness by preventing BT from gaining experience in the mass provision of broadband services, and limiting customer choice in the long run by creating entrenched local monopolies in some areas, and inadequate services in others.[9]

The way a popular vision can move technology policy up the political agenda was demonstrated when Tony Blair, leader of the opposition Labour Party, placed the 'information superhighway' at the centre of his proposals for regenerating Britain. He announced a plan at his Party's 1995 Conference, in the lead up to a general election, to wire-up schools, hospitals, and other public facilities. He said BT had agreed to assist in reducing the cost of linking these organizations to advanced ICT networks, provided restrictions on BT's capacity to deliver broadcast entertainment services using its existing network were removed by a future Labour Government. This turned the 'BT versus cable debate' into a major mass media issue, with the government counter-claiming that it was already implementing 'information superhighway' policies.

Germany

Like the European Commission, representatives of the German Government have preferred to speak of moving towards an Information Society, and avoided the highway metaphor. Nevertheless, the German Federal Government deliberated almost two years after publication of the Bangemann Report before it was able to present its own national action plan. One reason for this delay was that former governments had developed similar programs and important reform projects, such as telecommunications liberalization, that were already underway. Therefore, many questioned the need for any new government initiatives within Germany.

In 1974, the social-liberal government set up a Commission for the Development of Technical Communication to define which communication services

---

9 The 'BT versus cable' focus of UK telecommunications policy has blurred important distinctions between the promotion of the interests of nationally-based ICT suppliers and users of the networks. Chapters 18 and 20 of Dutton *et al.* (1996) indicate that the latter may be more critical to economic growth.

were 'economically sensible' and 'socially desirable.' The main focus was on data communications and two-way cable television, both having just been introduced in the United States at that time (KtK 1976; also see Dutton et al. 1987). The German government reorganized itself and merged the ministry of research and technology with that of post and telecommunications in order to better address the convergence of computing and telecommunications. Programs were set up to support the development of a national computing industry, and the study of computer science.

There was also public support for large field trials of cable TV and videotex (Dutton, *et al.* 1987; Mayntz and Schneider 1988). However, the effects of these initiatives on both the economy and society were limited. The greatest changes for private households revolved around the introduction of cable and, later, satellite television, along with commercial TV channels.

In 1984, the conservative-liberal government submitted a report entitled *Information Technology* (BMFT 1984), designed to coordinate the work of four ministries key to the development of IT, which included economic affairs, defense, research and technology, as well as post and telecommunications. The Deutsche Bundespost (DBP) was to invest more than DM 300 billion within 25 years to set up a national broadband network — a nationwide fiber optic network connecting every business and private home and providing telephone, dat,a and video services, as well as broadcasting.

As an intermediate step, the DBP was to install digital switching throughout the telephone network and adopt Integrated Digital Service Network (ISDN) standards. The proponents of a national broadband network anticipated major markets for new multi functional terminals, like the video phone. They also expected the technology to spur innovation in the delivery of services, such as in facilitating telebanking and teleshopping. Proponents also saw the potential for interorganizational networking — an aspect of the 'virtual organization.'

Within a few years, however, aggressive plans for fiber to every home were abandoned. The uncertainty of demand for broadband infrastructures became an issue in Germany and in other nations. This experience contributed to a strategic shift, leading the government withdraw from efforts to force technological innovation, such as through the planning of the telecommunications infrastructure, and to rely on market forces to drive decisions on telecommunication infrastructures and services.

In 1985, an important commission was convened to make recommendations for the liberalization and privatization of telecommunications (Neuordnung der Telekommunikation, 1987). These recommendations led to a reform of telecommunications in 1989; followed by a second set of reforms in 1993.

In parallel, Germany has been engaged in a continuing debate over the reform of broadcasting. The provision of commercial television channels had been restricted until 1984 (see Kleinsteuber 1996), when the government sought to encourage the development of cable and satellite communications. In response, the federal constitutional court formulated in 1986 what is now called the 'dual order of broadcasting,' which explicitly required public broadcasting as a means to contribute to the pluralism of opinions, and the democratic process.

With these reforms already underway, the Bangemann Report did not present a new direction for Germany, nor require an action that was not on the government's present agenda. The main task for the federal government was to develop a consensus within Germany that could overcome partisan differences between the Federal government and the German states. The federal government was formed through a coalition of the Christian Democratic Party (CDU) and the Free Democratic Party (FDP), while most states had Social Democratic Party (SPD) majorities. The states had to approve the telecommunications reform bill, and they are charged by the German Constitution with broadcasting as one aspect of their responsibility for cultural policy.

With efforts to liberalize broadcasting and telecommunications, the federal government received criticism by industry associations for not taking a stronger lead in the formulation of R&D and technology policy. This criticism heightened in the aftermath of the US NII initiatives and the Bangemann Report, which many read as a signal for a government-led industrial policy. In response, Chancellor Helmut Kohl announced moves to increase dialogue between industry, the scientific community, and the state on questions of research, technology, and innovation (Deutscher Bundestag 1994). He convened a Council for Research, Technology and Innovation, that included 20 representatives from universities, industry, and trade unions, as well as, four federal ministers, and one state minister. The Council's first topic was Germany's own route to the information society, in response to US and EU initiatives (Der Rat für Forschung, Technologie und Innovation 1995).

The federal government also decided to renew pressure for liberalization, setting up a working group on the reform of Deutsche Telekom and a series of meetings with representatives of the states to address the reform of the broadcasting law. All three initiatives were woven together in a report entitled *Info 2000: Germany's Path to the Information Society* (BMWi 1996).[10]

The Social Democratic Party wished to participate in this national debate and, therefore, established of a study commission — an enquete commission — in the Federal Parliament.[11] In January 1996, the enquete commission on "The Future of the Media in Economy and Society: Germany's Way to the Information Society" began the development of a working program.[12]

Consensus evolved across parties and levels of government on the value of liberalizing telecommunications and broadcasting, but disputes developed over the regulation of new electronic media and services. State governments claimed that most new services were most analogous to broadcasting and, therefore, fell within their jurisdiction. The Federal Government argued that the new services were analogous to other telecommunication goods and services and, therefore, subject to federal laws governing commerce. This led to a compromise in late 1996, when the Federal Government and the heads of state governments agreed on a parallel process of legislation with a Federal law covering the services of individual communication, and a state treaty dealing with these services addressed to the general public (Kubicek 1996). They also agreed that there should be no licensing, not even a system for registering, these new services.

---

10 This report was due in late 1995, but published several months later, in February 1996, to allow time to resolve disagreements among federal ministries as well as between federal government and the states. *Info 2000* almost completely follows the recommendations of the Council of Research, Technology and Innovation (BMWi 1996).

11 Enquete commissions of the federal parliament consist of an equal number of members of parliament and experts nominated by the parliamentary parties. They are expected to submit a report to parliament showing possible options for action in areas that fall outside, or cross the traditional areas of responsibility of the standing parliamentary committees.

12 The first author of this chapter is a member of this commission. For a full list of members, working programme and interim reports, see http://www.bundestag.de/enquete/enqueber.htm.

International Initiatives: A Global Information Infrastructure

Despite differences in approach and symbolism, both the EU and US recognized that a coherent, balanced, and mutually-supportive set of transnational measures would be critical to the success of their own initiatives. In a speech at the International Telecommunications Union (ITU) in Buenos Aires in March 1994, Vice President Gore argued for world wide cooperation to extend the project of the NII to a Global Information Infrastructure (GII). This proposal was later endorsed at a 1995 meeting of ministers from the G7 group of leading industrialized countries. This agreement was important as a means to facilitate multinational efforts to co-ordinate the work of global bodies like the World Trade Organization (WTO), World Intellectual Property Organization (WIPO), and International Telecommunication Union (ITU), on issues relevant to the GII (see Chen 1995).

The GII is also regarded as a key element of economic development and industrial policy in many developed countries as it creates opportunities for reaching international markets (Dutton, Blumler *et al.* 1994: 25-26). However, there is a general acceptance that implementation of a GII will involve a long and complex process, given the number of players involved, and the different opportunities and threats that each nation perceives. Moreover, many countries will require huge investments in order to catch up with the leading industrial nations.

New Technological and Economic Paradigms

One major force behind all these national and international initiatives has been a growing consensus on the major outlines of emerging technological and economic trends. A widely shared set of beliefs about the information revolution and its economic implications — a 'techno-economic paradigm' — forms the basis and the environment for the technological visions and programs of governments and industries around the world (Freeman 1996). These belief systems are socially constructed in that they develop through discussion about the future of ICTs and the economy. Nevertheless, they limit the discretion and shape the strategic choices of governments.

Worldwide debate about the revolution in ICTs has helped create widespread agreement on major social, economic, and technological trends. When intelligent people see themselves faced with very similar problems, it is not surprising that they arrive at similar solutions (Bennett 1988; Dutton and Vedel 1992). Some of the most general worldwide trends include the centrality of the ICT revolution, the convergence of digital media, globalization, the strategic role of ICTs in economic development, and the advantages of a market-led approach. These features of a new paradigm are guiding policy responses in the EU and North America and are further described in the chapters that follow.

The ICT Revolution

One of the most relevant perceptions has been the nonlinear explosion in the power of core ICTs, accompanied by a continuing decline in their cost. The price-performance-ratio of microprocessors, for example, has improved dramatically over the last decades and is not expected to stop improving. It has not only enabled the production of microcomputers for the desktop that can out perform mainframe computers of the past, but it has also made ICTs a key component of innovations in telecommunications, broadcasting, consumer electronics, and in nearly every other sector of the economy.

Many other developments have signaled dramatic change in ICTs. One other example has been advances in the technology and markets for wireless communications (Institute for Information Studies 1996). Wireless systems, such as cordless phones and cellular telephony, have extended the utility and mobility of telecommunications. Moreover, wireless systems hold out the potential to connect private homes to terrestrial and satellite communication systems without the expense of bringing another wire into the home.

Globalization

Satellite broadcasting has changed fundamental assumptions of the television business and limited the discretion of national broadcasting authorities across Europe (see chapter 5). The internationalization of computer networking is another step that is eroding the sovereignty of national regulations and contributing to the globalization of new business and industries. These networks will have consequences that move beyond communications to the regulation of economic and business affairs more generally.

Convergence of Digital Media

The digital storage and transmission of all kinds of signals, representing data, text, graphics, images and sound has not only changed the technology of each of these sectors but also is expected to lead to their technological as well as industrial convergence. In a narrow sense, convergence means that all signals will be represented in a digital form. This type of technical evolution is reflected in emerging digital storage and transmission facilities. Radio and television programmes are distributed via the telephone networks and may be received by computers and stored on the same media as text and graphics produced on a personal computer. Likewise, voice telephony and data transmission can be provided over cable communication networks.

However, this potential can be used to expand the range of applications that can be provided over each medium, whether cable, telephone, or satellite network, for example. It need not create a convergence of industries.

There are also steps toward network convergence, such as the potential to replace separate cable and telephone networks with one broadband network to homes and businesses. This has become more technically feasible with advances in such areas as switching and digital transmission technology, in particular ATM (Asynchronous Transfer Mode), but is unlikely to become economically viable in the 1990s.

Technical trials of fully integrated, switched, broadband networks based on fibre optic cable were launched in the 1980s. They provide the potential for providing all kinds of electronic communication services over one pipe into the households and businesses. However, the cost for this move has remained prohibitive. For example, there has been no economic solution to the costs for digging the trenches to bring new fibre optic cable to every home. In addition, there is no proven consumer demand for the services that would justify this investment (see Chapter 8).

Some have argued that the superiority of this technical path will lead to the convergence of industries, heralding the end of traditional television and telephone companies (Gilder 1994). However, even if there were an integrated network for the delivery of all kinds of digital signals, other obstacles remain to the convergence of industries (Garnham 1996). In particular, the content, training and skills, production facilities, and marketing of these media — not just the visions of technicians — will shape the design of ICTs. Many technological innovations in ICTs take twenty or more years to diffuse to a substantial proportion of the public.

Despite these obstacles, the idea of convergence has become more central to visions of the future of communications, largely because most forecasts of the future of ICTs are technologically deterministic, and downplay the role of social, cultural, or even economic factors that do not fit well within a given scenario.

A Growing Faith in Market-led Industrial Strategies

The vision of a post-industrial society formulated by Daniel Bell (1973) and others was conceived not only as economically based on the new knowledge industries, but also as a system that governments might steer, employing the new information technologies and knowledge gained through the application of such methods as systems analysis and simulation. On this knowledge intensive society, government should use information technology to better understand and manage social and economic development.

This view of government fits well with some elements of the European Social Welfare State and also with American faith in technology and formal methods, as exhibited during the Kennedy years in the development of Planning and Budgeting Systems. If ICTs were strategic to the economic development of the advanced industrial nations, then governments needed to support innovation in ICTs and its widespread diffusion as a key to national industrial policy. State support for major research institutions and technological infrastructures, including telecommunications infrastructures, were a natural response to this logic.

However, an alternative model became prominent in the US and Europe in the 1980s. In Britain, Conservative governments began to reject state intervention and rely on the ´wisdom´ of market forces. Their vision was that of an economy which was freed from any kind of state intervention, where the supply of goods and services would follow demand. This rationale led to the privatization and liberalization of monopolies, including telecommunications.

Great Britain was followed by Germany, the Scandinavian Countries and the Benelux-States (see Grande and Schneider 1991).

The European Commission accelerated this change of thinking across Europe. Originally only responsible for the free exchange of goods and services within the European Economic Community, it declared not only telecommunications but also television to be just an ordinary good or service which falls under the treaty, thereby starting the deregulation of television which in some European countries such as France, Germany, and Britain, is highly regulated because of its attributed cultural and political significance.

This political trend of deregulation takes the form of state withdrawal from areas which formerly were regarded as infrastructures that had central social, cultural, and political significance, such as broadcasting. In the 1980s, conservative governments were identified most closely with a faith in market forces, distrusting the political bodies and bureaucracies as instruments of industrial or technology policy. By the late-1990s, there is more widespread agreement than ever before, across the political spectrum, in the wisdom of market forces. The end of the East-West conflict and thereby the lack of competition between political systems has made the market-protagonists stronger, with governmental institutions reducing their size and influence, while some variations remain. This tilt away from government-led initiatives has influenced approaches to the ISH on both sides of the Atlantic.

The Social Shaping of Policy Issues

The NII and EU Action Plan target very common policy issues as critical to the realization of their respective visions. This again illustrates the degree to which similar technologies create similar problems that yield similar solutions (Bennett 1988). However, historically anchored social, cultural, and administrative traditions often mean that the same issue has a somewhat different meaning and solution across national and regional boundaries.

Telecommunications Reform

There is cross-national agreement that competition should be introduced across all telecommunications markets, for local, and long-distance networks, and services, and for all kinds of terminal equipment. There is consensus also that the further development of telecommunication infrastructures must be financed increasingly by the private sector, while the role of government should be limited to providing the appropriate regulatory environment for fair competition, such as minimizing restrictions on the entry of new providers.

By 1997, most member states of the European Community had liberalized their telecommunication markets — that is, introduced competition. The European Commission supported and pushed this process by a number of directives. Most importantly, the EC's telecommunication ministers agreed that by 1998, full competition must be realized in every member country. Germany changed its telecommunication law in 1996 allowing for almost unrestricted market access for providers.[13] In the same year the Telecommunications Act of 1996 was passed in the US Congress, after several earlier attempts at telecommunications reform, which sought to introduce competition through deregulation.

Despite support for telecommunications reform, the success of policy actions remain uncertain. The Internet, which is often taken as the technological model for an ISH, is a better example of government-inspired rather than market-led innovation. It was initially funded, from 1968, by substantial public investments from the US Department of Defense's Advanced Research Projects Agency (ARPA) (see Denning and Lin 1994: 123-36). Its growth to cover tens of millions of users in the 1990s was encouraged largely through the provision of 'free' access to academic and research users, which also receive much support from public funds. The same is true for the Teletel-system in France, better known as Minitel (see chapter 6). There is mounting evidence in support of the role of competition in lowering costs and promoting innovation in telecommunications (Baer 1996). However, more regulations were often required to achieve competition, and, therefore, deregulation might not achieve the levels of competition expected, not provide for the broad access required to create new mass markets.

---

13 Licenses are required only for establishing transmission ways and providing basic telephone services.

Intellectual Property Rights

EU and US plans assume that property rights on electronic media content have to be secured in order for the private sector to invest in the production of content. In the past, intellectual property rights were connected to the physical media and the reproduction of a text, a picture, or a piece of music. However, digitalization loosens the connection between content and any physical medium. A text can be printed, but it can also be put on discs and distributed in computer networks. Over these networks it may be read and is inevitably copied. On both sides of the Atlantic, expert groups are struggling over new ways to adapt existing laws to the electronic media (Mansell and Steinmueller 1996). All nations see the need for international rules, given the global networks at issue, and, therefore, support efforts of the World Intellectual Property Right Organization (WIPO) to create global standards.

The European Commission (1995) presented a Green Paper on "Copyright and Related Rights in the Information Society" as well as a position paper on the "Legal Protection of Databases". A directive on the legal protection of databases was then passed, which defined a copyright for compilations of data in the broadest sense, such as in a database, or on a CD-ROM. A consultation process identified major issues that remain, including: reproduction rights, legal protections of technical schemes to identify and protect works from illegal use, distribution rights, and the management and enforcement of rights (European Commission 1996*d*).

In the US, the Administration released a White Paper on "Intellectual Property Rights and the National Information Infrastructure" (IITF 1994d). Corresponding legislation faces opposition from different interest groups such as authors, on the one side, and librarians and providers of online services, on the other [14]

These efforts strive to make incremental changes in existing law. For example, they generally adhere to the idea that pieces of knowledge or works of art are goods, on which one can, and should, hold and control individual property rights. However, this accepted practice has been questioned on a normative as well as a pragmatic level. Property rights to information and

---

14 See chapter 2 and the Websites of the Creative Incentive Coalition (http://www.cic.org) and the Digital Future Coalition (http://www.ari.net/dfc) with a comprehensive and up-to-date collection of documents and statements.

knowledge grants the right to decide who may get access and who may not. Traditionally, this has applied only to a small segment of the whole corpus of information and knowledge. Academic research and classical literature, for example, are governed by different regulatory traditions (Spinner 1994). There is therefore a risk that the commercialization of knowledge will build new economic barriers to access, when the promise of the information society has been to extend access to information.

The Electronic Frontier Foundation, among others, has argued that individual property rights can no longer be controlled over global computer networks, and that, therefore, new regulatory systems have to be developed, which give up the notion of permanent property relations, and instead define access as a service that may be paid for (de Sola Pool 1983). The provision of computer software as 'shareware' and 'freeware' are examples of how new concepts of IPR might be emerging.

The Internet, generally, does not provide the model for future information markets. Rather it reflects 'important historical American values of sharing, generosity, and neighbourliness which are the antithesis of modern market values' (Dutton, Blumler *et al.* 1994: 31). This derives not only from the public funding provided to it but also from the investment of a great deal of intellectual labour and creativity that was given for free by users from research-oriented communities. While these public and personal investments are unlikely to be as forthcoming in a more commercial market, the US government has placed a high priority on commercializing the Internet as an example of how public support can be translated into a viable commercial enterprise (Kahin and Keller 1994)

Privacy, Data Protection, and Security

Security concerns the protection of data and communications against unauthorized access. On contrast, privacy, referred to as data protection in Europe, concerns the unauthorized disclosure or use of personal information that might be legitimately held by a government agency, for example.

There is overall consent that security is a necessary precondition for the widespread use of computer networks for business transactions. Since the late eighties, governmental bodies round the world have been developing technical standards for improving the security of data and electronic transactions. The most important initiative in this area is encryption. The dissent is not between Americans and Europeans, but rather within both governments between the proponents of electronic markets who demand the free use of encryption technologies on the one hand and the guardians of public safety, who argue that these concerns must be balanced with the need for the state to conduct lawful surveillance, such as involved in wiretapping.

The European Commission (1990) suggested criteria and evaluation methods for information technology security (ITSEC), but without special reference to security in open networks, like the Internet. Questions of state control over encryption has been left to the national governments. In France, the private use of end-to-end encryption in telecommunications has been forbidden by law. In Germany the issue has not been resolved between different ministries. In the US, the Administration released a draft report "NII Security: The Federal Role" (IITF 1995), recommending that government retain a means to access any encryption keys. After strong opposition - the so-called 'Clipper Chip' debate - Vice President Gore announced a slight modification of this position (see chapter 2).

With regard to privacy, there are differences among the member states of the EU, but larger differences between Europe and the US (Flaherty 1989; OECD 1994). After a long period of negotiation, the European Council and the Parliament passed a directive in 1995 which was to be implemented by national law within one year. It aimed to harmonize data protection rules among the member countries in order to support the development of a common information market and also establish rules for the transmission of personal data to countries outside the European Union (Directive 1995). With regard to the transmission of data from member states into the US, a commission will have to evaluate whether there is an equivalent level of data protection. If there is equivalence, then transmission will be allowed generally. If not, each transmission must be approved. In addition, a special directive was issued to ensure privacy of telecommunications provided over mobile and digital networks.

While actions such as these have been taken, technological change has challenged the entire basis for privacy protection within Europe and the US. European approaches to data protection are anchored in assumptions of earlier decades, when a limited number of organizations stored and processed data in well-defined files and according to well-defined procedures. The rights of individuals and inspection bodies defined for this environment are difficult to apply to the situation of a more open, global network, like the Internet. If millions of Internet users can be collecting, storing, and processing personal data, registration and oversight become untenable. The US approach is anchored in the assumption that individuals will be able to know and understand when their privacy has been violated, since enforcement depends on litigation initiated by the injured party. This might also be less feasible.

In the US, after a two-year consultation process, the NTIA published a White Paper that focused on the collection, use, and dissemination of telecommunications-related personal information in the private sector (NTIA 1995). This report recommended that the US maintain its tradition of voluntary frameworks, instead of adopting the European tradition of legislation that would force formal notification and inspection procedures. In cooperation with private sector representatives in the NII Advisory Council, the Administration has developed "Principles for Providing and Using Information" — a code of fair information practice that is suggested for the public and the private sector.

Content Regulation and Control

There is also a growing sense that a balance has to be found between freedom of expression, on the one hand, and control over the dissemination of illegal or offensive content, on the other. The distribution of pornography over the Internet, for example, has raised concerns among parents over how to safeguard their children. Within the context of the US Telecommunications Bill of 1996, the Communication Decency Act introduced an attempt to regulate content on the Internet, but it has been challenged on First Amendment grounds for its broad and vague treatment of indecency. A more prominent approach has been to support self-regulation by the providers and users of services, such as households. To facilitate this, governments are asking the private sector to develop rating criteria and procedures as well as the technical means, such as the Violence-Chip (V-chip), which allow parents to better control their children's access to content. In late 1996, the European Commission provided draft reports on this issue arguing that present legislation is sufficient to cover the electronic media. The main problem, according to the Commission, is one of applying existing law.

Universal Service and Public Access

The NII initiative emphasized benefits for all Americans, and therefore noted the need to update and broaden the concept of universal service and public access. The NTIA undertook a number of steps, such as the conduct of public hearings, to develop an appropriate concept of universal service (see chapter 13). The Administration received strong support from Public Interest Groups, which led to corresponding legislation in the first years of the Clinton Administration. The election of a Republican majority in the 1994 mid-term elections led to some retreat from the original goals of the Administration, but the Telecommunications Reform Act of 1996 nevertheless contained strong measures aimed at extending access (see chapter 10).[15]

In Europe, the Bangemann Report, the Commission, and most of the member state governments stressed that there should be no gap between information haves and have-nots, but they expected the liberalization of markets to lower the costs of services and provide for universal access on their own. They did not see a need as yet for state intervention or special regulation (see chapter 14). In Germany, for example, recent legislation contained an ex post facto procedure for enacting universal service obligations in the event of an insufficient supply of basic telephone service.

Education, Libraries, and Other Applications in the Public Interest

Beyond universal service, the Agenda for Action stressed the importance of access for schools and libraries. The Telecommunications Act of 1996 also contained special regulations for bringing advanced telecommunications services to these institutions and offering services at affordable rates.[16] NTIA, through its Telecommunications and Information Infrastructure Assistance Program (TIIAP), provided about US $80 million to seed ISH developments in schools, libraries, and other-non commercial organizations. In its first

---

15 In addition, the Joint Federal State Board, enacted by the law, has published its recommendation to the FCC, which will decide in 1997 on the definition of Universal Service, what it will encompass and how it will be financed. See the www-site of the FCC (http://www.fcc.org).

16 The Joint Federal State Board , enacted by the Telecommunications Act 1996, has presented recommendations for discounted rates.(http://www.fcc.org).

years, the programme provided matching funds for hundreds of demonstration, access, and planning projects (see chapter 11).

The connection of schools to the Internet has been support directly by Vice President Gore and President Clinton. They launched what would be a series of Net Days in 1995, designed to enroll volunteers to wire schools, and at the end of 1996 introduced the Technology Literacy Challenge and the 21st Century Teachers Initiative to provide teacher training.[17]

There was not a comparable level of activity focused on these issues in Europe. Not for three years since the Action Plan, in its revised plan, did the European Commission try to better link reform initiatives in the public sector with its technology push.

The Bangemann Report stressed the need to demonstrate the benefits of the information society to the public and, therefore, recommended pilot projects in ten areas such as teleworking, distance learning, road traffic management, air traffic control, and trans-European public administration networks. However, these pilots failed to excite public interest. A trans-European public administration network, for example, is oriented toward the exchange of statistical or tax data between governmental organizations, which is quite another matter than 'wiring the schools'.

NII initiatives included projects aimed at improving access to governmental information for citizens and providing electronic delivery of governmental services, which directly involve the public. The NII was also coordinated with other lines of activity, such as the National Performance Review. The Government Information Technology Services Working Group within the IITF, for example, set up an Interagency Kiosk Committee, a coalition among several federal agencies, which developed a concept and an implementation scheme for an electronic multimedia kiosk by which a number of public services would be available to the citizen in a one-stop-mode (Interagency Kiosk Committee 1995). The management of a feasibility study, with some prototyping involved, was given to the U.S. Post Office.[18]

Improving the quality of public services became a new priority of the revised Action Plan. However, the structure of the EU is one factor that makes

---

17 See the web sites of the Department of Education (http://www.ed.gov/ Technology/) and of Benton Foundation (http://www.benton.org (http://www.benton.org)

18 The results of this work have been presented over the Internet, under the name WINGS. See http://www.wings.usps.gov.

it difficult for the European Commission to take concrete actions in Brussels, that will materially affect the quality of services at the local government level in the member states. Clearly, as this review suggests, much of the activity in Washington D.C. and Brussels has been focussed on creating visions and plans that will help orchestrate the decisions of private and public actors at all levels.

Overview of this Book

This book builds on the issues raised in this chapter to illuminate the many social dimensions of the Information Superhighway. The first two chapters of Part I are contributed by representatives of administrations in the US and Europe. Each provides a personal perspective on these initiatives. Thomas Kalil, Senior Director to the White House National Economic Council, summarizes the main elements of the NII. Michael Niebel, a member of the cabinet of EU-Commissioner Martin Bangemann, summarizes the EU Action Plan.

The next two chapters discuss critical technical issues of an ISH. Tom Spacek, responsible for the NII-related activities at Bellcore, argues that the Internet provides the most valuable model for the ISH. From a European perspective, Hans J. Kleinsteuber argues that it is still open whether the Internet or broadcasting satellites will become the dominating technological infrastructure for the majority of Europeans.

Part II draws attention to similar initiatives in the late seventies and early eighties and tries to draw some lessons from the past. Michel Berne from the Research Institute of France Telecom analyses the Minitel case, which is said to be one of the few successful innovations of telecommunications for everyday life. Tarja Cronberg deals with Social Experiments with Broadband Technology in Denmark, and Bill Dutton looks back at wired cities projects and similar initiatives in order to draw lessons of relevance to ISH visions and strategies.

The papers of Part III are devoted to the different economic, political, and social bases of ISH policy responses. Victor Bekkers, from the Netherlands, sets out the background for governmental actions related to constructing the Electronic Superhighway. Claire Lobet-Maris and Marie d'Udekem-Gevers, from Belgium, compare US and EC programmes to determine the relevance of public interest applications in the two settings. Herbert Burkert, senior researcher at a German public research institute and head of the Legal Advisory Board for the Information Market to the European Commission, takes a look at the assumptions about the "Information and Communication Citizen" who is said to benefit from the ISH. And Paschal Preston from Dublin City University reminds us that there are big regional differences within the European Union and analyses what the less developed regions may expect from the Commission´s activities.

Part IV takes up the issue of access to the information superhighway. James McConnaughey, a Senior Advisor at the NTIA, summarizes the efforts of the Administration to conceive and implement an enhanced concept of universal service. Marcel Haag and Louisa Gosling summarize the position and action of the European Commission. Bill Drake analyzes the role of public interest groups in the US, particularly in the process of telecommunications legislation. Richard Civille from the Center for Civic Networking shows that there is no contradiction between systems in the public interest and business. Instead, he argues that applications in the public interest are necessary preconditions for the broad commercial success of the Information Superhighway.

Finally in Part V authors turn back to the broad comparison of developments in the EU and US. Robin Williams begins by providing the theoretical and methodological foundations for this kind of comparison by introducing the social shaping approach of technology-oriented social research, and illustrating its application to the study of ICTs in general and the ISH in particular. Volker Schneider from the Max-Planck-Institute for Social Research concludes with a systematic comparison of the goals, strategies and the process of the NII and the EU Action Plan.

References

Advisory Council (1995), United States Advisory Council on the National Information Infrastructure: Common Grounds. *Fundamental Principles for the National Information Infrastructure*. First Report (Washington, D.C.: NTIA), March.

Advisory Council (1996a), United States Advisory Council on the National Information Infrastructure: Common Grounds. *KickStart Initiative: Connecting America´s Communities to the Information Superhighway* (Washington, D.C.: NTIA), January.

Advisory Council (1996b), United States Advisory Council on the National Information Infrastructure: Common Grounds. *A Nation of Opportunity: Realizing the Promise of the Information Superhighway* (Washington DC: NTIA), October.

Baer, W. (1996), Telecommunication Infrastructure Competition: The Costs of Delay, in: Dutton (1996): 353-370.

Baker, K (1982), The Impact of Information Technology, in Björn-Andersen, N., Earl, M., Holst, O. and Mumford, E., *Information Society - For Richer, For Poorer* (Amsterdam, New York, Oxford: North Holland) 77-80.

Bangemann, M. (1995), *Policies for a European Information Society*, in: PICT (1995), 5-12.

Bangemann Group (1994), High-Level Group on the Information Society, *Europe and the Gobal Information Society, Recommendations to the European Council*, Brussels, May 26.

Bekkers, V., Koop, B.-J. and Nouwt, S. (1996) (Eds.), *Emerging Electronic Highways. New Challenges for Politics and Law*, (The Hague, London, Boston: Kluwer Law International).

Bell, D. (1973), The Coming of Post-Industrial Society: A Venture in Social Forecasting (New York: Basic Books; Harmondsworth, UK: Penguin).

Bennett, C.J. (1988), Different Processes, One Result, Governance 1(4), 415-41.

Blumler, J., McLeod, J.M., and Rosengren, K.E. (1992) (Eds.), *Comparatively Speaking* (Newbury Park and London: Sage).

BMFT (1994), Bundesministerium für Forschung und Technologie, Informationstechnik: Konzeption der Bundesregierung zur Förderung der Entwicklung der Mikroelektronik, der Informations- und Kommunikationstechniken (Bonn: BMFT).

BMWi (1996), Bundesministerium für Wirtschaft, *Info 2000: Deutschlands Weg in die Informationsgesellschaft* (Bonn: BMWi), February.

CCTA (1994), The Government Centre for Information Systems, Information Superhighways: Opportunities for Public Sector Applications in the UK (London: CCTA).

Chen, Ching-chih (1995) (Ed.), *Planning Global Information Infrastructure* (Norwood, New Jersey: Ablex).

Denning, D.E., and Lin, H.S. (1994) (Eds.), *Rights and Responsibilities of Participants in Networked Communications*, (Washington, D.C.: National Academy Press).

Der Rat für Forschung, Technologie und Innovation (1995), *Informationsgesellschaft: Chancen, Innovationen und Herausforderungen. Feststellungen und Empfehlungen.* (Bonn: Bundesministerium für Bildung, Wissenschaft und Technologie), December (http://www.kp.dlr.de/BMBF/rat/).

Deutscher Bundestag (1994), *Bericht der Bundesregierung zur Intensivierung des Dialogs zwischen Wirtschaft, Wissenschaft und Staat zur Forschung, Technologie und Innovation.* BT Drs. 12/6934 (Bonn: Deutscher Bundestag).

Dierkes, M., Hoffmann, U., and Marz, L. (1992), *Leitbild und Technik* (Berlin: Sigma).

Directive (1995) *Directive of the European Parliament and of the Council concerning the processing of personal data and the protection of privacy in the telecommunications sector, in particular in the Integrated Services Digital Network (ISDN), and in the digital mobile networks.*

Drake, W. J. (1995) (Ed.), *The New Information Infrastructure: Strategies for U.S. Policy* (New York: The Twentieth Century Fund Press).

DTI (1988), Department of Trade and Industry Communications Steering Group, *The Infrastructure for Tomorrow: Communications Steering Group Report* (London: Her Majesty's Stationary Office).

DTI (1991), Department of Trade and Industry, *Competition and Choice: Telecommunications Policy for the 1990s*. White Paper, Cm 1461 (London: Her Majesty's Stationary Office).

Dutton, W. et al. (1996) (Ed.), *Information and Communication Technologies — Visions and Realities* (Oxford and New York: Oxford University Press).

Dutton, W., and Vedel, T. (1992), *Dynamics of Cable Television in the U.S., Britain, and France'*, in Blumler et al. (1992): 70-93.

Dutton, W., Blumler, J. G., and Kraemer, K. L. (1987) (Eds.), *Wired Cities* (Boston: G. K. Hall, MacMillan).

Dutton, W.H., Blumler, J.G., Garnham, N., Mansell, R., Cornford, J., and Peltu, M. (1994), *The Information Superhighway: Britain's Response*. Policy Research Paper No. 29 (Uxbridge: Brunel University, PICT).

European Commission (1993), *White Paper on Growth, Competitiveness, and Employment: The Challenges and Ways Forward Into the 21st Century*. COM (93) 700 final, Dec. 5, (Brussels: Commission of the European Communities).

European Commission (1994), *Europe's Way to the Information Society: An Action Plan* COM(94) 347 (Brussels: Commission of the European Communities).

European Commission (1995a), *Directive of the European Parliament and the European Council on the Protection of Individuals with regard to the Processing of Personal Data and on the Free Movement of such Data*, October 24, (Brussels: Commission of the European Communities).

European Commission (1995b), *Green Paper on Copyright and Related Rights in the Information Society*, COM (95) 382 final, July 19, (Brussels: Commission of the European Communities).

European Commission (1996a) (Ed.), *A European Information Society for All. First Considerations of the Group of Highlevel Experts*. Interim Report. DG V, January, (Brussels: Commission of the European Communities).

European Commission (1996b), *Living and Working in the Information Society. People First*. Green Paper COM(96)389. Draft, July 23, (Brussels: Commission of the European Communities).

European Commission (1996c), Communication *The Information Society - From Korfu to Dublin - New Priorities*. COM (96) 395 (final), (Brussels: Commission of the European Communities).

European Commission (1996d), *Follow-Up to the Green Paper* on Copyright and Related Rights in the Information Society. Communication from the Commission, COM (96) 568 final, Nov. 20, (Brussels: Commission of the European Communities).

European Commission (1996e), *Europe at the Forefront of the Global Information Society*. Rolling Action Plan, Communication from the Commission COM (96) 607 final, Nov. 27, (Brussels: Commission of the European Communities).

Flaherty, D. H. (1989), *Protecting Privacy in Surveillance Societies* (Chaple Hill, NC/London).

Forum Information Society (1996), *Information Society: Networks for People and their Communities. Making the most of the Information Society in the European Union.* First Annual Report to the European Commission from the Information Society Forum. (Brussels: European Commission, Information Society Activity Center) June.

Freeman, C. (1996), *The Two-Edged Nature of Technical Change: Employment and Unemployment* in Dutton (1996): 19-36.

Garnham, N. (1996), *Constraints on Multimedia Convergence,* in: Dutton (1996): 103-119.

Gilder, G. (1994), *Life After Television,* Revised Edition (New York: W. W. Norton & Company).

Gore, A. (1991), *Infrastructure for a Global Village,* Scientific American, 265 (September), 108-111.

Gore, A. (1993), Speech to the Press Club, http://www.hpcc.gov./white-house/gore.nii.html

Graham, A. (1996), *Public Policy and the Information Superhighway. The Case of the United Kingdom,* in: Kahin and Wilson (1996), 349 - 386.

Grande, E., and Schneider, V. (1991), *Reformstrategien und staatliche Handlungskapazitäten. Eine Vergleichende Analyse insitutionellen Wandels in der Telekommunikation in West-Europa,* Politische Vierteljahresschrift, 32, 452 - 478

Helmers, S., Hoffmann, U., Canzler, W. (1995), *Die Datenautobahn,* Forum Wissenschaft, Vol 12, No. 1, pp 10-15.

IITF (1993), Information Infrastructure Task Force, *National Information Infrastructure: Agenda for Action* (Washington D.C.: National Telecommunications and Information Administration).

IITF (1994a), Information Infrastructure Task Force, *National Information Infrastructure. Progress Report September 1993-1994.* (Washington D.C.: Office of the Vice President, The Secretary of Commerce)

IITF (1994b), Information Infrastructure Task Force, Committee on Applications and Technology, *Putting the Information Infrastructure to Work.* (Washington, D.C.: National Institute of Technology (NIST), May.

IITF (1994c), Information Infrastructure Task Force, Committee on Applications and Technology, *The Information Infrastructure: Reaching Society's Goals* (Washington, D.C.: National Institute of Technology (NIST), September.

IITF (1994d), Information Infrastructure Task Force, Working Group on Intellectual Property, *Intellectual Property´ and the NII. Working Group Report* (Washington, D.C.: National Telecommunications and Information Administration), June.

IITF (1995), Information Infrastructure Task Force, *NII-Security. The Federal Role* (Washington, D.C.: National Telecommunications and Information Administr.) Sept.

Institute for Information Studies (1996) (Ed.), *The Emerging World of Wireless Communications* (Nashville, TN and Queenstown, MD: Nortel North America and The Aspen Institute, Annual Review of the Institute for Information Studies).

Interagency Kiosk Committee (1995), *The Kiosk Network Solution: An Electronic Gateway to Government Service.* Prepared for the Customer Service Improvement Team of the Government Information Technology Services Working Group. (Washington, D.C.: NTIA), April.

ITAP (1982), Information Technology Advisory Panel to Cabinet Office, *Report on Cable Systems* (London: Her Majesty's Stationary Office).

Kahin, B., and Keller, J. (1995) (Eds.), *Public Access to the Internet* (Cambridge, Mass. and London: MIT-Press).

Kahin, B., and Wilson, E. (1996) (Eds.), *National Information Infrastructure Initiatives: Vision and Policy Design* (Cambridge, Mass. and London: MIT-Press).

Kleinsteuber, H. (1996) (Ed.), *Der 'Information Superhighway'*, (Opladen: Westdeutscher Verlag).

KtK (1987), Kommission für den Ausbau des technischen Kommunikationssystems). *Telekommunikationsbericht.* Bonn: Bundesminister für das Post- und Fernmeldewesen, 1976.

Kubicek, H. (1996), *Multimedia. Germany's Third Attempt to Move to an Information Society,* in Kahin and Wilson (1996), 387-422.

Mackintosh, I. (1986), *Sunrise Europe* (Oxford: Basil Blackwell).

Mansell, R. (1993), *The New Telecommunications: A Political Economy of Network Evolution* (London: Sage)

Mansell, R. (1996), *Innovation in Telecommunication Regulation,* in Dutton (1966): 371-386.

Mansell, R, and Steinmueller, W. E. (1996), *Intellectual Property Rights: The Development of Information Infrastructures for the Information Society,* ENCIP Working Paper (Montpellier: ENCIP).

Mayntz, R., and Schneider, V. (1988), *The Dynamics of System Development in a Comparative Perspective,* in: Mayntz, R. and Hughes, P.T. (Eds.), The Development of Large Technical Systems (Frankfurt am Main/Boulder, Col.: Campus Verlag/Westview Press 1988) 263-298.

Neuordnung der Telekommunikation. Bericht der Regierungskommission Fernmeldewesen. (1987), Vorsitz Eberhard Witte (Heidelberg: R. v. Decker's).

Noam, E. (1992), *Telecommunications in Europe* (Oxford: Oxford University Press).

Noll, M. (1995), *Highway of Dreams* (Los Angeles: Annenberg School, University of Southern California).

NTIA (1995), *Privacy and the NII: Safeguarding Telecommunications-Related Personal Information* (Washington, D.C.: U.S: Department of Commerce), October.

OECD (1994), *Privacy and Data Protection: Issues and Challenges* (Paris: OECD).

OTA (1993), Office of Technology Assessment. *Advanced Network Technology.* Background Paper OTA-BP-TCT-101 (Washington, D.C.: US Government Printing Office).

PICT (1995), Programme on Information and Communication Technologies, *1995 Charles Read Lecture: Policies for a European Information Society.* A Summary of the Speeches (Uxbridge: Brunel University, PICT)

Riis, A. M. (1996), *The Information Welfare Society: An Assessment of Danish Governmental Initiatives Preparing for the Information Age,* in: Kahin and Wilson (1996), 424 - 456.

Spinner, H. (1994), *Die Wissensordnung. Ein Leitkonzept für die dritte Grundordnung des Informationszeitalters.*(Opladen: Leske + Budrich)

Vallance, I. (1995), in PICT, 16-18.

Vedel, T. (1996), *Information Superhighway Policy in France: The End of the High Tech Colbertism?* in Kahin and Wilson (1996), 307-348.

2. The Clinton-Gore National Information Infrastructure Initiative[1]

Thomas A. Kalil

The power of information and communications technology is exploding. The same computing power (one million instructions per second) that cost $800,000 in 1975 is available in 1996 for less than $14. The Internet, which connected 6,000 computers in 1985, a mere decade later connects more than 9.4 million computers and tens of millions of users, and is doubling every year. Satellite and wireless networks will enable us to communicate anytime, anywhere, and new fiber optics technology has the capacity to carry all of the phone traffic on Mother's Day on a single strand of fiber. The Clinton-Gore Administration believes that new information and communications technologies will have a profound impact on the way in which people work, learn, and interact with each other. This technology has the potential to increase the competitiveness of the U.S. economy, reduce the administrative costs associated with our health care system, improve student performance by making learning more exciting and engaging, and make government more efficient and responsive. For this reason, the Administration has made the promotion of the National Information Infrastructure (NII) - also known as the Information Superhighway, Cyberspace, the I-way, the Net, and the Infobahn - a top priority. There are as many definitions of the NII as there are analysts and pundits who talk about it. In the Administration's NII Agenda for Action, we refer to it as 'a seamless web of communications networks, computers, databases, and consumer electronics that will put vast amounts of information at users' fingertips' (IITF 1993).

---

1   This article is a revised and updated version of 'Public Policy and the National Information Infrastructure' which appeared in *Business Economics*, October 1995.

Of course, we already have an information infrastructure. Today's information infrastructure includes the telephone network, the Internet, cable networks, wireless and satellite systems, and over-the-air broadcasting. Although it is impossible to predict exactly how the NII will evolve, it is clear that over time, it will become more powerful and ubiquitous. Services that are difficult or impossible to deliver in 1996 (e.g., video conferencing, video on demand, retrieval of large multimedia files, access to shared virtual environments) will become possible once high-speed networks are deployed to homes and businesses.

Administration Philosophy

Before describing the Administration's policy agenda, I would like to describe some of the Administration's core assumptions and beliefs:

- The NII should not be viewed as an end in itself, but as a tool for accomplishing a wide variety of economic and social objectives, such as economic growth, job creation, higher productivity, a more efficient health care system, and a more open and responsive government.
- The NII should be built, owned, and operated by the private sector. Vigorous competition amongst firms is the best way to ensure lower prices, more customer choice, and faster rates of technological innovation.
- The government can help to promote the development of the NII by reforming the nation's telecommunications laws and regulations, making better use of spectrum, being a better user of information and communications technologies, investing in R&D and testbeds, establishing policies in areas such as privacy and intellectual property, and opening foreign markets for U.S. goods and services in the information and communications sector. The government also has an important role in ensuring that this technology does not polarize American society into information haves and have-nots.
- The Administration is technology-neutral. We do not care whether the bits are transported over fiber, coaxial cable, copper, or wireless links. We do have a strong preference for what Mitch Kapor has called a 'Jeffersonian architecture'. We would like to see an NII that:

- allows individuals to be producers as well as consumers of information;
- supports many-to-many communications and a wide range of applications;
- has low barriers to entry to network service providers; and
- is open to rapid technological change.

- It is very difficult to make predictions about the future. The pace of change is so rapid, and so many uncertainties abound about what the NII will ultimately look like, and what consumers will be willing to pay for it, that policy-makers need to act with a good deal of humility. Industry leaders are also having a difficult time predicting future market developments. In 1977, Ken Olson, founder of Digital Equipment Corporation, stated that 'There is no reason anyone would want a computer in their home'. In 1995, many telecommunications companies slowed their investment in broadband networks to the home because they were not sure whether new services would generate enough additional revenues to cover the cost of deployment. Many of America's leading information technology companies, including Microsoft, underestimated the importance of the Internet, and are scrambling to catch up.

Telecommunications Reform

One of the most important roles for government is to create a legal and regulatory environment that will promote competition and private sector investment. On February 8 1996, President Clinton signed the historic Telecommunications Act of 1996, a much-needed overhaul of the Communications Act of 1934. The Act:

- Preempts state laws that prohibit entry into local telephone service;
- Establishes the conditions for competition for local telephone service by requiring that local telephone companies interconnect with other carriers, allow resale, provide access to rights of way, unbundle the functionality of their networks, and provide number portability and dialing parity;
- Eliminates restrictions that prevent cable and telephone companies from entering each others' business;

- Gives the Federal Communications Commission (FCC) broad authority to forbear from regulating companies that do not have market power;
- Allows the Regional Bell Operating Companies (RBOCs) to enter the long-distance market when there is competition in the local telephone market; and
- Requires the FCC to continue to update the definition of universal service, and to provide discounted service to schools and libraries.

The Administration believes that the legislation will promote competition, lower prices of telecommunications services, increase customer choice, and accelerate the deployment of an advanced telecommunications infrastructure.

The benefits of competition in telecommunications markets are well documented. Since 1984, following the break-up of AT&T and the emergence of competitors such as MCI and Sprint, residential long-distance rates have declined by more than 50 per cent. Four carriers now have nationwide, digital networks. In 1994, more than 25 million residential customers changed long-distance carriers. Although there is undoubtedly more room for competition in the long-distance market, the existing level of competition has lowered prices and motivated carriers to provide higher levels of service, as measured by new features, clarity of transmission, and reductions in call blockage. The need for competition is greatest in the market for local telephone and cable television services. Analysis of the local telephone market, for example, reveals that competitive access providers such as Teleport and MFS Communications have less than one per cent of the market. Now that the President has signed the legislation, the action has mobilised the FCC and the state public utility commissions, which will have to implement the bill.[2]

Applications

Much of the press coverage on the Information Superhighway has focused on applications such as 500 channels of television, video on demand, networked games, and home shopping. These are all commercially important services that may help drive the deployment of residential broadband networks. The

---

2 The Federal Communications Commission web site (http://www.fcc.gov) has a wealth of information on the implementation of the Telecommunications Act of 1996.

Administration, however, believes that the NII will have a far more pervasive impact on our economic and social life, and has been active in promoting applications such as health care, education, electronic commerce, manufacturing, delivery of government services, intelligent transportation systems, digital libraries, telecommuting, geographical information systems, access for Americans with disabilities, and community networks. The Administration has identified ways in which it can help promote these applications by sponsoring pilot projects, eliminating legal and regulatory barriers, and making the government a more adept user of information and communications technologies. Below is a brief description of a few of the most important NII applications.[3]

Health Care

Although the health care sector is highly information-intensive, it is trailing the rest of the economy in its efforts to adopt information technology. In 1996, for example, 11 per cent of laboratory tests had to be reordered because of lost results, 40 per cent of the time a diagnosis was not recorded, and 30 per cent of the time a medical record was completely unavailable during patient visits. The NII has the potential to reduce administrative costs, enable consumers to make more informed decisions about their health care needs, and improve the quality of care in underserved urban and rural areas. Health care applications of the NII include tele-medicine, computer-based patient records, unified electronic claims, personal health information systems, and access to the latest medical literature.

Education

Education is one of the most exciting NII applications. Already, some students are using these technologies to collect and share real environmental data, model the energy efficiency of their homes on remote supercomputers, take "virtual" field trips to online museums, and publish their school newspaper on the World Wide Web. Introducing networks to the classroom can help

---

3   More information is available in IITF (1994a, b, c). These and other NTI documents are available on the World Wide Web at http://nii.nist.gov.

introduce curricula based on active learning and increase interaction between parents and teachers. President Clinton and Vice President Gore have created an ambitious Educational Technology Initiative to 'put the future at the fingertips of our children.'[4] The initiative seeks to:

- Connect every classroom to the Internet and other advanced telecommunications services by the year 2000;
- Give teachers the professional development they need to be as comfortable with computers and other technology as they are with the chalkboard;
- Increase the number of multimedia computers in the classroom; and
- Promote the development of high-quality educational software and applications.

Reaching these goals will require an investment of tens of billions of dollars. Although the federal government cannot meet this challenge alone, it can serve as a catalyst. For example, on February 15 1996, the President unveiled a proposal for a 5-year $2 billion Technology Literacy Challenge at the Christopher Columbus School in Union City,New Jersey. This fund, which the President included in his seven-year balanced budget, is designed to help leverage state, local, and private sector efforts to meet educational technology goals in computers, connections, teacher training, and educational software.[5]

Similarly, on March 9 1996, the President, Vice President, and over 20,000 volunteers all over the state of California participated in "NetDay" - an all-volunteer effort to wire thousands of California schools. Several companies agreed to provide free access to the Internet to every school in California. A NetDay "marketplace" was created that allowed companies to advertise hardware and software that they are providing for free, or at cost, to schools. A database created by NetDay organizers included an online map of California that allowed people to zoom down to the street level and see who had volunteered at their school. This allowed people with a shared interest in upgrading the technology in their school to discover each other in a grassroots, self-organizing fashion, and it also helped focus future efforts on schools that have not been helped. NetDay was so successful that similar efforts are being organized in other states as well.[6]

---

4   See http://www.whitehouse.gov/edtech.html for more details.
5   See http://www.ed.gov/Technology/Plan/
6   See the NetDay web site at http://www.netday.org.

Electronic Commerce

Increasingly, all firms will have to use information and communications technology to lower costs, improve quality, and reduce time-to-market. These technologies are also changing business-to-business and business-to-customer relationships, and altering the way work is organized within the firm. For example:

- Ford has developed a Global Design Studio connected by high-speed lines that allows its engineers from the United States and Europe to view and critique the same CAD (Computer-Aided Design) drawing simultaneously, slashing months from its product development time.
- The U.S. fiber, textile, and apparel sector now has the ability to adjust more rapidly to changes in consumer demand by virtue of a Quick Response system that links manufacturers and retailers electronically.
- Potential customers of Digital Equipment Corporation can test-drive a workstation over the Internet, using their own software and applications before making a purchase decision.
- Firms are experimenting with ways to increase the productivity of their workers by creating shared-knowledge repositories, delivering just-in-time training over corporate networks, and re-engineering business processes using groupware and workflow software.
- Amazon.com, a small start-up bookstore on the Web, has no inventory but is able to offer over one million titles for immediate delivery. It also offers a free personal notification service that alerts customers when a book on a particular subject, or by a particular author, has been released.

Information Policy

The NII will not realize its full potential unless we resolve a number of important information policy issues, including privacy, security, and intellectual property rights. Computer-based patient records will not be socially acceptable unless privacy and confidentiality can be ensured. Firms will not transmit sensitive, proprietary information across networks if it can be easily intercepted. Owners of copyrighted materials will not make content available on the network if they believe those rights will be violated. In addition to attempting to resolve these policy challenges, the Administration is also seeking to increase substantially the electronic dissemination of government information.

Privacy

In the context of the NII, privacy refers to 'an individual's claim to control the terms under which personal information - information attributable to an individual - is acquired, disclosed, and used' (NTIA 1995). Privacy will become an increasingly important issue as more individuals use the NII to communicate, purchase goods and services, and obtain information. Moreover, technology is making it increasingly easy to store, analyze, and re-use data generated by NII transactions. As more information is available online, it will be easy and inexpensive to build detailed profiles about individuals by combining information from a variety of databases. In the 1970s, privacy concerns focused on collection of information about individuals by government agencies. Today, consumers are more concerned about information collected by corporations, and polls show that three out of four Americans believe that they have lost control over the way in which information about them is circulated and used. Working with its private sector NII Advisory Council, the Administration has developed *Principles for Providing and Using Information* (IITF 1995b). These principles are designed to provide a code of fair information practice that will apply to both the public and private sector. For example, the Administration believes that individuals should have the right to obtain their personal information, correct this information when it is inaccurate, maintain the confidentiality of their communications and transactions, and remain anonymous when appropriate. The Administration believes that organizations that collect personal information about individuals have an obligation to:

- Provide notice about why they are gathering it, how they plan to use it, and how they intend to protect its integrity and confidentiality;
- Use technical and managerial controls to protect its confidentiality and integrity; and
- Not use it in ways that are incompatible with the individual's original understanding of how it will be used.

In the real world, implementation of these principles will require making trade-offs against other societal values, such as legitimate law enforcement objectives, freedom of speech and freedom of the press, and the benefits of the free flow of information. The Administration is considering whether to create an organization within the Executive Branch that would serve as a champion for these principles.

Security

People will be reluctant to use the NII unless they know that it is reliable, that information cannot be maliciously altered or destroyed, and that the confidentiality of information can be maintained. In June 1995, the Administration released a draft report entitled *NII Security: The Federal Role* (IITF 1995a). The report contains a number of recommendations for increasing security on the NII, including conducting threat and risk assessments, making security technologies developed for government use available to the public, strengthening laws against computer-related crime, investing in long-term security-related R&D, and making the government a model user of secure computer and communications systems.

The most controversial security-related issue has been encryption policy. Although unbreakable encryption can help protect privacy and confidentiality, it can also undermine legitimate national security and law enforcement interests. For example, a law enforcement agency could obtain a court-approved wire-tap, and still be unable to conduct electronic surveillance against criminals or terrorists using strong encryption. The Administration's first attempt to balance these competing interests (the Clipper Chip) met with strong opposition from businesses and civil libertarians. The Clipper Chip provides strong encryption, but also allows law enforcement organizations, when legally authorized, to obtain the keys that unlock the encryption. Under the Administration's original proposal, the keys would be held by two separate government agencies. On October 1, 1996, Vice President Gore announced that the Administration would allow short-term liberalization of export controls on some commercial encryption products, provided that industry was willing to develop products that support key recovery[7]. Under this proposal, trusted private sector parties would verify digital signatures and hold spare keys to confidential data. These keys could only be obtained by persons or entities that have lost their own keys, or by law enforcement officials acting under proper authority.[8]

Intellectual Property Rights

The emerging digital networked environment raises a host of questions related to intellectual property rights. Copyright owners are concerned that it will be easy for individuals to make illegal copies of songs, software programs, movies, magazines, and other protected works available to millions of users. Scholars and librarians want to know how fair use will be defined in the digital age. Some companies are concerned that allowing firms to patent critical NII interfaces will slow efforts to deploy an interoperable NII. In July 1994, the Administration released a draft report on *Intellectual Property Rights and the National Information Infrastructure* (IITF 1994d). The report concluded that the existing Copyright Act required only fine tuning to keep up with advances in technology. For example, it calls for the prohibition of devices that remove technological methods used to protect copyrighted works. Legislation has been introduced that would implement some of the recommendations of the White Paper that has the strong support of copyright holders, but it faces opposition from groups such as librarians and some segments of industry (e.g., online service providers, and telecommunications companies).[9]

Although only minor changes may be required in copyright law, many experts believe that new technologies and contractual arrangements will be required to enforce and manage these rights (Ebersole 1994). These requirements may include the ability to identify each work and its copyright status, meter usage, collect payment, and encrypt works so that only authorized users may receive them. Companies are experimenting with technologies such

---

7 See "Statement of the Vice President", Office of the Vice President, The White House, October 1, 1996.
8 See "Administration Statement on Commercial Encryption Policy." July 12, 1996.
9 Dueling Web sites explain the arguments for the bill (Creative Incentive Coalition - http:/www.cic.org) and against it (Digital Future Coalition - http://www.ari.net/dfc) .

as "headers," which might contain a publisher's electronic address, a digital signature that can be used to verify that the document has not been altered, and the prices associated with uses such as display, copying, or preparation of derivative works. New business models may also emerge in the networked environment. Companies such as Netscape and Adobe are giving away copies of their client software for individual use to strengthen their position on the server side - the modern equivalent of giving away the razor and selling the razor blades. Publishers are giving away multimedia magazines on the Internet and charging sponsors who wish to advertise on their World Wide Web sites. Other software companies make money selling freely-available software by providing training, technical assistance, and customization.

Dissemination of Government Information

One of the Administration's NII priorities is to increase the dissemination of government information. President Clinton recently signed the Paperwork Reduction Act of 1995 which calls for improvements in the 'quality and use of federal information to strengthen decision-making, accountability, and openness in government and society.' In October 1994, Vice President Gore unveiled *Welcome to the White House; An Interactive Citizen's Handbook*. This Internet-based service allows people to read all Presidential speeches and White House documents, take a "virtual" tour of the White House, send e-mail to the President and Vice President, and listen to audio clips of Socks, the First Cat.

Other federal agencies are rapidly expanding their use of the Internet to disseminate information and provide services. NASA (National Aeronautics and Space Administration) is providing real-time information on space missions. The Department of Labor has partnered with state employment services to create a national online job bank with over 100,000 hard-to-fill jobs. The Department of Energy has created OPENNET, an index of 250,000 recently declassified documents. The National Cancer Institute's CancerNet system is making valuable information available to thousands of patients and doctors. The Small Business Administration is providing entrepreneurs with information about starting or expanding a business. To help citizens navigate through this large and rapidly growing information space, the Administration has directed agencies to implement a Government Information Locator Service.

Research and Development

Historically, research partnerships between government, industry and academia have played an important role in the development of the U.S. computing and communications industry. Government-supported research has helped foster innovations in areas such as time-sharing, computer graphics, networking, workstations, design of integrated circuits, and storage technology. Federally-funded research has also created a pool of trained people who start companies or are employed by existing firms. Continued federal investment in computing and communications R&D is essential. A study by the National Research Council concluded that ten to fifteen years elapse between initial research on a new idea and commercial success, and that 'few firms will invest for a payoff that is ten years away' (Brooks and Sutherland 1995).

The Internet is a good example of the impact that government research can have on the development of the computing and communications sector. Today's Internet is an outgrowth of the ARPANET, which was started in the late 1960s. ARPA (the Defense Department's Advanced Research Projects Agency) sponsored the development of protocols that allow multiple networks to interoperate which are still in use in 1996. In the 1980s, the National Science Foundation created the NSFNET for the university research community. In the late 1980s and early 1990s, a number of companies were created to provide Internet connectivity on a commercial basis. The number of computers connected to the Internet has increased from 5,500 in 1985 to 9.4 million in January 1996, and the Internet has helped catalyze a $15 billion data communications business.

Leading researchers in government, industry, and academia have identified a host of technical capabilities that will be needed to build the National Information Infrastructure. These include:

- High-speed, reliable networks capable of delivering two-way voice, video, and data to homes and businesses at affordable rates;
- Search mechanisms that will allow people to locate and retrieve the information they are looking for, and filters that will prevent people from being overwhelmed by "info glut";
- Electronic payment mechanisms such as digital cash that are resistant to fraud, and protect privacy;

- Products and services that are easy to use for individuals with a broad range of cognitive and physical capabilities; and
- The ability to develop rapidly new applications with little or no programming by gluing together software components. (EDUCOM 1994)

The Administration´s major programme for supporting R&D related to the NII is the $1.1 billion High Performance Computing and Communications (HPCC) initiative. The original focus of the program was the technologies needed to solve "Grand Challenges" which require advances in supercomputers and high-speed networks, e.g., scientific and engineering problems such as forecasting the weather, predicting global climate change, modeling oil reservoirs, and designing new drugs. Since 1993, the scope of the program has been expanded to include support for the NII applications and technologies discussed above. On October 10, 1996, President Clinton announced the Next Generation Internet initiative. This initiative will connect more than 100 universities and national labs with networks that are 100 - 1000 times faster than today´s Internet. It will also be used to experiment with cutting-edge applications such as tele-immersion, collaboratories (laboratories without walls), and real-time visualization of large quantities of data.[10]

Global Information Infrastructure

America´s National Information Infrastructure will be part of a much larger Global Information Infrastructure (GII). In a March 1994 speech before the World Telecommunication Development Conference, Vice President Gore called for the nations of the world to promote the GII by encouraging private sector investment, promoting competition, providing open access to the network by information users and providers, creating a flexible regulatory environment, and ensuring universal service. The United States has been successful in getting other countries to adopt these principles through bodies such as the International Telecommunications Union, the G-7 summit of advanced industrial nations, APEC, and the Summit of the Americas. This development is important, given that the telecommunications infrastructure of many countries are still dominated by state-owned monopolies. The United States is also

---

10 For more information, see http://www.hpcc.gov/white-house/index.html

pushing this market-oriented agenda in the World Trade Organisation negotiations on basic telecommunications services, and in discussions on the restructuring of international satellite organizations (Intelsat and Inmarsat).

Recently, Vice President Gore unveiled the Leland Initiative, a five-year,
$15 million program to expand Internet access in 20 African countries. The
goal of the initiative is not only to promote physical connectivity, but to increase the availability of training for engineers and end-users, and to promote
Internet applications that will advance Africa's economic and social development.

Conclusion

Readers can be forgiven for tiring of the hype surrounding the Information
Superhighway. There is a real danger that it will be oversold as the cure for
every ill of modern society. But there can be little doubt that this technology is
important, and that used wisely, it can strengthen our economy and improve
our quality of life. Although market forces will drive the deployment of the
National Information Infrastructure, public policy has a significant role to
play. For this reason, the Clinton-Gore Administration will continue to make
the promotion of the NII and its applications a top priority.

References

Brooks, P. and Sutherland, E. (1995), *Evolving the High Performance Computing and
    Communications Initiative to Support the Nation's Information Infrastructure*,
    National Research Council.
Ebersole, Joseph L. (1994), *Protecting Intellectual Property Rights on the Information
    Superhighways.* Information Industry Association.
EDUCOM (1994), *R&D for the NII: Technical Challenges.*
IITF (1993), Information Infrastructure Task Force, *National Information Infrastructure:
    Agenda for Action* (Washington D.C.: National Telecommunications and Information
    Administration).
IITF (1994a), Information Infrastructure Task Force, *National Information Infrastructure.
    Progress Report September 1993-1994.* (Washington D.C.: Office of the Vice President,
    The Secretary of Commerce)

IITF (1994b), Information Infrastructure Task Force, Committee on Applications and Technology, *Putting the Information Infrastructure to Work*. (Washington, D.C.: National Institute of Technology (NIST), May.

IITF (1994c), Information Infrastructure Task Force, Committee on Applications and Technology, *The Information Infrastructure: Reaching Society's Goals* (Washington, D.C.: National Institute of Technology (NIST), September.

IITF (1994d), Information Infrastructure Task Force, Working Group on Intellectual Property, *Intellectual Property and the NII. Working Group Report* (Washington, D.C.: National Telecommunications and Information Administration), June.

IITF (1995a), Information Infrastructure Task Force, *NII-Security. The Federal Role* (Washington, D.C.: National Telecommunications and Information Administration), September.

IITF (1995b), *Privacy and the National Information Infrastructure: Principles for Providing and Using Personal Information*, Information Infrastructure Task Force, June 6.

NTIA (1995), *Privacy and the NII: Safeguarding Telecommunications-Related Personal Information* (Washington, D.C.: U.S: Department of Commerce), October.

3. The Action Plan of the European Commission

Michael Niebel

Introduction

A revolution is coming based on information, itself the expression of human knowledge. Technological progress now enables us to process, store, retrieve, and communicate information regardless of the form it takes, and unconstrained by distance, time, and volume. This revolution adds huge new capacities to human intelligence and constitutes a resource which changes the way we produce, work, learn, and live together. Awareness of this revolution - whether we call it the Information Superhighway, the Infobahn, or the Information Society - has rocketed within a relatively short period of time. This chapter considers the European Commission's response to this revolution.

The Emergence of an Action Plan for the Information Society

The notion of "electronic highways" first appeared in European policy-making in 1988, in a communication of the European Commission to Parliament and Council. This was a largely technical paper dealing with broadband networks - one of the possible backbones of an information infrastructure. Later, in the early '90s, the Commission launched the idea of transEuropean networks, in the context of the creation of the internal market. One of these mooted networks was the transEuropean telecom network.

However, broader discussion was only triggered with the publication of the White Paper on *Growth, Competitiveness and Employment* which, in 1993, took on one of Europe's most burning problems: unemployment (European Commission 1993). In this context the Commission felt it necessary to react to the rapid progress being made in information and communication technologies (ICTs). Developments in digitisation and compression were not only leading to basic changes in the relevant industries, but were starting to have a much wider impact.

This realisation led the Commission to select the term "Information Society" for its deliberations. It felt that the Superhighway or the Infobahn only described the elements of higher speed, and larger volumes, and that these terms neglect that new ICTs not only enable you to do things faster, but also introduce fundamental qualitative changes in how things are done: they have a profound influence on economic interactions, and on society at large. Thus, by the Information Society, the Commission wished to express a comprehensive and integrated view of the new phenomenon. Equally important, the Commission wished to give a political message, i.e., that whilst technological advances drive developments, they do not constitute a purpose in themselves but must be harnessed to serve society.

Following the White Paper, the member states (through the European Summit of Heads of State and Government in Brussels) asked a group of high-level representatives of relevant sectors to make proposals for the European route to the Information Society. This group, under the chairmanship of Commissioner Bangemann, presented its report to the European Summit in Corfu on the 24th and 25th June, 1994 (Bangemann Group 1994).

The report stressed the importance of commercial competition in driving developments, and requested a liberalisation of telecommunications markets. Only through competition could communication costs be reduced to a level where citizens could take full advantage of the information society's possibilities, and where European economic operators were no longer at a significant price disadvantage compared to those in the United States. The group also demanded a common regulatory framework especially as regards standardisation, the protection of intellectual property rights, respect of privacy, and the security of data transmission. Finally, it identified ten areas for pilot applications to be tested.

European Heads of State and Government welcomed the report and asked the Commission for an Action Plan. This plan - presented only three weeks later - was organized along four axes (European Commission 1994):

- the regulatory and legal framework
- the networks, services, applications, and content

- the social and cultural aspects
- the promotion of the information society (European Commission 1994)

Important progress has been made since then regarding the regulatory framework for telecommunications. As of the 1st January 1998 the European telecommunications sector will be fully liberalized. I should also mention - as it is important to the social shaping of the information society - that one leitmotiv of the liberalisation discussion in the Union has been the aim to safeguard universal service in the process. Therefore the European Commission has proposed rules and procedures to guarantee and finance universal service in a liberalized environment, where such mechanisms are most needed.

The momentum created by the information society discourse played a vital part in progressing the emergence of the action plan. This was especially true for the decision to liberalize infrastructures, for which a specific Council meeting on the information society proved instrumental. In addition, the rapid dynamics of both technological and market developments led to the European Commission shortening the transitional periods that some Member States had initially requested.

Another regulatory area where work is progressing is in the field of copyright. In the new market environment, the rights of creators as against the interests of users have to be kept in balance. Legislation, globalisation, and the separation of content from the carrier, all pose a number of new problems. In this regard, by November 1986 the Commission - following a consultation based on a Green Paper on *Intellectual Property Rights in the Information Society* - had outlined principles for the approach it intended to take. Legislative proposals were expected to follow in 1997.

The role of the public sector is, however, limited regarding networks, generic services, applications, and content. Financing the networks is essentially a task for the operators. In the creation of generic services, the Commission, to some extent, has a coordinating function. With its R&D support, the Community can play a catalytic role for the development of technologies, services, and applications.

It is remarkable that a large number of the pilot projects originated at local and regional levels, and typically involved some kind of public-private partnership. In many cases, these initiatives organized themselves across national borders, cooperating with each other in the exchange of experience and best practice. In themselves, they offer evidence of a new form of networking.

The Social Dimension of the Action Plan

As we discuss the social shaping of the information society, I would like to concentrate on the third axis of the action plan: its social dimension.

One of the major elements of the European Union's debates is the fear that the information society will cost jobs, a fear that is extremely difficult to dispel. It is easy to identify the jobs most threatened by the emergence of ICTs. For example, as the telecom sector undergoes restructuring, the shrinking of the work forces of the incumbent monopolists is highly visible. Similarly, jobs lost due to the automation of machinery are also clearly identifiable. Compensation for such job losses - through job creation by newly emerging competitors, or from outsourcing - is not always evident. It is also difficult to demonstrate how many jobs have been saved, or created, across the entire economy, thanks to cheaper and more efficient means of information and communication delivery. Despite these difficulties, it has to be made clear that we have no choice except to take advantage of the opportunities of the new ICTs.

An increasingly pressing issue surrounds discussion on the globalisation of economic activity, i.e., the impact of the diminishment of the relevance of distance or physical presence, on jobs that used to be sheltered by geographical proximity. A specific example requiring public and policy discussion is teleworking. Teleworking offers a number of opportunities:

- it improves the chances of working closer to, or in, the home;
- it reduces space requirements in densely-populated areas;
- it can integrate less-favoured regions;
- it can reduce traffic, which benefits the environment, saves energy, and cuts infrastructure costs.

However, that begs the question as to whether employers regard telework as dependent, or independent, work. Teleworking affects labour market legislation in areas such as working hours, wage agreements, and workers' protection and, thus, calls for a reappraisal by the social partners. The Commission has set up a group of high-level experts to look into these issues which has already presented its first report. On this basis the Commission has published a Green Paper which, after consultation, could lead to concrete proposals (European Commission 1995, 1996a).

There is also a fear that cyber-encounters may replace personal contacts, or teleshopping replace visits to the store, thus leading to increased social isolation. On the other hand, the new ICTs offer excellent opportunities to (re)integrate sick or disabled persons. For the elderly, especially, they create the possibility of more frequent contact with their families, and improved participation in social life. We should also not forget that - despite the image of the global village - cultural differences will remain strong even amongst industrialized countries. Whether we come from a drive-in culture, or we are used to mixing on the Piazza or Agora, will continue to influence our behaviour in the information society. Even within the European Union, differences in the use of ICTs between member states will remain significant.

Another major social issue generated by the information society debate is the fear that we may create a two-tier society of information "haves" and "have nots". To prevent this, education and training are of paramount importance. Modern ICTs make effective distance-learning possible, and facilitate everyone's access to knowledge. A continued, life-long, learning process is an essential requirement for individuals to thrive in the rapidly-changing work environments of the information society. Private teaching and learning methods will not only complement, but will also compete with, what is on offer in the public sector.

In the European Union, access to teaching across borders (e.g., foreign language teaching via multimedia networks) must not be the preserve of an elite. It must be part-and-parcel of normal education. It would, however, be wrong to attempt to train new generations to become computer specialists: a lot of people can drive but very few are car mechanics. What is required is our readiness to learn quickly, and to adapt continuously.

New technologies should not work to aggravate inequalities in educational opportunity, but rather they should serve to bridge gaps that may exist today. At the G7 Conference in Brussels on the Information Society, the late Ron Brown, U.S. Secretary of Commerce, illustrated the positive effects of new ICTs when he described a visit to his former school in the Bronx. This school, in an underprivileged area, used to be characterized by frequent absenteeism and by pupils' lack of motivation. With the introduction there of new ICTs, attendance increased dramatically, and the motivation of teachers and pupils alike improved considerably.

This example illustrates how new ICTs can be used to help create better chances for the socially disadvantaged. They can also help to negate the disadvantages of living in remote areas. More radically, they provide our education systems with the means to develop more than a single disciplinary perspective; through the new ICTs, we can tap into the full potential of scholars who use differing kinds of intelligence, and who deploy different intellectual strengths.

For the European Commission, education and training for the information society is an important objective. In the near future it may well be the case that, for the first time, teachers are confronted by pupils who know more about a subject than they do themselves. In the European Union, education and training policies are primarily separately devised and implemented by each of the member states. However, the Commission is in a position to launch a number of initiatives, including industry's participation in education. Therefore, at the request of the Heads of State and Government in Florence, the Commission presented an Action Plan on *Learning in the Information Society* (European Commission 1996b). In addition, the Commission has created a Task Force on multimedia educational software to broaden and accelerate the range of educational tools on offer.

Early European Union policy discussions centred on questions of technology, of industry, and of the legal framework. To expand the spectrum of input - preparatory to formulating the political agenda - the Commission has created an Information Society Forum, consisting of representatives from different groups in society. Their recommendations cover a wide range of subjects such as Public Services, Culture, and Consumer Protection (Forum Information Society 1996).

On 27 November 1996, the Commission adopted a Rolling Action Plan for the Information Society which builds on completed, pending, and ongoing actions (European Commission 1996c). This plan calls for a number of new actions to be initiated, with a particular emphasis on the chapter of "people at the centre".

No nation can develop the information society in isolation. A first step towards international cooperation was taken at the G7 Ministerial Conference, hosted by the Commission, in February 1995, which agreed on a shared vision and common principles, as well as on piloting 11 global test projects. Following that came the Conference on the Information Society and Development in which was held in South Africa, with representatives from the different regions of the world. International conferences on specific topics like Standardisation Aspects of the Information Society, and Conditions for Use and Misuse of Global Information Networks followed throughout 1997.

The European Union places particular emphasis on cooperating with its neighbours. In 1995, it joined forces with Central and Eastern Europe at a ministerial level, and launched a concrete work programme through a first Forum Meeting. In 1996, it initiated dialogue on the information society with the Mediterranean countries.

Our guiding principle must be to create an information society for all people. We must work together to avoid the spectre of information "haves" and "have nots" within our countries, and between the countries of the world.

References

Bangemann Group (1994), High-Level Group on the Information Society, *Europe and the Gobal Information Society, Recommendations to the European Council*, Brussels, May 26.

European Commission (1993), *White Paper on Growth, Competitiveness, and Employment: The Challenges and Ways Forward Into the 21st Century*. COM (93) 700 final, Dec. 5, (Brussels: Commission of the European Communities).

European Commission (1994), *Europe's Way to the Information Society: An Action Plan* COM(94) 347 (Brussels: Commission of the European Communities).

European Commission (1995), *Green Paper on Copyright and Related Rights in the Information Society*, COM (95) 382 final, July 19, (Brussels: Commission of the European Communities).

European Commission (1996a), *Follow-Up to the Green Paper on Copyright and Related Rights in the Information Society*. Communication from the Commission, COM (96) 568 final, Nov. 20, (Brussels: Commission of the European Communities).

European Commission (1996b), *Learning in the Information Society. Action Plan for a European Education Initiative 1996 - 1998*. Communication from the Commission (Brussels: Commission of the European Communities)

European Commission (1996c), *Europe at the Forefront of the Global Information Society*. Rolling Action Plan, Communication from the Commission COM (96) 607 final, Nov. 27, (Brussels: Commission of the European Communities).

Forum Information Society (1996), *Information Society: Networks for People and their Communities*. Making the most of the Information Society in the European Union. First Annual Report to the European Commission from the Information Society Forum. (Brussels: European Commission, Information Society Activity Center) June.

For an inventory of documents see http://ispo.cec.be

4. How Much Interoperability Makes an NII?

Thomas R. Spacek

Introduction

The existing National Information Infrastructure (NII) consists of a wide variety of networks and applications including wireline and wireless telephony, 800-based information services, cable TV, the Internet, online services, and others. These networks, separately and in some cases jointly, provide a wide array of useful information access, computing, and communications applications which are socially and commercially beneficial. As we look forward to an advanced NII as articulated by the Council on Competitiveness (C on C 1993), the Computer Systems Policy Project (CSPP 1993), and the Clinton/Gore Administration (IITF 1993) questions remain as to whether the full vision of this advanced NII will require more than the extension of existing networks and applications to multimedia forms. In particular, one must address the issue of full, seamless connectivity and interoperability amongst networks and the associated applications which will form the next generation NII (CSPP 1994).

Important characteristics of an NII include: meeting urgent societal needs, focusing on market-driven applications, attaining maximum interoperability and interconnectivity, providing universal access and service, assuring global interconnectivity, being user-friendly, and requiring a framework for development, growth, and improvement in an on-going economically sustainable way (Spacek 1994). This paper touches on several of these important characteristics, but focusses predominantly on interconnectivity and interoperability, without which the visions of an advanced NII may not be achievable.

Background and Vision

We have a "voice telephony NII" in 1996, and one can view the current Internet as a model for a data (or perhaps broader) communications NII. Telephony, the Internet, or perhaps other existing network approaches represent good starting points from which an NII may evolve; however these may not naturally evolve into an NII as envisioned by the Council on Competitiveness, the CSPP, the Clinton/Gore Administration, and others. Although business and technology convergence is taking place in the communications/information industries, it is not at all clear that current market forces will be viewed by major players in these industries as creating the incentive for making necessary investments and cooperative agreements to evolve the current array of networks in a way which will achieve such a vision (CEOs 1993; RBOCs 1993; Spacek 1994).

The three key NII visions referenced above are quite similar in intent although they differ somewhat in emphasis. The following is the *Vision for a 21st Century Information Infrastructure* by the Council on Competitiveness, May 1993: 'The infrastructure of the 21st century will enable all Americans[1] to access information and communicate with each other easily, reliably, securely, and cost-effectively in any medium - voice, data, image, or video - anytime, anywhere. This capability will enhance the productivity of work and lead to dramatic improvements in social services, education, and entertainment.' It will consist of: 'a set of widely accessible and interoperable communications networks, digital libraries, information databases and services, easy-to-use information appliances and computer systems, and trained people who can build, maintain and operate these resources.'

---

[1]   This is a vision of an NII in the US and thus the reference to "all Americans". One can view each country (or in some cases, groups of countries) in the world having a vision of its "network of networks" or NII and a timetable for evolving toward that vision. A GII then consists of a "network of NII networks" where the NIIs of countries throughout the world interconnect and interoperate. For this to occur, the timetables and the capabilities of each country's NII do not have to be the same, however common protocols need to be followed.

Distinguishing Characteristics of NII Applications

Some of the key properties in this vision, which we will refer to later, include: 'all Americans' - implying an NII should be ubiquitous; 'voice, data, image, or video'; and 'widely accessible and interoperable communications networks.'

An NII includes applications in the areas of health care, education, digital libraries, intelligent manufacturing, intelligent transportation systems, interactive entertainment, advanced telecommuting, access to government information, electronic commerce, and others. There are existing applications, experiments, and trials in all of these areas. But what characteristics distinguish future NII applications from LAN (Local Area Network) or local computing applications? An NII application eliminates distance. It facilitates virtual communities to form and function without the need for the physical presence of the community members. Some of these communities may otherwise not have formed. It provides for remote access of a wide variety of information sources. Further, applications can be fully shared in an NII. So for example, if a pilot education trial in Colorado Springs were successful, it could be readily available in other parts of Colorado as well as throughout the country. In addition, functionalities are shared in an NII. For example, remote diagnosis in health care and distance learning in education may have many application and network functions in common (such as video telephony) that can be shared, resulting in reduced costs.

Reaching the NII Vision

These distinguishing characteristics of NII applications together with the key properties of NII visions noted above, imply that seamless interoperability among networks and applications is needed to achieve an advanced NII. Whether or not full seamlessness can be achieved, it is clear that the advanced visions and application characteristics make such interoperability the target to shoot for.

The difficulty of achieving network interoperability will depend, in large part, on whether the constituent networks are heterogeneous or homogeneous. Network interoperability can more easily be achieved amongst homogeneous networks. However it is unlikely that such networks will be ubiqui-tously deployed. There is a very large embedded base of both privately and publicly available networks with varying technologies. Firms may be neither able nor willing to trade out their networks and build new ones with a par-ticular technology just to be connected to an NII. Many firms may even choose not to connect to an NII until security problems are solved. However, these problems are currently being addressed by active research and develop-ment programs.

Competitive firms are constantly developing new technologies with new capabilities employing new approaches. Such competition is healthy, but is not likely to lead to homogeneity. Further, advanced technologies like ATM (Asynchronous Transfer Mode) may potentially become widespread, but per-haps not ubiquitous. Thus it is more likely that an NII will require seamless interoperability among heterogeneous networks, many of which are already in existence, perhaps with subtending homogeneous sub-networks.

How do we achieve such interoperability? There are two classes of techni-cal approach to this problem, although there may be many different solutions within each class. The first class involves translations. If there are n tech-nologies, then it takes $n \times (n-1)$ translations (or encapsulations in some cases) for the networks employing these technologies to communicate with each other. In addition, each network needs to have knowledge of properties of every other network in order to perform the translation required to communi-cate with them. The second class involves a protocol that can operate over any of the n technologies. This approach requires only 2n translations or encap-sulations, and perhaps more importantly, knowledge about other networks is not required. Examples of such protocols are the Internet Protocol (IP) which is in widespread use and the next generation IP protocol, IPv6. The latter is planned to be available in routers by 1998 and will have enhanced routing, addressing, and congestion control capabilities that will support real-time voice and video. Protocols such as these allow for heterogeneous network substrates to work together.

Such protocols facilitate seamless interoperability among networks to transport packets and streams of information. Potentially, a more difficult problem is seamless interoperability between applications and networks, and amongst applications. However the complexity of application-to-network interoperability is reduced by a "spanning layer" as discussed by David Clark

(Clark 1995). An example of a spanning layer is the open bearer service of the National Research Council's open data network architecture (CSTB 1994). Clark notes that if there are m applications and n network technologies, the complexity of the interoperability problem is m x n, whereas with the spanning layer the complexity is reduced to m + n. Although it is beyond the scope of this paper, it is worth noting that there are some economic concerns that arise for firms operating at the bottom layer of the open data network architecture model (Srinagesh and Gong 1995; Varian 1995).

Four Interoperability Scenarios

To address the issue of how much interoperability is needed for an NII, we will discuss four potential NII scenarios. The first is where multi-media networks providing voice, data, image, and video are fully interoperable. This is similar to the Council on Competitiveness' NII vision quoted earlier. Users just plug their appliance into the wall and have full connectivity and interoperability to all NII applications. Although this is a nice aim, one must look carefully at variants of this scenario which perhaps may act as evolutionary steps toward the full vision (Srinagesh 1995).

Does everything really need to be seamlessly interconnected regardless of cost? For example, suppose HDTV (High Definition Television) were available. This morning I am sitting at my laptop writing a paper, and it would be a perfect addition to my paper if I inserted a frame from a HDTV movie I viewed last night. So I do it. This may cost me a dollar or perhaps 20 dollars; but I am not asking the question of the cost or people's willingness to pay to take this action. Rather, I am asking what is the cost to make this capability available in the first place, i.e., the cost of this level of seamless interoperability. If the cost is low, such capabilities should be incorporated. The intent here is not to focus on HDTV, but rather to make the point that for each such capability, we need to weigh the cost of providing that capability in a seamlessly interoperable NII against the benefits, where the costs include not only financial considerations but also time delays in having an NII broadly available.

For the second potential NII scenario, let us assume it is two years from now. The model is the Internet with the IPv6 protocol supporting limited, but much improved, voice and video capabilities. Perhaps the voice and video applications are well enough supported to meet the needs of a significant portion of the business-to-business desktop multi-media market. Although some voice and video applications are supported on the advanced Internet, in this scenario the preponderance of voice communications is carried by traditional telecommunications networks, and the preponderance of entertainment video is offered over cable and video dial tone networks. There are gateways between these predominantly voice networks and video networks and the evolved Internet.

Connected to, and fully interoperable with, the Internet in this scenario are many homogeneous sub-networks, e.g., ATM sub-networks, which may or may not be geographically contiguous. Such an ATM sub-network could be small or large - ranging from a medium size firm's network to the size of a state or multiple states. In fact, depending on how successful and widespread ATM becomes, it is conceivable that over time these homogeneous sub-networks become larger than the Internet from which they subtend, based on some measure or other, e.g., when the volume of traffic carried by the subtending networks exceeds the volume of traffic sent over the Internet, or perhaps the number of switches vs. number of routers. Depending on one's perspective, these subtending networks would be considered part of the Internet, and the term "larger than" above is meant to imply an increase in sub-network homogeneity over time.

For communications within a homogeneous sub-network, there is no need to go up to the IP layer; the communication is handled completely within the sub-network[2]. However, when a communication from a sub-network is leaving that network, then the communication does go up to the IP layer for transport to the destination network(s) which may be based upon different technology from the originating sub-network. IP handles the communications among these heterogeneous networks. Although this scenario is not totally

---

2   For this discussion, such an existing sub-network need not be homogeneous consisting predominantly of the same technology, but it could be an existing network with differing technologies which are interoperable via some mechanism such as translation, multi-protocol routers, etc. Such mechanisms are not easily broadly extensible to a wide variety of network technologies that will exist in an NII. However, if an existing network is already interoperable via such mechanisms, it can be viewed in the same way as we view a 'homogeneous sub-network' in this discussion.

seamlessly interoperable since there are two functional gateways, it may be viewed as a significant step leading toward an advanced NII.

The third scenario is perhaps a "non-NII" scenario where multiple networks of different types proliferate and do not interconnect or interoperate. There may be independent voice telephone networks, the Internet, video dial tone networks, cable systems, satellite systems, intelligent transportation systems, ATM networks, etc. Each offers applications it was designed to support, and perhaps adds other applications if the costs of doing so are low enough.

The fourth scenario is a vertical or "stovepiping" scenario which involves a small number of firms (or partnerships) each creating its own NII with each having seamless interoperability vertically throughout its networks, applications, and exclusive information content, and having either no connectivity or perhaps some gateway connections to its rival NIIs. Such connections may or may not adequately handle real-time services. An even more significant issue with this type of gateway model is the potential inability of competitors to insert new technologies, services, and applications within vertically-integrated solutions without the cooperation and permission of the vertically-integrated providers. Each firm (vertically-integrated provider) vies for customers for its own NII. However, this scenario may not satisfy the major NII visions and may not meet the requirements for NII applications described earlier in the paper. Note that even though this scenario and the second one (positing an advanced Internet which provides multimedia desktop services, homogeneous sub-networks, with traditional telecommunications networks carrying the preponderance of voice, and with cable and video dial tone networks handling the preponderance of entertainment video) have gateways, they are very different types of gateways. This fourth scenario involves relatively closed systems with gateways between network service providers each providing its own proprietary NII. The second scenario involves relatively open systems with gateways between some functions that may not be fully interoperable early on.

Closing Remarks

Stovepiping may occur if current trends continue. Moreover, lack of applications-to-network interoperability may itself lead to stovepiping. For example, why should a network provider seek to interoperate with other networks if there are not sufficient applications available to work in that environment? After all, people use applications, not networks. For stovepiping to be avoided, competing firms or partnerships will need to vigorously compete on quality, service offerings, applications, prices, etc., while cooperating to achieve interoperability. The economic incentive for such competition/cooperation is that firms must believe they have greater potential profitability, e.g., with NII capabilities people will spend more money on communications than otherwise, and that they will be willing to spend sufficiently more to cover the costs and risks of providing seamless interoperability. Although there may be some historical examples, lots of speculation, and some relevant work (Economides 1995), the author is not aware of any studies that would convince providers that economic incentives to create a fully seamless interoperable NII presently exist.

Government, industry, and academia must recognize the potential economic waste of the stovepiping approach. Due to lack of interoperability and connectivity amongst customers who might want to use new advanced interpersonal communications capabilities, or who would use multiple applications although only some are available on their provider's NII, the market may not expand. The system could collapse over time only to be re-built with a more horizontal and open approach years later. The benefits of an interoperable NII may provide the potential for firms and partnerships to be more profitable as well as to provide significant societal benefits, but this still needs to be demonstrated sufficiently to affect the investment decisions of network service and applications providers if we are to achieve the visions of an advanced NII.

References

C on C (1993), Council on Competitiveness, Vision for a 21st Century Information Infrastructure (Washington, DC: C on C).

CEOs (1993), CEOs of 14 major US telecommunications firms, Policy Statement (on the NII) (Morristown, NJ: Bellcore).

Clark, D. (1995), 'Interoperation, Open Interfaces, and Protocol Architecture', draft, MIT Laboratory for Computer Science, presented at NII 2000, Washington, DC.

CSPP (1993), Computer Systems Policy Project, Perspectives on the National Information Infrastructure: CSPP's Vision and Recommendations for Action (Washington, DC: CSPP).

CSPP (1994), Computer Systems Policy Project, Perspectives on the National Information Infrastructure: Ensuring Interoperability (Washington, DC: CSPP).

CSTB (1994), Computer Science and Telecommunications Board, National Research Council, Realizing the Information Future - The Internet and Beyond (Washington, DC: National Academy Press).

Economides, N. (1996), 'The Economics of Networks', International Journal of Industrial Organization,14: forthcoming.

IITF (1993), Information Infrastructure Task Force, Department of Commerce, The National Information Infrastructure: Agenda for Action (Washington, DC: Dept. of Commerce).

RBOCs (1993), An Infostructure for All Americans: Creating Economic Growth in the 21st Century (Washington, DC: RBOCs).

Spacek, T. R. (1994), 'Building Consensus for a US National Information Infrastructure: A Telecommunications Industry Perspective', Association of Research Libraries Proceedings of the 123rd Meeting: The Emerging Information Infrastructure: Players, Issues, Technology, and Strategy (Washington, DC: ARL). Also in International Society for Technology in Education, Educational IRM Quarterly, 3 spring/summer 1994: 37-40.

Srinagesh, P. (1995), , 'Internet Cost Structures and Interconnection Agreements', in Brock, G. (1995) (ed.), Toward a Competitive Telecommunications Industry: Selected Papers from the 1994 Telecommunications Policy Research Conference (Hillsdale, NJ: Lawrence Erlbaum).

Srinagesh, P. and Gong, J. (1995), 'Economics of Layered Networks,' presented at NII 2000 Washington, DC.

Varian, H. (1995), Department of Economics, University of Michigan, presentation at NII 2000, Washington, DC, (currently at U. of California, Berkeley).

5. Crippled Digitalization

Superhighways or One-Way Streets?
The Case of German Digital Television

Hans J. Kleinsteuber

Introduction

This chapter begins with a brief review of the U.S. National Information Infrastructure (NII) and then continues with an analysis of German (and European) developments in the light of the logic and intention of the American example. The purpose is not to dwell on the situation in the U.S., but rather to provide a comparison for understanding recent German developments: the central thesis of this chapter is that the German context for the application of new digital technologies is quite different from the American one. This is the case, even though developments in both countries are based on similar technologies, viz personal computers and their components, digitalization of networks, and digital transmission and compression. Differences will be explained in terms of how the leading actors in both countries employ digital technologies, what their intentions are, and how they try to translate their interests and strategies into specific technologies.

A comparative perspective is taken here which is explicitly concerned with exploring the differences between the two countries so as to highlight Germany's specific history. This should prove to be a particularly fruitful approach since Germany exemplifies European trends in this respect, while the U.S. typifies developments in non-European countries such as Canada or Japan. That said, it must be stressed that an American-style Information Superhighway can be identified in some German developments, and a German-style specification of digital television - as will be described in this chapter - can also be found in certain U.S. developments. An example of the former would be that the American 'highway' policy constitutes part of German

Telekom's strategy (albeit on a much smaller scale), and it is also pursued by some of German Telekom's competitors, e.g. Vebacom. An example of the latter would be RCA's America's Digital Satellite System (DSS), with providers like DirecTV. The interesting question, though, is why these respective approaches have been reduced to a minority position in each others countries.

Facing the Challenge: Digital Media Technology

The term "digital revolution" refers to the merger of new digital computer logic with the conventional technologies of radio and television. On the surface, this convergence only seems to require some marginal adjustment, because the screen (whether television or computer) remains as the essential interface to the user. But in the digital future, every screen will be fed by binary 1-0 commands. By means of the digital signal, the computer's logic gradually creeps into the technology of television transmission and the resulting changes are truly remarkable.

Apart from other innovations, digital technologies pave the way to full interactivity (Neuman 1991: 104ff). Interactivity describes a technical as well as a societal structure in which bi-directional communication is possible, that is, the roles of the sender and the receiver become interchangeable; the participants may take turns to become active or passive during the exchange. Interactivity, understood as bi-directionality, is not just a technological principle. It also refers to the way communcication is structured in a society.

Conventional analogue television follows a centralized and hierachical pattern, forcing the viewer into passivity. The traditional analogue interactive principle is best represented by the telephone system. Digital technology offers the chance for the user to become active, if desired. This marks a clear advance over the passive consumption of broadcasting communications which pertains today. The American metaphor of the "Information Superhighway" refers to interactivity; one-way streets are naturally incompatible with the concept of a highway (Kleinsteuber 1996).

Online computer services (and especially the Internet) represent the most developed and most widespread application of digital interactivity (Negroponte 1995). Currently these services are only available on narrowband. The ideal material for broadband interactive networks seems to be optical fibre, but it will take several decades before the major countries establish a fully optical infrastructure. Developments in ISDN or "fibre to the curb" (main lines in fiber, lines to the home coaxial), or possibly the telephone line, might offer intermediate steps towards the world envisaged in the Info-Highway. However, what is common to all these highly interactive networks is their terrestrial nature (MediaGruppe 1995). Orbital communication via satellites might be able to offer interactive services to the general public in the future, but, at the moment, their utilization for private purposes is prohibitively expensive; Direct Broadcasting Satellites (DBS) - as presently used, or as may be applied in the foreseeable future - are restricted to one-way transmission only. However, it is the presence of such satellites which makes for the major infrastructural difference between this and the other side of the Atlantic.

Besides the promise of interactivity, a second feature which we associate with the American-style vision of the Info-Highway is its universal access, again depicted in the metaphor of a street network with many entrances and exits that are open to all. The way users may enter and leave the infrastructure is basically egalitarian, since everyone is subject to the same "traffic" rules of the net.

This interactive and egalitarian model is individual and personal in principle. The very idea of it clashes with our historical experience of media technologies whereby just a few content providers deliver centrally-produced programmes to a large mass of consumers. Some American thinkers hold that, in the digital age, this historical concentration of power will become obsolete (Gilder 1994). The argument is that this agglomeration of media power in only a few centres - technically, in the sender stations, and, economically, in the media companies - must wither away; interactivity will reduce one-way communications and so will potentially put the individual communicator on an equal footing with the old centres.

This chapter suggests otherwise. What follows is a short description of how new media technologies have been introduced in Germany, and the thesis of the author is that Germany is entering the digitalization era without changing its basic pattern of passive and receptive broadcasting. Digital television in this context means the delivery of more-of-the-same programming, and interactivity is not intended.

The Beginnings of New Media in Germany

Germany has always prided itself on being one of the leaders in developing new media technologies. However, the most recent one to actually succeed dates back to 1967 with the introduction of PAL colour television, which was eventually adopted by about 50 other countries (Bruch and Riedel 1987). Since then, a number of new technologies have been tried out including a DBS TV satellite, a videotex system called BTX (Bildschirmtext), and a Digital Satellite Radio (DSR). Even though all these developments were heavily subsidized by public funding, they have not taken off. Their failure may be attributed to the fact that all of them were conceived by small elites, each of whom specified their innovation in a top-down fashion, without having knowledge of, or interest in, the demands of the market or the needs of consumers.

It is interesting to recall that as early as the 1970s West Germany had entered into a debate on the possibilities for using coaxial cable systems to create two-way television through a back channel. In a comprehensive Telecommunications Report of 1976, the concepts of the "wired city", and of "cable democracy" - stimulated by American studies and projects like Qube in Ohio - were extensively discussed (KtK 1976). None of the proposals of that report were ever tested, let alone realized, and interactivity remained a chimera. With hindsight, it seems clear that the concept of a two-way cable served mainly to make cable technology look attractive and to reduce widespread scepticism about its value. In fact, extensive cabling only began in 1982 following a change to a Conservative-Liberal government in Bonn, and, even at that, its main purpose was to offer a new means of transmission to Germany's nascent commercial television industry. The last thing this industry was interested in was experimenting with interactivity through back channels. Since then, this chapter argues, the commercial television industry quickly became a major player with the power to decide which technologies to adopt or reject. It has never had a substantial stake in interactivity.

The Major Actors

ASTRA and Direct Broadcasting Satellites in Europe

Central to the introduction of digital television in Europe is the ASTRA system of DBSes which can deliver programmes Direct-To-Home (DTH) or via head stations into cable systems. The first ASTRA 1A-satellite was launched in 1988. ASTRA began as an American business initiative in Europe but was taken over by European investors, mainly due to the successful resistance mounted by the European telecom companies. A Société Européene des Satellites S.A. (SES) was established in 1985, based in Luxembourg.

All ASTRA satellites are manufactured by Hughes Communications in California, as they offer a high number of TV-transponders (16 of them, at the outset) and a footprint that covers the entire European continent. With this capacity, ASTRA has come to dominate the DBS market, which originated in Europe through TV-Sat in Germany and a similar system in France. These latter DBS initiatives have partially failed to capture the European market, since they offer a low number of transponders (a maximum of 5) and a smaller footprint. In addition, ASTRA has marginalized the satellite services offered by EUTELSAT (the European organization for the various national telecoms).

ASTRA currently holds an absolute hegemony in Europe by controlling more than 90 per cent of the European DBS-market. In early 1995, SES managed four satellites with analogue technology (ASTRA 1A-1D) which offer more than 60 TV programmes that go DTH to about 15 million households in Europe (ASTRA 1995). Most of the programmes are in English and German, the two most attractive language markets of Western Europe. Up to nine million German households (out of 33 million German households with TV) have installed an ASTRA receiver antenna comparatively cheaply (prices start at around DM 300).

	TV-Households	Satellite and Cable	Satellite only
Germany	32.140 Mio	23.470 Mio	9.230 Mio
Austria	3.000 Mio	1.967 Mio	1.063 Mio
Switzerland	2.881 Mio	2.564 Mio	0.253 Mio

Table 1: *Cable and Satellite in the German-speaking part of Europe (Middle of 1995) (Source: ASTRA 1995: 8)*

The quoted figures are published by ASTRA itself and so may reflect a favourable view of ASTRA's activities. However, the overall trend is clear. ASTRA claims that it reaches more than 23 Mio of all German households with TVs via cable and/or satellite, and that amounts to a market share of about 73 per cent. In all German-speaking countries together, the system reaches about 38 Mio households, which means that the market share amounts to about the same figure.

Name	Year of Launching	Number of Transponders
1 A	1988	16 analogue
1 B	1991	16
1 C	1993	18
1 D	1994	18
1 E	1995	18 digital
1 F	1996	22
1 G	1997	32
1 H	1998	32

Table 2: *The ASTRA-system*

In October 1995, SES launched the first digitally-equipped satellite - ASTRA 1E - into orbit. Each of the 18 transponders of that satellite can transmit between five and ten digitally-compressed TV programmes (Schulz 1995). Another satellite with digital capability - ASTRA 1F - was launched in March 1996, this time with 22 transponders. Two more digital satellites - ASTRA 1G and 1H - are scheduled for 1997 and 1998 with an even higher number of transponders. By 1998 the ASTRA system alone may offer Europeans between 500 and 1,000 additional digital TV channels. Most of the available digital transponders have already been leased to two alliances - Kirch and Bertelsmann - interested in the introduction of digital television.

In addition, EUTELSAT is also actively involved in DBS technologies with its EUTELSAT and HOT BIRD satellites. Digital-encoded programmes may be found on EUTELSAT II-F1 and on HOT BIRD 1, and in April 1996 the first European digital package became available (the French "bouquet numerique"). EUTELSAT plans to have five HOT BIRD satellites working by 1998, each of which will carry between 16 and 22 transponders (EUTELSAT 1996). So far, the EUTELSAT system comes a poor second to ASTRA's though this may change once the digital television era fully blossoms. EUTELSAT dominates the Southern European digital programming market including France and, in the future, Italy. However, its relevance for developments in Germany will probably remain minimal.

The German Telekom

The German Telekom emerged in 1990 from the former Bundespost and it must be seen as a very special case. Ranking only behind AT&T and the Japanese NTT, it is the third largest telecom organization in the world and the largest in Europe. For a long time, it enjoyed complete monopoly rights, some of which disappeared in the 1980s, and the last of which will go in 1998, as stipulated by the European Union (EU). The German Telekom was privatized in 1996 and is currently attempting to demonstrate its commercial competence in new communications technologies, including terrestrial networks, cable, and satellite. The German Telekom claims to have the largest coaxial cable network in the world; very few cable systems are privately owned in Germany. The German Telekom also purchased a share of about 17 per cent in SES, thus becoming the largest investor in ASTRA.

By 1995 the ASTRA satellite system could offer more TV channels, cheaper, than German Telekom's cable network could (the German Telekom then charged up to DM 22,30 per month). In addition, the satellite system has emerged as a superior means for transmitting TV programmes. All major German TV programmes - public and commercial - may be received via ASTRA, though local programming is not possible. The problem for the German Telekom is that it finds it rather difficult to sell new cable subscriptions. Viewers prefer ASTRA DBS; for an investment of a few hundred Deutschmark, they can receive about 60 programmes. ASTRA's attractiveness applies especially to East Germany. The German Telekom only started cabling there in 1990, following unification, in a context where many households had already installed an ASTRA antenna. Therefore, it is the German Telekom's policy to reserve all remaining unoccupied channels in its cable system for digital television.

To protect its tremendous investment in cable and satellite, German Telekom has adopted a step-by-step-strategy to expand its existing systems via digital compression. For this reason, the company is a natural ally of actors who are betting on digital television. In addition, it claims to be very advanced in ISDN and has laid more optical fibre than any other telecom company. These networks could, in principle, be utilized for an American-style highway strategy, though German Telekom has shown little interest so far. All things considered, German Telekom's present policy is somewhat incoherent, probably because of its privatisation in late 1996.

Kirch and Bertelsmann

Besides ASTRA, the leading players in European digitalization are its largest media organizations. Over the last decade, two conglomerates, Kirch and Bertelsmann - each under the leadership of a large transnational corporation - have taken over commercial TV in Germany (Wulf 1996). They have been named as the two "sender families" in Germany (Röper 1995), and each operates in close collaboration with one of the major political parties in the country.

The Kirch Group is personally controlled by the aging film trader, Leo Kirch. He made his fortune by providing public service broadcasters with (mainly American) film material. Today Kirch owns by far the largest stock of film and TV material in Europe and, as such, he is ideally placed for Pay-TV initiatives. As Kirch is a long-standing member of the CSU party - the Bavarian sister-party of the CDU, which governs Bavaria and part of the Bonn coalition - he has enjoyed strong protection from the conservatives. He steers his activities from Munich, the capital of the conservative state of Bavaria.

Some of the Kirch Group's investment activities are controlled by his son, Thomas Kirch. To avoid charges of cartelism, the group claims that the son's activities are completely independent from the father's. Both companies own varying capital shares in the following TV channels: Sat1; Pro7 (Thomas Kirch only); DSF (sports); Kabel 1; H.O.T. (teleshopping); and, Premiere (Pay-TV).

Amongst its many other ventures, Kirch controls the largest publishing house in Europe, Springer. Furthermore, the Kirch Group is active in other European states (Spain and Switzerland); Kirch has bought into Berlusconi's Mediaset in Italy and he is also a major shareholder in Telepiu, the Italian Pay-TV company.

The Bertelsmann company, the third largest media conglomerate in the world, has its headquarters in Gütersloh/Northrhine-Westphalia, traditionally a Socialdemocratic state which, since 1995, has been governed by a Red-Green Coalition. Bertelsmann controls one of the major magazine and newspaper publishers in Germany (Gruner + Jahr) and is active in all media markets. Most of Bertelsmann's broadcasting activities started from Northrhine-Westphalia, and some from Hamburg, which is another traditional Socialdemocratic state. Bertelsmann started up the most successful German commercial TV channel, RTL, in association with Luxembourg's CLT. For years CLT and Bertelsmann struggled for the control of RTL.

In April 1996, Bertelsmann's daughter-company for all its radio and television ventures, UFA, and the CLT decided to pool their European activities and merge. This fusion of two major European players was quickly accepted by the EU. The CLT/UFA venture controls TV channels in the Netherlands, Belgium, France, the United Kingdom, and Germany. The merger ended the power struggle over RTL (Berschens and Wulff 1996). CLT/UFA have significant shares in the following German TV channels: RTL; RTL2; Super RTL (together with Disney); Vox (together with Murdoch); and Premiere (Pay-TV).

For the German market, this means that CLT/UFA is now the largest provider of programming with a market share of more than 25 per cent. Kirch controls between 15 per cent and - if Pro7 is included - 25 per cent. The public service channels (ARD, ZDF and Third Programmes) control up to 40 per cent. Thus, Kirch and Bertelsmann each control one "family" of commercial

TV programmes that, between them, constitute the bulk of commercial television in Germany.

Both companies compete against each other in all relevant media markets, be it radio, TV, or print. They have only co-operated in one enterprise: the establishment and management of Germany's sole Pay-TV venture - Premiere - which they jointly control with the French company, Canal Plus, the most successful Pay-TV provider in Europe. Premiere presently offers a programme of films and sports and charges around DM 44,50 per month for its services. It claims to have about 1.4 million subscribers.

Since 1994 these major actors have been preparing for the introduction of digital television. Before their strategies are analysed, digital television will be briefly described.

Digital Television: The Technology

The ASTRA satellites allow for the transmission of TV programmes that are digitally compressed, based on MPEG 2. To decode these digital signals into the analogue "language" of conventional TV receivers, a decoder - or set-top-box - has to be installed between the antenna and the TV set (Hamann 1996). As each transponder (or channel) transmits between five to ten programmes, they are packaged and sold in "bouquets". Bouquets consist of a mix of commercial programmes that are not available through the cable networks, or Pay-TV. However, there is not much demand for additional material, as more than twenty channels are already available on the German TV market.

In addition, the advent of digital television makes it feasible to offer services such as Pay-Per-View, teleshopping, and time-shifted programmes which allow for Near-Video-On-Demand, etc. (Prognos 1995).

How the set-top-box is specified is extremely important for shaping the nature of digital television. It is equipped like a small computer and, through it, viewers may use a (valid) chip card to avail of services such as Pay-Per-View. Thus, whoever controls the set-top-box has direct access to participating households and can monitor their consumption patterns in detail.

Digital television is a technology which both increases the number of programmes that may be transmitted to the viewer, and which can collect payment where appropriate. When it is designed to operate with a predominantly one-directional agenda, it becomes a one-directional technology only. There may be one exception to this: it may be possible to link the set-top-box via modem to the telephone system, thus allowing for a digital back signal that may be received by the commercial centres of the system, e. g., at TV stations for Pay-Per-View, or at mail order companies for teleshopping. It is telling that the set-top-boxes introduced in late 1996 contain a small modem (2,400 bps) that only allow for simple communication with centres, but offer no access to online services or to the Internet. The set-top-boxes cost less than DM 1,000 when mass produced. By comparison, a modem that allows access to online services only costs about 10 per cent more. It should now be clear that interactivity is technically possible but is simply not part of the design.

If digital television is picked up from a DBS satellite, it may also be fed into existing cable systems. It is feasible to fill one channel with a package of five to ten digitally-compressed programmes, and German Telekom has reserved about 15 channels in the hyperband of its cable systems for this purpose. This offers them the transmission capability to send as many as 150 new programmes, though between 50 and 100 are more likely. German Telekom promised to deliver this service on a routine basis by 1995. To date, little of that has been realized, and the service has been confined to a few pilot projects in places like Berlin. Further policies are unclear at this time (Digitales TV 1995).

First Steps Towards Digital Television

MSG

By 1994 the technical opportunities afforded by digital television became clear to the large media actors. After years of delay, the three largest players in German communications - German Telekom, Bertelsmann, and Kirch - founded a joint venture, the Media Service GmbH (MSG), to provide digital services as outlined above. MSG was devised as a monopoly company, but it promised to offer services to all other interested parties on an equal basis.

MSG met very strong resistance from all other European media companies; they accused the MSG shareholders of constructing a virtual monopoly that would effectively keep competitors out. As MSG was based in Germany -

and received support from influential power centres within the country - opposition to the cartel could only come from abroad. This opposition centered around the EU and its newly enshrined anti-cartel policy. The MSG was banned by Brussels late in 1994, and this signalled the end of the rather precarious coalition that had shaped it. Kirch and Bertelsmann returned to their more familiar pattern of competitive in-fighting. Interestingly enough, Premiere, their only jount venture, was kept out of the MSG strategy.

Major Players: Kirch and Bertelsmann Lead New Alliances

In July 1995 it was made public that the major European media players had booked up nearly all the digital transponders on the scheduled ASTRA digital satellites (Peters 1995). In August 1995 Bertelsmann and Canal Plus announced that they were working together on the development of a set-top-box. Several other actors declared their intention to join this consortium; amongst them, the public service broadcasters ARD and ZDF, the Luxembourg CLT, and the German Telekom. They planned to establish a new company - Multimedia-Betriebsgesellschaft (MMBG) - to provide digital services. After a long period of negotiations, MMBG was finally set up, with headquarters in Berlin, by the Summer of 1996.

The Kirch Group kept out of this consortium and, instead, commissioned the development of its own set-top-box, produced by the NOKIA electronics group. A working model of this decoder was shown at the Broadcasting Fair in Berlin in Autumn 1995 where Kirch announced that they already had ordered a million set-top-boxes (Brockmeyer 1995).

Late in 1995 several months of hectic negotiations began between the major European adversaries, Bertelsmann and Kirch. The dealings between the families' representatives often took a dramatic or comical turn. Onlookers referred to the process as a game of poker (Kaiser 1996: 28). For example, at one point Helmut Kohl, Germany's Chancellor, wrote to the board of German Telekom complaining that they were cooperating with Bertelsmann instead of Kirch, his own favourite. Incidents of spying were even reported. It seems certain that MMBG did seriously attempt to accommodate Kirch's activities within their alliance. However, by March 1996, the wrangling ended with the public announcement by Kirch that he would pursue his own individual strategy (Ein Befreiungsschlag 1996).

By the summer of 1996, two European alliances had emerged, each of whom championed their own specification of a set-top-box. The two systems are similar, but incompatible. A viewer wishing access to all digital TV programmes must either buy two set-top-boxes or must buy additional equipment to make the systems compatible. In June 1996, EU Commissioner Martin Bangemann, invited Leo Kirch and a senior Bertelsmann's representative to discuss the matter further, but without results.

Between them, the two European alliances account for most of the large European actors. The Kirch Alliance, based on the d-box technology, includes: The Kirch Group (including Telepiu in Italy); Silvio Berlusconi (Mediaset, Canale 5, and Italia); and Johann Rupert/Richmond Group (Nethold). The Kirch Alliance operates with Vebacom - a daughter-company of the German utility company Veba, one of the future competitors of German Telekom - and with Metro - the largest German retailer, who will sell the d-box in its media market chain stores.

The Bertelsmann Alliance, based on the media-box technology, includes: Bertelsmann; CLT; Havas/Canal Plus (Pay-TV in France and several other European countries). The Bertelsmann Alliance operates with ARD and ZDF (the public service German broadcasting stations), German Telekom, and DEBIS, a company belonging to Daimler, the owner of Mercedes Benz.

In April 1996, Canal Plus in France became the first to operate a digital Canal Satellite Numérique, which is based on the MMBG standard. They plan to introduce their mediabox in Germany in the first instance and to move later to cover Italy and Spain. Kirch plans to introduce TV packages for his d-box in Germany and, following that, Kirch and Berlusconi plan to go digital in Italy with Telepiu, the Pay-TV venture. Belgian and Scandinavian broadcasting is most influenced by Johann Rupert's group, which joined Kirch's d-box Alliance (Freese 1996). Great Britain, meanwhile, is largely controlled by Murdoch and his BSkyB package of analogue TV programmes. Murdoch belongs to Bertelsmann's mediabox Alliance, but, in 1996, is reported to be unsatisfied.

Kirch started the first digital package, called DF 1 (DF stands for 'Digitales Fernsehen') in July 1996 it includes a standard offering of about twenty film formats, such as Action, Western, Children and 'Heimat' (German light romance). For an additional DM 10 two sports programmes are added. Pay-per-view is possible for DM 6 per movie. A later addition is an Erotic offering.

The purchase of the necessary set-top-box demands DM 890, a price which appears to be subsidized. At the end of 1996, Kirch planned to have sold 200.000 boxes, but in reality no more than 20.000 had found a buyer, if at all. Kirch is loosing heaps of money with digital television.

Bertelsmann and RTL had planned to offer a digital package of their own, but withdrew after Kirch's strong offensive in the fall of 1996. Not because they expected the disaster that Kirch is now encounting, but rather because they were unable to find the necessary film material as Kirch had bought up nearly all available movie and sport rights (see below). The withdrawel also stopped the MMBG-project. Kirch had to learn the hard way that digital TV of the DF 1-type is not viable. His strategy in 1997 seems to be to fight for the control of Premiere, the pay TV-company that lately has become quite successful. His intention is to merge the activities of both companies and deliver Premiere plus DF 1 through his digital decoder. But Premiere is still under the control of the competing alliance of Bertelsmann and Canal Plus and started handing out its own set-top-boxes, incompatible to Kirch's, in February 1997 (Premiere digital). Presently the battle between the two "sender families" is fought out in German courts. There is a possibility that Kirch wins the struggle, as his old ally Johann Rupert lately merged his company Nethold with Canal Plus, so becoming one of the top shareholders. He could use his influence to change alliances.

German Telekom, under strong pressure of liberalization and privatization, still seems to be undecided what to do. Plans have been reported to become a provider of digital tv-packages for their own cable systems in competition to Kirch. But the EU strongly proposed that German Telekom should divert itself from its cable systems as part of a pro-competition telecommunication policy. The German Telekom is a potentially strong actor, but lately without clear conception (Oppermann 1996)

Providing the Programming Software

For all actors involved, it seems clear that owning the film software to fill the programme packages is crucial to the success of digital television (Wulff 1996). On the whole, Kirch seems to be the best placed to capitalize on digital television, which explains his preference for going it alone. He already controls the largest stock of film rights in Europe, and recently added thousands more films to his stock in a large deal with Columbia Tristar Studio. In addition, he has strengthened his alliance with the American company, Viacom, to include his growing access to Paramount's films. Viacom's European programmes, MTV (which is presently encoded on satellite), VH-1, and Nickelodeon are due to be packaged through Kirch's d-box.

On Bertelsmann's side, Canal Plus struck a deal with Disney - a company which is also affiliated with CLT in Super RTL. Though Bertelsmann has been looking for years to buy one of the major studios, it has not succeeded so far and so cooperates mainly with independent U.S. film producers. In mid-1996, CLT/UFA and Kirch began bargaining - at extremely high prices - for MCA/Universal films.

The investment of all actors in digital television is immense and the risk very high. According to a Forsa public opinion poll, only 14 per cent of Germans know what Pay-Per-View means and just two per cent are prepared to pay DM 60 per month for Pay-TV (Thomsen 1996). By the end of 1996, Kirch hopes to have sold 200,000 subscriptions for his DF-1, though commentators doubt that this figure will be reached, since the struggle over the set-top-boxes is still on-going.

Conclusion

Looking at present developments in Germany, the following features emerge as dominant:

- The leading technological paradigm of the future is digital television, which is based on satellite transmission and digital compression and allows for the digital multiplication of conventional TV programmes.
- Future programmes will deliver the same kinds of TV material as today, but it will be marketed differently. "Free" television (i.e., financed by commercials) will be supplemented by different forms of Pay-TV.
- The development of digital television is mainly driven by the leading media companies and the ways in which they devise their market strategies.
- German Telekom is potentially a major player but it currently seems paralysed by its present challenges, viz the liberalization of telecommunication

markets and the privatization of German Telekom stock. To date, its policies appear short-sighted and incoherent.

- The public service broadcasting stations (ARD and ZDF) are no longer a major force. In fact, they do not seem to have a clear concept of the digital age.
- Digital television and online services are the two principal applications of digital technology. In Germany, these applications are emerging separately; convergence between them is not intended, even though both might be available from the same company (e.g., Bertelsmann and its joint venture with America Online-AOL).
- Kirch and Bertelsmann are a duopoly of two major "sender families" in Germany. Their rivalry has resulted in the development and marketing of two incompatible set-top-box specifications for digital television. Clearly this is not in the public interest, nor even in anything except the short-terms interests of the actors themselves.
- The introduction of digital television is taking place without any public regulation or control.

The general picture emerging is that it is industrial alliances, rather than public institutions, that are driving the next generation of TV technology - a process that runs counter to European tradition.

Despite the competition between the two sender families and their alliances, both depend on the same technical logic. Looking at the technology itself, MSG, MMBG and the set-top-boxes represent the idea of channel multiplication with very rudimentary (or no) interactivity . DBS satellites filter communication so that it travels in only one direction. This way of utilizing large-scale satellite technology ensures that the one-directional stream of information is controlled by technical (ASTRA) and industrial (Kirch, Bertelsmann) "centres", which position Germany and the rest of Europe as their "periphery". Thus, digital television reflects the intention of the leading media players to provide more-of-the-same TV programming. The low-capacity back channel of the set-top-box is designed in such a way that its main use is for settling accounts; the modem is too weak to enable entry into the Internet. The interactive potential of digitalization is only partially used. It is in this sense that digitalization, as exemplified by the German case, is "crippled".

There are fundamental differences between the development of the NII in the U.S. and German digital television. One of them is that the Information Superhighway incorporates more of the client-server logic of the Internet. As such, it offers a much greater potential for interactivity and individual choice. Another, which underpins the first major difference, is that the NII is based on terrestrial digital networks, not on DBS satellites. Even though ASTRA is an American product, DBS satellites like ASTRA have only been introduced in the U.S. after years of successful testing and marketing in Europe, and they remain a minority vehicle for delivery of services.

In economic terms, the construction of the American Information Highway is being driven by a loose coalition that incorporates actors from diverse industries such as telecommunications, cable, computers (hardware and software), and programme providers. Their various strategies are not identical, but they all share a common interest in conquering the lucrative markets of commercial television currently dominated by three networks - ABC, CBS and NBC. Interactivity in digital networks in America is understood to offer marketing advantages over conventional TV. Therefore a broad industrial alliance supports the aggressive move into substantial digitalization (Kleinsteuber 1994).

In Europe, the equivalents of these American actors (telecommunications, cable, computer, and entertainment industries) are comparatively weak. Instead, a few large media conglomerates, strong in commercial television - and as such resembling the American network companies - are pushing to introduce their concept of digital television. This chapter has described the fierce in-fighting they are currently engaged in. As there is no third force (e.g., Telekom, state supervisory bodies, or public service broadcasting) to check them, they offer two incompatible specifications of digital television. Between them, they are about to introduce a "crippled digitalization" to Germany and to Europe.

References

ASTRA (1995), ASTRA aktuell, Nr. 21, August (Eschborn: ASTRA-marketing GmbH).

Berschen, R., and Wulff, M. (1996), Multikultureller Laden, Wirtschaftswoche, 21, 46-48.

Brockmeyer, D. (1995), Digitalisierung dominiert, Medien Bulletin, 9, 14-16.

Bruch, W., and Riedel H. (1987), PAL - Das Farbfernsehen. (Berlin: Deutsches Rundfunk Museum).

Digitales TV (1995), Wettlauf um das Fernsehen der Zukunft, Tendenz, 3 (topical issue).

Ein Befreiungsschlag (1996), Der Spiegel, 11, 122-125.

EUTELSAT (1996), Das Hot Bird Satellitensystem für Europa (Paris: European Telecommunications Satellite Organization) (Also other information material by EUTELSAT was used).

Freese, G. (1996), Stoff für eine Serie, Die Zeit, 12, 28.

Gilder, G. (1994), Life after Television. The Coming Tranformation of Media and American Life. (New York: W. W. Norton & Company).

Hamann, K. (1996), 'Settop-Boxen - TV total', PC Professionell, 4, 18f.

Kaiser, L. (1996), Rivalen an der Box, Journalist, 1, 28- 30.

Kleinsteuber, H. J. (1994), Die Verheißung der Kabeldemokratie. Von der amerikanischen Datenautobahn und dem deutschen digitalen Fernsehen, Wechselwirkung, 12, 23-28.

Kleinsteuber, H. J. (Ed.) (1996), Der Information Super Highway, Amerikanische Visionen und Erfahrungen. (Opladen: Westdeutscher Verlag).

KtK (Kommission für den Ausbau des technischen Kommunikationssystems) (1976), Telekommunikationsbericht. (Bonn: Bundesminister für das Post- und Fernmeldewesen)

MediaGruppe München (MGM), Michael Hönig (Projektleiter), Interaktives TV. Tests, Projekte, Systeme. Ein Überblick. (München: MediaGruppe).

Negroponte, N. (1995), Being Digital. (New York: Alfred A. Knopf).

Neuman, W. R. (1991), The Future of the Mass Audience. (Cambridge MA: Cambridge University Press).

Oppermann, Chr. (1996), Rabiater Auftritt, Die Woche, March 8, 14.

Peters, R.-H. (1995), Digitales Fernsehen: Hauen und Stechen, Wirtschaftswoche, 44, 150-156.

Prognos AG (1995), Digitales Fernsehen. Marktchancen und ordnungspolitischer Bedarf. (München: Verlag Reinhard Fischer).

Röper, H. (1995), Medien im Multi-Fieber, journalist, 10, 14-19.

Schulz, D. (1995), Digitale Dienste über ASTRA, Infosat, 11, 24-28, 186-188.

Thomsen, F. (1996), Onkel Leo hat Spendierhosen an, Stern, 25, 120.

Wulf, M. (1996), 'Stark in Hollywood', Wirtschaftswoche, 16, 56-60.

6. French Lessons: The Minitel Case

Michel Berne[1]

Introduction

More than ten years after the large-scale launch of commercial videotex (Télétel) in France, it can be said that it has met considerable success at home - a success without parallel anywhere in the world. At the same time, Télétel has also failed in several respects and its future is now questioned. This chapter begins by recounting the history of French videotex upto the present day, goes on to consider Télétel's successes and weaknesses, and then proceeds to discuss options for the future in a context where information highways are drastically changing the broader picture for videotex. In the conclusion, the implications of the Minitel case for information highways are considered. Though technical, business, and regulatory environments have changed dramatically in recent years, there are lessons to be learnt from the French videotex case by the general public, by business, and by the national economy.

Télétel, Yesterday and Today

For the average French person, it seems that videotex has been part of every-day life for ages. The Minitel terminal is ubiquitous and its use widespread.[2] However, the commercial life of videotex has actually been rather brief as is clear when we consider that its main function - to act as an electronic phone book - only became available in selected French regions in 1983. Therefore,

---

1 This chapter presents the personal opinion of the author and does not necessarily represent the official point of view of France Télécom.
2 6.5 million Minitel terminals at the end of 1994 as well as 24 600 services.

we will first briefly relate Télétel's history and then concentrate on its present state.

Prehistory of French Videotex

Modern videotex is the heir of a variety of technical systems, some stemming from TV broadcasting - for example, CEEFAX or ORACLE in the U.K., and Antiope in France - and others from the telephone network - the ancestor being an ingenious device called SCT[3] (Service de calcul par téléphone). Sadly, the emergence of a single style of videotex was hindered from the beginning by lack of contact between the promoters of various systems; in the '70s, convergence amongst telecommunication, computer and media organisations was still to be put into practice. Later attempts at collaboration were blocked by a series of misunderstandings and ill-thought bouts of national pride. We know the results: all the major countries have developed incompatible standards and systems, and this has weakened the international diffusion of videotex.

It should be remembered that by the '70s, following a long period of stagnation which had left French telecoms far behind other countries, the French telephone network had been subject to a vast growth plan. At the end of the '70s, the Direction Generale des Télécommunications (DGT), which was renamed France Télécom in 1988, was looking for ways to maintain its own growth, and that of French telecom manufacturers. Plans were therefore examined for fax machines as well as for videotex .

During the same period the French government commissioned a report on the computerization of society (Nora and Minc 1978). The authors clearly stated the challenges and opportunities ahead, and their document was widely discussed. Nora and Minc coined the word "telematique" to represent the marriage of telecoms with informatics. In other countries one spoke of videotex (i.e., a new telecom system), but French people dreamed of "telematique" - a word which conjured up a vision of the information society as much as a particular technical system - in much the same way as we conjure with "information superhighways" now. And indeed, the ideas of Nora

---

3   With SCT, one could use the phone as a pocket calculator. The results were computed on a central computer and given back with a speech synthesis system - 1970, France.

and Minc quite accurately prefigure what we see today. Seventeen years later, "telematique" is the usual French word for videotex, though for the general public it has since lost most of its appeal.

A turning point came in 1978 when the DGT decided to launch a full-scale experiment in Velizy, a suburb close to Paris. This test started in 1981 and proved very useful from both technical and commercial points of view. Indeed, if we consider videotex as an interlocked innovation (Bouwman and Christoffersen 1992: 7), it requires: 'innovation on at least three levels:

- innovation in the communication infrastructure;
- innovation in the supply of new services; and
- social innovation in the way users fulfil their specific communication and information needs.'

The Velizy experiment clearly showed the interactions between these three points and the viability of the whole scheme.

At the same time, the DGT decided to replace the phone book with an electronic directory. Various reasons were given, ranging from the ecological (to prevent tree-felling) to the economic (to prevent phone books becoming too bulky). A trial was initiated in the Brittany town of Saint-Malo in 1980; the service was later extended to the surrounding region and then generalized to cover the whole of France. However, contrary to their original intention, the DGT left the subscriber with the choice of an electronic or a printed phone book. Those preferring the electronic directory were lent a Minitel terminal for free, while the rest continued to receive the traditional phone book. Even now, subscribers still get the Yellow Pages in book form.

1978	The DGT decides to launch videotex
July 1980	55 citizens of Saint-Malo (Brittany) experiment with using the Electronic Directory
July 1981	2,500 users experiment with Télétel
Oct. 1982	Opening of the first business 'gate' (3613); Opening of Gretel, the prototype of "messageries" (online messages)
Dec 1984	Opening of the "kiosk" system reserved for the media
May 1985	The electronic directory achieves national coverage
Sept. 1985	The general public gate 3615 achieves national coverage
Oct. 1987	Opening of the business gates 3616 and 3617
1987	At-home payment of services is allowed by the LECAM box
1989	France Télécom opens the electronic videotex mail-box MINICOM
1989	Intelmatique opens an international "bridge" to foreign videotex systems
1993	Creation of 'Conseil Superieur de la Télématique' (Higher Council of Telematics) and 'Comite de la Télématique Anonyme' (Committee of Anonymous Telematics)
1994	Opening of the high-speed service TVR (Télétel Vitesse Rapide)

Table 1: *Key dates in the history of French Videotex*

The Commercial Launch

Based on the results of the experiments, it was decided to extend the benefits of Télétel to all French subscribers, and the main technical and commercial options were chosen and implemented. This expansion phase went smoothly amidst considerable public interest. Initially, the media had been concerned by the apparition of a potentially powerful competitor (and, what is more, one controlled by the state). However, the DGT chose to collaborate with the media in developing applications for the general public and the relevant companies all quickly offered their services. Major suppliers of goods and services such as transportation companies, banks, mail-order companies, and the public services followed suit.

As can be expected when a new media appears, its use, once implemented, differs from the original plan. Télétel is no exception. At first, the public made immoderate use of game services and of "messageries roses" ("pink" online messaging) until very high bills sobered everybody.[4] At the same time, the DGT was anxious not to appear to be promoting sexual misbehaviour and it cracked down on the most explicit services. After this successful (but slightly embarassing) episode, the DGT promoted the use of Télétel in business, offering facilities to companies to set up services using professional databases, order-taking etc. Amongst the public, a generation of Minitel addicts emerged who were studied by sociologists and psychologists, much like the Internet addicts we see now.

The Present State of Télétel

One must see Télétel as a system comprising a network and specific terminals, information services, and ancillary services. Here we will examine the main elements in the system, excluding the more technical aspects of the network.

The number of Minitel terminals, services and hours of connection follow the well-known S Curve (see Graph 1). We can now regard Télétel as a mature system. Most of the figures quoted here come from a 1994 survey of users conducted by France Télécom (Bilan 1994).

The number of Minitels used by the public at the end of 1994 was a little under 6.5 million. Of course, it is possible to access Télétel from a microcomputer (400,000 units in 1993; 600,000 in 1994), a facility which is mostly used in office.[5]

According to the same survey, at the end of 1994, 68 per cent of the terminals used at home were still the Minitel 1 - the basic model that is freely loaned to users. The proportion of users having access to more elaborate terminals is steadily growing as new generations of terminal appear on the mar-

---

4   The tariff is based on duration of calls.

5   2.5 per cent of terminals in homes; 10 per cent of terminals used in offices. The total number of users could be 810,000 in 1994.

ket. However, the large proportion of users left with the old basic Minitel 1 will eventually create a replacement problem.

Thirty six per cent of the French population above the age of fifteen (nearly 16.5 million people) have access to Télétel at home or at work according the the same survey. About five per cent of Minitels are not used at all (around 170,000 terminals).

At the end of 1994 about 24,600 services were available on Télétel, offered by 10,200 service providers and hosted by 4,200 servers. The growth in services shows no sign of decreasing (Graph 1). Of course, a very large number of these services attract only a small amount of traffic, and some of them use multiple access codes. Seventeen thousand seems a good estimate of the number of "real" services, with a very high turnover in games and messageries.

At the other end of the spectrum, a very large facility, like SNCF's railway service, answers two million calls each month and processes sophisticated demands like seat bookings. All major companies and a very large number of organizations of all kinds[6] offer services of some sort, whether it is order-taking, online information, mailboxes, or televoting. It has been shown that videotex can help provide a competitive advantage to firms that can deliver faster and better services, and create virtual markets.[7] Besides the electronic directory (a service known and used by everybody), the major services, according to a 1993 survey[8], are: (La lettre de Télétel et de l'Audiotel)

- banking services (known by 84 per cent of users, called by 47 per cent);
- mail-order services (respectively 84 per cent and 38 per cent);
- transportation (75 per cent and 48 per cent);
- weather services (73 per cent and 34 per cent); and
- entertainment information (72 per cent and 36 per cent).

---

6   Government departments; public services; trade associations and all types of associations; special-interest groups... The use of Télétel to promote what can be called "tele-democracy" aroused considerable interest for a while both at local and national levels.

7   Well-known examples can be given in the transportation sector. The SNCF (railways) service allows round-the-clock order-taking with any Minitel. The Lamy service offers a virtual "freight exchange" where truckers can find loads to transport (Steinfield, Caby and Vialle 1993).

8   The corresponding 1994 survey differs from a methodological point of view, but its results are consistent with those of the 1993 survey.

Once popular services like messageries are now only called by four per cent of users (at least, this is the declared figure, according to the survey), news services are only called by 16 per cent of users, and professional databases by 20 per cent of users. It seems therefore that usage has become very rational. Most callers avail of value-adding services such as avoiding having to make a trip to the nearest station or bank, replacing a letter, or getting up-to-the min-ute information. Using Télétel for dating or as a forum has become rather marginal. The continuous decrease in the average duration of calls is consis-tent with this trend (Graph 2).

As the number of services is so large, France Télécom offer a videotex guide called "Les pages Minitel" as well as a paper directory, called ENVOI, of the most frequently-used services. France Télécom returns a proportion of its Télétel fees to the service providers[9]. Amounting to more than three billion francs in 1994, this sum keeps growing due to the continuous increase in use of the system, and to the graded means - the "kiosk" system - by which serv-ices providers pay for gaining access to the system. Indeed, following from this latter point, one of the major side-effects of Télétel is the emergence of a very active sector of service providers: ten to fifteen thousand jobs are said to be provided by Télétel services, though these are just estimates.

Leaving aside the use made of the electronic directory, French videotex marketing specialists have classified users of the system into six types (La lettre de Télétel et Audiotel):

- Players, who mainly use games, news and classified advertisements (15 per cent of the total number of users);
- Travellers, who mainly use transportation services (12 per cent o. t. total);
- Finance Users, who mainly use banking and finance services (15 per cent of the total);
- Consumers, (the majority are female or unemployed) who mainly use mail-order and consumer-oriented services (28 per cent of the total);
- Addicts, who use Télétel several times a day, mostly during working hours. They mainly use business services, transportation, and news serv-ices (23 per cent of the total); and,
- Utilitarians, who mainly use business services (seven per cent of the total).

---

9 The exact amount depends on the type of service, but it is, on average, a little less than 50 per cent of total income.

According to the same survey, 94 per cent of users are satisfied, or very satisfied, with Télétel. Eighty five per cent think that Télétel is a useful tool. Fifteen per cent declare that they could not live without it. However, opinion is more divided on the question of cost: 28 per cent of users believe Télétel is too dear. This percentage appears to be rising, as the 1994 survey suggests that a majority of users find the system too costly.

The electronic directory remained the most popular service in 1994, with 23 million connection hours and 784 million calls (representing one-fifth of total connection time). The directory offers White and Yellow Pages for all French subscribers. Yellow Pages accept requests written in natural language. Just like the paper counterpart, the electronic White and Yellow Pages carry advertisements and special information sections. The first three minutes of use are free. With this directory, it is also possible to access the electronic directories of other countries (including Germany, and the U.S.) though at a much higher cost.

As mentioned earlier, the emergence of different local standards has hindered the international diffusion of seamless videotex services. However, France Télécom has developed "bridges" which can link Télétel to over 15 videotex systems elsewhere in the world. International use is growing in three areas:

- Europeans (mainly from Italy, Belgium, and Switzerland) availing of French services (80 per cent of all international traffic);
- Companies using their internal videotex services from locations abroad (15 per cent of traffic); and
- French users calling foreign services, mainly the electronic directories of other countries.

However, in 1993, international connection hours still only accounted for three per cent of total connection hours (La lettre de Télétel et Audiotel).

Télétel is important to France Télécom. In 1994, the total turnover was more than six billion French francs. Of this, half was returned to the service providers. The remaining three billion was used by France Télécom to promote Télétel; to distribute Minitel terminals (produced by several manufacturers); and to pay for calls on the phone and packet-switching networks. Net returns to France Télécom amounted to 2.4 per cent of total turnover, including Télétel and Audiotel .

Bright and Dark Points

Key Features: the Pillars of Success

The success of Télétel rests on a limited number of choices that have over-come the well-known problem of No Services, No Customers; No Customers, No Services.

Most important of all, DGT had the technical expertise, the money, and the political clout to implement the videotex project. Technical expertise came from DGT's research centres, CNET and CCETT. Money was available through cross-subsidies from the general network. As to political clout, it derived from the combined commitment to the project of senior DGT executives and the various ministers in charge of telecommunications. Indeed, ministers saw videotex as a useful means to orchestrate short-term industrial policy in the telecom sector, as much as a long-term programme for the 21st century. By the beginning of the '80s, the DGT enjoyed the prestige attendant upon having succeeded in implementing a crash programme to rescue the telephone network. Thus, it was not looking for short-term returns.

Télétel adopted a simple and easily supervised standard. The French videotex system is based on simple and proven technologies. It uses a very low transmission speed, it allows for decentralization of servers, and it is entirely under France Télécom supervision.[10]

Minitel is a simple, user-friendly, and cheap terminal and its manufacture and mass distribution came at little or no cost to the user.[11] Thus, users experienced few barriers which might prevent their using the terminal. At the same time, they had an positive incentive to try it out since, from the outset, Minitel was the gateway to a variety of up-and-running services.

The system has enjoyed an adequate billing system. From the user's point of view, charging is based on the type of service being accessed, and on the duration rather than the distance of calls. Access to all services is offered anonymously, and without any prior subscription. From the service provider's point of view, the system provides for a remarkable equality of access

---

10 One major breakdown occurred in June 1985 when videotex traffic blocked the Transpac network, but this was an isolated incident.
11 The cost of each terminal was about 1000 FF in 1996.

to the customer base and a secure pay-back system in exchange for a modest initial investment (the so-called "kiosk" system).

It is difficult to rank the importance of the last three features. One can simply remark on the consistency of technical and commercial choices made, due to the unique position of the DGT. Service providers are obviously pleased with the system as shown by the huge number of services on offer. It is also difficult to pinpoint the impacts of the system on the economy or the country's social relations. After the initial exploratory period, when new behaviours and trends appeared, most people returned to a more rational and sedate use of Télétel. The same can be said of the system's economic impact, even though firms have accumulated experience in exploiting its possibilities and some of them have clearly built their success on an adequate use of Télétel.

Rate of Return Problem

One obvious consequence of the type of development chosen by the DGT was its financial cost in the short- and medium-term. On the debit side, the DGT has not only paid for developing the system and for building and distributing the terminals. It has also subsidised certain kinds of usage of the system, e.g, the electronic directory. On the credit side, the DGT did so in expectation both of generating additional traffic through Télétel, and of making savings on printing phone books.

As might be expected, a controversy arose as to the true costs and benefits of Télétel. The French Government Accounting Office (Cour des Comptes) wrote a report in 1989 on the topic. At the end of 1987, according to this report, Télétel generated costs of about eight billion francs and showed returns of about three billion francs (Salzman 1989). However, these figures are only meaningful when one takes a longer financial perspective on Télétel, where three factors assume significance. The first is the growth in usage over time. By 1995, this has stabilised. The second is the useful life of Minitel terminals. This is estimated to be seven or eight years. The third is the possibility of renting, as opposed to lending, Minitels. While renting was not implemented for the basic Minitel terminal, it is the case for newer and more sophisticated Minitels.

Since 1989, Télétel's annual expenses have been met by revenues generated, and it is expected that, by 1997, the total cost of the programme will be covered by cumulative revenues.[12] By then, the first generation of Minitel terminals will be obsolete. Thus, in 1996, we are now at a turning point for the French videotex system.

Legal Problems

Since the outset, it was obvious that France Télécom's legal position was debatable, since it is not the provider of most Télétel services. These are offered by the content providers, who sign a contract with France Télécom which stipulates that they accept sole responsibility for their services. Nevertheless, it is France Télécom which provides access to these services and, thus, is implicated if it so happens that the content of certain services is not legal. Vulgar advertising for these services on street billboards is also detrimental to Télétel's reputation.

Therefore two laws were passed in 1986 (September 30th and November 27th) to regulate access to Télétel. A Telematics Commission (Commission de la Télématique) had been set up. Since the decree of February 25, 1993, it has been replaced by a Higher Council of Télématics (Conseil Superieur de la Télématique, or CST) which governs a Committee of Anonymous Télématics (Comite de la Télématique Anonyme, or CTA), previously known as the Consultative Council of Phone and Telematics Kiosks. The Council is made up of representatives from all relevant parties: consumer associations, trade associations, regulators, etc. The main aim of the Council is to formulate ethical guidelines. France Télécom is not part of the CTA. The CTA advises on the content of services[13], based on the terms of the contract between France Télécom and the service provider. If the CTA is critical, France Télécom is entitled to stop the service.

Thus, one of the societal innovations which has accompanied the implementation of Télétel is that Télétel has become a testing ground for new forms of partnership between the operator and its service providers.

---

12 In 1991, another study was prepared by a consultant on behalf of France Télécom. It showed that the internal rate of return of the Télétel project ranged from 11 to 15 per cent over the 1984-2000 period, depending on the assumptions made.

13 At the request of France Télécom or service providers. In 1994, the CTA has issued 293 notifications, out of which 125 blocked access for services. Moreover one service was suspended and seven discontinued.

International Diffusion

It is not surprising that the international diffusion of Télétel has turned out to be difficult, given the multiplicity of competing standards, and the national industrial policies of most nations. The French government had great expectations about exporting Télétel to the rest of the world and no effort was spared towards this end. It must be said that no major export market appeared despite various experiments in several countries. Two such experiments were made in the U.S., one with Videotel/SouthWestern in Houston, the other in Omaha with US West.

In the previous section we quoted figures on levels of international traffic using Télétel, which show that neighbouring countries have a strong interest in the system. Since March 30th, 1990 when a European agreement was signed to link the videotex systems of seventeen countries, no significant incompatibilities amongst European standards for videotex remain.

And Now, What ?

While it is clear that Télétel enjoys popular success, it is also obvious that major changes are on their way. First, the old Minitel system is nearing the end of its life; new terminals have to be offered. Secondly, and perhaps more important, more recent network technologies render Télétel rather obsolete. Its slow speed and limited capabilities are now due serious attention. Three ways of addressing these problems have been, or are being, explored: the provision of new terrninals, audiotex, and an Internet corresponding to the four major families of communication - the phone, the Minitel, the microcomputer, and the TV set.

New Terminals

France Télécom regularly offers new terminals which exploit the latest technological advances. For example, the new Magis terminal can read smart credit cards and therefore can be used for more secure tele-shopping. Introduced in 1995, Magis shows very promising sales so far.[14] A mobile Minitel has also been offered in the past.

To make better use of networks, France Télécom also offers terminals working at higher speeds such as Minitel Photo, and TVR (Télétel Vitesse Rapide). One can also buy add-on cards or modems which allow microcomputers to emulate Minitels. The most recent of these, Kiosque Micro, also incorporates higher transmission speeds.

These immediate solutions are very useful, but they cannot really bridge the technical gap which now exists between Télétel and Internet services. The success of providing short-term solutions rests on the relative cost of services: for the time being, Télétel is a low-cost alternative which allows for secure payments to be made through smart cards.

Audiotel

Another possibility, offered by France Télécom, is audiotex (called Audiotel). The development of Audiotel has been extremely fast. By the end of 1994, the number of connection hours through Audiotel accounted for more than one-sixth of Télétel calls, and 5,800 services were offered. Audiotel is seen as simpler, cheaper and faster than Télétel. This is especially true of banking services. However, by definition, its possibilities are limited to voice services. For France Télécom, Audiotel and Télétel are more complementary than substitutable.

Internet

The tremendous developments of the Internet bring homes and offices a new generation of videotex, based on a recipe rather similar to that of Télétel, viz. a universal terminal - the microcomputer; subsidised price; and, decentralized services (although, the Internet is fully decentralized as opposed to Télétel which is firmly in the hands of France Télécom). Because the recipes are similar, both suffer from the same kinds of adverse effects. Competition between them will appear when service providers on the Internet offer services similar to Télétel, at a lower cost, and with a vastly improved user-interface.

---

14 100,000 Magis terminals sold in six months.

French organisations are now developing Web sites to complement their Télétel services. The Internet brings new possibilities such as pictures and access to a world-wide customer base, but also signals difficulties over order-taking and receiving payment for services. One idea being explored is to build bridges between Internet and Télétel services; some are already in operation for e-mail.

France Télécom has decided to be pro-active regarding the Internet. They offer access at competitive rates and access to the White and Yellow Pages. A France Télécom subsidiary (FT2M) is launching an online service called Wanadoo.

Short- and Long-Term Perspectives

The main challenge for service providers is to capitalize on the enormous customer base they currently enjoy to promote enhanced services whenever new channels appear. The French association of service providers, AFTEL (Association Francaise de Télématique) believes that competition between the Internet and Télétel will start soon, and it calls for two measures to be taken:

- the manufacture of a cheap modem enabling Minitels to work at eight times their current speed; and,
- a price decrease in selected services, within the context of a careful re-engineering of the kiosk system (La lettre de Télétel et Audiotel 1994).[15]

France Télécom has also written a report on the future of videotex (La Lettre de Télétel 1995). Between 1998 and 2000, France Télécom envisions that videotex services will be accessed from a variety of terminals: Minitels, tele-phones, micro-computers plus CD-Roms, and television sets. Depending on the type of service, customers will use one or other of these media. For ex-ample, shopping is easier using mail-order catalogues on CD-Roms, but buying trains tickets is easier, safer, and quicker with a Minitel. And of course, one can watch telemarketing TV channels. Videotex will, in addition, have to meet the challenge of mobile communications and will have to interact with the personal digital assistants now under development. For 2001-2004, it is reasonable to predict the widespread use of speech recognition in

---

15 Indeed, if the kiosk billing system is well adapted to launch a large variety of services, it can be fairly expensive for customers and excludes bulk rates or flat fees.

videotex systems, as well as the emergence of "virtual supermarkets". For France Télécom, the major challenge rests with managing the consequences of European deregulation of infrastructures and networks. Mastering networks is as important as offering services. All options on that front are still open-ended.

Conclusion: Videotex and Information Superhighways

French Initiatives

It is important to outline French government initiatives to promote information superhighways. In 1994, Gerard Théry (the head of DGT at the time of the crash programme in the '70s) was asked by the then Prime Minister, Mr. Balladur, to present a policy orientation paper on the topic.[16] His report, which was made public at the end of 1994, set out two objectives:

- All citizens should be linked to information superhighways by the year 2015; and,
- The existing telephonic universal service should be extended to include access to information superhighways.

Meeting these two goals requires four actions to be taken:

- Building optical fibre networks as quickly as possible, i.e., at a rate of four or five million lines per year. (By 1995, the French network had about 32 millions lines in total);
- Launching "platforms" to experiment with the development of software, the delivery of services, and the testing of markets;
- Promoting the development of services (network management software as well as multimedia software); and,
- Intensifying the development of ATM (Automatic Teller Machines).

In turn, these four actions require:

---

16 Moreover, the Ministers of Interior and Economic Development had asked T. Breton (1994) to prepare technical reports on teleworking and teleservices. These reports assumed the market for teleservices to be worth 33 billion Francs in 1993 and to grow to between 86-195 billion francs in 2005.

- A mobilisation of all Ministries, together with France Télécom, to agree on priorities;
- the use of existing networks, in particular, cable networks;
- a European-wide approach; and,
- an extensive information campaign aimed at the general public.

A forum was organized at the end of 1994 where everybody paid tribute to this remarkable report. However, dissenting voices were heard as to the size of the investment required to carry out such a programme, as well as to the need to pay more attention to services and rather less to infrastructure.[17]

Following the report's publication, the French Ministries of Industry, Posts and Telecommunications, and External Trade launched a very wide call for proposals. Five hundred and twenty five proposals - totalling a staggering 12 billion French Francs - were submitted to a jury chaired by Mr. Théry. Forty nine projects were selected, mostly on the basis that they needed little or no financing. One third of them were infrastructural projects; the rest, service projects. France Télécom was awarded nine of them, including a few dealing with the evolution of videotex. All of these projects are now in the implementation phase.

Lessons from the Télétel Case

The French videotex system, Télétel, has proved its ability to deliver an enormous range of services, at low cost, reliably. Its social impact has been important. However, its profitability has been low and it is fast becoming obsolete given new developments in online computer services. So what are the implications of the Minitel case regarding information superhighways? We have to be very careful in this respect. Technical progress has been tremendous since the early days of Télétel; the telecommunications sector is being fully deregulated; and, the business environment has changed.

---

17 France has a long tradition of active industrial policy, with mixed results. Indeed, in the communications sector, the videotex program was a success while the cable network programme - Plan Cable - was a failure. Attention to the provision of services largely explains these results.

However, there might be useful lessons for the general public, for business firms, for network operators and for the national economy. For the general public, as well as for business firms, two points have to be stressed.

- There is a two-stage learning curve. During the first stage of Télétel, some people believed that it could be used for every purpose: shopping, education, social life, information, etc. Some even became addicted to using it. Then came a second stage when people became more realistic about the added-value of the services offered. By the end of this stage, it became clear that most people are rational users, who appreciate the interactivity and possibilities of Télétel, and who would not consider living without it.
- These new tools spur social inventiveness. In the Minitel case, there was great enthusiasm for "teledemocracy", for example, or for messaging. Again, over time it became clear which applications offer more value-added.

Business firms look more specifically for the competitive advantage they can get from exploiting new media. For them, the key issues are to be guaranteed a large number of users; to be provided with a safe system, allowing electronic commerce; and, to be able to set up virtual markets.

Network operators (France Télécom in the Télétel case) have to deal with financing problems and, therefore, they must establish adequate billing systems. They can also take advantage of new services to foster new kinds of relations with business partners as well as customers. Finally, they can enter the value-added services market.

For the national economy, one has to be very modest in assessing Télétel's impact on GDP, employment, and external trade. However, the present situation might well be different, if Télétel did not exist (Minc 1995). Indeed, the projects currently under way may spur consumption in the fields of education, entertainment etc. In any event, all the relevant actors are looking for ways to make good use of the tremendous experience accumulated through more than ten years of commercial operation of videotex. It is too soon to say what the outcomes will be, but time is now of the essence, and the next few years will be crucial for the future of videotex in France.

We may conclude by recalling Nora and Minc's vision of "télématique":- 'Télématique' networks, contrary to electrical networks, do not transport electric current, but information, that is power. 'Télématique' networks will not be more networks, but networks of another nature (...): they will transform our cultural model' (Nora and Minc 1978: 11). The major challenge is therefore less about the future of videotex, than about the future of our society when confronted with the advent of information superhighways. The history of Télétel shows that social effects always differ from those expected.

References

La lettre de Télétel et Audiotel, every 2 months, France Télécom (created in 1984 as La lettre de télétel, now La lettre des Services en Ligne).
Messages, monthly, Ministère des Postes et Télécommunications (the name of the ministry has varied over time).
Réseaux, every two months, CNET.

especially:

AFTEL (1994),: Association Française de la Télématique, La télématique française en route vers les autoroutes de l'information (Paris: Les éditions du Téléphone).
Alten, M. (1995), De la léléinformatique domestique au Minitel (1960-1978), Quatrième colloque sur l'histoire de l'informatique, Rennes 14-16 novembre 1995.
Ancelin, C. and Marchand, M. (1984) (eds), Le videotex - contribution aux débats sur la télématique (Paris: Masson, Collection CNET-ENST).
Bilan 1994, June 1995 L'avenir de la télématique: 1994-2004, Hors série N° 12, 1994.
Bouwman, H. and Christoffersen, M. (1992) (eds), Relaunching Videotex (Dordrecht, Nl: Kluwer Academic Publishers).
Breton, T. (1994), Les téléservices en France, quels marchés pour les autoroutes de l'information? (Paris: La Documentation Française).
du Castel, F. (1993) (ed), Les télécommunivations (Paris: X,A Descours-Berger Levrault) .
Colonna d'Istria, M. (l990), 'Minitel: les autoroutes électroniques', Le Monde, (Paris), 17 Feb. 1990: 9.
Jouët J. (1991), 'L'amour sur Minitel', in Bougnoux D. (1993) (ed), Sciences de l 'information et de la communivation (Paris: Larousse), 784-789.
Jouët J. and Celle, N. (1985), La communivation au quotidien (Paris: La Documentation Française, Collection CNET-ENST)
Marchand, M. (1988), The Minitel Saga (Paris: Larousse).
Marti, B. (1994), Histoire du videotex dans le monde et du Minitel en France. In: Feneyrol M. and Guérard, A. (1994) (eds), Innovation et recherche en télécommunivations (Paris: Eyrolles), 211-247.
Minc, A. (1995), Perspectives. In: Fondation Idate (1995), La Société fave au Multimedia (Montpellier: Fondation Idate).
Ministère de l'Industrie, des Postes et Télécommunications et du Commerce Extérieur (1994), Les autoroutes et services de l'information - contributions aux débats des journées des 7 et 19 décembre 1994 (Paris: Ministère de l'Industrie, des Postes et Télécommunications et du Commerce Extérieur).

Neveu, E. (1994), Une société de communication? (Paris: Montchrestien, ClefsPolitique).

Nora, S. and Minc, A. (1978), L'informatisation de la société (Paris: Points-Seuil) Annexes, (Paris: La Documentation Française); in English (1980), The computerization of society, (Cambridge, MA: MIT Press).

Ponjaert M., Georgiades, P. and Magnier, A. (1983), Communiquer par Télétel (Paris: La Documentation Française).

Salzman, C. (1989), Anatomie d'un scandale, L'informatique professionnelle, (Paris, 76: (Août-Sept), 3-12.

Steinfield, C., Bauer, J.M. and Caby, L. (1994) (eds), Telecommunications in transition: policies, services and technologies in the European Community (Thousands Oaks, CA: Sage).

Steinfield, C., Caby, L. and Vialle, P. (1992), 'Internationalization of the firm and impacts on videotex networks', Journal of Information technology, 1992-7: 213-222.

Théry, G. (1994), Les autoroutes de l'information (Paris: La Documentation Française).

ANNEX

Source: France Télécom, La lettre de Télétel et Audiotel (June 1995)

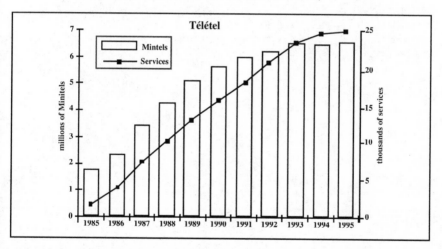

Graph 1: *Minitels and services*

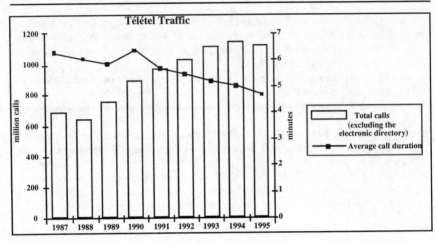

Graph 2: *Call duration*

7. Reshaping the Danish Information Society: 1984 and 1994

Tarja Cronberg

In 1994 I was elected to be a member of the reference group for the Danish Information Society: The Info-Society Year 2000. The group was constituted to support the work of an Info Society Committee, which was to draft plans for managing the related social change.

At the first meeting of the committee I suggested that we should start by learning from our earlier experience, which dated from discussions held in 1984 about the Information Society in Denmark. At that time a decision was made to build a broadband network - or, rather, a combination of high speed optical cables with local cable aerial antenna systems - a so-called "hybrid network". The decision to build this first step towards an information super-highway was coupled with a decision to initiate an accompanying social ex-periment. Local communities were given the opportunity to assess their tech-nological needs and to devise new organisational forms to meet those needs, given that change implies the use of information and communication tech-nologies. In these trials, some 50,000 Danes participated in using the new technology in libraries, schools, local information technology centres, and in homes.

As I had evaluated these experiments (Cronberg et al. 1991) and retained an interest in the subject, it seemed reasonable to remind the participants of Info Society Year 2000 that the best springboard for entering new discussion was to consider what we had already learnt from our recent past. However, the response from the Commission's Chair was astonishing: "The situation is new", she said. "We should not dwell on earlier experiences. At that time there was no cyperspace." Although she had followed the debates on infor-mation technology in the '80s - as a parliamentarian she had approved the hybrid network - she wanted to simply forget our past failed efforts. (I mean that they failed only in the sense that the technical, economical and social visions built into the broadband network did not materialize). Her point was that the construction of the Internet demanded a new beginning: cyberspace implied a different information society from the one posited in1984. As the Committee for the Info Society for the Year 2000 did not want to start by remembering, in this chapter I attempt to do so by comparing the two information society discourses in Denmark; the first on the broadband network decision in 1984, and the second on the plan for the Danish Info Society Year 2000.

My starting point is the social construction of technology, specifically the shaping of the information society. Who negotiates it? Who defines the issues and sets out the arguments? How is this new society conceived, what are the visions attached to it, and how are these formulated in discussion? Before embarking on a comparison of the first and second waves of Danish information society discourses, I begin with some words about the social construction of the information society.

Information Society Discourses

By the end of the '70s the Japanese were experimenting with an information society. The call was to become the world's leading nation in information and communication technologies (Cronberg 1981). Two towns, Taman New Town and Higaschi-Ikoma, were selected as experimental sites which would reveal the contours of an information society based on technical experimentation with optical cables. These were used for TV transmission, pay-TV, interactive learning, videotex, and the like. A wholistic Japanese society was envisaged by Yonedi Masuda who described a future where an information community was to be combined with local communities in a new information and communication space (Masuda 1981).

In The United States, Alvin Toffler presented his Third Wave Society vision where standardization and mass production were to be replaced by an orientation on the consumer and closer cooperation between users and producers. Telecottages were to emerge where families would work together.

Representative democracy would be replaced with a more direct democracy with due regard to ethnic and other minorities (Toffler 1983).

France, under Mitterand's socialist government of the early '80s, developed an urgent interest in formulating a vision of society based on information technology. France was late in introducing an effective telephone system and so, by the late '70s, French Telecom was an organisation which had become ripe for introducing new information technology, and Nora and Minc´s report on the information society provided a timely intellectual framework for how the French information society could be established (Nora and Minc 1978)[1]. The ensuing debate, which highlighted the need for social experimentation to accompany technical change, proved influential in Denmark and set the scene for the discussions of 1984.

The latest wave of information society discourses has been triggered by President Bill Clinton and Vice-President Al Gore who, in their campaign in 1992, set out to faciliate the creation of information superhighways. It was proposed that by 2015, every home, business, laboratory, classroom, and library would be connected through a National Information Infrastructure (NII). By means of digital online services, a wide array of public documents, databases and learning materials would be available to the majority of US citizens. A new American industrial policy would emerge which would replace the Cold War's military engagement in R&D with a civilian technology effort. A keyword in NII has been "interactivity" and, towards that goal, a wave of trails has been initiated.

Europe has followed America's lead. The European Commission has prepared its own plan for the information society and member countries have drafted similar national agendas; the Danish Info Society 2000 provides just one example. Methods have been designed for how to implement change at regional and local levels. A landmark was reached in February 1995 when the European Commission hosted a G-7 Ministerial Conference on the Information Society. This meeting endorsed a series of principles that should guide the world's entry into the information age (EC Information Society Project Office 1995). European rhetoric is less about industrial policy, and more

---

1   The French telephone situation is an interesting case in itself on how technologies do not just emerge. Different countries show a very different access curve for telephones, which is not only dependent on income. For a discription of the French case, see for example Cronberg (1988).

about conditions of work, especially teleworking, whereby people may work whereever they happen to live. Teleworking is seen as favouring underprivileged regions, and helping to solve unemployment problems.

Shaping Technologies, Building Societies

The title of this section, reflecting Wiebe Bijker and John Law's book (Bijker and Law 1992), expresses a theoretical approach towards the infomation society. Technologies are shaped, and through this process, a new society is built. This could, in fact, be interpreted as technology determinism; new technologies lead to a new society, technological change needs social change. However, the social shaping of technology or the social constructivist approach to technological change is interpreted differently. Technologies are malleable and technological change is not predetermined. Individual technologies and technological artefacts are formed in a negotiation process. Actors participate in these negotiation processes and for that reason their outcomes are not knowable in advance. This theoretical approach to technical change is called the Social Construction of Technology (SCOT) or the Actor-Network Theory.[2]

When we agree that actors shape technologies in negotiation processes, new issues emerge in our understanding of technological change. It is no longer enough simply to observe technological change, we must also look at who participates in the process; which actors mobilize to shape a certain technology; what their arguments and motivations are; and how they form alliances in the process. In addition, the meaning attached to a particular technology is of importance. An emerging technology is black-boxed, i.e., its power relations are stabilized within the technology as the actors participating in the negotiations agree on its particular meaning. Consequently, when understanding how information societies are created (whether American or European versions), our focus of attention should be on who argues for and against an idea, as much as on the specific arguments used.

---

2   The social shaping or the social construction of technology focuses on actors, negotiations and arguments rather than on technologies and technological properties. Technology is not given, but merges as a result of a social process. See further Bijker and Law (1992), Latour (1987,1991), and Cronberg and Sørensen,(1995).

The leading actors in the first phase of information society debates were the telecommunication agencies, computer engineers and future oriented researchers and writers scuh as Alvin Toffler. The second wave, in contrast, involves public servants and policy-makers and is marked by massive government investment in planning and infrastructure at the same time as telecommunication networks are being liberalised. While the information society in Toffler's or Masuda's versions could be described as possessing specific, fixed, characteristics, the discourse of the second wave can offer no such closure for this discourse is about the very shaping of the information society. A quote from the EU Commissioner, Martin Bangemann, in a speech delivered in1996, serves as an example:

'We are not passengers on the information train, but drivers. The Informational Society is not something that will simply happen - it must be created and shaped. And each individual can play a part in making it come about. There is no reasonable alternative to the Information Society. But there are differing ways.' (Bangemann 1996)

The Danish Information Society: 1984 Model

Let us return now to the Danish scene and the domestic debate on the information society in 1984. A principal actor at this time, although standing in the background, was the government's Media Commission. The Media Commission had, in the early '80s, prepared a report on how to receive satellite TV on earth, and on how many TV channels Denmark should have in the future (there was only one at the time). The Commission suggested - in the tradition of Danish public service - that a publicly-owned broadband network be built which would encompass neighbourhoods but not individual households. Through the "hybrid network" mentioned at the beginning of the chapter, it proposed to connect the obtical cables of the main highways with the cable aerial antenna systems of the neighbourhoods.

In 1982-83, the newly-elected conservative government was extremely interested in this proposal and established an intergovernmental committee (TMU) to prepare legislation on the broadband network. The teleadministrations (of which there are three in Denmark) were mobilized and they prepared a report on the matter. According to this much publisized report, the future broadband network would only reach communities with more than 250 households. This, in fact, meant that 400,000 Danish households, i.e. 1.4 million out of a population of 5 million, would be excluded from the future information society.

This issue mobilized the Ministry of the Environment for this proposal was not in accordance with the equal development of the country as a whole. The Ministry did not question the value of information technology; the query was about access. Its concern was that everybody should have access, particularly in the thinly populated areas, since the claim made of the electronic highway was that it would reduce the importance of distance, rather than work to support existing population concentrations. Actors from scarcely populated areas, particularly the Mayors of cities in Jutland, promoted the idea of a broadband network but only given that it would benefit peripheral areas.[3]

By 1984 there was a broad consensus amongst the parties in Parliament that the broadband network should be built, and a decision to that end was made in December of that year. The conservative government was in favour, as was the opposition of mainly Social Democrats. All the Ministries were in favour, although there were disagreements about who should transmit satellite TV. The teleadministrations were in favour, for it would broaden their market and break the monopoly of the P&T which had, until then, the sole right to receive satellite signals. The Ministry of Environment, the only opposing Ministry, became enrolled once the Hybrid Network Act allocated funds for social trials.

The only actors opposed to building the hybrid network were, in fact, the manufacturers and owners of aerial antenna systems. The latter was constituted particularly by people living in large residential areas who were afraid that they would be financially penalised on that account given the government's decision to impose an equal taxation policy. The net itself would be self-financing. A heated debate took place on whether or not there was a risk that telephone users would, in fact, pay for TV viewers' access to new channels. However, the appropriate Ministry underlined that this would not be the case.

---

3   The debates in 1984 between the Ministry of Environment and other actors have been analyzed in more details, in Cronberg (1990).

Learn to live with it

This Danish vision of the information society in 1984 was no more elegant than high-speed transmission of data and of live pictures. The need for these two things was never questioned. They were simply seen as the road to the future. As stated in a report by the Ministry of Public Works:

'As always, a technical revolution implies an element of risk, a risk that the technology will run ahead of our ability to adapt ourselves to the new facilities in an appropriate way. Are we able to make this large machinery available without endangering essential values of social life? Such questions may be posed, but should not stand in the way of intrepid attempts to develop and provide the best new technology can offer. It is no use turning our backs on a future that will come anyway. You have to learn to live with it, manage it and put it into the service of society[4]. *'*

On the micro level the issue was foreign TV. As Danish viewers had only one national channel, access to a multitude of international TV programmes through communication satellites would provide a varied supply. The decision to build the hybrid network, however, never included any analysis of what kind of TV programmes viewers were potentially interested in, nor of consumers' willingness to pay for choice, despite the fact that residential areas with aerial antenna systems already had access to satellite TV. The aerial antenna system taking down satellite signals directly was both a cheaper and an already established technical solution which the government had to (and did) prohibit in order to make the hybrid net commercially viable. Building a public network to be run on a commercial basis required the exclusion of another cheaper alternative.

Finally, both the macro level vision of needing high-speed data transmission in the information society, and the micro level issue of pursuading viewers to pay, supported the main agenda of the government, i.e., industrial development. It was assumed that building an optical network would promote Danish industry, support the emergence of a domestic market, and consequently provide competitive advantages for product development. Danish cable producers and TV producers, as well as other electronic industries, would have access to the future-oriented services of the information society.

---

4   Quoted from the ministerial report, Ministry of Public Works, May 1983, presenting the Hybrid Net plan to the government.

With the exception of one Danish cable producer, who saw a domestic market for optical cables, and a Danish TV producer, for whom it was important that its engineers work in an environment with a more varied supply of programmes, industry actually remained silent on the question of a broadband network.

Local communities shape technology

The key to passing the Hybrid Net Act was the acceptance of social experimentation. In social constructivist terms this was the critical point of passage where alliances could be formed and negotiations completed successfully to allow for the Act to be acceptable to all. These trials were carried out in 1987-1990. There were 16 of them in different local communities, and funding of about $20 million. They had to be approved by the TMU, which administered the experimental programme and the precondition for inclusion in the test sites was that there had to be local involvement. Departing from many other international experiments - for example, the Japanese ones of the '70s which were technology-led - it was officially underlined that the social experiments were not about new technology. The social experiments in the Danish context were about finding new local organizational forms to allow the technological changes to take place. In fact, local communities were called upon to construct the organizational and social context for the application of information technology.

Nor was the specific information technology defined. Which technologies were to be experimented with was an open question, once they remained within the boundaries of information, transmission of data, or visual communication. Interestingly enough, it was assumed, both when passing the Hybrid Net Act and during the experimental phase, that the technology was ready to be implemented. Neither the teleadministrations nor other technical experts ever questioned the technical feasibility of transmitting high-speed data or pictures at a distance.

When the local communities started to experiment in 1987-1988 it was technology that turned out to be the problem. With the exception of simple PC applications (e.g., in a local information centre where people could just come in and use a computer) very few of the advanced applications were ready for use. Local networks between institutions such as libraries and schools, or x-ray picture transmission from the dentist's office to the dental university did not function. It took at least a year for most of the more advanced applications to become operational. Although this meant that a number of potential users were frustrated and left the experiments, thousands of Danes participated and tried to find out whether information technology was something for them.

Boys between the ages of 9-14 and farmers turned out to be the most active users, though women and older people joined in during the later phases. The applications most frequently identified were mostly fairly mundane bookkeeping, secretarial work on WordPerfect, or accounting functions for small enterprises. Very few applications of high-speed data transmission of live pictures were implemented, and even fewer turned out to be of interest. One of the few examples was some farmers who experimented with visual communication between their stables and the vetinarian, or between their fields and the agricultural councellor. Even here it turned out that the broadband functions were not yet technically or economically feasible, and the farmers had to return to the transmission of still pictures.

The experiments resulted in an increased awareness of, and experience with, new information technology and in the production of some new applications which were shaped cooperatively by users and producers, e.g., library information systems and special transformers. Meanwhile the hybrid net which was being built in the larger communities turned out to be an economic disaster. The population, in the expected numbers, was just not interested in connecting itself to the many TV channels. Telephone subscribers ended up paying some of the bills, and the only sign of the information society was more passive TV watching.[5]

The Danish Information Society: 1994 Model

Inspired this time, not by the French but by the Clinton-Gore initiative on information superhighways, the Danish government decided in 1994 to create a new programme for the information society. A two-person committee was

---

5 The results of the experiments have been analyzed by a group of researchers (see Cronberg et al. 1991) and the economic consequences reported in a magazine Børsens Nyhedsbrev, Aug. 27, 1994.

selected, one woman and one man. The woman was an MP, the wife of the Prime Minister and the head of the Board of the Danish Datacentralen, the government-owned computer firm. The man was a high official in a Danish region as well as being a member of the Board of Datacentralen. To secure democratic representation, a reference group was formed whose members were drawn from all the Ministries, as well as from industry and research. I myself participated as a researcher. There was an almost equal representation of men and women. Although it included a wide distribution of individuals, it was weighted in favour of government officials, industry and research. Future citizens of the information society and those most likely to suffer from any of its negative aspects, such as the unemployed, were not represented.

The work was carried out over four months. The reference group met twice during that time. The result was a report *Info Society Year 2000*. It did not reflect any of the 1984 experience of the hybrid net implementation, or its related social experiments. In fact it assumed a totally new situation, where the American vision of the information superhighway was translated into the Danish context.

The vision was no longer one of high-speed data communication and visual transmission of pictures. The main objective now was to establish how the Danish public sector could be mobilised as a locomotive for the information society. That information society was taken for granted. It was not to be questioned, it simply was to come. Maybe it was even already there. But it could be formed and shaped, and the public sector should take responsibility for this to enforce its priorities. The main issues of the report were how to promote the use of information technology in schools, in health care, in administration, etc. A high priority was given to research. In spite of all the discussions about the emergence of cyberspace, the focus was on access to personal computers, not on networks, global information spaces, or the Internet.

The report discusses the two- thirds of the Danish population who do not yet have access to PCs in their homes, and expresses worries about them being excluded from the information society. In the Danish welfare tradition *Info-Society Year 2000* points practically on every page to the risk of polarization; of the division into A and B persons. However, it does not actually promote any ideas on how to fight this potential risk - other than ensuring access to personal computers. Although it promoted the role of the user of information technology in the public sector, the report did not advise that any funds should be allocated in support of this end. A new resource allocation was expected to take place within the existing financial frameworks of each sector. This was perhaps the most (and the only) controversial point of the report.

Info-Society Year 2000 with the subtitle *From Vision to Action* led in 1996 to a governmental action plan for the information society, *Info-Society for All - the Danish Model.* This action plan sets out three goals:

- Accepting social responsibility for ensuring that everybody may participate in the info-Society, so that it is a reality for all.
- Facilitating the means for a broad dialogue to take place, following which, all actors will accept their measure of responsibility for taking action.
- Building up a future-oriented infrastructure which will be implemented once the second goal is reached.

Before 1996 is out, over half of all Danish households should have at least one PC in the home. Denmark would then overtake the United States as the country which has the broadest dispersion of PCs in the home. Although the focus is on PCs, the action plan also underlines that it should be attractive for Danes to be on the Net. This implies a liberalization of the telecommunications sector, as well as development of the Internet, so that it should be as easy to use as the existing telephone system. Furthermore, security in the Net will be guaranteed by legislation on digital signitures and secure communication keys. A citizen's card is on the programme as well as electronic data exchange between companies. The Ministry of Research is responsible for implementing the action plan.

1984 and 1994 Compared

The information society of 1984 was a technology push. The potential of technology was taken for granted. It would induce organizational and social change which could then be studied in social experiments. Although it turned out that the information and communication technologies were not ready for use, they were black-boxed as something to be taken for granted. No one in the 1984 debate questioned the ability of technology to perform. Negative social consequences could be avoided since the social experiments provided an arena to organize the information society according to good welfare state practices. This reflected the understanding of technology in Denmark at the time: technology was technique, hardware but also organizational software.[6] Although technology was not seen as socially constructed, its organizational context was seen as malleable. New organizational forms could be created that would make adaptation to the technology both easier and more beneficial.

Compared to the 1984 situation, the 1994 model is also a social push. It is not just the technology which is taken for granted, but also the role of the public sector. The public sector should, in all activities, promote the use of information technology and at the same time guarantee citizens' access to its benefits. Access is the key to avoid polarization. The risk of polarization is seen one-dimensionally; inscribed as access to PCs, preferably at home. The second best alternative is the library or the school. Access is not problematized in terms of what people should use information technology for; what needs might arise in the future; or what learning processes are involved in order to be able to master the new technologies. (Maybe the third time the information society becomes a hot topic, it will be a question of the cultural push. Maybe in 2004 we will have found out that the social push was not enough. Cultural acceptance of information technologies, and cultural problems related to it, may then appear on the agenda.)

In the 1984 model high-speed data transmission and visual communication are talked about in abstract terms. Advanced technical solutions are taken for granted and the global village, local networks, and visual transmission of live pictures are assumed to be the future. The 1994 vision is more cautious. Although cyberspace and the Internet exist, access to PCs is seen as key. We hear no more talk about advanced technical solutions although, according to the action plan, researchers in particular are guaranteed access to the Internet. And although tele-surgery and other more exotic distance-transcending functions are on the agenda, it is the citizen card - an individual card with personal information - which becomes the symbol of the new Info-Society Year 2000. It is seen as a practical everyday thing. The Prime Minister's wife stated on

---

6 The Danish definitions of technology were discussed at a conference organized by the Social Science Research Council, a report of which has been published as Teknologi-opfattelse og teknologibegreber, Publication nr. 6. Teknik-Samfund Initiativet, Det Samfundsvidenskabelige Forskningsråd, 1987.

TV, when presenting Info-Society Year 2000, that she thought it was easy to get married with the citizen card (she was engaged to the Prime Minister at the time). This card could prove her eligibility to get married without having to wait in offices for the necessary documents.

Why this shift from the global village to the individual citizen card? Furthermore, this in a situation where the Internet is creating a global information space combined with local networks. By 1994 the Internet is already taken for granted. Small modifications may be made, such as the proposed Danish security measures, but as a whole it is not seen as problematic. The problem is the person using it, or rather all those not using it. A citizen card is a smart way of securing the spread of information technology through the back door. It is an easy entry to a society where data is accessible, transmitted quickly, and is easily controlled.

But is technology - or the info-society - socially shaped? In spite of the efforts to construct a society where the transmission of pictures would be an important element, the expectations of 1984 have not yet materialized. Although the farmers in Jutland actively participated in unique transmission experiments, they could not mobilize the necessary economic support for a broadband network of 2 Megabits/sec from door-to-door. Consequently, they had to settle for still-picture video transmission. Whether in 1996 or beyond, the sectorial Ministries are willing to give the necessary priority to investments in technology instead of other activities, in order to become the Danish locomotive for the info-society is still an open question. But technology may well be socially shaped even if the politicians' efforts to construct a future are not successful.

Through the experience of 1984 we find that there is no evidence for a technologically-determined understanding of social change. Technology does not just come and all we can do is "learn to live with it". In fact, the technological imperative is socially constructed, and takes different forms depending on the historical and social context and on which actors are mobilized, viz. Denmark's focus on public sector involvement as opposed to the US's preference for private enterprise.

The information societies of 1984 and 1994 are shaped by different actors. Parliament, the teleadministrations and Ministerial officials were key actors in 1984. Public debate was only initiated in terms of the need for TV channels, and who should pay for them. In 1994 the group participating in the Info-

Society Year 2000 is more heterogeneous with representatives from industry, the Ministries, researchers, politicians and even citizen movements. On the other hand, the small two-person committee is more homogeneous although equal representation of the sexes is guaranteed.

The public debate now is about the citizen card and about whether or not Ministries should prioritise the use of information technology rather than other activities. More critical voices were heard in 1984 about the nature of the information society. It was not yet taken for granted, and doubts were expressed as to whether it was only an illusion created by the electronics and media industries. In 1994 the frame of discussion is more massively adapted to the information society; it will be there, but is to be shaped. We are not talking about any other kind of society. More critical researchers, like myself, are actively involved within the actor-networks which support the information society rather than standing outside the dominant discourse.

References

Bangemann, Martin (1996) Information Society. Intervention at the 10th World Congress "Technology and Services in Information Society". Reuter EU-briefing (4th June 1996, European Commission).

Bijker, W., Hughes, T. and Pinch, T. (1987), The Social Construction of Technological Systems (Cambridge: MIT Press).

Bijker, Wiebe E. and John Law (eds.) (1992), Shaping Technology/Building Society. Studies in Sociotechnical Change (Cambridge: MIT Press).

Cronberg, T. and Sangregorio I-S. (1981), More of the Same: The Impact of Information Technology on Domestic Life in Japan. Development dialogue, 2, 68-79 (Uppsala).

Cronberg, T. (1988), Ved Skillevejen. Det informationsteknologiske spillerum i hverdagen. (At Crossroads. Information Tehnology and Freedom in Everyday Life). (Copenhagen: Social Science Monographs).

Cronberg, T. (1990), Experiments into the Future (Fremtidsforsøg). An evaluation of the Danish government´s experimental programme for information technology in local communities. (Copenhagen: Academic Publishers) (in Danish).

Cronberg, T., Duelund, P., Jensen O.M. and Qvortrup, L. (1991), Danish Experiments - Social Constructions of Technology. (Copenhagen: New Social Science Monographs).

Cronberg, T. and Sørensen, K.H. (eds) (1995), Similar Concerns, Different Styles? Technology Studies in Western Europe. Social Sciences COST A4. Vol. 4. (Luxemburg: European Commission).

European Commission, Information Society Project Office (1995). Information Society Trends, Special Issue "An Overview of 1995 is Main Trends and Key Events".

Forskningsministeriet (1986). Infosamfundet for alle - den danske model. (Info Society for all - the Danish model).

IT-politisk redegørelse 1996 til Folketinget og IT-politisk handlingsplan 1996. København.

Latour, B. (1987), Science in action. (Milton Keynes: Open University Press).

Latour, B. (1991), The Impact of Science Studies on Political Philosophy. Science, Technology and Human Values. Vol. 16. No.1. 1991, 3-19.

Mazuda, Y. (1981), The Information Society as Post-Industrial Society. World Future Society. (Washington D.C.).

Ministry of Research, 1994. Info-Society Year 2000. Copenhagen.

Nora, S., Minc, A. (1979), L'informatisation de la Société. (Paris: Ed. Du Seuil).

Toffler, A. (1981), The Third Wave. (Pan Books).

8. Multimedia Visions and Realities[1]

William H. Dutton

Introduction

Visions of information superhighways, global networks, and virtual communities, combined with concrete technological advances and huge multimedia mergers, have rekindled interest in video phones, interactive television, and all sorts of other new services over the Internet (Burstein and Klein 1995; Emmott 1995; Negroponte 1995). On occasion, proponents of new multimedia services will acknowledge the controversial history of earlier innovations, such as the Picturephone. However, few draw lessons from this history to inform discussion on the future of communications (some exceptions are Elton 1991; Elton and Carey 1984; Greenberger 1985, 1992; Noll 1985, 1992; and Rogers 1986).

Past efforts to introduce video telephones, video conferencing systems, interactive cable television, and videotext provide at least two types of insight valuable to new media developments. First, they suggest areas of continuity and discontinuity with the past; in many ways the offerings of today are not new. It is useful to isolate these genuinely new features, if we wish to draw appropriate analogies between the past and present. Second, they offer an empirical basis to the often ungrounded debate amongst media pundits over the future of telecommunications, which the Internet has brought into full swing.

---

1 An earlier version of this chapter appeared as `Driving into the Future of Communications? Check the Rear View Mirror' in Emmott, S. (1995) (ed.) Information Superhighways: Multimedia Users and Futures (London: Academic Press): 79-102.

Continuities and Discontinuities

Discussion of information superhighways, global multimedia mergers and the "fibersphere" suggests revolutionary change in the making (Lucky 1989; Gilder 1990; Burstein and Klein 1995). However, there are fundamental areas of continuity in the visions and services central to these new ventures, while there has been a noticeable shift in the geographical scope and backgrounds of the key players.

A Return to Earlier Visions

Despite revolutionary developments in communications technology over the last several decades, the dominant images of the future of telecommunications recapitulate earlier themes. Optimistic 1960s scenarios of all kinds of electronic services reaching all households and businesses of the major industrial nations emerged again in the 1990s (Gore 1991).

In the 1960s, the development of online interactive computer systems fostered proposals for a public information utility (Sackman and Nie 1970; Sackman and Boehm 1972). These computer utilities had many features in common with the idea of an information superhighway. Technology has changed, ie., personal computers replace dumb terminals and gigabyte networks replace dial-up access, but the underlying conception of public access to huge electronic stores of information is remarkably similar. Also in the 1960s, advances in cable systems spawned discussion of interactive cable television (Smith 1970; Dutton et al. 1987). This was illustrated particularly by the development of coaxial cable — literally defined as the information highway of that time - and the idea of marrying this with interactive computer technology. Academics and journalists outlined the exciting prospect of people being able to compute, shop, vote, send electronic mail, get medical assistance, and access information, radio, television and films over coaxial cable. This convergence of services over a single medium, albeit using analog versus digital signals, became popularized as the "wired nation" in which all households and businesses would have access to an integrated array of all kinds of electronic information and communications services (Smith 1970, 1972; Goldmark 1972; Dutton et al. 1987).

Grand visions of the future of interactive communications could not withstand the perceived market failure of interactive cable-TV in the early 1980s, particularly with the growing sense that a number of commercial videotext services were also floundering. They were replaced by more technocratic visions.

One was the push for an integrated services digital network (ISDN). This concept did not capture the imagination of a nontechnical constituency and even became a focus of jokes within the technical community, as everyone came up with their own words for renaming this acronym, such as "Incredible Services We Don't Need". Yet many services centrepieced by the promoters of ISDN were strikingly similar to those later promoted by the developers of multimedia. Promotional videos of ISDN often showcased business colleagues, far removed from each other, simultaneously editing a document while consulting over a video conferencing link.

Since the mid-1980s, the idea of a Broadband-Integrated Services Digital Network (B-ISDN) had a brief period of ascendence related to dozens of fibre-to-the-home trials in the US and abroad (McGilly et al. 1990). Most of these were limited to technical trials with less than 200 subscribers. Driven by a few telephone companies and manufacturers, over two-thirds of the fibre-to-the-home (FTTH) trials focused on voice telephony services, comparable to the services provided over twisted wire pairs. Another 19 per cent experimented with cable TV as well as telephone services. Only about one in ten experimented with broadband telecommunication services (McGilly et al. 1990).

In the 1960s, telecommunications was viewed, and later regulated, as a vehicle for social and political reform. One reason is that the concept of a wired city in the U.S. was developed in the context of Lyndon Johnson's so-called Great Society. In the 1980s, communication came to be viewed and deregulated as a vehicle for international trade and economic development, during a period in which policy arguments were dominated by economists wedded to competition versus regulation as the most efficient means to control prices and service. Public service visions were muted in favour of more nuts-and-bolts technical trials. In the 1990s, at least in the U.S., there has been continuing interest in telecommunications as an industrial strategy, but also a renewed commitment to using telecommunications to again pursue various social goals and objectives under a new Democratic administration.

The Pursuit of Convergence

Multimedia and the Internet are new and have become the labels for journalists writing about almost any new development. This reflects the frenzy surrounding the Internet and the prominence of the multimedia personal computer as a defining technology of the mid-1990s. In the early 1980s, videotext was often used in the same way - as a generic term for new media developments - until its market failure. The Internet and multimedia personal computer have caught attention because they embody the idea of convergence - the integration of the once separate technologies and industries of print, broadcasting, and telecommunications.

The eventual realisation of convergence, along with the transformation from analog to digital systems, might well enable many old services to be provided in ways that fundamentally change the way we use the media. The vision of Nicholas Negroponte and others at MIT's Media Lab, for example, entails a shift from mass to more personalised media services as more intelligence can be embedded in telecommunication networks (Brand 1987; Negroponte 1995). Nevertheless, the idea of convergence is not new to the telecommunications industry.

The wired nation of the 1960s was anchored in the idea that radio, television, telecommunications, and electronic mail would all be conveyed to the business and home over the same coaxial cable infrastructure (Dutton et al 1987). Digital technology was not essential to convergence (as sometimes suggested) but, analog or digital, convergence is far more than a technical issue of multiplexing signals within a single conduit. It entails industrial as well as technological restructuring and therefore has been far more difficult to achieve than the technical issues alone would lead us to believe (Garnham 1996).

Familiar New Services

Many applications said to be enabled by the new multimedia are also familiar to those tracking field trials and experiments over the years. Specifically, technological advances such as in compression, switching and storage media, are expected to facilitate the provision of video telephony and conferencing, interactive television, video-on-demand, video and audiotext services, electronic mail, and conferencing as well as applications of virtual reality. These services are in addition to conventional telephone, facsimile, cable, and broadcasting services, which should be available at higher levels of fidelity and resolution in a fully digital future.

Since the 1960s, the major applications promoted today, including video-on-demand, multimedia, home shopping and video communications, were piloted around the world. Table 1 provides a selected list of some of the trials and offerings that might inform current discussion of each type of service enabled by advances in information and communication technologies.

Type of Service:	Selected Trials, Prototypes & Offerings:
Video telecommunication	AT&T's Picturephone
	AT&T's VideoPhone 2500
	France Telecom's Biarritz Trial
	Confravision
	AT&T's Picturephone Meeting Service
Two-way, Interactive	Interactive cable TV experiments (NSF, Hi-OVIS)
	Warner's QUBE
	Interactive television network
	GTE's Main Street
	Screen phones
Video on demand	Hi-OVIS
	Fiber to home trials (eg., Cerritos)
	Time Warner's Full Service Network, Maitland, Florida
	World Wide Web (WWW)
	Video rental stores
Electronic mail & conferencing	Videotext (Prestel, Times Mirror and others)
	Arpanet, the Internet
	Public and private bulletin boards
Multimedia Personal Computer or Game Machine	Videotext (Prestel, Times Mirror and others)
	Columbus, Ulysses
	Games (eg., Nintendo and others)
	Multimedia Kiosks (eg., Info California)

Table 1: *Types of Service in Selected Trials*

In 1994, for example, video-on-demand trials in the U.S. and U.K. vied for recognition as the first in the world, when video-on-demand was a central feature of the Hi-OVIS (Highly Interactive-Optical Visual Information System) project in the early 1980s (Kawahata 1987). Hi-OVIS was an interactive cable television experiment in Higashi-Ikoma, Japan. They offered a video-on-demand service for about five years, although it was called a "video request service" and was limited to three channels - what today is sometimes called "near video on demand". Nevertheless, it was sophisticated enough to utilise a robot in the cable studio that would retrieve video cassettes and insert them in the video tape monitors for play-back to the home. A decade later, a trial of video-on-demand in the U.S. depended on a human being fetching video cassettes for play-back to only four homes included on the network.

As noted above, multimedia personal computers are new, but there have been earlier introductions of multimedia terminals, such as in France Télécom's Biarritz trial, and there are ways in which the history of videotext services can inform discussion of multimedia services. Perhaps the best example of continuity of service offerings is the cycle of attention given to interactive television services.

Awakening a Passive Audience

Interactivity has regained a great deal of currency. Interactive television, interactive cable - even interactive Teddy Bears - are among the range of new services of the 1990s. Again, however, interactive services have a quite interesting history over the last several decades (Dutton et al. 1987).

In the early 1970s, "wired city" experiments were tied most directly to both governmental and corporate investments in interactive cable television projects in the U.S. and Japan. In 1973, the Japanese Ministry of Posts and Telecommunications initiated a local cable TV experiment in Tama New Town, which was followed later by the Ministry of International Trade and Industry's launch of the Hi-OVIS project.

In 1974, the U.S. National Science Foundation (NSF) supported a series of experiments with interactive cable, which joined academic researchers with cable operators in Reading, Pennsylvania; Spartanburg, South Carolina; and Rockford, Illinois (Becker 1987). As technical trials, they demonstrated that a variety of public and commercial services could be provided over two-way cable systems (Brownstein 1978). But these same experiments also cast doubt over any widespread consumer interest in new information services, suggesting that interactive offerings were only marginally, if at all, more effective than conventional broadcasts - but significantly more costly (Becker 1987; Elton 1980).

Even by the time these early NSF experiments and trials were operational, glamorous images of consumer response to interactive cable had begun to fade. Nevertheless, in 1977, Warner-Amex, a subsidiary of Warner Communications, introduced QUBE, a 30-channel interactive cable television system, on a commercial basis (Davidge 1987). It was launched in Columbus, Ohio because this city was a test market for a number of products. A primary business rationale behind QUBE was to use interactive cable for audience research. QUBE offered two main interactive capabilities: it permitted viewers to send an up-stream data signal for polling or ordering a Pay-TV programme and it permitted the cable operator to continually sweep homes to monitor who was watching what channel.

This second feature of the interactive network was the most central to their trials of new programming ideas, eventually leading to the national launch of such programmes as Nickelodeon, a children's television programme, and MTV, a video music channel (Davidge 1987). Its live and interactive programmes were able to regularly draw nearly a quarter of QUBE subscribers, but they were never profitable given the costs of the productions for a local audience (Davidge 1987: 84-85). Warner-Amex pulled the plug on QUBE in 1984 in large part because of the losses which its parent company, Warner Communications, incurred with its Atari game subsidiary, when sales fell below forecasts.

Hi-OVIS was in operation from 1978 to 1986. During its initial phase, the trial tested technical aspects of the system while, after 1980, they turned their attention to the market for, and commercial viability of, the services provided over the system, including retransmissions of television signals, character and still picture information services, video request services, and two-way interactive voice and video services. The trial was terminated in March 1986, failing in the sense that the system was not diffused to other communities as a commercial venture.

As early as the 1970s, requiems were written for the wired city and interactive television. Yet even in the mid-1990s, the future of interactive TV remains uncertain and the vision continues to motivate new service offerings (Burstein and Klein 1995). Some new interactive television projects piggyback on existing broadcasts of game shows and sporting events as opposed to being produced from scratch as interactive productions. The California-based Interactive Network Inc. uses a hybrid communication system. This combines broadcast television, FM radio and telephone systems to allow viewers to, say, play along with game shows from their homes, using a hand-held terminal that can receive the radio signals. A different system, marketed in the U.K. by Interactive Network Ltd, uses on-screen graphics, a vertical blanking interval rather than FM radio, and provides four cheap handsets so that members of the household can compete with one another as well as the larger audience as they view TV game shows. These systems raise new possibilities for establishing an audience over time.

Discontinuities

One discontinuity has been a shift in the geographical orientation of new media from local to more national and global networks, best exemplified by the World Wide Web (WWW) on the Internet. In the 1960s, the wired city was built on a foundation of local as well as interactive cable TV, in which the local orientation of systems was as significant as the notion of interactivity. In Britain, for example, this period was marked by experiments in community cable TV rather than interactive cable. This local orientation was in part driven by the early history of cable systems, which began as local community antenna systems (CATV), as well as the belief that cable technology was inherently local since the attenuation of signals downstream limited the area covered by early CATV systems. In the U.S., it was also supported by a tradition in broadcasting that favoured, but failed to foster, localism. In fact, the arrival of satellite-linked cable systems in the late 1970s was the major impetus to the wider diffusion of cable systems in the U.S.

The advocates of superhighways for the 21st Century seem more focused on national information infrastructures, but with clear ambitions for extending them to a more global scale through Global Information Infrastructure (GII) initiatives. This was driven by a variety of factors including the greater value of any network that could provide similar levels of service around the world, as was the case with Internet or ordinary telephone networks. There are some exceptions to this global orientation, such as the emergence of local electronic bulletin board systems like Santa Monica, California's Public Electronic Network and, in the UK, Manchester's HOST system, where a local orientation is a central feature of the services. But these too would move globally by moving onto the Internet.

Another exception is the emergence of successful initiatives to launch neighbourhood television, such as in New England, U.S.A. (Dutton et al. 1991). Yet these remain the exception, despite the fact that localism remains one of the few strategic advantages of wired over wireless systems, such as direct satellite broadcasting.

Discontinuity is found also in the centrality of the "techies". They represent a new set of players - technically-adept networkers within the Internet community - who have risen to take a leadership role in debates over the future of communications. David Ronfeldt of the Rand Corporation refers to the experts in computer networking as "cybercrats". Clearly, the cybercrats influenced thinking within the Clinton-Gore administration, and leaders within the computing industry, such as Bill Gates of Microsoft, have become key visionaries, reaching outside the computer industry per se. While leaders within the computing world were important to visions of a public information utility in the 1960s, and some like James Martin have remained key to discussions of the future of telecommunications, they seem to have been less central than leaders of the cable and telecommunications industry until recently (Burstein and Klein 1995).

The rise of players from an industry not previously well-connected to entertainment and information services to the public at large, is one factor undermining lessons from past experience. In the 1970s, cable enthusiasts included many investors and journalists unfamiliar with the broadcasting industry and therefore less sceptical than they might have been about the promise of local and interactive television. In the 1980s, most telephone company executives considering the provision of video-on-demand via fibre to the home were not closely involved with cable and broadcasting services. Likewise, many of the computer techies of the 1990s were not even alive when their predecessors advocated the construction of a public information utility, and are also distanced from cable and broadcasting services.

Visions and Realities: Some Reflections

Some recurring issues cut across this history of telecommunication trials and commercial offerings. They are only a subset of any list that might be culled from this history.

The Importance of Visions

Vice President Al Gore and President Bill Clinton captured the attention of politicians and journalists in the U.S. and abroad in the early 1990s with their evolving concept of an information superhighway. Public officials have subsequently knocked down all sorts of barriers between cable, telephone, and broadcasting that might constrain the construction of a modern information infrastructure. Like the wired city concept, the idea of an information superhighway gained a great deal of legitimacy in debate within industry and policy circles (Dutton 1996b; Sawhney 1996). As in the past, this vision played an important role in shaping public policy, particularly U.S. telecommunications policy. A journalist, Ralph Lee Smith, popularised notions of a wired city in ways that helped convince key people at the Federal Communications Commission (FCC) that the long-term social and economic benefits made it worth the known risks to the broadcast industry to knock down regulatory barriers to the development of cable, and create regulation aimed at achieving the technological infrastructure of the wired city.

Based on these visions of a wired nation, local and interactive cable TV experiments were undertaken in a number of nations in the 1970s. These visions led several companies to construct interactive systems on a commercial basis, such as QUBE. The axing of QUBE in 1984 reflected a general sense that local and interactive cable systems were not commercially viable at that time. Nevertheless, the cable TV industry moved into a more central role in broadcasting, at least in the U.S. and Canada, if not in Britain, France, and Germany.

A BBC Horizon programme, entitled *Now the Chips are Down,* provided a compelling view of the challenges confronting the British economy, and provided a vision of Britain seizing opportunities to create new industries and compete internationally in areas such as software development where the U.K. might enjoy a competitive advantage. This programme, and its vision, played a significant role in convincing key ministers and civil servants in Britain to develop policies aimed at addressing the industrial implications of the microelectronics revolution in information and communication technologies. In fact, the chip might have been as powerful a symbol in Britain during the early 1980s as the superhighway has become in the U.S. a decade later.

In the case of fibre to the home (FTTH) trials in the U.S., the lack of any compelling vision of the future of communications mattered greatly. Promoters of FTTH promised little beyond the targeting of video-on-demand as a source of revenue for constructing new telecommunication infrastructures. In this case, the lack of a compelling social and economic vision left the telephone companies with little support within the FCC and Congress, who saw no reason to jeopardise the cable television industry to create a video juke box. It was only when new telecommunication infrastructures became tied more closely to national economic competition - in part, by way of the information highway metaphor - that the telephone companies gained more support amongst regulators and politicians.

The idea of a wired city captured the imagination of regulators and reconfigured communication policy in the United States. Contemporary discussion of multimedia superhighways has had a similar influence, if not always in the ways their promoters and originators expected or hoped.

Predictions of the Unpredictable

Those who have tracked the history of innovations in information and communication technology learn to distrust nearly any forecast (Elton 1991). Forecasters have had a remarkably poor track-record. On the one hand, exciting forecasts of major markets for interactive cable television, the videophone, and videotext services were not fulfilled. On the other hand, dreary forecasts of a limited future for the facsimile machine, wireless telephony, and video cassette recorders proved to be wildly off the mark as well.

Video telecommunications is a case in point. The idea of a telephone that transmits and receives images on a screen is at least as old as television. Bell Labs began experiments with video telephony in the 1950s, leading to the display of a prototype at the 1964 World's Fair in New York City. A number of major telephone equipment manufacturers designed video phones in the

1960s, including Nippon Electric Company, Stromberg-Carlson and the British Post Office (Dickson and Bowers 1974).

AT&T developed the Picturephone for the commercial market in the late 1960s, forecasting a market of up to one per cent of all domestic and three per cent of all business phones by 1980 (Martin 1977). It was to become a business status symbol. The Picturephone was even equipped with a signal that would indicate if the person called did or did not have a video phone, hoping to elicit the kind of social pressure exerted around the answering machine in the 1990s: `You don't have an answering machine?' Picturephone never reached this stage. Faced with an exceedingly limited response from business, AT&T withdrew the Picturephone in 1973 after investing from $130-500 million in its development (Dickson and Bowers 1974).

In 1979, France Télécom, the government-owned telecommunications monopoly, chose Biarritz, a resort and tourist centre in the South-West of France, as the site for an experimental fibre optic network providing voice, video, and data services. The government's objectives were to develop the technical know-how for building and installing fibre optic systems, and also to showcase French technology. France Télécom hoped also to explore the market for broadband services. The first 50 subscribers were connected in 1984, and all 1,500 residences covered by the project were connected by the summer of 1986.

The Biarritz system provided distributed services, including 15 cable TV channels and 12 stereo sound channels, and switched services, including video telephony. Subscribers were provided with a multi-service integrated (multimedia) terminal with a video monitor, camera, keyboard, and telephone handset. The terminal could be used as a video telephone to transmit still or full-motion images. Subscribers could consult on-line image and data banks and access any of the thousands of videotext services provided over the Télétel system (better known as Minitel). Subscribers were charged a monthly tariff for cable service and both a monthly fee and a usage-sensitive rate for switched services.

France Telecom found that only a minority of connected households in Biarritz used their terminal as a videophone or picturephone, and only after a fairly long period of adaptation (Gérin & Tavernost 1987). Later, in 1992, AT&T reintroduced a video phone, calling its product the VideoPhone 2500. Other companies - including Mitsubishi, Sony, and BT - launched similar products in the 1990s. As before, the public's response to these video telephone services (in the short-term at least) has been far below the expectations of its developers.

Perhaps the public does not need or want video telecommunications (Noll 1992). However, it is difficult to make any definitive judgement about the future of video telecommunications on the basis of such trials. Not only are both the technology and market changing, but there are also multiple explanations for why each product has failed within the marketplace, e.g., the absence of trigger services, human factors' design issues, the lack of a critical mass, concerns over privacy, and cost.

If the existence of uncertainty is acknowledged, then industry and government can take a long-term perspective. Policies could aim at stimulating more field trials, encouraging more experimentation, accepting more failures, and supporting continued research and development rather than targeting sure winners.

Capturing the Public's Interest

When I first demonstrated digital video to my class at the University of Southern California I was astonished by their response. I had just shown them over 30 seconds of motion video with text and sound - all stored on a 3 and 1/2 inch diskette! All they had to say was: 'Television is better'. Many trials of new services experience the same reaction. In 1996, when I showed my class an interactive CD-ROM designed by Bill Gates (1995), my undergraduates were only interested in seeing the tour of his home! Enthusiasm for many breakthroughs in video over telephone wires, multimedia, and interactivity reflect more than technological advances. The personal computer was in some respects a technological breakthrough in microelectronics. However, its success beyond the hobbyist market was based on its provision of trigger services, such as word processing and spreadsheets, which individuals would purchase a personal computer in order to use. Many of the new media have yet to offer this so-called trigger service or infamous "killer ap" that will create a demand for the technology.

The hype that surrounds most new media ventures creates expectations of improved services that often do not square with the reality. Interactive cable was one case in point where great expectations were dashed by actual systems, which were generally limited to simple audience response systems permitting the polling of individuals from their homes. While interactive cable TV was judged to be a marginal success for some types of programming, these systems cost cable operators nearly three times the expense of installing a conventional cable network. Likewise, video-on- demand is based on the proven market for Hollywood movies. Television viewing and video rental stores support that claim. But the public is unlikely to be satisfied with lower quality video, even if available on demand, and even if they can beat the price at the video rental store.

In the early 1990s, the multimedia personal computer remained more of a technological than market breakthrough. It is conceivable that the multimedia personal computer could provide the facility for accessing all of the new services, from video telephony to personal computing, at least in business. A multitude of applications have been promoted for this technology in business (training), education (hypertext archiving and searching) and entertainment (games). But none of these offers the clear trigger service for the public at large, comparable to word processing or spreadsheets for the personal computer.

The most enthusiastic promoters of multimedia see the public interfacing with huge electronic libraries and video juke boxes through a multimedia window in which they control what, and when, they watch. In many respects, this scenario makes problematic assumptions about the public's interest in information, which I discuss below, and in exerting greater control over content. As experiments with interactive TV suggest, it is not clear that individuals wish to actively become involved in the control of video, particularly as a medium for their entertainment.

The desperation surrounding the search for a trigger service is evident in the claim that prurient interest will propel the multimedia market. Sex and violence is often suggested as the trigger for multimedia with quite incredible figures about the proportion of CD-ROMs, for example, that are devoted to pornographic material. High tech "peep shows" are claimed to be the new killer ap (New York Times, Jan 9, 1993). Others argue that the impact of this market has already been felt (Greenberger, 1992: 142). Experience with other media underscores this point. Adult films were among the most popular pay-per-view movies on QUBE (Davidge 1987), but they were not popular enough to generate a profit for QUBE, or a market for interactive cable TV.

Adult sites have been among the most popular on the World Wide Web in its early years, but far more is required to make this a mass medium.

Changing Media Habits

Many innovations in information and communication technology, such as flat screen displays and portable telephones, simply make it easier to do what users are already in the habit of doing - working at a computer or talking on the phone. But many trials of new media have bumped up against the existing media habits of the general public. As Hazel Kahan (1984), who worked with the QUBE system, put it: you should never underestimate the difficulty of getting someone to do something they have never done before, such as talk to their TVs, particularly if it's something they don't like to do. In the case of interactive television, most people watch television quite passively, sometimes treating the TV as the modern equivalent of the fire place. Habits change slowly.

In U.S. and Japanese trials of interactive cable, providers could constantly monitor channel selections. One thing they learned was that even an activity as limited as channel selection took years to change from a habit of watching one channel all evening to more frequently switching from one channel to another. For better or worse, we take it for granted in the 1990s, particularly in multichannel environments like the U.S., that many people often graze through programmes, watching TV more than they watch individual programmes. But this pattern took over a decade to develop and was not an immediate impact of remote control devices. And grazing through channels is not the engagement required to participate in an interactive programme.

Of course, developers of new services often challenge existing communication habits even when they believe they are building on them. For example, developers of video telephony sought to emulate face-to-face communications. Instead, they created a quite different medium calling for new rules, a new etiquette, and a change in communication habits. Even early studies of the Picturephone found that video phones distort normal face-to-face communications as well as normal telephone use (Dickson and Bowers 1974). This videophone moved the image of the other person to well within the conventional social distance that Americans are used to maintaining, and created an abnormal level of eye contact between the users. Americans were not accustomed to being within three feet of those with whom they are speaking. Nor are they used to someone looking directly at them for a sustained period of time, even if the cameras fail to provide a sense of direct eye contact.

Likewise, the developers of interactive television believe that they are building on an activity people already like to do - watching television. Or, are they introducing the mass audience to something they do not do, and do not like to do - 'talking to their TVs' (Kahan 1984)? Similarly, the developers of the UK's Interactive Network, which allows viewers to play along with game shows, believe that they are complementing the existing habits of viewers watching game shows who shout out answers and try to outwit the contestants.

Communication versus Information

Any survey of literature on multimedia encyclopedias, and other huge stores of information, illustrate the degree to which the industry remains convinced that there is a widespread interest in getting access to information per se. Likewise, early visions of the public information utility were based on the assumption that the public is interested in information. In fact, many assume that the public is composed largely of avid information seekers.

However, this assumption might well be a misleading guide to the development of services. Experiments with electronic services have reinforced an observation made by many involved in the early market trials of videotext services, which is that the public might be more interested in specialized services and in communication than in information per se (Hooper 1985, p. 190). Videotext trials in the U.S., and the French Minitel system, underscored the centrality of interpersonal and group communication to electronic networks.

For example, Times Mirror's commercial offering of its Gateway videotext service found a growing interest in electronic mail among its subscribers. But Times Mirror was a publisher interested in the future of the newspaper business. Realising that it would be quite some time before videotext competed with the newspaper, Times Mirror saw no reason to continue with Gateway. The logic seemed to be that if there was a market for electronic communications, then let the telephone companies provide it.

This point is striking from research on electronic bulletin boards, such as the Santa Monica PEN system, as well as from usage of the Internet, the success of which has been a major driving force behind the promotion of an information superhighway. In fact, arguments about the rapid growth and saturation of Internet capacity is central to proposals for the next generation of infrastructures to support this service. Arpanet, which later became Internet, was developed to support remote access to computing services, permitting students and researchers at one university to use computing facilities at other universities. The actual use of Arpanet did not support remote computing. The network evolved instead to become primarily a medium for interpersonal communications - e-mail. Despite growing interest in the World Wide Web, which is similiar to broadcasting, individuals use Internet facilities primarily to send e-mail and manuscripts to their colleagues at local and distant locations. Communications remains the trigger service for these computer networks.

All of the most successful computer-based information services for the public, such as SeniorNet and CompuServe, have made e-mail and conferencing a central aspect of their operations (Arlen 1991). The popularity of electronic bulletin boards in the U.S. are again anchored in the value of communication, not accessing information.

Given the potential value of communication versus information services, it becomes quickly apparent that one of the most central problems facing the new media is getting to a point at which there is a critical mass of users. The value of any telecommunications network increases in a nonlinear fashion as more people are connected to the network. France Télécom's experiment with video telephony in Biarritz quickly discovered that a small number of video telephones in a local community failed to incorporate a critical mass (Gérin and Tavernost 1987).

All of the trials and experiments with the video phone and other new interpersonal communication technologies are limited by the lack of a critical mass of users. This is not a design problem but one of how to subsidize users until a critical mass of users exists, at which point the need for a subsidy would diminish.

In 1996, however, we were presented with unbelievable statistics on the 10 per cent per month growth of Internet that suggest e-mail and conferencing is diffusing to a rapidly expanding base of users. It might well have moved beyond a point of critical mass and become significantly more valuable to new users. Nevertheless, there are problems in accessing these claims. The actual use of e-mail and conferencing systems is often substantially different from any formal measures of registrations, official users, or account sign-ups. Also, the Internet's use is subsidized to the point that many users often realise no costs. In addition, despite major strides, the user interface on most e-mail networks is difficult and nonintuitive for a large proportion of users. Finally, some existing systems that have moved outside the university setting and into the public at large are already experiencing difficulties with their regulation, with respect to privacy, speech, and access (Dutton 1996). All of these problems raise cautions and suggest the need for more systematic and disinterested research on actual usage patterns over time.

Reality Costs

The Clinton-Gore campaign staff posted a simple message on their wall to remind everyone that they should focus on the economy. In the main offices of a major U.S. aerospace firm, which is developing computer simulations for training applications, a notice reminds its staff that 'Reality Costs'; simulations can be closer and closer to reality, but as they move closer to reality, they will cost more. In a narrow sense, this is a lesson learned by a history of trials with new media, which are often based on the assumption that users want to more closely approach face-to-face human communication.

For instance, a number of experts lay the failure of video phones on their cost, which in the case of Picturephone was about 10 times the cost of an ordinary telephone call (Martin 1977). Price remains substantial. AT&T's VideoPhone 2500 was introduced at $1,500, 100 times the cost of an ordinary telephone. Even if the use of a VideoPhone 2500 costs no more than an ordinary call over the telephone network, the equipment costs remain substantial for residential customers.

The issue of cost was one major factor leading AT&T to move away from video telephone services for individuals in the 1970s to the use of its Picturephone technology in supporting video teleconferencing for executives. Its major cost justification was as a telecommunications substitute for travel to executive meetings. However, trials of AT&T's Picturephone Meeting Service (PMS), which continued into the early 1980s, made a transition from

Picturephones to full motion, broadcast-quality video conferencing systems, which AT&T provided on a trial basis well below actual cost. PMS as well as other publicly accessible video conferencing facilities, such as Confravision in the UK, met with similar problems of building a viable customer base of repeat users. Individuals would use these rooms, often expressing quite positive opinions about the experience, but then not return on any regular basis.

There are numerous explanations for this failure to build a video conferencing market in the 1980s. Few executives feel they travel too much, and few wish to substitute a video conference for travel unless it is to an unpleasant site (Johansen 1984). One of the only successful public applications of video conferencing in the U.S. is between the courts and prisons, and between police stations and district attorney offices, making it possible for victims of a crime to talk with the district attorney's office without travelling to the office (Dutton et al. 1991).

Generally, business executives and managers do not perceive that visual information is critical to most meetings nor that video communications is critical to most of their business conducted over a distance (Johansen 1984). They also face critical mass problems as well as the difficulties entailed in travel to a video conferencing facility. While PMS facilities were located in a number of major cities in the U.S., is it not an exaggeration to note that travel within metropolitan areas such as Los Angeles and New York City is sometimes more difficult than long distance air travel!

Issues of convenience and critical mass might be overcome by permanently installed, private video conferencing facilities within the key offices of major corporations. The trade literature frequently claims that privately installed rooms are now quite common place. However, there are few systematic, non-proprietary studies of the utilization of these privately installed facilities.

Taking Account of Social Concerns

Trials highlighted the potential significance of enduring social concerns, such as privacy, equity of access, and freedom of expression. The Picturephone and other video telephones, for example, were perceived to be an intrusive technology that invaded the privacy of the user (Dickson and Bowers 1974: 102). The most common concern raised by those with whom I discuss video communications is being on camera in their homes. Almost uniformly, individuals draw analogies to when and where they use their telephones - such as when they step out of the shower - to raise concerns over being seen. Here again, design changes such as smaller screens and locating phones in offices and in the windows of computer screens might address this issue. But these solutions then raise other problems, e.g., making telecommunications less versatile, portable, and convenient (Dutton 1992).

HI-OVIS was arguably the most innovative of the interactive cable television trials, particularly in offering two-way video communications. A video camera installed on the TV set of the Hi-OVIS households permitted live video from the home to be transmitted to the cable head-end and then broadcast to the other HI-OVIS households (Kawahata 1987). Households were broadcast live on local cable television. Families literally cleaned their homes and dressed up for television. Critics argued that this kind of participation clashed with cultural traditions in Japan that discouraged individuals from attracting such attention to themselves. But in any culture, the design and use of the system highlighted the intrusive potential of video communications in the household.

Lessons Learned

Looking back at early trials and experiments might be discouraging: the history related in this chapter does not demonstrate a proven mass market for multimedia or interactive video communications per se. But neither does this history provide solid ground for the opponents of new media ventures. Any failure is a matter of debate and is open to alternative interpretations.

Nevertheless, understanding the history of new communication media provides some valuable lessons that suggest ways forward. The following points seem most critical from this overview:

- New media have histories. There are continuities with the past as well as discontinuities. The way information and communication technologies are designed, and taken up over time, tend to be evolutionary rather than revolutionary.
- The history of new media developments shows that visions like the wired city or the information superhighway can be influential in shaping industrial strategies and public policy, even in ways unintended by the visionaries. Words make a difference, particularly when - as in the case of the in-

formation highway - they help organise and focus an otherwise fragmented industrial and policy community around a more common goal.

- Uncertainty surrounds any forecast of the future of information and communication technologies. The key decision-makers in the U.S. (in contrast to Japan) predicted the fax machine to fail. And, for decades, it did fail to diffuse widely, before literally taking-off to become an almost ubiquitous medium within the space of a few years. Predictions abound in the communications field, but they remain problematic and contentious.

- For the most part, the public is uninterested in technological breakthroughs, such as digital video, but is excited by services that are markedly better than existing services. Media habits buttress existing services. Since many patterns of information and communication behaviour are habitual rather than merely instrumental (e.g, reading a newspaper or watching television) even real improvements in a service may take years - if not decades - to find widespread acceptance. New technologies demand that we change the way we do things, requiring social and institutional change that will inevitably lag behind advances in equipment.

- Trials and commercial offerings demonstrate that the public is more interested in communication than in information per se. This finding directs attention to the necessity of creating a critical mass of users if new media are to succeed. Public subsidy of the Internet may have solved the critical mass problem for e-mail, but it has still taken decades to be overcome.

- The actual (and perceived cost) of services can be critical to the success of new media. While there are multiple explanations for the failure of any new service, cost provides one major explanation for the failure of many. Cross-national differences in the diffusion of some media, such as electronic bulletin boards in the U.S. as compared with the UK, suggest that costs - real or perceived - might play a more influential role than is often recognised.

- Issues of privacy, freedom of expression, equity of access, and other social concerns are critical to the take-up and long-term viability of information and communication services. Privacy concerns have emerged as an issue in video communications and in new services such as call-line identification. Free expression is raising problems for electronic communities. Public responses to new media offerings truly affect the bottomline (Silverstone 1991), and are ignored at real cost to the industry.

References

Arlen, G. (1991), `SeniorNet Services: Toward a New Electronic Environment for Seniors', Forum Report, No. 15. (Queenstown, Maryland: The Aspen Institute)

Becker, L. B. (1987), `A Decade of Research on Interactive Cable', in Dutton et al. (1987): 102-123.

Brand, S. (1987), The Media Lab (New York: Penguin Books).

Burstein, D. and Kline, D. (1995), Road Warriors: Dreams and Nightmares along the Information Highway (New York: Dutton).

Davidge, C. (1987), `America's talk-back television experiment: QUBE', in W. Dutton (1987): 75-101.

Dickson, E. M. with R. Bowers (1974), The VideoTelephone (New York: Praeger).

Dutton, W. H. (1992), `The Social Impact of Emerging Telephone Services,' Telecommunications Policy, 16(5): 377-387.

Dutton, W. H. (1995), `Driving into the Future of Communications? Check the Rear View Mirror' in Emmott (1995): 79-102.

Dutton, W. H. (1996a), `Network Rules of Order: Regulating Speech in Public Electronic Fora', Media, Culture and Society 18(2): 269-290.

Dutton, W. H. (1996b) (ed.) Information and Communication Technologies - Visions and Realities (Oxford and New York: Oxford University Press).

Dutton, W. H., Blumler, J. G., and Kraemer, K. L. (1987) (eds.), Wired Cities (Boston: G.K. Hall).

Dutton, W. H., Guthrie, K., O'Connell, J., and Wyer, J. (1991), `State and Local Government Innovations in Electronic Services', unpublished report for the U.S. Office of Technology Assessment, December 12, 1991.

Elton, M. C. J. (1980), `Educational and other Two-way Cable Television Services in the United States' in Witte (1980): 142-55.

Elton, M. C. J. (1991), `Integrated Broadband Networks: Assessing the Demand for New Services', unpublished paper presented at the Berkeley Roundtable on the Industrial Economy, New York: Columbia University.

Elton, M. C. J. (1992), `The US Debate on Integrated Broadband Networks', Media, Culture and Society, Vol. 14, pp. 369-395.

Elton, M. C. J. and Carey, J. (1984), `Teletext for Public Information: Laboratory and Field Studies' in Johnston, J. (1984): 23-41.

Emmott, S. J. (1995), Information Superhighways: Multimedia Users and Futures (London: Academic Press).

Garnham, N. (1996), `Constraints on Multimedia Convergence' in Dutton (1996): 103-120.

Gates, B. (1995), The Road Ahead (New York and London: Viking).

Gérin, F. and de Tavernost, N. (1987), `Biarritz and the Future of Videocommunications', in Dutton et al. (1987): 237-254.

Gilder, G. (1990, revised edition 1994), Life After Television: The Coming Transformation of Media and American Life (New York and London: W. W. Norton).

Goldmark, P. C. (1972), `Communication and the Community', In Communication: A Scientific American Book (San Francisco: WH Freeman).

Gore, A. (1991), Infrastructure for the Global Village', Scientific American, 265 (September): 108-111.

Greenberger, M. (1985) (ed.), Electronic Publishing Plus (White Plains: Knowledge Industries Publications).

Greenberger, M. (1992) (ed.), Multimedia in Review: Technologies for the 21st Century (Santa Monica, California: The Voyager Company and Council for Technology and the Individual).

Hooper, R. (1985), 'Lessons from Overseas: The British Experience' in Greenberger (1985): 181-200.

Johanson, R. (1984), Teleconferencing and Beyond: Communications in the Office of the Future (New York: McGraw Hill).

Johnston, J. (1984) (ed.) Evaluating the New Information Technologies (San Francisco, CA: Jossey-Bass).

Kahan, H. (1984), 'How Americans React to Communications Technology: Technological Craps', paper presented at the wired cities forum, Annenberg Schools of Communications, Washington D.C.

Kawahata, M. (1987), 'Hi-OVIS', in Dutton, W. et al. (1987): 179-200.

Lucky, R. W. (1989). Silicon Dreams (New York, NY: St. Martin's Press).

McGilly, K., Kawahata, M., and Dutton, W. H. (1990), 'Lessons from the Fibre-to-the-Home Trails'. (Los Angeles, CA: Annenberg School for Communication, Un. of Southern California).

Martin, J. (1977), The Future of Telecommunications (New York: Prentice-Hall).

Negroponte, N. (1995), Being Digital (London: Hodder and Stoughton).

Noll, A. M. (1985), 'Videotex: Anatomy of a Failure', Information and Management 9: 99-109.

Noll, A. M. (1992), 'Anatomy of a Failure: Picturephone Revisited', Telecommunications Policy 16(4): 307-316.

Rogers, E. M. (1986), Communication Technology(New York: The Free Press).

Sackman, H. and Nie, N. (1970) (eds.), The Information Utility and Social Choice (Montvale, NJ: AFIPS Press).

Sackman, H. and Boehm, B. (1972) (eds.). Planning Community Information Utilities. (Montvale, NJ: AFIPS Press).

Sawhney, H. (1996), 'Information Superhighway: Metaphors as Midwives', Media, Culture and Society, 18(2): 291-314.

Silverstone, R. (1991), 'Beneath the Bottomline', PICT Policy Research Paper, No. 17 (Uxbridge, Brunel Un: The Programme on Information and Communication Technologies).

Smith, R. L. (1970), 'The Wired Nation', The Nation, May 18.

Smith, R. L. (1972), The Wired Nation: Cable TV: The Electronic Communications Highway (New York: Harper and Row).

Witte, E. (1980) (ed.), Human Aspects of Telecommunication. (Berlin: Springer Verlag).

9. The Emergence of the Electronic Superhighway: Do Politics Matter?[1]

V.J.J.M. Bekkers

Introduction

It is only since 1994 that information and communication technologies (ICTs) have reached the front pages of the major journals. Now, those headlines speak about the electronic superhighway as the symbol of an emerging information society, based on a revolution in the way we communicate. Through this superhighway we may connect all kinds of information processing devices like personal computers, fax machines, television, CD-ROM, CI-I, telephone, and video. The use of digital network technology will enable users of the superhighway to combine, in an interactive way, images, sounds, and texts according to their own preferences. Now, at the end of the 20th century, progress is promised. New challenges lie ahead, challenges and developments which will change the way in which our daily life is organized.

The reality in which we actually live and work is complemented by a virtual reality. Through the increase in communication possibilities, the necessity for people to be physically present at the same time in order to communicate effectively is put into perspective. For instance, computer technology enables us to walk through the city of Florence in the 16th century, and Internet applications like World Wide Web enable us to search for policy documents in the Library of Congress, or to walk through the Louvre in Paris and look at the paintings within the museum, on the monitor of our personal computer. McLuhan's dream of a global village, consisting of cosmopolitans who surf through cyberspace, has come true.

---

1 This chapter contains parts which have been earlier published in: Bekkers, V., Koops, B. and Nouwt, S. (1995) (eds).

However, not everyone is optimistic about this new information age and society. Some people talk about the myth, the hype. When we look at the available infrastructure and applications, the superhighway more closely resembles a sandy path. Scepticism about the technological state of affairs prevails. Other people point out the dangers of this new society. A society which is organized around the technical and intellectual capacities to process and control data will create a new class of deprived people: the information "haves" and "have-nots".

Before the dream of a cyberspace world comes true, it is necessary to modernize the infrastructure which permits interactive data exchange. All kinds of policy initiatives have been launched during the last two years. We can think of the National Information Infrastructure (NII) Initiative of U.S. Vice-President Gore, and the European Initiative of the Global Information Society (GIS). Not only does the construction and modernisation of a network of (super)highways involve a number of technological desiderata, but a large number of political and administrative hurdles must also be jumped. The deployment of such an infrastructure involves a number of parties who may either gain or lose by it. We can think of national and international governments, telecom operators, application providers, and consumers. Their interests and domains are at stake, and they will try to influence the outcomes of the policy initiatives regarding the establishment of the superhighway according to their own preferences.

The first section of this chapter will address the question of which parties will win or lose on the superhighway. Who are the most important stakeholders, what are their interests, and what kind of strategies will they pursue to maximize their profit? Since every party follows its own interests, deadlock situations in developing and deploying the superhighway can occur. The solutions found will be of critical importance to the superhighway's success, so in section two a number of potential deadlocks will be described. In section three, the issue of whether politics affect the emergence of superhighways will be considered. In the final section, some observations about the social shaping of the superhighway will be formulated.

Mapping the Playing Field of the Superhighway

Although many of the markets for infrastructural communication services throughout the world are national monopolies, the playing field of the super-highway is international in scale. First, the providers of services are mostly multinational corporations, like AT&T, Alcatel, IBM, Microsoft, and Philips. They operate across many countries, yet the effective and efficient delivery of information and communication services is often obstructed by protective national regulatory regimes. The superhighway offers possibilities for pene-trating new markets. Moreover, it is the international and multinational private sector which makes most use of these services and applications. Companies like Shell and Nedlloyd use ICTs to optimize their logistic operations. Royal Dutch Airlines uses satellite technology to transfer their administrative opera-tions to India, where wages are much lower and comparative advantages can be realized.

Second, the market culture for these services is global. The world of in-formation and communication services, notably entertainment like MTV, is an illustration of McLuhan's "global village": people all over the world, espe-cially the younger generation, share a number of values, norms, symbols, and rituals (McLuhan and Powers 1989). There is a cult of information, and of information technology (Roszak 1986)

When we look at the most important players in the superhighway field, three groups can be identified: providers, users, and regulators (Huigen and Bekkers 1994; King and Kraemer 1995; Bekkers 1995).

There are three types of providers. The first type is the owners of the con-duit such as (mobile) telephone, cable, cellular, satellite, and broadcast televi-sion. Within this group special attention should be paid to the telecom opera-tors, mainly the telephone companies. They operate under different regulatory regimes. In the USA they compete freely against each other. In some coun-tries, national telephone companies have a monopoly position in the telecom market, while in others such as the U.K., the Netherlands, Sweden, and Finland, the monopoly of the national telecom operator is - or will be - re-placed by a duopoly. In deploying the superhighway, these companies and operators have an important competitive advantage because the highway, to a large extent, uses telephone lines. The second type of provider is the manu-facturers of information appliances such as television sets, telephones, com-puters, and software. We can think of computer hardware companies (e.g.,

IBM, Apple, and Compaq), computer software firms (e.g., Microsoft, IBM, and Apple), and companies which produce TV and electronic devices (e.g., Philips, Ericsson, Sony, and Panasonic). The third type of provider is the suppliers of content such as movie studios (e.g., Disney, Universal, and Sony); television stations (e.g., NBC, CBS, CNN, and RTL); national broadcasting companies (e.g., BBC); publishers of newspapers, books, and magazines (e.g., Elsevier Reed, Bertelsmann, and Murdoch); cable-TV companies; and on-line data services (e.g., Reuter).

These providers compete aggressively in a market that is very uncertain. Nobody can predict exactly which services or products will succeed. Will it be video-on-demand, electronic shopping, or something else entirely? Moreover, none of the providers know how individual consumers or households will access the highway. Will the gateway be a personal computer, connected by a modem and telephone lines to a worldwide communication network, or will it be interactive television? In the Netherlands, a struggle is ensuing between the Dutch PTT-Telecom which is betting on telephone lines as ultimate gateway, and the cable-TV companies in cooperation with the electricity companies, which are betting on the television as the winning device.

The result of this uncertainty is that each provider tries to shape the future of the highway according to their own market position. To reduce market turbulence, providers search for strategic alliances in order to preserve a wide range of options on markets that might take off (Huigen and Bekkers 1994; King and Kraemer 1995). We see all kinds of joint ventures, takeovers, and mergers in the increasingly competitive telecommunications sector. Dutch PTT-Telecom collaborates with Swedish Telia and Swiss Telecom in a joint venture called Unisource. Unisource is itself allied to AT&T, the American giant, to improve its position in America and Asia. German and French Telecom see each other as interesting partners. In the Netherlands, a joint venture, EnerTel, was established by a diverse range of companies in order that they might get a license to act as a telecommunications operator. EnerTel's constituents were the Dutch railway company, which has its own communication network running parallel to the major railways; a number of regional cable firms; electricity companies which exploit the cable-TV network (a network which is currently only used to exchange TV and radio signals, but which has spare capacity); and an American Regional Bell company - Bell South - that wanted to penetrate the European market. By 1996, EnerTel had fallen apart but this example still serves to show that many companies see the liberalisation of the telecommunications market as a winning opportunity.

A second group of players is the end users, who come in all shapes and sizes. We can think of libraries, schools, businesses, and households. The heterogeneity of the user group implies a proliferation of wishes and needs (Huigen and Bekkers 1994). For instance, schools and libraries hope that the highway improves interactive and long-distance learning, while individual households will use the highway to access video-on-demand or electronic games. King and Kraemer (1995) point out that creating services that households really desire could require huge levels of investment, and might force providers to substantially recoup their costs. Providers hope to raid other industries in order to speed up market development, but it is quite possible that this strategy will fail. Households are already well-provided for, and are satisfied with traditional services. The successful exploitation of services for households will hinge on the added-value of new services compared to traditional ones (Huigen and Bekkers 1994).

The final group of players is government organisations. In the initiatives described in the introduction, the government's role is limited. The deployment of the superhighway is considered to be the business of the private sector. Government action is restricted to facilitating the creation of a market, and to setting out the rules of the game in such a way that free competition amongst all kinds of providers can take place - free competition being seen as a necessary condition for the effective and efficient functioning of the superhighway.

However, in some countries the smooth execution of this role is being obstructed by a kind of hypocrisy. Although many countries pay lip-service to the idea of deregulation and privatisation of the telecommunications market, simultaneously they often try to protect their own industry. In a number of countries (e.g., France with its 'filière electrique'), the interests of the government, the national telecom operator, hardware and software companies, and R&D firms are closely interwoven. They form an iron circle difficult to break.

Deadlocks on the Superhighway

As we have just seen, the superhighway can be understood as a playing field in which a number of parties with diverse interests, agendas, and wishes compete. This situation can give rise to conflicts, and deadlock situations can occur. In this section, I will describe some issues which can descend into deadlock (see Huigen and Bekkers 1994; Bekkers 1995).

The first is price-fixing. In information and communication services this issue is often complicated and opaque. A number of remarkable examples of extreme price-fixing by telecom operators can be given. One concerns a municipality in the Dutch province of North Holland, which invited Dutch PTT-Telecom to tender for a high-speed communication line between two buildings. Their offer was Dfl.160,000 (US$100,000). The alternative option was to use the services of the local cable-TV company. After this was reported to the PTT-Telecom, the price dropped by half and, in the end, the connection was established for Dfl.40,000. This example shows how free competition might prevent this kind of practice.

One reason for price-setting by many telecom operators is the huge investments they must make to develop the superhighway's infrastructure. The existing network of telephone lines has to be replaced by fibre-optic cables, digital switchboards have to be installed, and mobile telephone networks have to be established. The private sector must fund these investments: the Bangemann report is quite explicit in this respect. So, for telecom operators, an important element in setting a price is the return on investment. In a monopoly market, price-fixing is not a problem and the return on investment is relatively high. However, this changes when the monopoly is replaced by competition. Competition therefore increases the uncertainty for telecom operators as to whether, and how soon, their investments will pay off. This uncertainty - and the way it is perceived and handled by the operators - can obstruct the smooth deployment of the superhighway.

If the return on investment for modernising the infrastructure becomes uncertain, the next question is who pays the price? Who is left holding the baby? Telecom operators markedly differentiate between how they charge their domestic and their business users. Competition is roughest in the latter arena, because the big revenues are generated there, e.g., Philips' data communications are served by British Telecom (BT), and not by Dutch PTT-Telecom. However, it is private households who foot the bill. In 1994, Dutch PTT-

Telecom raised its household rate in favour of its international rate, which works to the advantage of the private sector. BT provides another example. Although it was privatized, it was structurally forced to reduce its rates for some years. The privatized BT wanted to secure its price-setting, as if it were a monopoly. This strategy obstructed the entry of Mercury, a new operator, into the British telecom market since setting high prices in a captured market acts as an important entrance barrier for possible new providers. Government intervention resolved this situation.

The second issue which might lead to deadlock is the relationship between price and the number or quality of services and infrastructures to be delivered. Will the superhighway offer a minimum level of service for a minimum price? If turnover is low, the willingness of service providers to invest will be modest. Every party involved in the establishment of the superhighway - providers, government, and users - is affected by this problem, and it will become a critical issue for its successful deployment. Two considerations are important in this respect.

First, there is a financial issue. As discussed before, huge investments have to be made in a market that is very uncertain and turbulent. Second, there is a marketing issue. As mentioned earlier, it is unclear which products and services will be successful on the superhighway, because of the variety of user wishes. In the end, a deadlock situation might occur in which users demand a wide range of products and services, yet providers postpone making the necessary investment in order to minimize their risk. Meanwhile, governments depend on the eagerness of the private sector to invest in the superhighway. Therefore a situation can occur in which every player is waiting for someone else to make the necessary moves such that, in fact, nothing happens. In game theory and public choice theory, this situation is often described as the "prisoner's dilemma". In essence, it can be described as follows. Parties are deprived of certain benefits because they fail to exchange information about their wishes and motives. They go their own way, although cooperation between them would be mutually profitable, had each only known what the other was up to. This dilemma can be resolved if governments act as brokers to show the other parties that, for each of them, the deployment of the superhighway carries more benefits than drawbacks.

Another issue is user access to the superhighway. The access question is critical for the successful exploitation of the superhighway, because its resolution will profoundly shape how providers will compete to penetrate the consumer market. Three aspects to the question can be discerned.

The first refers to physical access to the superhighway. Which device will enable individual users and households to walk through cyberspace? Some people - seeing the Internet as the precursor of the superhighway - believe that the computer will be the dominant delivery mechanism. Other people doubt this: they see the TV set, expanded with a set-top box, as the main device. This set-top box will transform the television into a computer so that, through our remote-control, we can go teleshopping, or give our opinion about public issues, etc. (See Chapter 5, for a discussion on the set-top box). Which device emerges as the "winner" will have important political and economic consequences, if we compare the number, and distribution, of personal computers and televisions amongst households.

This brings us to the second aspect of the access issue: intellectual and economic access. Using a personal computer as the gateway to the Internet requires certain skills. In their evaluation of the Digital City of Amsterdam (a virtual community, or Freenet) Schalken and Tops (1994) show that the inhabitants of this city are highly educated. About 72 per cent enjoy, or have enjoyed, a college education; students constitute a major group within this virtual community. They are also very young; about 58 per cent of the inhabitants are younger than 30, and about 91 per cent are male. So, it is possible that the superhighway will engender a new division in society: the information "haves" and "have-nots". However, the possibility that many people may be intellectually and economically excluded from using the superhighway will be ameliorated should its gateway be interactive television. The spread of television is almost universal - which cannot be said for the personal computer - and most people will find a television set, expanded with a set-top box, easier to use than a computer.

The third aspect of access to the superhighway is a legal one. There is a risk that some sparsely-populated areas may be poorly served relative to populous and economically vibrant areas. For example, as a result of BT's privatisation, the investment needed to modernize the telecommunications infrastructure in some of Britain's sparsely-populated areas was not made (Taylor 1993). In many countries, telecommunications regulations explicitly aim to safeguard rural communities against being deprived of certain communications services precisely because the level of investment required to deploy an infrastructure in a thinly-populated area is so high, relative to its use. Government-level specifications of the superhighway (including the American, European and Dutch versions) all endorse the legal right to universal access. Notwithstanding that endorsement, it is the private sector which is primarily responsible for the deployment of the superhighway. Private enterprise may well be inclined to limit its investment to serving major metropolitan areas, because the return on investment is obviously highest in thriving urban regions. Clearly, there is an on-going tension between the legal right to universal access and the profitable deployment of the superhighway.

The final potential deadlock situation to be addressed here is how the infrastructure will connect with the communication and information services which rest upon it. The superhighway may be understood as a "network of networks" which integrates different networks and services. However, there are bottlenecks. Entry barriers offer just one example.

Although telecommunications markets are being liberalized to enable new operators to enter, these newcomers must use the telecommunications infrastructure which was formerly owned by the national telecom operators. There is a risk that the old operator (who, in most cases, had previously had a monopoly) will create barriers against any company wishing to make use of, or connect to, the existing infrastructure. This can be illustrated by considering the British case mentioned earlier: for some time BT prevented the smooth interconnection of its network with Mercury's. Because of the dominant position of the incumbent ex-monopolist telecom operator - and the huge investment new entrants have to make - newcomers will often be dependent on the services of the traditional operator. An asymmetrical dependence relationship exists between them, which can obstruct full and honest competition.

A second bottleneck may occur around the issue of standardisation. The development of standards is essential for the smooth interconnection of infrastructures and the operability of services within and between them. Standardisation is seen as an important goal for liberalising the communications market for, by that means, economies of scale can be realized. An important question, however, is whose standards will be the winning standards? If a market is standardized, newcomers' products and services can only succeed if they conform to existing standards. Once again, there is a risk that ex-monopolist telecom operators will define standards which may act as further entry barriers against newcomers.

Do Politics Matter?

In the previous sections we saw that a number of convergent and divergent interests are at stake in establishing the "network of networks"; in realising the superhighway. All kinds of strategic alliances are created, and coalitions are built or fall apart. One possible result is that a prosperous superhighway will simply fail to emerge. Deadlocks may occur which may lead to stalemate, with everyone waiting for everyone else. For some people, such a scenario calls for strong political leadership: political intervention is being requested. The question is, do politics matter?

Before answering that question, it is helpful to review some of politics' relevant functions, and some of the domains in which political intervention is necessary. In general, politics fulfils four functions. A classic political function is to regulate who gets what, and how, and when. It refers to the authoritative allocation of rights and duties. A second function is that of establishing, and maintaining, a balance between competing interests. A third relates to the creation of institutions, arrangements, and processes for political decision-making. A fourth is the preservation and legitimation of the political system.

If we look at the domains in which these functions are performed for our present purposes, we can distinguish between policies which address the establishment of the superhighway, and those which address the permissible interactions between people on that superhighway. Do politics have a role in creating, and monitoring, the playing rules which regulate the behaviour of people and organisations? Let us examine the functions of politics within these two policy domains.

Do Politics Matter? Establishing the Superhighway

In the policy documents of the U.S. Government and the European Commission, the private sector is charged with responsibility for the design, deployment, and operation of the superhighway because it is the private sector which benefits most from the opportunities thereby created. The role of government is rather limited. The establishment of the superhighway is primarily market-driven.

Given the actors involved, and the diversity of their motives, interests, and strategies - in combination with the complexity, turbulence, and uncertainty of the various telecommunications markets - it would be naive to think that government could effectively manage and control the activities of the private sector which are necessary to create a network of superhighways. Moreover, in several policy documents, laissez-faire is seen as a necessary condition for the establishment of the superhighway. All documents plea for liberalising the several telecommunications markets. However, we can readily see that deregulation and privatisation hugely increases the uncertainty and turbulence of the enterprise.

This rather chaotic process influences the first two functions of politics. If the role of government is limited as to the actual establishment of the superhighway, that does not imply that governments should shy away from focusing on key related issues. An important task is agenda management. Politics has a role to play in ensuring fair access and basic levels of service, in encouraging interoperability, in guaranteeing privacy and security for the superhighway's participants, and in tackling the possible division between the information "haves" and "have nots".

The second function is balancing between interests. In establishing the superhighway, an important governmental role is to act as a broker, mediating between the interests at stake. This is important because, as we saw in the last section, a number of deadlocks can occur. This broker's role could also include acting as a referee: earlier we saw that the British government intervened in the dispute between BT and Mercury. However, this dual role is controversial. In many countries, the government remains closely implicated in the functioning of the national telecommunications market, because these markets had been controlled by state-owned monopolies. Furthermore, these very monopolies provided a crucial arena for realising other governmental policies such as R&D and employment. Although governments can emphasize the importance of deregulation, this is not the same as liberalisation. One can deregulate and, at the same time, try to protect nationally-owned telecom monopolies. This kind of history of political involvement stands in the way of governments' ability to fulfil the role of neutral broker and referee.

A third function of politics is to formulate rules for decision-making. In this respect, as with the previous function, governments' historical involvement in their telecommunications markets implies that there is a tension between a government's detailed involvement with telecom affairs and its involvement as a referee. In some countries, the liberalisation of the market forces governments to withdraw. The combination of roles leads to a certain degree of role perversion and of misuse of power and influence. In the Netherlands the roles of supervisor and of referee are being transferred to a politically neutral agency. So, in establishing arrangements and rules with respect to the emergence of the superhighway, governments have to choose. They must either claim a substantial level of involvement, or they must create decision-making rules, which incorporate concepts of checks and balances, and misuse of power etc.

The fourth political function is the reproduction of the political system itself: governments aim to preserve and legitimate their own existence. From this perspective, the superhighway offers the political system both new chances for renewal and new threats (Bekkers et al 1995). The superhighway offers citizens new services, delivered in new ways. For instance, we can think of civic service centres, the electronic handling of tax assessments, and the introduction of public service information services. All of these enhance the transparency and openness of government. Through community networks, or digital cities, network technology offers citizens a forum for public political debate (Schalken and Tops 1995). However, network technology also promotes the idea of direct democracy which may transform traditional representative democracy into a "push button" democracy.

In sum, it is not easy to judge whether politics matter with respect to the establishment of the superhighway. A moderate position should be welcomed, for two reasons. First, looking at the power play which accompanies the emergence of the superhighway, the parties involved, and the interests at stake, there is no central force - not even in the political arena - which can plan and monitor the outcome of this play. Second, governments have had a rather dubious history of involvement in telecommunications, stemming from the conflicting roles they have played in the past.

Do Politics Matter? The Establishment of Playing Rules

Recent discussions about pornography on the Internet illuminate weaknesses of the superhighway. Many people agree that it is high time that playing rules on the superhighway should be introduced. Indecent or criminal behaviour which we condemn in "real life" should also be outlawed in the virtual world of cyberspace. Political intervention is often called for, because politicians have the power to make, and impose, rules and regulations. However, the problem is that the digital world of the superhighway challenges our traditional concepts of rule-making, and of the law. Therefore governments' role in formulating rules for cyberspace is limited. Let us examine why this is the case (Bekkers et al 1995).

One problem is that as soon as information is digitalized, it behaves as if it were an inkblot, or as radiation. It spreads, and it is often very difficult to detect its origins. Another problem is that geographical boundaries become obsolete. The superhighway is a global technology, which crosses many countries and continents. Meanwhile, however, political rule-making and law-enforcement are still largely linked to notions of national sovereignty and territoriality. The superhighway challenges traditional forms of political regulation, and new means must be sought for establishing a code of behaviour which guides users' actions. Alongside the state as a physical entity, there is a shadow "virtual state" (Frissen 1996), within which government has yet to find a new role. In a world which exploits network technology, and where society increasingly resembles a network without a centre, we must begin to question the primacy of the political arena in our arguments.

The Social Shaping of the Superhighway: Challenges for the Science of Public Administration

The emergence of the superhighway, the liberalisation of telecommunications markets, and the risk of deadlocks lead to all kinds of (de)regulation games, in which stakeholders (government, the private sector, consumers, etc.) try to secure a favourable starting position in establishing that superhighway. National and global information infrastructures affect the domain, and the interests, of a wide variety of parties. The resulting power struggle will influence the content and shape of the superhighway which results.

Therefore, the deployment of the superhighway offers public administration scholars a unique opportunity to rethink the development and use of large technical systems, or "big technology", as Mayntz and Hughes (1988) put it. Particularly worthy of study are the interactions of the most important players (government, providers, and users), and the ways they perceive and solve the deadlocks described earlier. The superhighway's complex dynamics lead us to consider the social shaping of technology, and the development of policies which address it. For some time the development and use of technology has been romanticized. We all know the heroic histories of major inventors like Thomas Alva Edison. Their ingenuity and persistence has led to important discoveries and inventions, although the technological harnessing of their work tends to be taken for granted. Technology is seen as a black box. This is a narrow view of technology, as a number of sociologically-inspired technology studies show (Hughes 1983; Bijker et. al 1987). No technology - however autonomous - is developed outwith an economic, political, and intellectual context (Ellul 1980).

Discovering the meaning of the context within which a technological system is developed and implemented has important consequences for how we conceptualize that technology. That is, the characteristics of the environment in which the technology is formulated, developed, tested, and implemented are reflected in the technology itself. For this reason, Pinch and Bijker (1987) conceptualize technology as a social construct. While the development of technology can be understood as an answer to a problem, that begs the question: whose problem? The lack of a clear definition of the problem to be solved leads to divergent solutions. But what solution is selected as the definitive answer to a specific problem?

In answering this question, Pinch and Bijker (1987) and Callon (1987) suggest that it is fruitful to identify the relevant social groups and tease out their interests, goals, and opinions. Every group defines the problem, and its resolution, according to their own frame of reference. The strategic interaction between those groups, or stake-holders, leads to a shared and/or dominant definition of the problem and its technological solution. Winner (1988) also pleads for a stake-holder approach. He argues that the flexible nature of technology is well-suited to maintaining particular power positions and relations.

The perception of the superhighway as a set of instruments and strategies to achieve a number of goals, is also interesting from another perspective. The metaphor of a network of highways is a powerful one (Bekkers et al 1995 and chapter 1). It inspires people, and mobilizes the release of financial resources. However, this challenging metaphor of a superhighway can also be dangerous, because it narrows our perception of a number of issues concerning the communications revolution: it defines problems and solutions in a biased way. These issues are being approached from an engineering perspective, as if the superhighway is something which can be monitored from one central apex point. Deploying the superhighway, when it is seen as the construction of roads according to a blueprint, implies that society can be moulded from a central and superior point; a master plan which can be developed and controlled by politics.

At the same time, the word "super" as a prefix to highways evokes an image of progress. But is this image of planning and progress adequate to describe how the superhighway will develop? I do not think so. If we look at the turbulence and uncertainty of the communications and information services market, at the interests at stake, and at the dual role of governments in liberalising the telecom market and in protecting national interests, the development of the superhighway will not proceed as a perfectly orchestrated and harmonious symphony. It will more likely be a chaotic and incremental process, a cacophony. Maybe decisions about its development will feature elements of the "garbage can" model of decision-making. In this model, decision-making is not a rational process. Four streams can be discerned - problems, solutions, participants, and choice opportunities - and decision-making is seen as the relatively arbitrary process of matching these four streams together (Cohen, March and Olsen 1972).

This makes the study of the shaping of the superhighway all the more interesting, because the outcome is uncertain and cannot be enforced. It offers an opportunity to study complex and rather chaotic decision-making processes. Moreover, the fuzzy character of the deployment of superhighway - both in how it is established and how its participants interact - puts the supposedly dominant role of politics into perspective. This is a rather challenging perspective, because it stimulates politicians, civil servants, and academics to look for new conceptions of regulation and self-regulation within a world which is increasingly virtual and transnational.

References

Bangemann Group (1994), High-Level Group on the Information Society, *Europe and the Gobal Information Society, Recommendations to the European Council*, Brussels, May 26.

Bekkers, V.J.J.M. (1995), The playground of the electronic superhighway. Players, interests and deadlocks, in: Bekkers, V., B. Koops & S. Nouwt (eds.), Emerging electronic highways. New challenges for politics and law (The Hague/London/Boston: Kluwer International Law) 9-26.

Bekkers, V.J.J.M, Koops, B. and Nouwt, S. (1995), Emerging electronic highways: Epilogue, in: Bekkers, V., Koops, B. and Nouwt S. (eds.), Emerging electronic highways. New challenges for politics and law (The Hague/London/Boston: Kluwer International Law) 173-184.

Bijker, W.E., Hughes, Th.P. and Pinch, T.J. (1987) (eds.), The social construction of technological systems (Cambridge Mass.: MIT Press).

Callon, M. (1987), The society in the making, in: Bijker, W.E., Th.P. Hughes & T.J. Pinch (eds.), The social construction of technological systems (Cambridge Mass.: MIT Press).

Cohen, M., March, J.G. and Olsen, J.P. (1972), A garbage can model of organizational choice, in: Administrative Science Quaterly, vol. 17., pp. 1-25.

Ellul, J., J. (1980), The technological system (New York: Basic Books).

Frissen, P.H.A. (1996), De virtuele staat (Schoonhoven: Academic Service).

Hughes, Th.P. (1983), Networks of power (Baltimore: John Hopkins University Press).

Huigen, J. and Bekkers, V. (1994), Wegwijs op de digitale snelweg. Over belangen en impasses, in: Bekkers, V. (red.), Wegwijs op de digitale snelweg (Amsterdam: Otto Cramwinckel Uitgever).

King, J.L., and Kraemer, K. (1995), Information infrastructure, national policy and global competitiveness, in: Information infrastructure and Policy, vol. 4, pp. 5-28.

Mayntz, R. and Hughes, Th.P. (1988) (eds.), The development of large technical systtems (Frankfurt a/M: Campus Verlag).

McLuhan, H.M. and Powers, B.R. (1989), The global Village (Oxford: Oxford University Press).

Pinch., T.J. and Bijker, W.E. (1987), The social construction of facts and artefacts, in: Bijker, W.E., Hughes, Th.P. and Pinch, T.J. (eds.), The social construction of technological systems (Cambridge, Mass.: MIT Press).

Roszak, Th. (1986), The cult of information (New York: Pantheon Books).

Schalken, K. and Tops, P. (1995), De digitale stad. Een onderzoek naar de achtergronden en meningen van haar inwoners, in: Bekkers, V. (red.), Wegwijs op de digitale snelweg (Amsterdam : Otto Cramwinckel Uitgever).

Taylor, J. (1993), Telecommunications infrastructure and public policy development. Paper presented at the 1993 EGPA Conference at Strassbourg, Strathclyde.

Winner, L. (1988), Do artefacts have politics, in: Kraft, M.E. and Vig, N.J., Technology and politics (Durham/London).

10. Public Interest Groups and the Telecommunications Act of 1996

William J. Drake

Introduction

The role of public interest groups is an important but understudied aspect of the U.S. National Information Infrastructure (NII) debate. Traditionally, analysts of many theoretical and political persuasions - from Marxists, to liberals, to public choice theorists, and beyond - almost exclusively have focused on the power, interests, and bargaining strategies of governmental and corporate actors in explaining policy choices. Viewed then in the context of the historical evolution of U.S. policy, it is a noteworthy development that groups from society's "third" or non-profit sector have mobilized during the 1990s to try to influence the decisions of the U.S. Congress and the Clinton Administration. No less noteworthy is that they have sometimes succeeded - including on hotly-contested issues where they were opposed by powerful interests.

In parallel, the role of public interest groups in the U.S. NII debate is notable from a comparative perspective. Public interest groups have usually been a much less important actor in European NII debates than other historically progressive organisations like trade unions and social democratic parties, and the evidence suggests that this is true elsewhere in the world. Of course, independent activist groups are far from being an exclusively American phenomenon; in Europe and elsewhere around the world, they have been important players in a wide range of arenas like human rights, environmental, arms control, and social policies - often to much greater effect than their American counterparts. But in the specific case of NII policies, it is clear that consumer groups, privacy advocates, progressive churches, the educational and library communities, advocates for people with disabilities, alternative media groups, Internet user communities, and so on have been more organized and influential in the United States than they have elsewhere. These cross-national variations raise a number of interesting analytical and political questions about the social shaping of information infrastructures in countries with different institutional structures, interest configurations, political cultures, and so on.

This chapter explores the role of public interest groups in the Congressional deliberations that culminated in the recent enactment of the Telecommunications Act of 1996. I will show that when the Congressional debate was taking shape, and progressive or populist Democrats were in control of the policy-making process, advocacy groups were able to register significant gains that, if adopted and implemented, would have promoted the interests of citizens and non-commercial institutions to an extent that many observers may not appreciate. But the Democrats ultimately failed to carry the legislative game to its conclusion, and a Republican electoral triumph in November 1994 totally changed its rules. The new Republican majority rejected the mixed commercial/non-commercial model advocated by public interest groups and pushed hard instead for a narrower approach designed solely to liberalize market entry and benefit major corporations. Nevertheless, to win bipartisan support for final passage and enactment of their legislation, the Republicans made a number of concessions to positions advanced by public interest groups and liberal Democrats on the shaping of liberalisation. In the end, the Telecommunications Act represents a missed opportunity to devise a new and inclusive policy architecture, but within the narrower parameters of promoting competition, it is only a partial disaster.

Gearing Up

Public interest group involvement in U.S. communications policy is not a new phenomenon. At least since the 1960s, activist groups have been engaged in reform debates about traditional telephone, cable television, and broadcast media. To take some examples, the United Church of Christ was instrumental in obtaining legal standing in Federal Communications Commission (FCC) proceedings for stakeholders who did not have a direct financial interest in its decisions; the Consumer Federation of America has been an important voice for affordable telephone service in legislative and regulatory debates; a number of activist groups participated in a loose coalition with a new generation of liberal politicians to press for the liberalisation of telephony, and the reform of broadcast content in the 1960s and 1970s; and public, educational, and governmental (PEG) programmers have successfully lobbied many municipal governments for public access channels to be set aside as part of local cable television franchises. In a few instances, public interest groups were independently influential in bringing about policy changes that would not have happened without their efforts. But more often, their role was as supporting actors who added weight to the positions being adopted by reformists in government.

Since the late 1980s, the character of public interest activism has changed in at least three ways that are significant for the NII debate. First, advances in information systems, the rise of broadband networking, and above all, the mass popularisation of the Internet have raised many new issues, and thus broadened the agendas of activists and other non-commercial stakeholders. Hence, when the Clinton Administration took power in January 1993 and began to talk up the notion of an "information superhighway" and the need to revise the 1934 Communications Act of America, public interest groups were handed a useful conceptual and political umbrella under which to press for their expanding agendas. The discourse on information infrastructure envisioned - in an often vague, or at least multivalent, manner - some sort of emerging environment in which media convergence, broadband pipes, networked computer servers, multimedia services, and the Internet would collectively constitute a new type of interactive and user-empowering media system that required a new legislative architecture. Public interest groups' varying concerns were thus hooked to a larger and integrating vision of a new overarching model that would more effectively balance commercial and non-commercial stakeholders and uses, than did the segmented policy models for telecommunications, broadcasting, and cable television[1].

Second, and in parallel, as the scope of issues expanded from the 1980s onward, so too did the number and diversity of public interest groups that

---

1 For a discussion of the historical context and broad parameters of this debate, see, William J. Drake, "Introduction: The Turning Point," in Drake (ed.), *The New Information Infrastructure: Strategies for U.S. Policy* (New York: The Twentieth Century Fund Press, 1995) pp. 1-27.

were pressing them. New organisations specialising in communications is- sues - like the Alliance for Public Technology, the Center for Media Educa- tion, the Center for Civic Networking, the Center for Democracy and Tech- nology, Computer Professionals for Social Responsibility, the Electronic Frontier Foundation, and the Electronic Privacy and Information Center - were created, often with the Internet as a central policy concern and advocacy tool. At the same time, organisations from the non-commercial sector that previously had not been heavily involved in communications policy - such as the American Library Association, the National Writers Union, and People for the American Way - came to see the importance of the NII for their objec- tives, and devoted staff and resources to tracking and taking positions on the issues. These new entrants, together with existing organisations with spe- cialized expertise like the Alliance for Community Media, the Consumer Fed- eration of America, and the Media Access Project, gave the public interest community a profile on matters that extended well beyond the traditional con- cerns with rates, television programme content, and so on.

Third, and despite this new heterogeneity, in the 1990s public interest groups have worked to expand their cooperation with each other. In search of strength in numbers, they have often sought support from their peers on spe- cific policy problems and campaigns, whether in the form of joint lobbying or, less ambitiously, simply signing onto position statements and letters to the Congress and the Clinton Administration. To institutionalize such cooperation on a wider scale and press the case for progressive legislative reform, over 40 public interest groups launched an informal peak association called the Tele- communications Policy Roundtable (TPR) in July, 1993. The TPR holds monthly meetings in Washington D.C. that have attracted representatives of over one hundred organisations and it has an Internet listserv for discussion at roundtable@cni.org. The TPR mechanism facilitates information-sharing, consultation, and in some instances, active collaboration on joint campaigns.

To be sure, many non-commercial organisations expressing views on the NII have not been major players in lobbying the Congress and the Executive Branch and often do not represent politically-potent constituencies. Indeed, most of the heavy lifting on federal policy questions has been done by a com- paratively small core group of organisations like the Alliance for Community Media, the American Civil Liberties Union, the American Library Associa- tion, the Association of America's Public Television Stations, the Benton

Foundation, the Center for Media Education, Computer Professionals for Social Responsibility, the Consumer Federation of America, the Electronic Frontier Foundation, the Media Access Project, OMB Watch, People for the American Way, and the Taxpayer Assets Project. Nevertheless, that a wide range of organisations have, at times, supported the core group of Washington insiders gave the latter's efforts greater weight with politicians and bureaucrats than they might have had otherwise.

How have public interest groups pressed their views in the political sphere? Indirect and comparatively passive channels of influence have included, inter alia, newspaper op-editorials and magazine articles, occasional appearances in broadcast media, conference circuit presentations, and participation in Internet discussion groups. To the extent that relevant politicians and bureaucrats pay attention, or attach any significance, to the wider public debate on the issues, these avenues of expression may play a diffuse but important role by broadening the discourse and injecting considerations into minds that otherwise would not have registered them. But more direct and active engagement in the forms of letter- writing campaigns, lobbying, Congressional testimony, and participation in regulatory proceedings are, of course, infinitely more salient to the political world, particularly if the groups involved can claim to represent a significant political constituency. As such, while the institutionalisation of awareness, activism, and an alternative policy discourse amongst a variety of groups from around the country may provide a base for future campaigns (including at the state and local levels), to date the main story of public interest group involvement in national policy has revolved around the core group playing the Washington D.C. insider's game.

A Window of Opportunity

The years 1993 and 1994 were the high point of public interest group influence on the NII debate in general, and federal law reform in particular. At least three important factors converged to open a window of opportunity for advocates of a new policy architecture. First, technological and market trends like media convergence, broadband networking, and the rapid mass popularisation of the Internet created a sort of liminal moment when reconceptualising and redesigning the nation's communications systems and policy in some respects seemed possible, and in which competing visions of the future were more able than usual to get a hearing. Public interest groups pounced on the opportunity by stepping up their advocacy and attempting to forge united fronts on certain issues. Second, a new Democratic administration had taken over the Executive Branch, announced an administration-wide commitment - spurred on by Vice-President Al Gore - to growing the NII and reforming the Communications Act, and was expressing an unprecedented openness to public interest group's participation in policy discussions and to some of their legislative goals.

Third, liberal and populist Democrats who were receptive to public interest concerns were chairing the committees and subcommittees of the House and Senate that would be responsible for drafting and pushing through legislative reform. This gave activists a direct channel through which to lobby politicians and their staffs, focus letter-writing campaigns, and submit draft legislative provisions. The support of key legislators, especially Edward Markey, Chairman of the House Subcommittee on Telecommunications and Finance, and Ernest Hollings, Chairman of the Senate Commerce, Science, and Transportation Committee, also provided public interest groups and other non-commercial players with an important opportunity to testify in Congressional hearings and thus make their concerns part of the calculi of legislators who might otherwise have ignored them.

In consequence, alongside a multitude of business representatives debating the costs and benefits of greater competition in various markets, the Democratic-controlled 103rd Congress also heard testimony from: the AFL-CIO, the Alliance for Community Media, the Alliance for Public Technology, the American Civil Liberties Union, the American Council of the Blind, the Center for Media Education, the Consumer Action Network, the Consumer Federation of America, the Electronic Frontier Foundation, Hear Our Voices!, the International Center for Deafness, the Markle Foundation, the Media Access Project, the National Education Association, the National Education Telecommunications Organization, the National Association of State Utility Consumer Advocates, the New York Public Library, Television Viewers of America, the Video Action Fund, and the United Church of Christ, as well as various representatives of libraries, public television stations, and K-12 and higher education (including students). In addition, submitted for Congressional consideration, and inserted into the record of testimony, were letters from the Benton Foundation, the Center for Responsive Law, the George Lucas Educational Foundation, the National Association of Development Organizations, the National Coordinating Committee and FORUM on Technology in Education and Training, the National School Board Association, the Taxpayers' Assets Project, and the TPR. Legislators also heard from a variety of state and local governments and their regulatory and consumer agencies, as well as from the Communications Workers of America and representatives of small communications businesses, both of whose views occasionally dovetailed with those of the public interest groups.

Not since the failed battle to set aside a non-commercial broadcast spectrum in the 1934 Communications Act had so many activists testified before, and lobbied, the Congress in the pursuit of a policy model that would accommodate non-commercial players and make direct concessions to consumer and citizen interests.[2] And the working relationship between activists and progressive politicians actually did result in legislation coming out of the House and Senate committees that contained a significant amount of language favoured by public interest groups, including some that they had drafted.

Of course, Congressional observers might be tempted to conclude that the inclusion of such provisions, particularly in the early stages of the legislative process, was not entirely serious and might eventually have amounted to little. After all, it is not unusual for sympathetic committee chairmen to include language favoured by some constituency, knowing full well that it will be watered down - or deleted entirely - in the bargaining that goes on first when bills go to the full chambers for a vote, and second when bills passed on the floors of the House and Senate go to conference committee for reconciliation between the two versions prior to the final floor votes, and submission for the President's signature. And indeed, watering down, or deletion, along the way were the fates met by some of the provisions promoted by public interest groups. But even so, the language that remained intact at the end of the aborted legislative process of the 103rd Congress was potentially significant, and in some cases, it enjoyed enough support from key legislators that it would not have disappeared in the later stages of the process without a fight.

---

2 On this earlier episode, which has parallels with the struggle over the Telecommunications Act, see, Robert W. McChesney, *Telecommunications, Mass Media, and Democracy: The Battle for the Control of U.S. Broadcasting, 1928-1935* (New York: Oxford University Press, 1993).

How significant were public interest group's gains? As passed by the full House on a surprisingly overwhelming vote of 420 to four, the House version of reform, H.R. 3626, included the following provisions pushed (and often drafted) by activists:[3]

Legislative Purpose: Section 1 of the Communications Act was amended to state that it is the government's objective "to make available, so far as possible, to all the people of the United States, regardless of location or disability, a switched, broadband telecommunications network capable of enabling users to originate and receive affordable high quality voice, data, graphics, and video telecommunications services....[and] to ensure that the costs of such networks and services are allocated equitably among users and are constrained by competition whenever possible..."[4]

Open Platform Service: The term means "a switched, end-to-end digital telecommunications service that is subject to title II of this Act [e.g. regulated as common carriage] and that 1) provides subscribers with sufficient network capability to access multimedia information services, 2) is widely available throughout a State, 3) is provided based on industry standards, and 4) is available to all subscribers on a single line basis upon reasonable request."[5] The FCC was to initiate an inquiry to consider the regulations and policies needed to make open platform services available at reasonable rates.

Universal Service: A new Federal-State Joint Board on Universal Service was to be created. The board was to promote access to advanced services, including open platform services, and to consider whether lack of access to advanced service would unfairly deny individuals educational and economic

---

3 For a discussion of the broader thrust of the Democrat's NII legislation beyond these provisions, see William J. Drake, "The National Information Infrastructure Debate: Issues, Interests, and the Congressional Process," in Drake (ed.), *The New Information Infrastructure*, pp. 305-344.

4 United States Congress, H.R. 3626, *Antitrust and Communications Reform Act of 1994*, 103rd Congress, 2nd Session, August 1994, p. 30 [Internet version]. The texts and committee reports on all the legislation discussed in this chapter are available on the world wide web at http://thomas.loc.gov.

5 United States Congress, H.R. 3626, *Antitrust and Communications Reform Act of 1994*, p. 31.

opportunities. Further, universal service was to be made available at just and reasonable rates; specific and predictable financial support mechanisms were required; and all service providers were to make equitable and non-discriminatory contributions to its funding.

Preferential Access for Non-commercial Entities: To the extent that common carriers rolled out advanced services, the Joint Board was to ensure that such services (other than video platforms) be made available - at preferential rates, recovering only the costs of providing them - to government agencies, non-profit educational institutions, health care institutions, public libraries, public museums, public broadcasters, and charitable organisations both as users and as providers to the general public of non-commercial telecommunications and information services. Further, the National Telecommunications and Information Administration (NTIA) was to conduct an annual survey of access to advanced services by educational institutions, health care institutions, and public libraries, and the FCC was to adopt regulations enhancing such access.

Information Services and Electronic Publishing: The Bell Operating Companies (BOCs) were to participate in these markets through separate subsidiaries, subject to a number of pro-competitive safeguards. In addition, they were to provide independent content providers with non-discriminatory and unbundled access at just and reasonable rates.

Cable Television and Common Carrier Video Platforms: Limitations were placed on the ability of BOCs to buy out, or operate, traditional cable systems within their telephone service areas. If they built new video platforms, the BOCs were to provide services through separate subsidiaries and to offer adequate capacity to independent programme providers under non-discriminatory conditions and at reasonable rates. The FCC was to extend similar capacity and rate requirements to any cable companies that installed switched broadband delivery systems. The FCC was also to ensure that the BOCs provided the capacity, services, facilities, and equipment for PEG access at preferential rates.

Set-top Boxes and Other Critical Interfaces: The FCC was to examine the costs and benefits of requiring open interface architectures and to determine how set-top boxes and other interactive devices could be sold by competing vendors and retailers.

Civic Participation: The FCC and NTIA were to study policies promoting civic participation in the NII, including the social benefits of flat-rate pricing for access to computer networks, and the appropriate role of common carriers in the Internet environment.

Ownership Diversity: The FCC was to promote lower entry barriers for small businesses, businesses owned by minorities and women, and non-profit entities seeking to provide telecommunications and information services.

The Senate version of reform, S. 1822, was reported out of committee on a vote of 18 to two in August, 1994. However, smelling victory in the coming November elections, and hence the ability to pursue legislation more to their liking in the next Congressional session, Republicans led by Bob Dole shifted to strong opposition to S. 1822, which led Senator Hollings to give up on pursuing passage by the full Senate. This put an end to the 103rd Congress' efforts and was a major disappointment for public interest groups which, as with H.R. 3626, had won inclusion of a number of significant provisions:

Legislative Purpose: The introductory findings section stated, inter alia, that "access to switched, digital telecommunications service for all segments of the population promotes the core First Amendment goal of diverse information sources by enabling individuals and organisations alike to publish and otherwise make information available in electronic form.."[6]

Telecommunications Competition: S. 1822 imposed stronger requirements on the BOCs than H.R. 3626 had done to open the local loop to competition before allowing them out into the long-distance and equipment manufacturing markets. Many public interest groups supported these provisions, although the primary political forces behind them were the incumbent long-distance carriers, or "inter-exchange" carriers (IECs), and other industry factions that would be affected by BOC entry.

---

6   United States Congress, S. 1822, *The Communications Act of 1994,* 103rd Congress, 2nd Session, August 11, 1994, p. 4 [Internet version].

Universal Service: The bill's general requirements were more detailed but broadly in line with the intent of H.R. 3626.

Preferential Access for Non-commercial Entities: The universal service provisions also included the obligation "of all telecommunications carriers that use public rights of way to permit educational institutions, health-care institutions, local and State governments, public broadcast stations, public libraries, other public entities, community newspapers, and broadcasters in the smallest markets to obtain access to intrastate and interstate services provided by such carriers at preferential rates."[7] The FCC was to prescribe regulations implementing this intent, and to enhance the availability of advanced services to all "public and non-profit elementary and secondary classrooms, health care facilities, libraries, museums (including zoos and aquariums), public broadcast stations, and any other class of public institutional telecommunications users identified by the Commission..."[8] The Joint Board and the FCC were to ensure that consumers in rural and high-cost areas attained access to advanced services for health care, education, economic development, and other public purposes. Carriers were also to ensure accessibility by persons with disabilities wherever feasible.

Moreover, another section of the bill stated that in exchange for the carrier's use of public rights-of-way, up to five percent of telecommunications network capacity was to be reserved for eligible institutions to deliver information services to the general public at incremental cost-based rates. These entities included elementary and secondary schools, public telecommunications entities, public and non-profit libraries, and non-profit organisations involved in non-commercial educational, informational, cultural, civic, or charitable activities. If the FCC determined that a network had a sufficiently open architecture, capacity, and non-discriminatory access to cater to such entities' needs, the set-aside would not be applicable.

Information Services and Electronic Publishing: The bill's requirements were more detailed than, but broadly in line with, those of H.R. 3626.

---

7   United States Congress, S. 1822, *The Communications Act of 1994*, p. 7.
8   United States Congress, S. 1822, *The Communications Act of 1994*, p. 60.

Cable Television and Common Carrier Video Platforms: Telecommunications and cable television firms were limited to a five percent financial interest in each other within their existing operating areas, and other pro-competitive safeguards like separate subsidiary requirements were established. BOC video platforms were to make capacity available to independent programmers on non-discriminatory terms, but there was no specific provision regarding PEG access.

Four observations are necessary here. First, the inclusion of such language demonstrates that public interest groups had an important influence on Congressional actions. In both the House and Senate versions, the language used to set the national goal of evolving toward switched broadband networks that would allow all segments of society to create and disseminate voice, data, graphics, and video messages was pushed by organisations like the Alliance for Public Technology and the Electronic Frontiers Foundation. The two bills' universal service language was also heavily influenced by organisations like the Consumer Federation of America and, in the case of advanced services at preferential rates for non-commercial institutions, the National Education Association, the American School Board Association, and the American Library Association. Their requirement that BOC video platforms have adequate capacity to accommodate independent programmers (and, in the House version, offer PEG access at preferential rates) were won by a coalition including the Alliance for Community Media, the Alliance for Communications Democracy, the Media Access Project, and People for the American Way, as well as local and state government organisations like the National League of Cities, the National Conference of Mayors, and the National Association of Counties.

H.R. 3626 reflected public interest group influence in other ways. For example, the open platform provision was drafted by the Electronic Frontiers Foundation. The open set-top box language was pushed by the Taxpayer Assets Project and computer firms like Sun Microsystems and Oracle. The provision on civic participation was drafted by the Taxpayers' Assets Project. In parallel, S. 1822's requirement that up to five percent (originally 20 percent) of network capacity be set aside for non-commercial public spaces was drafted largely by the Media Access Project and pushed strongly by America's Public Television Stations, People for the American Way, and the Center for Media Education. Moreover, even though they were eventually removed prior to committee passage, some additional provisions promoted by public interest groups were central to the debate for months. An example of this was S. 1822's language banning the "red-lining" of low-income neighbourhoods in the construction of common carrier video platforms, which was provided by the Center for Media Education with support from the Minority Media Telecommunications Council, the National Association for the Advancement of Colored People, and People for the American Way.

A second point that should be noted is that the public interest group victories listed above were on non-trivial issues. True, the most contentious questions addressed by the Democrat's legislation (and by the final Telecommunications Act as well) involved media convergence and the rules that would govern competitive cross-entry between formerly separated industries, e.g., cable television companies' provision of telecommunications services; the BOCs' provision of cable television, or video platform services; the public utilities' provision of telecommunications services; the BOCs' entry into equipment manufacturing and electronic publishing; the broadcasters' provision of ancillary digital services; and above all, the local and long-distance telecommunications carriers' entry into each other's markets. And true, on these big-money items, it was largely inter-industry bargaining and lobbying that drove the process; public interest groups supported pro-competitive provisions and denounced what they saw as anti-consumer power grabs, but their positions on such matters generally were not independently central to the deals Congress struck. Nevertheless, it would be a mistake to conclude that the issues activists introduced, and won on, were inconsequential to industry players and their supporters on the Hill.

Consider the case of the five percent capacity set-aside for public spaces in telecommunications networks. Leaving aside the question of whether this was a technologically workable proposal, it was public interest groups that got the issue onto the agenda and battled for its inclusion in S. 1822 over the strenuous objections of the BOCs and their Congressional friends. Similarly, although in the end it would be consumers, rather than the carriers' bottom lines, that would have had to cover the cost of providing advanced services to non-commercial institutions at preferential rates, the carriers were hardly chomping at the bit to take on this new obligation. Far from it; some lobbied actively against an expansive approach to universal service, and they had a number of legislators on their side. Nor could progressive Democrats have won this on their own without the backing of mobilized social constituencies. It was public interest groups that raised the matter and helped friendly legislators build a winning coalition among their colleagues. The same could be said of switched broadband networking and open platform services, access for PEG programmers to Regional BOC (RBOC) video platforms, competitively-provided open set-top boxes, and so on.

These issues mattered not only to the companies that would have been affected, but also to the social shaping of the NII. Had the provisions listed above been enacted in law, implemented by regulatory agencies, and survived any challenges in the courts, the new policy framework would have embodied an historic bargain between two different agendas. On the one hand, the various corporations, demanding to be freed of outdated barriers to entry, could now compete in new markets. But on the other hand, in exchange for acquiring these rights, some of these firms would also have been subject to new social obligations that might have made their systems a bit more like the Internet. That is, they would have had to provide the general public with the ability to disseminate, as well as receive, all forms of information - voice, text, data, and video - at rates that were reasonable and even (in the case of non-commercial institutions) preferential. Of course, in cases like the proposed video platforms, the BOCs could have simply refused to invest in building out the requisite networks and services if they found the obligations concerning capacity provision, PEG access, and so on to be disincentives. But in other cases like universal service, they would have been obliged to incorporate the new objectives into their planning regardless of whether this was their first preference.

Our third point concerns something that is not evident from the language cited above. As the legislation evolved between January and the summer of 1994, there were dozens of changes to the precise wording of contested provisions that could seem insignificant to people outside the process but which nevertheless had major implications. And in this process of "pulling and hauling" amongst competing players, public interest groups sometimes succeeded not only in inserting, or preserving, language that they favored, but also in softening, or eliminating, language that they opposed. By contacting the press, spreading the news on the Internet, and meeting with friendly legislators, public interest groups were able to "blow the whistle" on preferential language that corporate lobbyists and their Congressional allies were trying to slip into the bills with little fanfare. Particularly when this involved blatantly obvious favouritism, or "give-aways", to specific firms (e.g., some proposed broadcast ownership reforms) but also on complex issues where a more technically informed and nuanced case had to be made (e.g., service rates, or access to platforms), activists were able to rally their Congressional allies enough to pull the bills back a bit toward the pro-competitive and pro-consumer side of the ledger.

Fourth, while public interest groups achieved a good deal more than many observers may have expected, or even realize, today - hence, this chapter - they also lost on many issues. It could hardly be otherwise: tens of billions of dollars in revenues per year were at stake in the battles between industry contestants. The corporate lobbying campaigns were extremely aggressive and well-financed, and public interest groups had little hope, or expectation, of being a primary force in shaping the provisions that laid out the terms on which huge companies could compete with each other. Activists took positions on many of these issues, and sometimes played a minor supporting role, but in general, questions involving inter-corporate rivalries were decided by the Congress in consultation with those who had a financial stake in the matter. Public interest groups were far more influential on issues that directly involved the non-commercial sector's interests and, to a lesser extent, consumer protection, which is precisely what one would expect.

The Window Slams Shut

Everything changed after the November 1994 Congressional election. The Republicans took control of the House and Senate in a landslide victory that was widely seen as a stern repudiation of President Clinton and the Congressional Democrats. Robert Dole, who had played the lead role in killing S. 1822 and was a close ally of the BOCs, became the new Senate Majority Leader. Newt Gingrich, a far-right proponent of radical deregulation without consumer or pro-competitive safeguards became the Speaker of the House. Soon after the opening of the 104th Congress in January 1995, Gingrich called together a small group of top executives from the largest companies for closed-door meetings to see what they wanted in a new telecommunications reform effort. The Democrats were excluded from these consultations with the major players, who soon began to contribute millions of additional dollars to the Republican's campaign coffers while substantially cutting back their contributions to the Democrats.

In parallel, the public interest community's avenues of direct influence quickly narrowed. The new Republican majority showed little interest in catering for, or even talking to, public interest groups. Liberal Democrats continued to meet with activists, and to try and inject public interest concerns into the process, but they no longer controlled the committees that would be writing the new bills. Nor did they have the voting majorities needed to insert provisions that either Republicans or conservative or centrist Democrats opposed, or simply did not care enough about to fight for. Any victories on the public interest agenda, therefore, would have to come on "mom and apple pie" issues that might appeal to enough voters around the country to assemble a bipartisan coalition. Comparatively uncontroversial initiatives like promoting universal service in rural districts, providing schools with access to advanced services at discounted rates, or encouraging the accessibility of equipment and services by persons with disabilities might be able to survive in close votes. But any proposal that imposed strong new social obligations on the private sector, or could be characterized as a mere give-away to some purportedly self-interested liberal constituency, would have a difficult time making it into the bills. So too would anything that could be labeled as being simply the pet project of some self-interested activist group that lacked significant membership or supporters around the country. Conservatives and libertarians increasingly derided such beltway activists as "self-appointed guardians of the public interest" who represented nobody but themselves, which was a clever way to delegitimate them as mere "special interests," a term less frequently applied to the private sector.

The Congressional leadership instructed the new committee and subcommittee chairmen to write the legislation and move it through the process quickly, and this they did. In March 1995, Larry Pressler, the Chairman of the Senate Committee on Commerce, Science and Transportation, produced a draft bill that was to become S. 652, *The Telecommunications Competition and Deregulation Act* of 1995. A mere two days of committee hearings were held, and the only public interest advocates allowed to testify were from the Markle Foundation and the Consumer Federation of America. In May 1995,

Representative Craig Fields, Chairman of the House Subcommittee on Tele-communications and Finance, introduced what became H.R. 1555, The Communications Act of 1995. Three days of hearings were held with slightly broader public interest representation by the National Association of State Utility Consumer Advocates, the American Council of the Blind, Telecom-munications for the Deaf, the Media Access Project, and the Consumer Fed-eration of America. Also testifying was the National Association of Counties, which shared with activists a desire to preserve local control over rights-of-way, and the Communications Workers of America, which took just a couple of positions that were broadly compatible with those of the public interest community.

S. 652 and H.R. 1555 shared with the previous Democratic bills a preoc-cupation with balancing divergent corporate interests in setting the rules for cross-market entry and convergence. But they differed from their predeces-sors on both the pro-liberalisation and the new social obligations agendas mentioned above. Regarding the former, the Republican bills took a far more deregulatory approach but deleted many of the detailed safeguards the Demo-crats had established in hopes of promoting real and sustainable competition among unequal firms. In this sense, the new legislation favoured encouraged greater concentration of ownership and market power in some crucially im-portant instances. Regarding the latter, gone were the provisions on: the na-tional goal of building-switched, two-way broadband networks; open plat-form service; cost-based preferential rates for advanced service access by a wide variety of non-commercial institutions; the set-aside of five percent of network capacity for non-commercial institutions to provide services to the public; the FCC inquiries into civic participation in the NII and flat-rate pric-ing for Internet access; the rules on access by independent content providers BOC information services platforms; and, in the Senate version, the require-ment that television set-top boxes be architecturally open, and competitively provided.

In short, the new legislative architecture for the NII was to consist largely of a deal between the major corporate players about the terms and pace of competition, rather than also embracing a broader deal that would accommo-date the United States' burgeoning non-commercial sector. Nor would the legislation make direct concessions to consumer interests by imposing social obligations on the private sector; in most cases, the market would be the main determinant of whether, and when, new networks and services would be made available. To be sure, there were exceptions to this narrowed thrust: for example, S. 652 required that primary and secondary schools and libraries would receive, at preferential rates, those services designated by the Federal-State Joint Board and the FCC to be within the evolving definition of universal service. But on the whole, in the view of public interest groups, the bills fell far short of the marks set by the 103rd Congress and were a bitter disappointment after years of effort. Moreover, as the parameters of the possible contracted, many of the activists' Congressional allies were backing away from their previous stances and limiting their objectives primarily to improving the language on liberalisation. Most were also signing on to support the legislation in order to enhance their bargaining positions, be on the winning side, have a successful conclusion to their own years of effort, and so on. Not surprisingly then, some in the public interest community felt not only that the legislation was a major loss, but also that they were being deserted by their friends on the Hill.

The Telecommunications Act of 1996

S. 652 and H.R. 1555 were reported out of their respective committees by substantial margins and, in the summer of 1995, passed by the full chambers on votes of 81 to 18 and 305 to 117, respectively. In October a conference committee was convened to reconcile differences between the two versions, and very intensive line-by-line negotiations (primarily among the Congressional staff) ensued which lasted until January 1996. In a classic example of the sort of shifting tides that often characterize Congressional action, the Republican majority made numerous concessions that shaved off some of the sharpest edges of deregulation. There were several intertwined reasons for this turn of events: the Republicans very much wanted a legislative victory they could point to, in dealing with corporate campaign contributors and the electorate; President Clinton was threatening to veto the legislation if he received it unchanged; a strong bipartisan vote was desired for numerous reasons, not least of which was Clinton's threat; Democratic staffers in some cases were simply more knowledgeable of the issues, and better negotiators; and after almost 20 years of debating varying reforms of the Communications

Act, and especially after the intense battles of the last two sessions, there was a very strong desire for Congress to finally pass something and get this issue off the Congressional plate. In consequence, the conference report that emerged was a bipartisan compromise on liberalisation with a few pro-competitive and consumer safeguards added in.

On February 1, 1996 the full Congress voted on the conference report now called S. 652, *The Telecommunications Act of 1996*. The House voted 414 to 16 in favour, while the Senate voted 91 to five in favour. On February 8, President Clinton signed the Act into law at the Library of Congress, sending a copy of his signature out over the Internet via a special electronic pen. It was an oddly chosen gesture: the law Clinton was extolling contained an unconstitutional provision censoring the Internet which was vehemently opposed by users, suppliers, and Internet activists.

The Telecommunications Act is a lengthy law containing many complex provisions that would be well beyond the purpose of this chapter to summarize here. But regarding some of the major issues on which public interest groups fought, the Act does the following:

Local Telecommunications Competition: All common carriers must interconnect with each other, and all local exchange carriers (LECs) must allow service resale, number portability, dialing parity, and access to rights-of-way, and must establish reciprocal compensation agreements with other carriers. In addition, all incumbent LECs (e.g., the BOCs, or GTE) must: a) negotiate interconnection agreements with other carriers; b) provide non-discriminatory access to unbundled-basis network elements under fair conditions; c) offer for resale at wholesale rates, any telecommunications service that it provides at retail to subscribers who are not telecommunications carriers; d) provide reasonable public notice of changes in the information necessary for the transmission, routing, and interoperability of services; and e), allow equipment collocation under reasonable and non-discriminatory conditions. In addition, other sections of the Act allow cable television and public utilities like electric power companies to provide local telecommunications services.

While the Republican bills were viewed as victories for the BOCs and other LECs, the final Act does establish mechanisms that can be used to pry open local markets if the FCC and the public utility commissions (PUCs) use them aggressively. In August 1996, the FCC adopted rules implementing the provisions that could facilitate local competition from a variety of players, e.g., IECs, cable television companies, public utilities, wireless service providers, and specialized competitive access providers. Accordingly, in September 1996, several LECs and state PUCs filed successful legal challenges to block FCC action, and the matter will now be fought out in the courts as expected. Most public interest groups supported local competition (although some like the Consumer Federation of America worried about possible increases in basic telephone rates if traditional monopoly cross-subsidies were then withdrawn), but they were not generally a decisive factor in shaping the provisions.

Long Distance Telecommunications Competition: The BOCs may enter long-distance immediately in regions where they are not the incumbent LECs. In regions where they are the incumbent LEC's, a BOC can apply to the FCC to provide long-distance service via a separate subsidiary, if it has signed at least one interconnection agreement with an unaffiliated local competitor who provides switched service to both business and residential subscribers either exclusively, or predominantly, over its own facilities, in combination with the resale of another carrier's service. The interconnection agreement must meet the conditions of a reasonably demanding 14-point checklist. The FCC is to consult with the U.S. Attorney General and the relevant state PUC, and then decide if the application meets the checklist criteria and is in the public interest. If no potential competitor has requested such an agreement within 10 months of enactment, the BOC may go forward with an application to the FCC. A number of BOCs are already filing applications which, if approved, would mean more major players in an already competitive market. Most public interest groups supported BOC entry into long-distance only if they were first compelled to allow real competition in the local loop, but again, activists generally were not major actors in shaping the relevant provisions.

Universal Service: A Federal-State Joint Board is created that includes one consumer advocate. The board and the FCC are to adopt policies that, inter alia: ensure that consumers who are poor, or in rural or high-cost areas, have access to basic and advanced services at rates reasonably comparable to those charged in urban areas; and, require that carriers provide services, designated as universal, to elementary and secondary schools and libraries at rates less than those charged to other customers, as well as to rural health care facilities, at rates comparable to those charged elsewhere in a state. The FCC is also to enhance access by such institutions to advanced services. All telecommunications carriers are to provide funding towards universal service, and designated "eligible carriers" may receive support from the monies collected. The public interest community suffered major losses with the deletion of the 103rd Congress' expansive language on universal service and preferential access by a host of non-commercial entities, but fought hard to preserve the more narrow support for schools and libraries contained in the Act, and can count its retention as a victory under the circumstances. The same is true of the language specifying that universal service is an evolving concept that may be upgraded over time to encompass more advanced services.

Preemption: The Act preempts state legislative barriers to entry and some other local requirements and PUC regulations - moves opposed by some public interest groups as well as state and municipal governments.

Information Services and Electronic Publishing: Rules are specified only for BOC provision of electronic publishing services, not for the broader category of information services.[9] To enter the market, a BOC must establish a separate subsidiary and may jointly market inbound telemarketing or referral services only if they are available to all publishers on non-discriminatory terms. Moreover, a BOC can engage in an electronic publishing joint venture in which it does not control more than a 50 percent equity interest, or have a right to more than 50 percent of gross revenues (80 percent if the partner is a

---

9 Information Services are defined as "the offering of a capability for generating, acquiring, storing, transforming, processing, retrieving, utilising, or making available information via telecommunications, and includes electronic publishing, but does not include any use of any such capability for the management, control, or operation of a telecommunications system or the management of a telecommunications service." Electronic publishing is defined as, "the dissemination, provision, publication, or sale to an unaffiliated entity or person, of any one or more of the following: news (including sports); entertainment (other than interactive games); business, financial, legal, consumer, or credit materials; editorials, columns, or features; advertising; photos or images; archival or research material; legal notices or public records; scientific, educational, instructional, technical, professional, trade, or other literary materials; or other like or similar information. "Telecommunications *Act of 1996,* Public Law 104-104, February 8, 1996, pp. 110 STAT. 59 & 103.

small, local publisher). Basic telephone service must be provided to independent publishers at reasonable rates, but otherwise the open access scheme of the Democratic bills has disappeared. This could be viewed as a set-back to those public interest groups that advocated stricter rules but, in reality, the BOC's plans of a few years ago have largely been made irrelevant by the explosive growth and mass popularisation of the Internet as the preferred (open) platform for the provision of information services and electronic publishing to the general public.

Cable Television and Open Video Systems: Telecommunications and cable television companies can take up to a 10 percent financial stake in each other within their respective service areas, and more in rural areas. Outside their operating regions they can buy at will, subject to government approval. However, LECs can obtain a controlling interest in cable systems that are: not in the top 25 markets, not owned by one of the biggest cable companies, facing competition, and non-dominant in the market. The deregulation of upper-tier cable television rates is delayed for three years. Public interest groups generally opposed easing the rules on cross-ownership and rates, but the conference committee agreement won by Democrats made these provisions less objectionable to activists than those contained in the original bills.

Late in the conference committee, LECs lobbyists inserted a new scheme on new video platforms that is more permissive than the one contained in the prior Democratic legislation. The "open video systems" (OVS) language terminates the FCC's video dialtone rules and requires the Commission, *inter alia,* to: a) prohibit an operator from discriminating amongst video programme providers and ensure that the rates and conditions for access are non-discriminatory and reasonable; b) if demand exceeds the channel capacity, prohibit an operator and its affiliates from selecting the video programming for carriage on more than one-third of the activated channel capacity; c) permit an operator to carry on only one channel, any video programming service that is offered by more than one video programming provider; and d) prohibit an operator from unreasonably discriminating in favour of itself, or its affiliates, with regard to material or information (including advertising) provided to subscribers for the purposes of selecting programming. In return, OVS are relieved from both Title II common carrier regulation and Title VI cable regulations, including the need to obtain a local franchise license (although they could be subject to a locally-imposed fee). In particular, the language at first appeared to free OVS from the obligation to provide PEG access, which was one of several reasons public interest groups strongly opposed the new approach. However, the FCC subsequently adopted implementation rules that stated that PEG access was, in fact, required. In any event, given the cost of deployment, uncertain consumer demand, new competition from direct broadcast satellites, and other factors, it is at present very unclear whether anyone will be building OVS any time soon; buying into conventional cable systems currently appears to be the favoured method of LEC entry into video markets.

Set-top Boxes and Other Critical Interfaces: In consultation with industry standards bodies, the FCC is to assure the commercial availability from manufacturers, retailers, and other vendors not affiliated with the cable companies, of converter boxes and other equipment used to access programming and other services offered over video systems. However, such regulations (which sunset when a competitive market is achieved) cannot jeopardize signal security and property, and the FCC is required to waive its regulations if a video provider can show that this is needed for the introduction of new products and services. The provision does not actually require that boxes must have an open architecture; "competitive availability" could still result in the market dominance of a General Instruments/Microsoft box with a closed and proprietary architecture. As such, the provision contains loopholes that makes it weaker than the language public interest groups were supporting. The Act also says that the FCC may participate in industry standardisation processes concerning interconnectivity, although it is given no new powers to enforce open standards, which some public interest groups sought.

Broadcasting and Spectrum Management: The Act's provisions go well beyond the Democratic bills' calls for FCC consideration of rule changes. There are two key issues. First, the Act promotes concentrated ownership of traditional broadcast media by significantly raising the number of radio and television stations a company can own. Public interest groups strongly opposed the original - much more pro-concentration - language contained in the Republican bills, and here, too, Democrats in the conference committee were able to slightly scale back the damage. Nevertheless, most public interest groups still regard the provisions as a disaster from the standpoint of promoting a diverse public sphere.

Second, the section on spectrum flexibility requires that if the FCC decides to issue licenses for advanced television (ATV) services, it shall limit the initial eligibility for such free licenses to persons currently operating television stations - nobody else qualifies for access to this valuable real estate. The FCC is to allow such licensees to offer ancillary or supplementary services on the designated frequencies if it is consistent with the public interest. If the FCC grants a license for ATV services, it must require that either the additional, or the original, license be surrendered for reallocation or reassignment. Licensees must continue to operate in the public interest - including, implicitly, by continuing to provide free over-the-air broadcast television. And if a broadcaster provides an ancillary service on a subscription fee-basis, or receives compensation from a third party for transmitting material other than commercial advertisements, it is to make a payment to the U.S. Treasury as designated by the FCC.

Controversy over this language continues. Public interest advocates have argued strenuously that the plan amounts to a "give-away" of public property, and that any fees collected for subscription services will be set far below the real value of the spectrum. They have advocated instead for auctioning the spectrum and using the funds to support public interest applications and public television, and/or requiring the broadcasters to set up at least one channel as an open communication forum for independent video suppliers and PEG access. Activists found themselves in unusual company when former Senate Majority Leader Bob Dole began to decry the give-away. Dole was apparently motivated by the desire to reduce the federal budget deficit through an auction and, reportedly, his ire at broadcast networks over their coverage of the Republican Congress. As a condition for agreeing to the Act's passage, Dole extracted a commitment to further hearings with an eye toward possible supplementary auction legislation. Hearings were held by the Senate Budget and Commerce Committees and the House Telecommunications and Finance Subcommittee in the Spring of 1996, but they were heavily stacked in the broadcasters' favour and yielded no consensus for auctions. Broadcasters also launched a public relations campaign, running ads threatening to abandon free television if they did not get what they wanted, and encouraging voters to call their Congresspersons in support of their claims (which were not explained).

At the moment most analysts expect the auction proposal to die, but public interest groups are still working the issue and waiting to see how the FCC will respond.

Content Regulations: As is widely known, the Act imposes unconstitutional censorship on Internet speech that could be deemed indecent, as opposed to obscene (which is already illegal). Public interest groups lobbied vigorously and helped to mobilize a massive Internet letter-writing campaign to the Congress in an effort to delete the language, but neither the White House, nor many Internet-aware legislators, were willing to try to explain the problem to the general public and risk being labelled "defenders of pornography" in the 1996 election. The passage of the so-called "communications decency" provisions was a major defeat for the activist community. However, public interest groups, in alliance with portions of the Internet industry, stopped implementation in the courts, and the matter is now scheduled to be addressed by the U.S. Supreme Court. The Act also requires that television manufacturers build in "V-chips" that allow parents to block access to television programmes they deem inappropriate for their children, and that the programming industry devise a rating system to facilitate this blocking. Free speech advocates like the American Civil Liberties Union have opposed the V-chip scheme while some other activist groups have not.

New Funding: The Act establishes a Telecommunications Development Fund that is to use the interest on monies collected by personal communication services spectrum auctions, to promote small business participation in the telecommunications industry and support universal service. In parallel, the Act establishes a National Education Technology Funding Corporation to assist schools and libraries, although no funding source is specified. Public interest groups supported both of these provisions, although the actual benefits remain unclear.

In sum then, the new law represents a mix of wins and losses for public interest groups, although arguably the latter far outweigh the former. On the liberalisation agenda, the telecommunications competition provisions are better than many feared would be the case, especially if the Clinton Administration's FCC remains resolute in trying to pry open the local loop; the language on both OVS and information services and electronic publishing is inadequate, but increasingly irrelevant, as the Internet overtakes the BOC/cable company vision of an NII, based on pay-per entertainment; and the broadcasting provisions are awful. The agenda of building an NII which accommodates a range of non-commercial uses and voices has, however, largely disappeared. Moreover, its losses seem to have had a negative effect on the public interest community's overall levels of activism and enthusiasm. Nevertheless, a number of groups remain hard at work on the next wave of legislative and regulatory challenges, many of which directly involve the Internet - intellectual property, privacy and encryption, educational access, free speech, BOC proposals for service providers to pay fees for local loop access, etc.

Conclusion

How NIIs are to be organized and controlled is a question that has major consequences for the citizens and growing non-commercial sectors of North America and Europe. There is, of course, much about the American institutional landscape, policy-making process, and structure of civil society that is idiosyncratic and lacking strong parallels elsewhere. Nevertheless, the case of federal U.S. telecommunications reform suggests that advocacy groups can, at times, play an important role in promoting the interests of these stakeholders, especially if they are able to put forward concrete and well-informed proposals, work together, and forge alliances with progressive politicians. Scholars and activists alike might therefore benefit by further assessing the non-commercial sector's interests and roles in the social shaping of information highways around the world.

11. Non-Profit Applications of the Information Highways

Comparing Grant Programs of the European Commission and the National Telecommunications and Information Administration (NTIA)[1]

Marie d'Udekem-Gevers and Claire Lobet-Maris

Introduction

This chapter considers American and European policies relating to the design, or shaping, of the so-called "information society". In particular, we compare the political initiatives of the U.S. government and the European Commission which are aimed at stimulating telematics applications in non-profit sectors such as health care, education and training, culture, and administrative services. Traditionally, these sectors engage in a wide range of non-commercial activities which serve the public interest.

The key question raised in this chapter concerns the styles adopted by these two political institutions in building, or helping to build, innovative uses of information and communication technologies (ICTs). This question is important since the political style adopted influences the dynamism of the innovation process and the subsequent shaping of the information society. In our view, political style is more than a question of management. It is also a system of actions. This system of actions begins with the political vision engendered by the strategic interests of key actors in the debate - a vision which determines which actions will be endorsed; which procedures and regulatory devices will be invoked; and which roles will become available to states, industries, and users.

1 The authors thank Béatrice van Bastelaer for her comments, and the Belgian Federal Office for Scientific, Technical and Cultural Affairs (OSTC) for funding the research.

The first section of the chapter relates the strategic context and the political background of specific programmes launched by the U.S. government and the European Union in the non-profit sector. In the second section, these telematics programmes are analysed in terms of their objectives, structures, actions, and key players. In comparing their different styles, we highlight how the different political styles may profoundly affect the on-going shaping of the information society in the U.S. and in Europe.

Our methodology consists of a comparison of official documents such as public reports, agendas for action, programmes, and lists of funded pilot projects. That is, it is exclusively concerned with formal and official levels of discourse. The task still remains to interweave the findings recounted in this chapter with developments "on the ground".

The Information Society: Political Vision and Strategic Interests

The Political Contexts: Between Competitiveness and Democracy

In 1992, President Clinton and Vice-President Gore announced the U.S. National Information Infrastructure (NII) Initiative. This stated that technology policy constitutes a crucial component in U.S. economic policy, and that the NII - or superhighway - is one of the most important elements of that proposed policy. The NII *Agenda for Action* produced in 1993 by senior representatives of U.S. administrations, through the Information Infrastructure Task Force (IITF), itemised a series of actions and goals to be endorsed by the U.S. government to complement private sector initiatives already underway (IITF 1993).

As Dutton et al (1994) point out, the philosophy underpinning the NII is that government is not responsible either for commissioning, or for building, the superhighway - that is to be left to private enterprise - but that, nevertheless, a governmental role remains for carefully crafting particular kinds of action to assure the growth of an information infrastructure available to all Americans at a reasonable cost. This philosophy explains why the U.S. government actively participates in shaping particular facets of the NII such as regulating telecommunications markets; funding high-risk pilot applications; overseeing the general security provisions of the system; and taking an active role in smoothing the path towards the provision of universal services and non-profit applications.

In Europe, the publication of the White Paper in 1994 by Jacques Delors (then, President of the Commission) on *Growth, Competitiveness and Employment* (European Commission 1993) was the starting point for a series of actions to be taken by the Commission to facilitate a European version of the superhighway. In this White Paper, Delors pointed out the necessity to launch large technological programmes in the fields of transport and telecommunications in order to sustain Europe's growth, to assert its industrial competitiveness, and to address its serious unemployment problem. These objectives were quickly advanced by the Commission's gathering together of senior representatives of Europe's telecommunications and audio-visual industries to discuss the matter, resulting in a report by Martin Bangemann - the Commission's Director General for Industry - which was published in 1994 (Bangemann Group 1994).

Although the Bangemann report also strongly advocates that the building of a superhighway should be left to the private sector, and that the Commission should adopt a laissez-faire approach to developments in the telecommunications market, the proposed level of intervention - as itemised in the Commission's Action Plan (Commission Européenne 1994b) - is far more ambitious than that proposed by the U.S. government. The contrast is most obvious when we examine the Telematics Application Programme (TAP), which funds pilot applications which serve the public interest. In this programme, funding is not limited to the non-profit sector but also supports commercial projects. We may conclude that European initiatives actively aim to shape the market by means of supporting commercial ICTs. There is, therefore, a clear paradox in European policy: on one hand, the Commission argues for liberalisation and private enterprise and, on the other, it substantially finances those private initiatives.

Two Visions of the Non-Profit Sector

Major differences exist between U.S. and European policies in how they define and include non-profit concerns in their action agendas. In the U.S., the IITF has developed a specific programme aimed at promoting applications for the public and non-profit sectors, called the Telecommunications and Information Infrastructure Assistance Programme (TIIAP). In addition, the IITF has launched a separate programme for commercial infrastructural and applications projects, called the Advanced Technology Programme (ATP). By comparison, as we saw earlier, Europe's non-profit programme - TAP - does not distinguish between commercial and non-commercial endeavour in this field. The distinct ways in which non-profit concerns are formulated and addressed in policy programmes reflect more than the pragmatics of managing the relevant R&D: they also suggest important differences in how that field is envisaged and defined.

In U.S. policy, non-profit applications are synonymous with non-commercial applications which serve the public interest. In European policy, non-profit sectors such as health care, administration, education, etc. are treated as arenas within which profitable applications may be developed and sold. There is a clear divergence between the two definitions. In the U.S., programmes which fund pilot projects for the non-profit sector pursue two objectives. The first is to augment the social welfare of citizens directly, and the second is to inject a kind of "telematics culture" into the population at large so that, once in place, it will - of itself - generate a demand for commercial ICTs. This is not the case in European policy, where the non-profit sector is explored for its commercial potential. This may explain why Europe does not have programme dedicated specifically to non-profit - meaning, non-commercial - enterprise.

In the long run, both approaches are clearly oriented towards the market. The difference, rather, is that the U.S. vision encompasses the intermediary step of generating a user-led demand for ICTs by means of funding projects which deliver its citizens direct social value-added. In contrast, the European vision only supports steps which lead directly to the delivery of marketable applications. Crudely, the U.S. vision is oriented towards users and the demand side of the equation, while the European vision is oriented towards producers and the supply side of the equation. As we will see, these different visions lead to a tremendous divergence between the kinds of pilot applications supported, or funded, by U.S. and European programmes in the non-profit sector.

A Comparison of the U.S. and European Programmes

We will focus here on the major points of divergence between the American TIIAP and the European TAP, under the following headings:

- the general goals of the programmes;
- the main criteria for applicants' participation and eligibility;
- the funded domains for applications;
- budgets.

General Goals of the Programmes: Citizens versus Industries

The objectives of the U.S. TIIAP programme, as we have seen, are oriented towards users and the demand-side. The U.S. government aims to "promote the widespread use of advanced telecommunications and information technologies in the public and non-profit sectors in order to build a nation-wide, interactive, multimedia information infrastructure available to all citizens, rural as well as urban" (NTIA 1995b). By contrast, Europe's TAP programme has an industrial focus. Its prime objective is "to promote the competitiveness of European industry and the efficiency of services of public interest and to stimulate job creation through the development of new telematics systems and services in such areas as telework and teleservices" (European Commission - DG XIII 1994d: i).

Main Criteria for Applicants' Participation and Eligibility:
A Users' Community versus a Producers' Consortium

The U.S. TIIAP is geared towards the user communities of non-profit entities. Applicants are drawn from "state and local governments, health care providers, school districts, libraries, universities, social service organizations, public-safety services, and other non-profit entities" (NTIA 1995d). The TIIAP works on the principle of matching grants: the U.S. government will fund up to 50 percent of the total cost of a project, providing the applicant can resource the remainder from the private sector. This principle helps to ensure that private companies hold a vested interest in the project's success, and in its timely return on investment.

The European TAP targets the producers of services and applications. The programme is "open to any 'legal entity'... Legal entities may include industrial enterprises, ... research organisations, educational institutions, users' organisations etc. The projects are open to national, regional and local authorities, appointed bodies, development boards and agencies" (European Commission - DG XIII 1994c: 7). In practice, most applications for support have come from industry, based on their assessment of likely user demand. TAP's funding principle is also based on cost-sharing although it can, and does, fund private companies. Thus, the TAP programme may dramatically affect whether a company retains a substantial interest in a project's success because it permits private risk to be substituted by public investment.

Another difference between the two programmes concerns how applicants may form consortia for the purpose of gaining project funding. In the TAP programme, the main criterion is that joint- or multi-applications must involve cross-national collaboration between member states (at least two states must be involved). In contrast, U.S. criteria emphasise that collaborating applicants should share similar social agendas. The European programme privileges projects which deliver something that will be transportable across member states. The U.S. approach is more contingent, focusing on applications which have a social proximity to each other for a defined group of users. If the concept of a "community of users" underpins U.S. criteria, those of the European programme are geared to strengthen the European Union by enforcing cooperation amongst member states whose social realities may sometimes differ profoundly. The policy underpinning TAP suggests that the building of the European information society relies on artificially-devised forms of cooperation.

Moreover, in contrast with the TIIAP programme which is stimulating the emergence of the information society in the U.S. through supporting applications which have a proximity of contents for a defined user group, the TAP programme promotes generic pilot applications that can be used all over Europe. Let us take an example from the field of health care. In the U.S., funding has been given to the Public Health Services of New York to assist their AIDS-prevention campaign. In Europe, TAP only funds generic disease-prevention projects, and would refuse to consider an application which benefited only one region (unlike the New York example we have seen) or only one illness (such as AIDS).

Funded Domains for Applications

Analysing the contents of both programmes (i.e., which projects are selected for funding) brings us to another important difference between U.S. and European policy. The European programme (European Commission - DG XIII 1994d) sets out complex criteria for the fields, and domains of interest, for which an applicant can make a submission. The programme offers support for ICT pilot projects which - when all are mapped together - combine R&D into applications for vertically-integrated markets, with horizontally-integrated research into related engineering activities. TAP thoroughly prescribes which range of applications fall within its remit; which markets and domains of interest count as eligible; and which methodologies must be followed. Applicants must meet these stringent constraints, if they are to succeed in their submissions. By contrast, the American programme is more open: it consists only of a list of potential application domains (NTIA 1995a; NTIA 1995c). Starting with this simple list, applicants define their projects according to their own frames of reference, leaving them greater freedom to define the project's scope.

To some extent, U.S. strategy is more liberal since it enables users to decide what development is relevant, according to their own perception of the problem being addressed. This difference highlights a contradiction in European rhetoric since, on one hand, the Commission advocates a laissez-faire approach to the building of the information society while, on the other, all submissions for funding must tally with TAP's prescribed remit for supporting ICT developments.

To compare the application domains supported by each programme, we will analyse the TIIAP 1994 awards (NTIA 1995c) and the TAP 1994 awards (European Commission -DG XIII 1994d). Despite the different scope of each programme, we can still identify some equivalences between the fields supported by both (see Table 1).

USA TIIAP 1994		EU TAP 1994 - 1998	
Domains	*Budgets* MECU	*Domains*	*Budgets* MECU (Call for Proposals)
Governments + Public Information	3	Administration	25
		Transport	117
		Research	26
K-12 Education + Higher Education	4	Education & Training	34
Libraries Services	1.5	Libraries	
Science	0.2		
Community Informa-tion	5.7	Urban & Rural Areas	25
Health	3.6	Healthcare	70
		Disabled & Elderly People	
		Environment	15
Arts & Culture	0.2		
		Other Exploratory Actions	
Social Services	0.7		
Public Safety	0.1		
		Telematics Engineering	
		Language Engineering	23
		Information Engineering	
		Programme Support Actions	21
		(Specific Measures for SMEs)	15
	18.9		*371*

Table 1: *Comparison between Domains and between Detailed Budgets (MECU) of the 1994 TIIAP and of the Telematics Applications Programme*

Some fields are identical. Both programmes support ICT developments for education (Education and Training in TAP, K-12 Education and Higher Education in TIIAP); for libraries (Libraries in TAP, and Library Services in TIIAP); and for health (Healthcare in TAP, and Health in TIIAP). Other domains which receive support are not identical, though they are correlated. To some extent, TAP's Administration category matches two categories of domain in the 1994 TIIAP i.e. Government, and Public Information. There are also some overlaps between the Community Information Sector in TIIAP, and the Urban and Rural Areas domain in TAP.

However, there is some lack of conformity between the two programmes concerning the fields which are eligible for support. The 1994 TIIAP supports the domains of Science, Arts and Culture, Social Services, and Public Safety. These have no equivalent in the European TAP programme. Equally, TAP supports the domains of Transport, Research, Disabled and Elderly People, Environment, Other Exploratory Actions, Telematics Engineering, Language Engineering, Information Engineering, and Programme Support Actions. These domains do not receive support from the 1994 TIIAP.

A full description of the differences between U.S. and European investments into specific application domains requires further analysis and is beyond the immediate concerns of this chapter.

Budgets: Catalyst versus Support

Before comparing their budgets, we must first point out a crucial difference between the two programmes concerning the length of projects. TIIAP timescales are shorter than TAP's are: projects funded by TIIAP last between 12 and 24 months (NTIA 1 995b), while TAP projects may last for upto four years (European Commission - DG XIII 1994c).

Concerning global budgets, the TIIAP grants awarded a total of $24.4 million (18.9 MECU) in 1994 (NTIA 1995d), and a total of $35.7 million (27.6 MECU) in 1995 (NTIA 1995e). In 1994, TAP's total budget was 843 MECU and a further 371 MECU was available for the Call for Proposals (European Commission - DG XIII 1994c). Thus, for equivalent periods, TAP's budget is more than nine times higher than TIIAP's budget. In this sense, the TIIAP budget can be understood as a "catalyst budget" which is geared to kick-start certain innovative applications, where the European budget is designed to offer full support for ICT developments over a much wider range of domains. Furthermore, there are other U.S. programmes besides TIIAP which overlap with TAP's remit. For example, the U.S. ATP - which supports private sector initiatives - distributes grants of between $20 million (14.7 MECU) and $50 million (38.7 MECU) per year (NIST 1994). Thus, we must be very careful in how we interpret differences between TAP and TIIAP budgets.

We will now turn to compare the proportion of each budget which is allocated to different domains though we must bear in mind that, at present, the only available budgetary break-down for TAP is that concerning TAP's Call for Proposals (European Commission - DG XIII 1994b). Table 1 highlights the differences between the two programmes with respect to the domains which have received grant support. In Europe's TAP, the best-funded domains are Transport (117 MECU) and Healthcare (70 MECU). By contrast, the domains which have received most support from TIIAP are Community Information (5.7 MECU) and K-12 Education and Higher Education (4 MECU).

Conclusion

This chapter compares the U.S. TIIAP with its nearest European equivalent, TAP. The two programmes are quite distinct (see Table 2). TIIAP's objective is to provide American citizens with access to the information society, whereas TAP's aim is to promote the competitiveness of the European Union. TIIAP funds are largely ear-marked for use by coherent non-profit entities, or by state and local government collaborators. TAP essentially serves industrial enterprise by means of supporting - artificially - cross-national collaborations. TAP's scope is the more ambitious of the two, and its budget is commensurately larger. Above all, we find a marked divergence between the approaches adopted by the two programmes. TIIAP funds bottom-up user group initiatives, whereas TAP exists to facilitate the top-down vision endorsed by the European Commission.

A comparison of TIIAP and TAP is useful precisely because it reveals the chasm separating U.S. and European political visions of the information society. The task still remains to measure the effect of these political differences over time as the information superhighway begins to move from vision to implementation.

	USA TIIAP	EU TAP
Goal	access for all citizens	competitiveness
Main funded participants	* state & local govern- ment/ non-profit entities * within spontaneous collaborations	* industrial enterprises * within trans-national an artificial collaborations
Scope	* only non-profit domains * limited and realistic	* no distinction between profit and non-profit * wide and ambitious
Budgets	1994: 18.9 MECU 1995: 27.6 MECU	1994- 1998: 843 MECU (global budget)
Approaches	bottom-up --> stress on the initiatives of applicants	up-bottom --> stress on the 'model' proposed by the EU.

Table 2: *Synthesis*

References

Bangemann Group (1994), High-Level Group on the Information Society, *Europe and the Gobal Information Society, Recommendations to the European Council*, Brussels, 26 May 1994.

Dutton, W., Blumler, J., Garnham, N., Mansell, R., Cornford, J. and Peltu, M. (1994), The Information Superhighway : Britaints Response, PICT Report, Policy Research Paper nr29, London.

European Commission (1993), *Growth, Competitiveness, Employment: The Challenges and Ways Forward Into the 21st Century*. A White Paper (Luxembourg: Office for Official Publications of the European Communities).

European Commission (1994), *Europe's Way to the Information Society: An Action Plan* COM(94) 347 (Brussels: European Commission).

European Commission - DG XIII (1994a), Telematics Applications Programme (1994-1998): Guidelines for Evaluators.

European Commission - DG XIII (1994b), Telematics Applications Programme (1994-1998): Call for Proposals.

European Commission - DG XIII (1994c), Telematics Applications Programme (1994-1998): Information Package .

European Commission - DG XIII (1994d), Telematics Applications Programme (1994-1998): Work-Programme.

IITF (1993), Information Infrastructure Task Force, The National Information Infrastructure: Agenda for Action.

NIST (1994), National Institute of Standards and Technology, Advanced Technology Program (ATP), 1994.

NTIA (1995a), National Telecommunications and Information Administration, Guidelines for Preparing Applications Fiscal Year 1995.

NTIA (1995b), National Telecommunications and Information Administration, Telecommunications and Information Infrastructure Assistance Program (TIIAP), Docket Number: 950124024-5024-01.

NTIA (1995c), National Telecommunications and Information Administration, TIIAP 1994 Awards by Subject Category.

NTIA (1995d), National Telecommunications and Information Administration, A short summary of TIIAP.

NTIA (1995e), National Telecommunications and Information Administration, TIIAP's 1995 Grant Round.

Analysed documents are available at the following addresses:

Commission Européenne
Programme APPLICATIONS TÉLÉMATIQUES
DG XIII-E
Bâtiment Jean Monnet (B4/35)
L-2920 Luxembourg
e-mail: telematics @ mhsg.cec.be

Commission Européenne
Programme APPLICATIONS TÉLÉMATIQUES
DG XIII-C
Avenue de Beaulieu 29 (BU 29, 4 41)
B- 1160 Bruxelles
e-mail : telematics @ dg 13.cec.be

TIIAP:
http://www.ntia.doc.gov
tiiap@ntia.doc.gov

12. Involving the Citizens: The Normative Model of the "Information and Communication Citizen"

Herbert Burkert

'*involve*': ...4. To entangle (a person in trouble, difficulties, perplexity etc.; to embarrass [...]; ...7. to roll up within itself; to overwhelm or swallow up [...]"
   The Shorter Oxford English Dictionary, Oxford, 1933.

'*Municipal Buildings*': [...] Public Gallery: The public gallery should have separate access either from the main entrance or from a special entrance and an alternative means of escape is desirable; [...] The seats should face the mayor's chair and should be arranged, if possible, in two or three rows only: this is not usually difficult, as the numbers are generally small. The seats should each have a reasonably good view of the members [...]. The seats are generally in the form of benches, fixed (to avoid noise) [...]. A space about 5ft wide is desirable behind the back row seats, for circulation and for attendants to supervise the gallery."
   Pierce, S. Rowland; Cutbush, Patrick: *Planning. The Architects Handbook.* 6th edition. London 1949, 269f.

"In the technically advanced countries of today, the desired two-way communication between citizens and government is made possible by the existence of two parallel communication systems with practically complete coverage of the population - the broadcasting system and the telephone system."
   Zworykin, V.K.: Communications and Government. In: Calder, N. (ed.): *The World in 1984.* Vol. 2. Harmondsworth 1964, 59.

"The open secret of electronic media, the decisive political element, that is suppressed till today or is waiting - mutilated - for its very moment, is its mobilizing force."

Enzensberger, Hans Magnus: 1970: *Baukasten zu einer Theorie der Medien* [*Toolkit for a Theory of Media*, Translation H. B.]. In: Palaver. *Politische Überlegungen (1967-1973)*. Frankfurt 1974, 92.

Involving the Citizen

Information infrastructures seek to involve the citizen. While this notion of citizen involvement clarifies the object of involvement, what remains vague is who exactly should do the involving. After all, citizens - by definition - should actively involve themselves rather than being involved. Given this vagueness of intent, "insufficient involvement" is typically turned into a problem of systems design: if only (sets of) applications were properly designed, the opportunities for citizen involvement could be overcome. But there is a lingering uneasiness about the question. Under current social conditions, it is often assumed that special incentives are needed to promote citizen involvement and, furthermore, that someone must take responsibility for promoting the process.

This assumption immediately evokes defence mechanisms amongst system designers: they do not wish to have to act as propagandists or paternalists. Even where planners and designers do accept responsibility for involving the citizen, they do so in terms of their own assumptions about what that means precisely. If, say, they try to involve the citizen in the design process they intimately confront the inherent pitfalls of participatory design. Chief amongst these is that there are power differences within participatory design structures, such that developers' own assumptions tend to strongly influence how a problem is defined by the team as a whole.

This process of "transference" within a participatory design team echoes the processes by which democratic societies generate strong internal pressure to achieve conformity with regard to basic normative assumptions about the democratic process itself. Against this background, designers and "their" citizens come to share the same assumptions about what the information and communication citizen should look like.

This chapter explores the normative model of the "information and communication citizen". In Europe, the dominant model distinguishes between administrative and political modes of communication, and that distinction is preserved in this discussion. In the first sections, each mode is examined in terms of its assumed information needs and interaction patterns, and each concludes with a consideration of how those issues are modified by information and communications technology (ICT) application projects. Since discussion about ICTs is international - and since ICTs themselves act to disseminate information about the models which underpin them - it seems likely that the dominant European model will come to conflict with alternative accounts of the citizen. In the concluding section, therefore, I briefly discuss which modifications of the European model are most likely to surface in the light of current U.S. approaches to ICT design.

The Normative Model of the Information and Communication Citizen

ICT projects which seek to incorporate "the citizen" into their design usually invoke a normative model of that citizen, which is rarely made explicit. The model of the citizen simply assumes that particular information and communication needs, and specific patterns of communication and interaction, exist.

Within the European context, one of the main characteristics of this model is the separation of administrative and political forms of communication. The citizen is presumed to operate in two distinct communication modes: one in the administrative sphere and the other in the political sphere, with each distinguished by their own information needs and interaction patterns. This is not to say that these spheres are not understood to be linked. Indeed, the linkage is perceived as a tactical opportunity: each communication mode is used by the communicating parties to either re-enforce, or consciously circumvent, the other. However, the very fact that a link is perceived to exist simply confirms the prior assumption that the spheres are separate.

A. The Normative Model of the Administrative Communication Mode

In the administrative communication mode, the citizen communicates directly with institutions which represent the state at local, regional, national, and international levels of governance.

Information Needs

The information needs of the citizen in the administrative realm are perceived to fall within either a subordination or a service sub-mode. Both modes share an action-reaction pattern: the administration demands something and the citizen responds, or the citizen asks for something and the administration responds. The difference between the two is one of positioning. In the subordination mode, both parties position themselves consciously in a hierarchical relationship, whereas in the service mode both position themselves in a relationship of equality - at least verbally - adopted from the customer/provider model of the private sector. In both submodes, citizens are understood to have needs that are not primarily information-related. Rather, information is seen as necessary but somewhat incidental. That is, information indicates which reactions are required; which services are available; under which conditions requirements must be met; and under which conditions services are available.

This secondary role of information is reflected in administrative law. A deficiency in the provision of information (e.g., false information, untimely information) cannot be remedied separately from the administrative action to which it is related. Deficiencies in information may lead - under grave circumstances - to the invalidity of the administrative action, but these deficiencies cannot be addressed independently of that action.

Information in this communication mode is supposed to be provided by the administration in advance, and - in the service submode, where possible - in a manner that does not create additional needs. Information should facilitate the delivery of a service or action, and render it more efficient. Information that is needed to resolve conflictual situations (e.g., arising from the refusal of a service, or from opposition to an administrative demand) and that goes beyond the mere explanation of the action in question, is usually not provided. Even the provision of explanatory information is a fairly new development.

In conflictual situations, the normative model assumes that citizens will seek professional help outside the communication mode. As professionals can deploy their own information resources, all further communication is then mediated through these professionals. The separation, in the public sector, between citizen and professional information has consequences for legitimising the economic value of information: it is regarded as illegitimate to charge for information that explains administrative action, but legitimate to charge for information that relates to professional mediation. Legal information services (particularly regarding tax law) are seen as an extra source of public sector revenue - whether directly generated by the public sector, or through public sector/private sector cooperative agreements.

Interaction Patterns

As already indicated, the prevailing interaction pattern follows the action-reaction principle. Information is only provided in response to a stimulus, and is limited to discourse on that particular interaction. Any additional information is seen to jeopardize the interaction either by delegitimising it, or by adding unwanted complexity. This reductionist stance is adopted by both communicating parties: do not tell the administration more than it needs to know; do not tell citizens more than they need to know.

Modifications in ICT Application Projects

Against this background, ICTs work to rationalize this relationship. Technology is used to facilitate message delivery in the terms dictated by these sub-modes. For example, citizens may gain an innovative means to return their tax declarations, but this only represents the insertion of an electronic interface between the citizen's and administration's existing internal information processing. Similarly, one-stop-shopping points between the parties work to rationalize the relationship of the administration to its citizens.

At a formal level, ICT applications in this arena aim to lower the entry threshold by increasing the number of access points and by improving the design of information presentation. More substantially, we find attempts to match what are perceived as the diffuse needs of citizens with a preexisting service profile. In this context, "involving the citizen" leads to a system design that defines the citizen as the outlet of the administrative information processing system.

B. *The Normative Model of the Political Communication Mode*

The political communication mode is primarily perceived as mediated communication. Mediating institutions differ according to the type of information exchanged.

Information Needs

Information needs in the political realm are divided into structural information and on-going information. The provision of structural information - that needed by the citizen to understand the mechanics of the political process - is generally left to educational institutions. The mass media are also involved in this sphere, to the extent that changes in existing structures have to be explained.

The provision of on-going information - the information that citizens need to follow the political process from day-to-day, and to evaluate the current performance of political actors - is seen primarily as the task of the mass media (and of media institutions which represent organized interests). The mass media enjoy special information relationships with political institutions and their actors. Only very rarely - and in specific historical and geographical contexts - does the political system deliver information directly to the citizen.

In some European countries (e.g., Switzerland) such information is sometimes exchanged directly through referenda. In countries with less direct participatory structures, it is only provided under special circumstances. For example, the intended change to the European monetary system has led to an increase of information provision, although this type of information may also be categorized as structural. To take another instance, there has been no broad public debate on constitutional changes in Germany following unification, again in contrast to Switzerland which is currently revising its constitution. The purpose of giving these examples is to illustrate that any departure from the normative political mode of communication would have to differentiate between differing democratic traditions within Europe, with consequences for any resulting ICT applications.

Furthermore, direct political information needs are understood to be primarily spatially determined. On-going political information is more pertinent at local and regional levels than at national and international levels. On-going information needs are also seen to be time-related. The real-time exchange of information (e.g., between a Member of Parliament and individual constituents within a parliamentary decision-making process) is seen to be necessary only immediately before, or after, special events - but not on a continuous basis.

Interaction Patterns

The information needs noted above reflect the communication pattern that is assumed to be at play in the political communication mode: the citizen receives mediated information, and reacts through the voting system.

This model is a reflection of, and is reflected in, constitutional texts in Europe. With few exceptions, the freedom to seek information is limited to information which is already available, and which is channeled through generally accessible sources. Amongst these generally accessible sources, the press and other mass media enjoy the privilege of a legal institutional guarantee. In turn, reaction to information is channeled through the election process: "All state authority shall emanate from the people. It shall be exercised by the people through elections and voting and by specific organs of the legislature, the executive power and the judiciary." (Federal Republic of Germany. Basic Law. Art. 20 (2)).

Modifications in ICT Application Projects

ICT projects - whether past, current, or planned - do not usually tackle the normative structural model underlying the mode of political communication. There is uneasiness about implementing ICT applications that allow for a constant, unmediated, and user-steered flow of on-going information. This is sometimes articulated as a fear that the citizen may suffer information overload, or that populist movements may manipulate the political decision-making process. This perception contrasts with the normative model of the consumer. Consumer protection requires legitimisation and is only provided by, for example, extending the time for decision-making. The provision of market transparency is regarded as part of the transaction costs borne by the consumer.

With regard to structural information, ICT developments are on the increase. Again, however, most of this information is pre-digested either by the mass media, by professional media agencies used by the public sector, or directly by public sector institutions. The general assumption is that structural information should be simplified and explained. Original sources like legal texts, or the full text of political statements, are still rarely offered. The mass media do not feel obliged to provide direct links to their primary sources, which might allow the citizen to check the acceptability of their summarized offerings.

Information directly provided by local communities through Internet-type communications remains descriptive. The agendas of town meetings are offered but only rarely the minutes of, or documentation relating to, the points on the agenda. Following the political process - in so far as it is visible at all - is left to mass media-type communication links (e.g., offering direct TV-coverage of town hall meetings). These links explicitly exclude interactivity (at those same town hall meetings, the camera is not directed by the viewer). To my knowledge, there are no European ICT projects which provide access to information relating to the voting behaviour of representatives at local, regional, national, or European Union levels. However, the provision of feedback channels is increasing, e.g., the facility to respond by e-mail to political events. The organized exchange of responses - together with respondents' ability to evaluate any political impact of their input - is left to individual initiatives, and receives no infrastructural technical support.

A Summary of the Normative Model

Changes in the information infrastructure have not, to date, led to a change in the normative model of communication between the citizen and the public sector, which is divided into administrative and political modes.

Administrative communication is case- or service-related, and does not deviate from the classic version of that relationship. Improvements in ICTs raise the efficiency of those communicative actions rather than broadening their scope. Political communication is divided into structural and on-going information. ICTs addressed at structural information tend to improve the quantity and presentational style of what is on offer. ICTs which support the provision of on-going information are still relatively scarce. In general, the provision of such information is seen as needing mediation if it is to be comprehensible to the citizen. Mediation is either directly undertaken by the public sector, or the primary source is filtered by, and through, mass media institutions. There are still few possibilities for citizens to evaluate mediation performances.

The normative model has remained fairly constant over the last twenty years at least. New ICTs, designed in the context of the European information society, do not fundamentally question this model, but equip it with improved technical means of delivery. The systems designs of national and regional information infrastructures tend to reconfirm normative models of the information relationship between the citizen and the public sector. It seems, therefore, that a familiar pattern of technological development is being re-enacted: neither the telephone nor, later, videotext significantly changed our normative assumptions as to how citizens' interactions with public sector institutions could, or should, be re-negotiated.

One element, however, seems to have changed. While states may always have understood themselves to be part of a competitive process, the new ICTs ensure that their own citizens are also aware of this competition. Opportunities have improved for receiving information on how - in this case - the communicative process is structured. Not only does this process lead to a convergence in shaping the normative elements of national infrastructures (e.g., the history of data protection, or of privacy laws) but there is also a convergence in demands made on the public sector.

New Demands

In this climate of change, certain elements of the North American approach to information infrastructures have already had some impact on European discourse. We can point to a few examples of a discursive shift:

- the line separating the service perspective and the political perspective is becoming more blurred;
- more attention is being paid to issues such as the transparency of political and administrative processes (and their desiderata at any given time), as

well as the transparency of political institutions, and the actions of their agents;

- the distinction between what is properly deemed to be professional information as against what should be commonly-available administrative and political information, is becoming fudged. This is leading towards a reconsideration of Europe's approach to the commercialisation of information;
- citizen information and communication is beginning to be understood as having a horizontal, as well as a vertical, axis. Civic networking is slowly beginning to assume some importance in European debate. The citizen's information and communication needs are increasingly seen to include the need to facilitate self-organisation, and to cross-check the actions and responses of individual political institutions or actors.

Some of these perceived shifts in European discourse may, to some extent, only represent the efforts of those seeking to change the terms of the debate. In general, however, the normative perception of the role of the citizen in the information and communication processes of the information infrastructure tend to reflect real differences between North American and European normative models. Such differences can be traced back to processes which pre-date the announcement of the U.S. National Information Infrastructure Initiative, (e.g., differences in political culture, and in constitutional law).

It is plausible to assume that the North American approach to involving the citizen in the design of new ICTs resembles the European approach, at least in so far as each approach reproduces its own pre-existing normative concepts of that citizen. For that reason, it seems likely that new ICT applications will - initially, at least - be modelled on those (separate) normative assumptions. The differences that currently exist between them are, therefore, not differences in approach, but differences in content: the legal, political, and cultural values that are projected into the U.S. and European information infrastructures vary, but the projection process as such, does not.

However, the distinct models underpinning the projection process become more liable to being shared as ICTs advance in scale and scope, and the new technologies are likely to become a vehicle for a growing mutual awareness of differences in substance. As ICT applications compete with each other for supremacy across different political cultures, we might well envisage a convergence of substance.

13. Access to the Information Superhighway

James McConnaughey

Introduction

Policy-makers currently find themselves in the midst of a complex electronic information revolution of great promise. In the United States, President Clinton has compared the potential economic and social benefits of the National Information Infrastructure (NII) Initiative for the 21st century, with what investment in the railroads accomplished during the 19th century. Vice President Gore has emphasised that it is critically important to the economic future of the United States (Gore 1993). The Administration established the Information Infrastructure Task Force (IITF) - chaired by the Secretary of the U.S. Department of Commerce - to articulate and implement the NII vision, in collaboration with other sectors in a public-private partnership.

The IITF issued its landmark *Agenda for Action* in September 1993 as a guide for implementing the NII, setting forth nine basic principles and goals of government action (IITF 1993). These goals address a variety of issues, including promoting private investment and legislative reform; ensuring network reliability; protecting information privacy and intellectual property rights; and providing for a more open and efficient government (IITF 1993: 3-12). As principal advisor to the President, Vice President, and Secretary of Commerce on telecommunications and information matters, and as a vigorous participant in the IITF, the National Telecommunications and Information Administration (NTIA) has been actively involved in developing policies relating to the NII.

One of the most important NII principles is to "[e]xtend the 'universal service' concept to ensure that information resources are available to all at affordable prices" (IITF 1993: 3, 8). What is the relationship between the NII and universal service? The information market place is substantial and growing. The telecommunications and information sector currently comprises more than nine percent of U.S. Gross Domestic Product (U.S. Council of Economic Advisers 1994). Two out of three American workers are in information-related jobs (IITF 1993: 5). In this country, the NTIA estimates that private investment in the telecommunications infrastructure approximates 50 billion dollars a year, which is not an inconsequential amount. Why is that important? Private investment, prudently directed, will yield technological innovations that will boost U.S. global competitiveness through higher productivity, and the provision of new products and services.

There are two types of benefit that may accrue if these actions are conducted properly: economic and social. Economic benefits could include the creation of highly-skilled, better-paying jobs; a fostering of economic growth; and achievement of an increased standard of living. Potential social benefits are new educational opportunities obtainable through distance learning hookups to classrooms via satellite; expanded medical applications via advanced telecommunications services ("telemedicine"); and "community empowerment" - a means for disadvantaged communities to improve their quality of life. These are goals that the Administration is striving to meet, and a growing number of Americans are already enjoying these benefits. A critically important policy question remains to be addressed, however. How will the "information poor" fare? Badly, of course, in the new era, and it is a primary focus of the NII initiative to help ameliorate their plight. The discussion that follows will examine the American experience, and how the Administration is addressing the need for a new universal service policy.

Universal Service in the Information Age: The Traditional Concept

Universal service in this country has been built on the foundations of the 1934 Communications Act. Specifically, Section 1 of the Act directs Federal and State policy-makers to: "...make available, so far as possible, to all the people of the United States a rapid, efficient, Nation-wide and world-wide wire and radio communications service with adequate facilities at reasonable charges."

This section has been interpreted to mean the "Plain Old Telephone Service" (POTS) - a voice-grade communications line and dial-tone. In practice, how well has this mandate been achieved? The national rate now approximates 94 percent and has been generally rising over the past decade. During 1984-1994 - that is, since the watershed divestiture of AT&T's local exchange carriers from its long-distance, manufacturing, and research operations - the proportion of U.S. households without telephones decreased by 26.1 percent. This occurred despite a growing number of households, and rising competition in service markets.

A closer look, however, reveals that groups exist today that have not attained high levels of telephone penetration (Belinfante 1995). For example, amongst the very poorest households - those with annual incomes of less than $5,000 - the rates are significantly lower. In March 1995, only 74.3 percent of poor households had telephones, and penetration for Blacks (66.4 percent) and Hispanics (64.6 percent) was even lower. These percentages represent an improvement since 1984 (71.2, 63.2, and 55.1 percent, respectively), but the penetration remains unacceptable to policy-makers today.

A Changing Perspective

With the emergence of the information age, the need has come to reassess the concept of universal service, including how best to measure its progress. It can be reasonably argued that gauging telephone penetration rates is necessary, but no longer sufficient, as a performance measure. As NTIA stated in its study, *Falling Through the Net: A Survey of The 'Have Nots' in Rural and Urban America* : "There are legitimate questions about linking universal service solely to telephone service in a society where individuals' economic and social well-being increasingly depends on their ability to access, accumulate, and assimilate information. While a standard telephone line can be an individual's pathway to the riches of the Information Age, a personal computer and modem are rapidly becoming the keys to the vault" (NTIA 1995a:1).

Using special survey data collected by the U.S. Census Bureau, NTIA has developed a more expansive profile of universal service in America, one that includes computers and modems as well as telephones, broken down by several demographic variables and - for the first time - by rural and urban settings. *Falling Through the Net* produced a number of interesting findings with respect to this profile. One of the most insightful pertains to personal computers (PCs), and to on-line access, for the so-called "have nots" in America. As one would expect, the relationship is direct: the lower the household income, the less likely it is that the household has a computer (November 1994 data). In addition, rural households at a given income level tend to have a lower incidence of PCs than do urban households at the same income level. For example, rural households with less than $10,000 in annual income have a lower PC penetration rate (4.5 percent) than their urban counterparts (8.1 percent), and a significantly lower rate than well-to-do rural households where incomes are $75,000 or more (59.6 percent) (NTIA 1995a Table 2).

Disaggregating the data by race and origin, NTIA's study found that households comprised of Black non-Hispanics, American Indian/Aleut/ Eskimo non-Hispanics, and Hispanics in both rural areas and central cities have lower PC penetration rates than other groups. Thus, rural and central city Blacks (6.4 and 10.4 percent, respectively), central city and rural Hispanics (10.5 and 12.0 percent), and rural American Indians et al. (15.3 percent) significantly trail rural and central city Asians/Pacific Islanders (33.7 and 35.9 percent) and White non-Hispanics (24.6 and 29.4 percent) (NTIA 1995a Table 5).

Our examination of on-line activity revealed some remarkable results. More than one in five Black, Hispanic, or (non-central city) American Indian/Aleut/Eskimo households with on-line access took courses electronically. This was higher than any other group. In contrast, less than one in seven White-non-Hispanic households engaged in similar endeavours. Comparing on-line activity by level of educational attainment, the study ascertained that those rural and urban on-line households with the lowest level of schooling (i.e., eight years or less) accessed such coursework more than any other group - 24.3 and 31.8 percent, respectively (NTIA 1995a Tables 20, 26). In essence, NTIA's analysis determined that many of the groups that are the most disadvantaged in terms of PC and modem penetration also appear to actively use on-line services that facilitate economic uplift and empowerment, when given the opportunity (NTIA 1995:3). This sanguine finding tends to be strongly supportive of the goals of the NII initiative.

The Administration also seeks to expand electronic access for Americans by working with the private sector to connect classrooms, clinics, libraries, and hospitals to the NII by the year 2000 (Clinton 1994, 1996; Gore 1994). In a universal service context, certain public institutions become important as means to provide access to those groups who would otherwise have to forego connection to the NII. Ideally, all households that desire such access should be able to achieve it, particularly those persons who would otherwise be information "have nots". This should remain a long-term national strategy. In the interim, it is not realistic to expect to achieve this threshold. To advance the goal of universal service, then, transitional arrangements need to made, utilising such institutions as public "safety nets". Schools, libraries, and other community access centres represent important means to accomplish this goal.

As measured by access to the Internet and other advanced networks, however, many schools and libraries are still information-disadvantaged. Based on an October/November 1994 survey, a study conducted under the auspices of the U.S. Department of Education's National Center for Education Statistics found that 75 percent of public schools have access to some type of computer network, and 49 percent to wide area networks, such as the Internet or commercial on-line database services (NCES 1995). Approximately 35 percent of public schools have access to the Internet, but only three percent of all instructional rooms are connected. For those 49 percent of schools with access to wide area networks (WANs), only three percent of students, and two percent of teachers indicated that they use the network to a 'large extent'. According to survey respondents, the most important barriers to the acquisition, or use, of advanced telecoms in public schools are funding (69 percent), equipment problems (50 percent), and too few access points in the building (47 percent) (NCES 1995 Tables 2, 3, 5, 11, 14).

Research has also shown that most libraries are not connected to the NII. A study undertaken for the National Commission on Libraries and Information Science revealed that only 21 percent of public libraries have access to the Internet (McClure et al. 1994). Disaggregated geographically, 79 percent of libraries in large urban areas and 13 percent of libraries in the smallest towns have Internet connectivity. Less than 13 percent of public libraries allow their users to directly access the Internet through public terminals. The study found that the most important barriers to the acquisition, or use, of advanced telecommunications in public libraries vary, depending on how urban the setting is. In rural areas the main barrier is the cost of the telecommunications link, whereas in more urban locales, it is libraries' lack of knowledge or interest in the Internet that hampers access (McClure et al. 1994: 39, Figures 5, 20, 66).

Partnerships: Illustrative Solutions

A core vehicle for developing and implementing a new universal service policy is the public-private partnership (IITF 1993: 6-7). The IITF - with assistance from a non-Federal Advisory Council comprised of representatives of industry, labour, public interest groups, academia, and state and local governments - has sought to provide the vision that can ensure that no American who desires to participate in the information age will be denied that opportunity. Examples of such partnering already abound (NIIAC 1996). A recent event, and an on-going activity involving NTIA, illustrate the utility of cooperative efforts.

A large-scale event held in Washington, D.C., demonstrates the potential usefulness of inter-governmental cooperation. On January 9, 1995, the IITF's Telecommunications Policy Committee (TPC) (chaired by NTIA's Administrator Larry Irving), and the Annenberg Washington Program co-sponsored a Federal-State-Local Telecom Summit. With the keynote address delivered by Vice President Gore, political leaders and senior government officials met in Washington, D.C., to address issues of mutual interest concerning the future of advanced telecommunications and the role of each level of government. In addition to a series of remarks presented by elected officials, break-out sessions on six major issues took place. The purpose of those sessions was to give federal, state, and local officials the opportunity to exchange views and to forge an agenda, or action plan, for going forward on the issues. One of the most successful of the break-out groups involved universal service. Agreed-upon principles included:

- access to a basic level of telecommunications capacity should be available at affordable, just, and reasonable prices. Any changes in legislation or regulation should continue the universal service policy objective first established in the Communications Act of 1934.

- federal and state universal service policies should ensure that telecommunications providers contribute to the maintenance of universal service on an equitable, and competitively neutral, basis.

Both became bedrock principles in legislative bills introduced by Congress and, ultimately, the Telecommunications Act of 1996.

An on-going Commerce Department grant program exemplifies a successful collaboration of public and private sector interests. NTIA's Telecommunications Information Infrastructure Assistance Program (TIIAP) is a competitive, merit-based, grant program that provides seed money for promising technology projects throughout the United States (see Chapter 11 for a detailed discussion of this programme). TIIAP provides these grants on a matching basis to non-profit organisations such as schools, libraries, hospitals, public safety entities, and state and local governments. During its first two years of operation (1994 and 1995), the program awarded 209 grants in 47 States, the District of Columbia, and several territories, with TIIAP monies equalling less than 60 percent of non-Federal (including private sector) funds. The grants are targeted to help children in rural areas and inner cities gain electronic access to information; bring improved health care to those who are frail or incapacitated, or who live in remote regions; provide worker training and new job opportunities in economically depressed areas; and enhance public safety by extending emergency telephone service throughout the country.

Universal Service Working Group

Under the aegis of the Administration's TPC, the Universal Service Working Group (USWG) has the broad mission to help ensure that all Americans have access to, and can enjoy the benefits of, the NII. The NTIA's Administrator chairs the USWG, whose members are federal officials. The group focuses on two basic activities: interacting with the IITF, and engaging in public outreach. In the latter capacity, the USWG conducted field hearings on universal service around the country. It is to this cooperative venture that we now turn.

During 1993 and 1994, the NTIA co-sponsored five universal service field hearings with several state governments (NTIA 1994a). The primary objective of the hearings was to determine how the concept of universal service could be made more consistent with the needs of Americans today and in the 21st century. Hearings were purposely held in diverse settings, including areas that could be characterized as rural and poor; inner city and low income; rural and high-technology; urban and high-technology; and, finally, a mixture of these demographics (in a city appropriately nicknamed "the Crossroads of America"). Each hearing featured a board consisting of the Commerce Department, the NTIA, the Federal Communications Commission, and state representatives (usually public service commissions). Witnesses numbered 230, involving 41 hours of hearings, and 1,400 pages of transcript. Attendance totalled 1,145. A variety of exhibitors held technology demonstrations during four of the five hearings. Benefits of the hearings and demonstrations included collecting useful information, and creating the opportunity to share knowledge with respect to policy analysis and technological advances.

Several basic themes arose during the hearings, which may have been unmatched historically in their breadth of outreach with respect to universal service issues. Most generally, researchers found that a consensus exists that government has an important role to play in ensuring that the goals of universal service and open access are achieved in a multi-provider environment. The testimony produced related themes that seem almost a cliche in 1997, but may not have been widely accepted then: local competition should be promoted where feasible; competition and universal service may coexist; and residential ratepayers should be protected where the market fails.

A number of themes relating to various facets of universal service characterized the proceedings. The record showed that despite the availability of affordable basic telephone service for many Americans, the traditional universal service, or "Plain Old Telephone Service" (POTS), goal has not been fully achieved. Many witnesses believe that the universal service goal should be redefined to include more than POTS. The hearings also brought forth evidence that rural areas pose special problems relating to high costs and unattractiveness of entry, as well as opportunities - such as economic development - for public policy. There was widespread support for the notion that all Americans, including those groups with special needs such as the disabled community, should be able to access the NII.

Funding became a particularly complex subject for participants. They testified that traditional funding mechanisms for universal service may not be adequate in the new competitive environment. Multiple service providers - some of whom are non-traditional - are beginning to emerge in local markets.

There is considerable support for requiring all service providers in a given area to contribute towards the maintenance of universal service. Many also asserted that any support should be targeted at those truly in need.

Public outreach did not end with the five field hearings. In November 1994, the NTIA and the TPC's USWG held one of the first-ever government-sponsored electronic - or "virtual" - conferences on various aspects of universal service and open access. The conference received more than 900 comments from private locations and 78 public access points around the country. The aforementioned Federal-State-Local Summit created the opportunity for the various levels of government to exchange views on universal service and other pressing issues. And informal contacts occur virtually daily on this most important topic.

Laying the Foundation

In the Fall of 1994, the NTIA issued a comprehensive Notice of Inquiry on universal service and open access, shaped by what the agency had learned during the course of the hearings (NTIA 1994b). Two developments spurred the need to re-examine the definition of universal service. First, information is a vital economic resource and a source of individual empowerment. Second, technological change - the convergence of computers and communications, and the deployment of high-capacity digital transmission facilities - placed new capabilities within reach of the public. Parties submitted some 98 comments, or reply comments, in the proceeding.

What did the inquiry discover? It revealed a system under stress. Current pricing policies are inefficient. The emergence of competition has undermined the existing subsidy structure. We found, anecdotally, that some important segments of the population are currently without telephone service, let alone access to advanced networks.

The Notice of Inquiry proceeding marked a turning point of sorts with respect to the Administration's efforts to modify the universal service concept: the primary emphasis began to change from solely public outreach to an approach which also stresses the development of empirical findings and, ultimately, specific policy recommendations. The aforementioned *Falling Through the Net* sought to identify in a systematic way which groups and geographic areas suffered from deficient access to telephone service and to the Internet (NTIA 1995a). After identifying under-served communities, the NTIA concluded that: "[t]hese communities need to know what technologies and applications are available, what existing infrastructure they have and need, and what has worked for similar communities..." (NTIA 1995b).

In response, the agency published its *Survey of Rural Information Infrastructure Technologies* (NTIA 1995c). The report describes what voice, computer, and video telecommunications services and information applications are available in rural areas. It also surveys various wireline and wireless systems and technologies that are being used, or might be used, to deliver these services to remote, or otherwise needy, areas.

Where Do We Go from Here?

Recent technological, economic, and societal changes have forced a fundamental re-examination of universal service as a standing public policy. The challenge for policy-makers is basically two-fold. First, there is a need to develop a concept of universal service that fits the challenges and opportunities of the information society. Second, a new mechanism must be found to provide support to the information-disadvantaged that is sustainable in a competitive environment. With the passage of a new Telecommunications Act, the dimensions of universal service in this country are being modified (see chapter 15). Access to advanced telecommunications and information services has reached an unprecedented level as a policy matter, and newly-designated participants in the modernized universal service - schools and libraries - have become eligible to receive preferential rates in acquiring connections to the NII. In participating in the public debate before the independent Federal Communications Commission - now charged with many facets of implementing the Act's provisions - the Administration will continue to help those who might otherwise be unable to access a new tomorrow.

References

Belinfante, Alexander (1995), Telephone Subscribership in the United States (Washington, D.C: Federal Communications Commission), December 1995.

Clinton, William J. and Albert Gore, Jr. (1993), Technology for America's Economic Growth: A New Direction to Build Economic Strength (Washington, D.C: U.S. Government Printing Office), February 1993.

Clinton, William J. (1994), State of the Union Address (Washington, D.C.).

Clinton, William J. (1996), State of the Union Address (Washington, D.C.).

Gore, Albert (1993), Remarks delivered at September 15, 1993 Press Conference announcing plans to create a new national information infrastructure, Washington, D.C.

Gore, Albert (1994), Remarks before the Academy of Television Arts and Sciences, Los Angeles, California, January 11, 1994.

Information Infrastructure Task Force (1993), National Information Infrastructure: Agenda for Action, 58 Fed. Reg. 49,025 (1993).

McClure et al. (1994), McClure, Charles R., John Carlo Bertot, and Douglas L. Zweizig, Public Libraries and the Internet: Study Results, Policy Issues, and Recommendations (Washington, D.C: U.S. National Commission on Libraries and Information Science), June 1994.

NIIAC (1996), U.S. Advisory Council on the National Information Infrastructure, Kick-Start Initiative: Connecting America's Communities to the Information Superhighway (West Publishing), January 1996.

National Telecommunications and Information Administration:

NTIA (1994a), NII Field Hearings on Universal Service and Open Access: AMERICA SPEAKS OUT (Springfield, Virginia: National Technical Information Service), September 1994.

NTIA (1994b), Inquiry on Universal Service and Open Access, 59 Fed. Reg. 48,112 (1994).

NTIA (1995a), Jim McConnaughey, Cynthia Nila, and Tim Sloan, FALLING THROUGH THE NET: A Survey of The `Have Nots' in Rural and Urban America (Washington, D.C.: National Telecommunications and Information Administration), July 1995.

NTIA (1995b), Irving, Larry, Remarks before Educom's National Net '95, Washington, D.C., April 6, 1995.

NTIA (1995c), Survey of Rural Information Infrastructure Technologies (Boulder, Colorado: National Telecommunications and Information Administration), September 1995.

NCES (1995), National Center for Education Statistics, Advanced Telecommunications in U.S. Public Schools, K-12 (Washington, D.C: U.S. Government Printing Office).

U.S. Council of Economic Advisers (1994), Economic Benefits of the Administration's Legislative Proposals for Telecommunications (Washington, D.C.: Executive Office of the President).

14. Universal Service in the European Union Telecommunications Sector

Marcel Haag and Louisa Gosling

Introduction

The telecommunications sector in the European Union (EU) is currently undergoing a process of rapid transformation. Following the political agreement by the member states in two Council resolutions of July 1993 and December 1994[1], the European Commission, between October 1994 and March 1996, adopted a series of four directives[2] introducing the legal obligation on member states to take the necessary measures to ensure the full liberalisation of the sector by 1 January 1998. The progressive opening of European telecommunications markets has resulted in the restructuring of telecommunications operators, and has encouraged the privatisation of the incumbent telecommunications organisations in a number of member states. At the same time, technological progress facilitates the emergence of new services and networks,

---

1   Council Resolution of 22 July 1993 on the review of the situation in the telecommunications sector and the need for further development in that market, OJ No C 213, 06.08.1993, p. 1; Council Resolution of 22 December 1994 on the principle and timetable for the liberalisation of telecommunications infrastructures, OJ No C 379, 31.12.1994, p. 4.
2   Commission Directive of 13 October 1994 amending Directive 88/301/EEC and Directive 90/388/EEC in particular with regard to satellite communications, OJ No L 268, 19.10.1994, p. 15; Commission Directive 95/51/EC of 18 October 1995 amending Directive 90/388/EEC with regard to the abolition of the restrictions on the use of cable television networks for the provision of already liberalized telecommunications services, OJ No L 256, 26.10.96, p. 49; Commission Directive 96/2/EC of 16 January 1996 amending Directive 90/388/EEC with regard to mobile and personal communications, OJ No L 20, 26.01.1996, p. 59; Commission Directive 96/19/EC of 13 March 1996 amending Directive 90/388/EC with regard to the implementation of full competition in telecommunications markets, OJ No L 74, 22.03.1996, p. 13.

leading to the rapidly growing importance of electronic communications for the general economy of the EU, and for numerous aspects of citizens' daily lives.

In line with these developments, and following the publication of its White Paper in 1994 on *Growth, Competitiveness and Employment*[3], the European Commission has prioritized the creation of the information society in Europe. In this context, the development and maintenance of a universal service in telecommunications has become a widely-discussed issue. This chapter describes the development of the universal service concept at the EU level; the implementation of universal service obligations in existing European Community (EC) legislation; and the current state of the debate.

The Origins of a Universal Service Discussion at EU Level

Before the liberalisation of the telephony and network provision activities of the telecommunications sector became an EU agenda item, the issue of universal service did not really surface as a topic. The 1987 Green Paper on Telecommunications only mentioned universal service in the context of justifying why, at the time, telephony services should not be liberalized: it stated that, in tariffing telecommunications services, a balance had to be found between the universal service obligations of telecommunications organisations, and the cost orientation of tariffs.[4] The reason for the absence of any in-depth discussion on universal service was that the issue was considered to be an internal national matter since, at the time, each member state still maintained special and exclusive rights over their national telecommunications organisations.

However, it should be noted that, from the outset[5], EC measures on Open Network Provision (ONP) included elements of a harmonized European defi-

---

3 European Commission, Growth, Competitiveness, Employment - The Challenges and ways forward into the 21st century, White Paper, Brussels-Luxembourg, 1994.

4 European Commission, Towards a Dynamic European Economy - Green Paper on the development of the common market for telecommunications services and equipment, COM (87) 290, 30.06.1987.

5 These elements are listed in the Commission statement concerning the Council resolution on universal service in the telecommunications sector, OJ No C 48, 16.02.1994, p. 8.

nition of universal service. From its beginnings in the 1980s, EC telecommunications policy also included regional policy objectives - for example, in the framework of the STAR programme[6] - and initiatives encouraging the development of trans-European communications[7].

The debate broadened after 1992, following the EC's review of the telecommunications sector in Europe[8], and the consequent political decision to fully liberalize that sector by 1st January 1998. This political decision implied that, despite the necessity to take national variables into account, the issue of universal service could no longer be entirely handled at the level of individual member states. Universal service obligations and financing mechanisms can create barriers to market entry and can distort competition. Therefore, it became essential to ensure that universal service obligations were based on common principles which conformed with the EC Treaty - in particular, the principles concerning the internal market objective, and the competition rules.

The discussion centered around a Communication from the Commission of 15 November 1993, which set out the EC's position on the issue[9]. This position was further elaborated in the second section of the Commission's Green Paper on the *Liberalisation of Telecommunications Infrastructures and Cable Television Networks*[10]. The Council of Telecommunications' Ministers[11] and

---

6 Cf. Council Regulation of 27 October 1986 instituting an EC programme for the development of certain less favoured regions of the EC by improving access to advanced telecommunications services (STAR programme), OJ No L 305, 31.10.1986, p. 1.
7 Cf. Council Decision of 25 July 1985 on a definition phase for an EC action in the field of telecommunications technologies - R&D programme in advanced communications technologies for Europe (RACE), OJ No L 210, 07.08.1985, p. 24.
8 European Commission, 1992 review of the situation in the telecommunications services sector, SEC (92) 1048, 21.10.1992; European Commission, Communication on the consultation on the review of the situation in the telecommunications sector, COM (93) 159, 28.04.1993.
9 European Commission, Developing universal service for telecommunications in a competitive environment, and Proposal for a Council Resolution on universal service principles in the telecommunications sector, COM (93) 543, 15.11.1993
10 COM (94) 682 final, 25.01.1995.
11 Council Resolution of 7 February 1994 on universal service principles in the telecommunications sector, OJ No C 48, 16.02.1994, p. 1; Council Resolution of 18 September 1995 on the implementation of the future regulatory framework for telecommunications, OJ No C 258, 01.03.1995, p. 1.

the European Parliament[12] then adopted resolutions which essentially confirmed the position taken by the Commission. For the purposes of the debate, universal service was defined as a minimum set of basic telecommunications services offered to all customers at an affordable price, including targeted schemes for groups of users with specific needs. The minimal definition of universal service excludes the concept of public access to information services.

This notion of universal service does not cover all public interest objectives that can legitimately be pursued in the telecommunications sector under EC law. It is limited to the definition of a universal service which can be financed through contributions generated by undertakings within the sector. In particular, it does not exclude that other offerings may be subsidized, or otherwise stimulated. The Treaty provides for a number of instruments in this respect. Examples can be found in the provisions on Social and Economic Cohesion (Articles 130a to 130e); on Trans-European Networks (Articles 129b to 129d); on Social Policy, Education and Vocational Training (Articles 117 to 127); on Culture (Article 128); and on Research and Technological Development (Articles 130f to 130p).

The debate generated by the Commission's communication of 1993 focused on four questions, which we consider in turn.

The Scope of Universal Service

The Communication argued in favour of a narrow definition of universal service, primarily to avoid creating excessive entry barriers against new competitors. Therefore, the Commission concluded that universal service should, in principle, cover a basic telephony service.

---

12 European Parliament, Resolution of 6 May 1994 on the communication from the Commission accompanied by the proposal for a Council resolution on universal service principles in the telecommunications sector (A3-0317/94), OJ No C 205, 25.07.1994, p. 551; Resolution of 19 May 1995 on the Green Paper on the liberalisation of telecommunications infrastructure and cable television networks - Part II (A4-0111/95), OJ No C 151, 19.06.1995, p. 479.

The Nature of the Definition

Given the rapidity of technological and market developments, an EU consensus emerged that universal service should be regarded as an evolutionary, rather than a static, concept. However, any widening of the agreed initial definition should be carefully assessed.

The Financing Mechanism

The principle was recognized that exclusive or special rights were not necessary for financing the provision of universal service. Unlike other areas such as the postal services[13], it was accepted that the telecommunications sector would benefit from invoking financial mechanisms other than the maintenance of special or exclusive rights over the provision of universal service. The problem identified was that that particular financial mechanism may restrict the economic freedom of other market participants, and that, therefore, it would be disproportionate to retain it.

During the discussions, the Commission indicated that it would give preference to the establishment of a universal service fund, but that it could also accept, under certain circumstances, the use of supplementary charges as a means of financing universal service. This should not, however, be confused with the maintenance of cross-subsidies to finance the access deficits caused by unbalanced tariffs. The Commission made clear that universal service obligations should not prevent telecommunications organisations from progressively re-balancing their tariffs.

Monitoring

There was a broad consensus that certain principles should be set out at EC level, but that the implementation and administration of a universal service

---

13 Cf. European Commission, Proposal for a European Parliament and Council Directive on common rules for the development of Community postal services and the improvement of quality of service, OJ No C 322, 02.12.1995, p. 22, and Draft notice from the Commission on the application of the competition rules to the postal sector and in particular on the assessment of certain state measures relating to postal services, OJ No C 322, 02.12.1995, p. 3.

framework should be a matter for national authorities. However, the Commission would act to ensure that member states were in conformity with EC law, in particular with regard to competition rules.

On the basis of this discussion, the Commission submitted draft directives to set out the legal requirements at EC level regarding universal service.

Universal Service in Community Directives

Community secondary law currently sets out a framework for the provision of universal service in telecommunications in three directives: in the Commission Directive of 13 March 1996 on full competition in telecommunications markets[14], and in the two proposed ONP Directives on Interconnection and on Voice Telephony.[15]

The main objective of the directive on full competition in telecommunications markets is to fully liberalize the telecommunications sector in the EU by 1st January 1998. In order to effectively achieve this objective, the directive is not just confined to requiring that member states lift all special and exclusive rights over their telecommunications networks and services. In addition, it also sets out some basic requirements of the regulatory frameworks that member states must put in place to permit new entrants to exploit the market.

The directive allows member states to introduce a national scheme to share the net cost of universal service obligations between operators. At the same time, member states are required to allow their telecommunications operators to re-balance their tariffs, in order to achieve a tariff structure based on real costs. The universal service scheme may take the form of a universal service fund, or a system of supplementary charges. However, according to Article 4c, the scheme may only apply to undertakings which provide public tele-

---

14 See footnote 2 above.
15 Proposal for a European Parliament and Council Directive on interconnection in telecommunications with regard to ensuring universal service and interoperability through the application of the principles of open network provision (ONP), OJ No C 313, 24.11.1995, p. 7, and Common Position (EC) No 34/96 adopted by Council on 18 June 1996, OJ No C 220, 29.07.1996, p. 13; Proposal for a European Parliament and Council Directive on the application of open network provision (ONP) to voice telephony and on universal service for telecommunications in a competitive environment, COM (96) 419, 11.09.1996.

communications networks, and must allocate the burden according to objective and non-discriminatory criteria, and in accordance with the principle of proportionality. The application of the principle of proportionality allows member states to exempt new entrants which have not yet achieved a significant market presence.

The directive requires member states to notify any universal service scheme to the Commission. In addition, it provides for the Commission to review the situation with regard to universal service financing schemes within the member states by 1st January 2003, i.e., five years after the full liberalisation date.

While the full competition directive sets out the minimum requirements necessary to ensure compliance with the competition rules of the Treaty, the two ONP directives harmonize universal service regulation at a more detailed level.

The proposed ONP Interconnection Directive sets out the rules for calculating the cost of universal service obligations, and for calculating the corresponding contributions to be made by telecommunications operators. In the proposed directive on the application of ONP to voice telephony, the scope of universal service is defined. According to the provisions of this directive, the universal telecommunications service that member states must ensure - and the provision of which may be financed through a universal service funding scheme - covers the following elements:

- a connection to the fixed public telephone network, which supports the sending and receiving of (inter)national calls, and which also supports speech, facsimile and/or data communications;
- access to publicly available telephone services;
- directory services;
- public pay-telephones; and,
- specific measures for disabled users, and users with special needs.

However, directory services may only be financed through a universal service financing scheme in cases where no organisation is willing to provide such services. Member states must ensure that these services are available throughout their territory at an affordable price.

Thus, between them, the three directives establish a comprehensive legal framework for a universal telecommunications service at EU level.

The Current Discussion of the Universal Service Concept at EU Level

Alongside the principles and framework for defining and financing universal service in a competitive environment which were set down in the Full Competition Directive and the ONP draft Directives on Interconnection and on Voice Telephony, the Commission has also published two theme papers in 1996 which feed into the discussion of the development of universal service in Europe. In March 1996 it published a Communication entitled *Universal Service for Telecommunications in the Perspective of a Fully Liberalized Environment*[16]. Later in that year the Commission issued a more general Communication on *Services of General Interest in Europe*[17] addressing the broader question of public services across various sectors in the changing environment of the late 1990s.

Let us first consider the contents of the March 1996 Communication. It addresses the context of the legal framework for universal service, and sets the underlying universal service concept in perspective. It discusses the need to clarify and limit the definition of universal service for the purposes of the 1998 regulatory framework. The definition covers the provision of affordable access to everyone to a network of voice, data, and fax transmission, together with a voice telephony service. It also includes targeted service to those in special need. The Communication explains that this limited concept is to underpin the framework of costing and funding universal service; it is to act as the "firm anchor for the regulatory reforms under way at a national level to achieve the full liberalisation of telecommunications." It highlights that if additional telecoms-related obligations are imposed by member states on certain operators, then the additional financial burden must not be funded out of the mechanism established for funding universal service.

It is, on the other hand, emphasised that universal service is recognized to be a dynamic concept which must evolve according to needs, demands, and technological progress. So although the scope is clearly defined and limited in the context of the initial 1998 regulatory framework, it is certainly not set in stone. Changing conditions need to be monitored and assessed. To this end, the Communication announces that the Commission will report by January

---

16 COM (96) 73, 13.03.1996.
17 COM (96) 443, 11.09.1996.

1998 "on the scope, level, quality and affordability of universal service in the Community and consider the need...for adaptation of the scope". The need, however, to maintain a predictable environment to facilitate sound investment decisions is also recognized.

The concept of public access is raised in this context, especially vis-a-vis new services - for example, interactive audio-visual, Internet, or on-line data services - not included in the definition of universal service. Specifically, this addresses the question of funding enhanced access points in public areas such as libraries, educational establishments, and hospitals. The Communication acknowledges that progress in this area should be kept under review.

However, it also recognizes that developing an "information society" raises many other issues which, while they are clearly important, are beyond the appropriate scope of universal service in telecoms. Policies which regulate the provision of universal service should not be relied upon to provide - nor be confused with - an overall EU policy for the information society. It is recognized that national policies aimed at education, healthcare, and social concerns (together with their associated government funding mechanisms) should have a significant role to play in this context.

As to affordability, the universal service Communication establishes that particular measures (e.g., price caps and targeted tariff schemes) can, and should, be taken to ensure affordability for all users, regardless of their physical or economic situation. It notes that the framework for financing universal service is laid down, as described above, in the Interconnection and Full Competition Directive. More specific EU guidelines for assessing national approaches to costing and funding were issued to the member states in October 1996.

We will now consider the second 1996 communication mentioned earlier. The Communication from the Commission on *Services of General Interest*[18]

---

18 The term "service of general interest" covers market and non-market services which the public authorities class as being of general interest, and subject to specific public service obligations. The term used in Article 90 of the Treaty refers "services of general economic interest" which is, in fact, a subset of the former - referring specifically to market services which the member states subject to specific public service obligations by virtue of a general interest criterion.

in Europe must be seen in the context of the 1996 Intergovernmental Conference and, in particular, of the lobbying by some interests for a Treaty amendment that might address the perceived tension between the goals of public service on the one hand, and those of liberalisation and the open internal market on the other. Alongside the telecoms sector, the Communication specifically addresses four other key sectors where general interest goals increasingly need to be made coherent with those of competitiveness and market liberalisation. These are: postal services, transport, electricity, and broadcasting.

The document is also a response to new worries about employment and economic and social cohesion, and to the implicit or explicit challenges to the substance, and use by the Commission, of Article 90 of the EC Treaty[19] in this context. It concludes that existing Treaty instruments adequately allow for a balance to be struck between the principle of open markets and public interest objectives.

The stated aim of the Communication is to "reaffirm the principles of [the Commission's] policies (vis a vis services of general interest) and set out its objectives for the future". It particularly emphasises the challenge of subsidiarity[20] on the one hand, and of adjustments to a rapidly changing context[21]

The more common term "public service" tends to be avoided since it is prone to ambiguity: it may refer either to the actual body providing the service, or to the general interest role assigned to the body concerned. Also, there is often confusion between the term "public service" which relates to the vocation to render a service to the public (i.e., referring to what service is to be provided), and the term "public sector" which relates specifically to the legal status of those providing the service in terms the ownership of the undertaking.

19 According to Article 90, public undertakings and undertakings enjoying special and exclusive rights granted by a member state are, in principle, subject to the rules of the Treaty, and in particular to the internal market and the competition rules. In allows the Commission to adopt Directives to ensure compliance with this principle. The Article has been used as the legal basis for the liberalisation of the telecommunications sector in Europe.

20 The Communication specifically notes:
"Respect for national choice over economic and social organisation is a clear example of subsidiarity in action. It is for the Member States to make the fundamental choice concerning their society, whereas the job of the Community is merely to ensure that the means they employ are compatible with their European commitments"

on the other. This adds new complexities to the question of coordinating the goals of public service and those of market liberalisation and competitiveness in these economically important sectors[22].

The EU concept of universal service, defined in terms of principles and practice, is set out. The principles are essentially those of equality, universality, continuity, and adaptability. Sound practices include openness in management, price setting and funding, and scrutiny by bodies independent of those operating the services.

The discussion in the Communication of broadcasting public services alongside that of telecommunications services is noteworthy. The main piece of EU legislation relating to the broadcasting sector is the so-called "TV Without Frontiers" Directive of 1989[23]. For the purposes of freedom of movement of TV programmes throughout the EU, it coordinates national rules regarding production and distribution, advertising and sponsorship, the protection of minors, and the right of reply. It also recognizes that national rules relating to other considerations concerning content - that is, those linked to moral, democratic, and cultural values - are outside the EU framework.

New interactive audio-visual services which blur the boundaries between telecommunications and broadcasting are addressed in the review of the 1989 Directive. Although not complete in 1996, the draft revision excludes these services from the remit of public service broadcasting (i.e., for the purpose of effective exemptions to EU competition and internal market rules). As already mentioned, the EU definition of telecommunications public service (i.e., for

---

Different circumstances and practice may constitute a challenge for European integration. The Communication stresses, however, that such diversity may also be seen as an advantage in terms of the opportunities for drawing up models, and evaluating various experiences, within the EU and thus identifying some sort of benchmark or "best practice" criterion. Thus, greater coordination and information exchange in this context should be encouraged.

21 Technical change, the globalization of the economy and users expectations.

22 Their significance, in particular to overall European competitiveness, is underlined. For instance, public sector companies, which provide only some of these services, account for around nine percent of employment, 11 percent of non-agricultural activity, and 16 percent of investment within the EC.

23 Council Directive on the co-ordination of certain provisions laid down by law, regulation, or administrative action in member states concerning the pursuit of television broadcasting activities, OJ No L 298, 17.10.1989.

the purpose of funding from the national universal service scheme) also excludes new services such as interactive audio-visual and Internet services.

The Commission highlights that, in order to effectively maintain the sensitive balance, and smooth interplay, between the requirements of the single market[24] and those of the "general interest", it is essential that thought is given to the question of the right tools for the right tasks. The specific mechanism to be put in place for ensuring universal telecommunications service in the context of liberalisation and encouragement of market entry (where there are already significant, and entrenched, barriers to entry) is clearly not the best mechanism for also addressing much broader goals concerning education, social cohesion, and the so-called information society.

The Commission's Communication concludes: "Article 90 has proved its worth in fully guaranteeing the beneficial interaction between liberalisation and general interest. It is best left untouched". However, it should be noted that alongside this, the Communication also advocates that a new reference might by inserted in the Treaty in Article 3, which would refer to "a contribution to promotion of services of general interest". This, in essence, would more clearly establish that general interest services are to be taken into account by the EU institutions when drawing up policy and planning activities. At the same time, it would not impinge on the application of the Treaty competition and internal market rules.

Conclusion

The EC's telecommunications policy is based on the position that ensuring universal service and creating a competitive environment are not conflicting objectives. Based on experience gained in a number of countries, the EC's approach consists in stimulating the provision of universal service through opening up the telecommunications market. In this context, universal service obligations, and the financing of their net cost, are intended to provide an instrument to buffer the possible negative impact of the full liberalisation of the market.

---

24 In terms of free movement, economic performance, dynamism and progress.

At the same time, the EC is committed to the promotion of a range of social, societal, and cultural objectives for shaping the emerging information society. It is crucial for the future development of the telecommunications sector in Europe that these objectives are not confused with the more limited goal of ensuring an universal telecommunications service, as this would have a negative impact on investment and growth in this market. The temptation to place additional heavy financial burdens on the telecommunications sector should be resisted.

Annex

Date	Action
Before 30 June 1996	Proposal for a European Parliament and Council Directive amending the Voice Telephony Directive
	Member states commence drafting authorisation schemes for voice telephony and public network providers as provided by the Full Competition Directive
	Member states concerned apply for derogations to the 1998 deadline, and provide all economic data necessary for the assessment of the justification of such derogation, as provided by the Full Competition Directive
	Common Position on the ONP Interconnection Directive (including principles for the costing and funding of universal service)
	Common Position on the proposed European Parliament and Council Directive on a common framework for general authorisations and individual licences in the European Community
Before 30 September 1996	Communication on the Commission criteria for costing and funding of the universal telephone service in the EC
Before 31 December 1996	Common position on the proposal for a Council and European Parliament Directive amending the Voice Telephony Directive
	Adoption of the ONP Interconnection Directive
	Adoption of the Licensing Directive
	Communication by the member states of authorisation schemes for voice telephony and provision of public telecommunications networks including obligations related to universal services

Before 30 June 1997	Decisions of the Commission on the authorisation schemes submitted
	Publication in the member states of information required by the Full Competition Directive with regard to licensing procedures and terms and conditions for interconnection
	Adoption of the proposal for a Council and European Parliament Directive amending the Voice Telephony Directive
Before 1st January 1998	Full liberalisation of telecommunications services and networks, subject to possible transitional arrangements for certain member states, where justified and subject to scrutiny
	First Commission Report on the monitoring of the scope, level, quality, and affordability of the universal telephone service in the Community

Table 1: *Time Table for EU Short Term Action (1996-1998) related to Universal Service*[25]

---

25 Source: European Commission, Universal Service for Telecommunications in the Perspective of a fully liberalized environment - An Essential Element of the Information Society, COM (96) 73 final, 13.03.1996, p. 25.

15. A High Wire Act in a Highly Wired World: Universal Service and the Telecommunications Act of 1996

Andrew Blau[1]

Introduction

In February 1996, the U.S. Congress passed historic legislation to rewrite the rules under which almost every part of the U.S. communications industry has operated since the Communications Act of 1934 was enacted during the Great Depression. The "Telecommunications Act of 1996"[2] provides a new, national policy framework that relies on competition and market forces to accelerate the deployment of advanced communications infrastructure throughout the country. Lawmakers are also counting on competition to lower prices, improve services, and stimulate the overall growth of this sector. In addition, the Act includes special provisions to extend telecommunications service to public schools, libraries, and rural health care facilities. The Act touches almost every aspect of communications from telephone services (including local, long-distance, and wireless), to free, over-the-air broadcast television, cable television, and content and programming on television and computer networks including the Internet.

---

1   The author would like to acknowledge the substantial contributions of Kevin Taglang, Policy Analyst on the Benton staff, who prepared much of the research upon which the sections that discuss the Telecommunications Act and regulatory interpretations are based. In addition, Susan Goslee, also a member of the Benton policy team, provided invaluable editorial advice and perspective. This work draws extensively on papers and resources in Benton Foundations's Universal Service Virtual Library (www.benton.org/cpphome.html).

2   Telecommunications Act of 1996, Pub. Law No. 104-104, 110 Stat. 56 (1996). Hereinafter, the "Act".

Like any complex legislation hammered out after years of effort, the Act reflects the unresolved conflicts and fragile compromises that allowed it to make its way through the legislature and gain the President's signature. In particular, the Act's attempt to balance competition as the favored policy tool against the political necessity of maintaining universal service schemes was seen by some as fundamentally inconsistent. Universal service had been part of the monopoly-based system, where low-cost, high-volume users (e.g., business users, urban users) subsidized those whose costs were higher (e.g., rural users) or those for whom it was a policy priority to keep service affordable (e.g., residences). Maintaining this balancing act was critical to passing the bill into law, even if implementing it, which falls to Federal and state regulators, will be difficult and likely to be contested in the courts.

This paper will sketch the history of the national commitment to universal service, as well as the pressures for increased competition and expanded services that forced U.S. policy makers to reframe how that commitment would be supported. It will then summarize the 1996 Act as it pertains to universal service, noting the new principles, priorities and institutions that Congress added to the universal service scheme. The paper will also briefly review the steps to develop these policies, including expected action by the Federal Communications Commission ("FCC"), the role of the states, and the prospects for legal challenges. Finally, it will outline an alternative approach to universal service that could accommodate a multicarrier, multiservice, fully competitive environment.

As we will see, the high wire act of balancing the pressure for open, competitive markets against the pressure for keeping basic communications services affordable and available to all will take the skills of accomplished regulatory acrobats in the increasingly "wired" world of converging technologies, services, and providers.

A Brief History of Universal Service, 1907 – 1995

The commitment to making basic, voice-grade telephone service universal originally came not from policy makers or consumers but from industry leaders. In particular, the first articulation of universal service as a policy goal is widely credited to AT&T's President, Theodore Vail, in the company's Annual Report for 1907.

As Mueller (1993 and 1996) reminds us though, this goal was principally dressing for an argument against the growing number of competing telephone networks that did not connect to one another. Ironically but importantly, the tension between an openly competitive market for telephony and the goal of universal service appears at the very invention of the term, and industry arguments for universal service have often cloaked efforts to stave off competition (Dordick 1991, 116).

The policy of universal service evolved beyond the interconnection controversy. By many accounts, the Communications Act of 1934 established a national policy of universal service in its preamble, which announced that the purpose of the legislation was

> to make available, so far as possible to all the people of the United States, a rapid, efficient, Nation-wide, and world-wide wire and radio communications service with adequate facilities at reasonable charges.

This language has been widely held up as evidence of a national commitment to both wireline and wireless services that extend to all people and which are affordable upon arrival.

That commitment began to take familiar shape in the early 1950s as the first outlines emerged of a system that used long-distance revenues to hold residential rates low.[3] The telephone company ratebase was split into interstate and intrastate jurisdictions, and growing profits from long-distance services were directed to subsidize rates for local service. The underlying system of "separations" was formally recognized with the adoption of the "Ozark Plan" by state regulators in 1970.

From such simple beginnings, the effort to meet universal service policy goals resulted in a proliferation of formal and informal arrangements involving both explicit and implicit subsidies. Noam identifies twenty such

---

3   U.S. Senate Majority Leader Ernest McFarland (Democrat. - Arizona), who also chaired the Senate Communications Subcommittee, pushed for such an arrangement, which was adopted by state regulators. AT&T supported it as well as a political bargain. See, Noam (1995) 115-116.

"contributory elements" in place by the early 1990s that together support universal service goals.[4] (Noam 1993)

The best known elements of the universal service support system include: the Universal Service Fund that interstate carriers pay into to assist telephone companies serving high cost areas; access charges set above cost on interexchange carriers to use local facilities; toll pools within states for intrastate rate averaging; higher subscription charges on business lines than on residential lines; above cost prices for business-oriented services such as leased lines; above cost charges for features such as touch-tone, call forwarding, and caller-ID; averaged access charges; Rural Electrification Administration loans; and direct revenue contributions by government. (see Noam 1993, 8, Goldstein and Gooding 1995)

In addition, in recent years Federal and state regulators have created special programs targeted for low-income subscribers. The majority of universal service efforts aimed to keep basic rates within the means of most Americans, but by the early 1980s, it was clear that the poorest needed additional assistance. For them, policy makers created the Lifeline program, to offer very low monthly subscription rates (in some places, such as New York as low as $1.00 per month for limited local service), and the Link-Up America program, to help people not on the network get connected. The Link-Up program waived deposit fees and allowed payments for connection charges to be spread out over many months, among other features.

The Mounting Challenge to Traditional Arrangements

By the late 1980s, however, pressures were mounting that would undermine the support system upon which universal service efforts were based. Those pressures included the economic and political friction among the participants in the subsidy mechanisms; the growing interest in promoting competitive markets for telecommunications services by liberalizing entry requirements; the political interest in expanding what services should be universal; the awareness that telephone penetration had stalled by 1980; and the interest in

---

4   Note, too, that despite this extensive inventory, Noam suggests that other contributions, both implicit and explicit, exist to support universal service, especially within states.

extending the network to institutions such as schools and libraries as a means of expanding public access to advanced network services. Thus, the public claims on the system were growing while the underlying support systems were unravelling and the explicit goals of the system (maintaining and extending residential service) were no longer being met.

1. The break-up of the Bell System meant that the transfers between local service and long distance revenue became more problematic. Before the break-up, the transfers mostly took place within a single firm (AT&T) that believed that the subsidy system protected its political interests. Following divestiture, the transfers took place between companies with competing financial interests in the size of the transfers. By the end of the decade, those companies saw each other as potential rivals in their traditional markets, so the competing financial interests were joined by openly competing political interests as well.

2. The growing competition in the long-distance industry, followed by the emergence of competitive access providers for local service and the booming cellular industry suggested an increasingly competitive marketplace for telecommunications services. Economists predicted and regulators rightly feared that the new entrants would seek out those markets where rates had been set above costs because it was in those markets where they could most easily undercut the incumbents. The resulting competition would drive down the rates that were supporting the universal service efforts and could drain off the high-revenue subscribers who were paying those contributory rates. Yet there was an emerging political consensus that promoting head-to-head competition would be the favored policy tool for stimulating investment in advanced network technologies. The political interest in promoting competition was fundamentally at odds with the equally political reliance on subsidies that had maintained universal service goals.

3. Yet this interest in fostering competition, which would necessarily destabilize the universal service regime that had evolved over the previous 30 years, occurred at the same time that telecommunications firms were linked in the public mind with an expanding array of services. In the 1980s, companies were promoting advanced networking services for business users (e.g., frame relay, SMDS, leased lines, centrex, "intelligent network" services, etc.), to stimulate interest in the "enhanced" or "competitive"

services that regulators did not control. As a related matter, there were also efforts to position telecommunications firms as providers of socially desirable "public interest" services, such as education, health care, economic development, delivery of government benefits transactions, and political participation where pre-existing claims to universality had strong public support. One side effect of these campaigns was growing public appreciation for higher speed transport services, and a strand of policy arguments that basic telephone service should evolve toward broader bandwidth services that available to all.[5]

4. Gains toward achieving traditional universal service goals had levelled off around 1980. Following 30 years of strong and steady growth following the end of World War II, residential penetration hit 93% and stalled.[6] As such, while penetration idled around 93% for 15 years, the goal of truly universal service seemed to recede in light of the stalled progress toward traditional goals and the new pressures to expand the definition of what every home should get.

5. Finally, in the early-mid 1990s, network services not associated with traditional telecommunications carriers became exceedingly popular (i.e., the Internet for electronic mail and surfing the World Wide Web), and public interest grew in providing public access to these services, especially in conjunction with the broad range of socially beneficial public and quasi-public services described above. One result was pressure to wire schools, libraries, health institutions, and other institutions to enable them to become points of public access and platforms for community service.[7] Doing so as a matter of social policy, however, meant expanding the traditional

---

5   One version of this argument is made by Hadden (1993): "I believe it to be most effective to start with a list of features we want the network to exhibit... These features are the ones we hear about, and because they are now technically feasible, the whole issue of expanded universal service arises. Broadband - able to carry video signals in both directions along with voice and data." See, also, Alliance for Public Technology, "Connecting Each to All" (undated): "We believe that our nation cannot reap the full benefits from advances in telecommunications technology unless everyone has full access to a network that is capable of providing informational and transactional services using voice, high speed data, graphics and two-way video."
    Available at http://apt.org/apt/principles.html

6   Compare, for example, Cooper (1996) at p. 7, and Figure 2.1. See, also, Federal State Staff (1995), Table 1.1.

7   S. Rept. No. 230, 104th Cong., 2nd Sess. 1 (1996).

universal service concept from the residential subscriber who had always been its sole focus, to a new array of institutions who had never been part of the regulatory mix.

Break the Logjam or Roll with it?

Against that background, an avowedly anti-regulatory, pro-business Republican Congress passed the Telecommunications Act of 1996 "to provide for a pro-competitive, deregulatory national policy framework" designed to accelerate the "deployment of advanced telecommunications services... to all Americans by opening all telecommunications markets to competition." Thus, rather than resolve the long-simmering tension between competition and universal service, policy makers asserted that it was a case of mistaken identity. Competition was not the enemy of universal service at all; it was the most effective tool policy makers could wield to reach universal service goals. FCC Chairman Reed Hundt captured the new consensus in a speech to British officials:

> "When governments intervene in markets in the name of guaranteeing universal service, they generally don't make anything universal... [C]ompetition – far better than regulation – will promote widespread availability of telcom services."[8]

Yet the strong anti-regulatory rhetoric should not distract observers from recognizing that the Act expanded universal service in important ways. For the first time, Congress made it Federal law to:

- establish an unambiguous legislative underpinning for universal service and explicit principles upon which it would be based.
- require regulators to address the needs of rural areas and low-income consumers.
- expand the range of services to which universal service will apply, and initiate a regular process to expand it over time.

---

8   "Hundt outlines 'seven commandments' for telcom competition." FCC press release, September 6, 1996 (speech to the Royal Institute of International Affairs, London).

- ensure that rates for universal service must be "affordable," not only "just and reasonable," as regulatory tradition had established.
- extend the universal service tradition to consumers with disabilities.
- add institutional users – schools, libraries, and health care centers – to the class of subscribers who would be entitled to universal service.

The Act created a Joint Board of three Federal regulators from the FCC, four state regulators from public utility commissions around the country, and (in an remarkable break with tradition) one consumer advocate to consider how these goals should be met.[9] The Act required the Joint Board to make recommendations to the FCC by November 8, 1996, as to what services should be funded by Federal universal service support mechanisms, what mechanisms should be used to fund universal service efforts, which telecommunications carriers should contribute to the fund and be eligible for support from it, and how to implement the Act's provisions to connect schools, libraries, and health care institutions.

Following a round of public comments and replies that received almost 250 sets of comments (most submitted by groups of commenters, as the Joint Board had requested) and a supplemental round of additional questions for public comment, the Board issued its recommendations to the FCC on November 7. The Board made recommendations on the services that should be supported, stressed competitive neutrality, expanded programs for low-income consumers, and outlined historic discounts for public schools and libraries. The following subsections describe the Act's key provisions and the Joint Board's recommendations to implement them.

Principles for the Future of Universal Service

The Act identified six principles the Joint Board and the FCC must use as the basis for any new policies to preserve and advance universal service. It also provided the opportunity for the Joint Board to recommend additional princi-

---

9   On March 8, 1996, the FCC appointed Chairman Reed Hundt and Commissioners Rachelle Chong and Susan Ness to represent the FCC; State Commissioners Julia Johnson of Florida, Kenneth McClure of Missouri, Sharon Nelson of Washington, and Laska Schoenfelder of South Dakota to represent the states; and Missouri Public Counsel Martha Hogarty as the consumer advocate to the Board.

ples if the Board found it desirable to do so. Congress directed regulators to pay attention to:

Quality and rates. Quality services should be available at just, reasonable, and affordable rates.

Access to advanced services. Access to advanced telecommunications and information services should be provided in all regions of the nation.

Access in rural and high–cost areas. Consumers in every region, including low-income consumers and those in high-cost areas, should have access to telecommunications and information services similar to those in urban areas and at rates reasonably comparable to rates charged for those services in urban areas.

Equitable and nondiscriminatory contributions by providers to the preservation and advancement of Universal Service. All providers of telecommunications services should make equitable and nondiscriminatory contributions to preserve and advance universal service.

Specific and predictable support mechanisms. There should be specific, predictable, and sufficient federal and state mechanisms to preserve and advance Universal Service.

Access to advanced telecommunications services for schools, health care facilities, and libraries. Elementary and secondary schools and classrooms, health care providers, and libraries should have access to advanced telecommunications services.

Additional Principles. Such other principles as the Joint Board and the Commission determine are necessary and appropriate for the protection of the public interest, convenience, and necessity and are consistent with the Act.[10]

The Joint Board took the opportunity offered by the "additional principles" provision and recommended one: "competitive neutrality" for support mechanisms and rules. The Board sought both to ensure that contributions to universal service would be technology neutral and to clarify that "universal service support should not be biased toward any particular technologies." In addition, the Board suggested that this principle should be "applied to each and every recipient of or contributor to the universal service support mechanisms, regardless of size, status or geographic location."

---

10 Section 254(b) of the Act, "Universal service principles." (This list contains slight modifications of the original language for brevity.)

What Services Should Be Universal?

In establishing the definition of universal service, the Act directs the FCC to consider the extent to which any telecommunications service meets four essential tests: is it consistent with the public interest, convenience, and necessity; is it essential to education, public health, or public safety: is it being deployed in public telecommunications networks; and, has it through market forces been subscribed to by a substantial majority of residential customers.

The Joint Board recommended that universal service support be provided for: 1) voice grade access to the public switched network, including, at a minimum, some usage; 2) dual-tone multi-frequency (DTMF) signalling (e.g., touch tone) or its equivalent; 3) single-party service; 4) access to emergency services, including access to 911, where available; 5) access to operator services; 6) access to interexchange (long distance) services; and 7) access to directory assistance (but not the service itself).

Defining "Affordable"

The Act mandates that rates for universal service be not only just and reasonable but also "affordable." The Joint Board recommended that affordability must take into consideration both rates and other factors, including the scope of the local calling area, customer income level, and cost of living considered on a local rather than nationwide basis. The Board deferred any more explicit definition and recommended that the states exercise primary responsibility for determining affordability because states were closer to local conditions.[11]

Targeting Low-Income Consumers

The Joint Board made several important recommendations to strengthen and extend current universal service programs that serve low-income consumers. Among those recommendations, the Board suggested that Congress's intent would best be served if all low-income consumers had access to Lifeline assistance. The Board further recommended that the Lifeline program cover the

---

11 Cooper offers an extensive analysis of affordability as it applies to telecommunications services. See Cooper (1996), op. cit at footnote 6.

same group of services described above as the basic package for all customers. In addition, low-income consumers should get free access to voluntary toll limitation or blocking services to help them control costs. Carriers receiving universal service support for providing Lifeline service should be prohibited from disconnecting the local service for non-payment of toll charges. In addition, the Board recommended:

- prohibiting telecommunications carriers from requiring Lifeline-participating subscribers to pay service deposits in order to initiate service if the subscriber voluntarily elects to receive toll blocking.
- that support for low-income consumers no longer be funded through charges on only long distance carriers, but that all telecommunications carriers that provide interstate service should contribute on an equitable and nondiscriminatory basis as a function of revenues.
- enabling all eligible telecommunications carriers, not just LECs, to be able to receive support for serving qualified low-income consumers.
- that the Commission eliminate the state matching requirement and provide for a baseline level of federal support ($5.25) that would be available to low-income consumers in all states.

Connecting Schools, Libraries, and Rural Health Care Providers

The effort to expand universal service to support public and nonprofit schools, health care providers, and libraries is a particularly important new element, since it adds a class of beneficiaries that had not been part of universal service policy. The Commission is expected to establish rules to provide both basic and advanced telecommunications and information services to these entities. The FCC will also define the circumstances under which a carrier may be required to connect these public institutions to its network and at what rates.

The Act's provisions for health care providers are slightly different from those affecting schools and libraries, and the Act appears to treat advanced services to these three types of institutions separately from the guarantee of basic service.

Health care providers in rural areas. Telecommunications providers shall supply services to health care providers that serve rural residents at rates reasonably comparable to rates charged in urban areas. These rates are yet to be determined. The provision includes "services which are necessary for the provision of health care," as well as instruction related to those services.

Educational providers and libraries. Telecommunications providers are to provide schools and libraries with services defined in the universal service proceedings "at rates less than the amounts charged for similar services to other parties. The discount shall be an amount that the FCC, with respect to interstate services, and the states, with respect to intrastate services, determine is appropriate and necessary to ensure affordable access to and use of such services by such entities."

Advanced services. The FCC shall establish competitively neutral rules to enhance access to advanced telecommunications and information services for public and nonprofit classrooms, health care providers, and libraries.

In defining the scope of these legislative provisions for schools and libraries, the Board made the following recommendations:

- All eligible schools and libraries may receive discounts of between 20 and 90 percent on all telecommunications services, Internet access, and internal connections, subject to a $2.25 billion annual national cap. Companies would be reimbursed by the fund to cover the discounts they provide. The discount program would begin at the start of the 1997 - 1998 school year.
- The discounts would apply to the lowest price the school or library can negotiate on "whatever package of telecommunications services they believe will meet their telecommunications service needs most effectively and efficiently." Carriers however are required to provide service to a school or library at a rate no higher than the lowest rate offered to "similarly situated non-residential customers for similar services." In the context of competitive bidding, this rate would be the ceiling on the price offered to schools and libraries.
- Schools and libraries may receive discounts on charges for internal connections, as well as for all commercially available telecommunications services and Internet access and other information services. Internal connections, which may include such items as routers, hubs, network file servers, and wireless LANs, but not personal computers, will be included in the discount program.
- Schools and libraries should comply with self-certification requirements to ensure that "only eligible entities receive universal support and that they

have adopted plans for securing cost-effective access to and use of all of the services they purchase."

- Schools and libraries that are eligible to receive discounts under these provisions may join in buying consortia with customers who are not eligible for those discounts in order to lower prices overall. As before, the discount for the schools and libraries would apply to the lowest price the consortium could negotiate. The Board recommends that state commissions take steps to enable such consortia to be formed.

Below is the Board's proposed matrix for determining the discount a school or library would receive. For example, an urban school (probably in a "low cost" area) serving a school population with 20% of the students eligible for the school lunch program[12] would receive a 50% discount on the rate bid by a local telecommunications provider.

DISCOUNT MATRIX			
	COST OF SERVICE (estimated percent in category)		
HOW DISADVANTAGED? based on percent of students in the national school lunch program (estimated percent in category)	low cost (67%)	mid- cost (26%)	highe st cost (7%)
< 1 (3%)	20	20	25
1-19 (30.7%)	40	45	50
20-34 (19%)	50	55	60
35-49 (15%)	60	65	70
50-74 (16%)	80	80	80
75-100 (16.3%)	90	90	90

Source: In the Matter of Federal-State Joint Board on Universal Service (CC Docket No. 96-45), Recommended Decision, 555.

---

12 In the U.S., children from families whose incomes are 130 percent or less of the poverty level qualify for a free lunch, while children from families whose incomes are between 130 percent and 185 percent of the poverty level qualify for a reduced price lunch. See 47 U.S.C. § 1758(b).

What's Next

The Act requires the FCC to issue new universal service rules by May 8, 1997. Public comments have already been filed on the Joint Board recommendations, and since three of the four sitting FCC Commissioners were also members of the Joint Board that developed and approved those recommendations, a final decision that substantially reaffirms the Joint Board's work is expected.

Of course, the Commission's approval merely concludes the first leg of a regulatory relay race to establish a new universal service framework. The Commission's action will hand off the baton to the 50 states to implement the rules and make them fit local circumstances. Individual states may also enact their own universal service rules as long as they include the Federal definition. It can go beyond that definition only if the state can maintain funding without burdening the federal support mechanisms. Every telecommunications carrier that provides services within a state can be required to contribute to a statewide universal service funding mechanism.

Given the financial stakes involved, as well as the potential to promote or block various firms' competitive positions through the implementation of these rules, vigorous legal challenges to the FCC rules – whatever their substance –are expected. The source of the challenges, as well as the nature of the claims, will depend on what shape the rules finally take. But within the Washington policy community, a legal battle is considered likely.

A number of issues present themselves for challenge. There was tension between state and Federal prerogatives throughout the drafting of the recommendations, and the tension between state and Federal authority in telecommunications regulation is a reliable source of litigation.[13] A group of states, joined by several LECs, have already challenged the Commission's interconnection order, adopted August 1, on the grounds that the Commission had exceeded its authority in dictating state pricing models. Similar states rights issues may appear when the FCC rules are adopted in areas such as whether the FCC can establish rules that direct flows of intrastate revenues, as these rules may be considered to do.

The recommendations also invite challenge in the sections that seek to offer discounts to schools and libraries. The decision to allow firms that do not pay

---

13 See Noam, op. cit. at footnote 3.

in to the universal service fund, such as Internet service providers and firms that offer routers or local area network wiring, to be compensated out of the fund for offering discounted service is likely to raise legal claims.

In any set of recommendations this complex, there will be fertile ground for legal challenges to delay implementation or to force reconsideration of points lost in the public comment process. As a result, the true implementation of a new universal service framework may still be years away.

The Future of the Future

While implementation of the current law may take years, it is not too early to begin to consider what the next round of universal service rules should look like. In particular, how can policy makers frame a commitment to universal service that really does accommodate the competitive environment that lawmakers are seeking to encourage and meet the political and social goal of serving all customers?

As a first step, any new definition of basic service must recognize that the target of traditional universal service support payments – connections – is increasingly meaningless as network intelligence migrates toward the margins of the network and networks become "bit pipes." The problem is that bit pipes do not deliver services. Bit pipes deliver bits, which become a service once they are off the network.

The rising importance of customer premises equipment in determining network functionality erodes the traditional unity between provider, facilities, and service, which makes centralized regulatory definitions of basic service arbitrary and thus fragile. Finally, the promised convergence of providers, technologies, and services will require the explicit harmonization of superficially unlike (and formerly distinct) traditions of universal service drawn from media beyond telephony.

In light of these trends, policy makers should move away from a universal service system that focuses on services and move towards a system defined by transport and termination requirements, without controlling what users will do with those facilities. Transport requirements concern the quality and capacity of transport media of whatever type and the their distribution over a specified area. Termination requirements mandate carriers connect a user with a specified destination on demand. Such an approach would allow for universal service policies without either specifying or implying specific facilities, architecture, or network topography and the carriers that are traditionally associated with those elements.

As such, a voucher system targeted for poverty and cost to serve may be increasingly desirable in the future. Vouchers could be provided that allow users to choose a basket of services that fits their needs from various providers over whatever facilities are the most cost effective in that area. The voucher would be bounded by some specified value to control exposure to potentially limitless claims of communications need.

The need for universal service mechanisms will continue, even as competition, and new configurations give consumers more options and lower costs. We can best promote that competition, encourage new configurations, and sustain our social commitment to universal service if we (1) pay attention to these technical, economic, and even social trends, and (2) create policies to work with them rather than ignore those forces.

References

Cooper, M. (1996), Universal Service: A Historical Perspective and Policies for the 21st Century. Joint publication of Benton Foundation and the Consumer Federation of America.

Dordick, H. S. (1991), Toward A Universal Definition of Universal Service. In: Universal Telephone Service. Ready for the 21st Century. Annual Review of the Institute for Information Studies (Queenstown, MD), 109-139.

Federal State Staff (1995), Federal State Joint Board, Monitoring Report, CC Docket No. 87-339, May.

Goldstein, M. and Gooding, R. Z. (1995), Universal Service to Universal Access: The Paradigm Shift in Citizens' Use of Telecommunications, International Research Center, State of Arizona Contract No. A6-0028-001.

Hadden, S. G. (1993), Universal Service Policies for the Public Interest Sector. Communications Policy Working Paper #3 published by the Benton Foundation. Available at www.benton.org/Library/PolicyOps/working3.html.

Mueller, M. (1993), Universal Service in Telephone History: a reconstruction. Telecommunications Policy 17, 5 (July 1993) 352-69.

Mueller, M. (1996), Universal Service: Interconnection, Competition and Monopoly in the Making of the American Telephone System (Cambridge, MA.: MIT Press).

Noam, E. M. (1993), NetTrans Accounts: Reforming the Financial Support System for Universal Service in Telecommunications. Paper prepared for Symposium cosponsored by Benton Foundation and Columbia Institute for Tele-Information, October 1993. Available at http://www.ctr.columbia.edu/vi/papers/nettrans.htm.

Noam, E. M. (1995), The Federal-State Friction Built into the 1934 Act and Options for Reform. In: Teske, P. (ed.) American Regulatory Federalism and Telecommunications Infrastructure (Hillsdale, N.J.: Lawrence Erlbaum Associates). pp. 113-123.

Telecommunications Act (1996), Pub. Law No. 104-104, 110 Stat. 56.

16. Global Consumer Markets for Civic Networking: Conditions, Indicators, and Strategies

Richard Civille

Introduction

This chapter proposes a strategic framework to understand emerging tele-communications market conditions favourable to what is often referred to as "civic networking". These conditions are beginning to appear in industrialized democracies in North America, Europe and the Pacific Rim. After discussing these various conditions and their characteristics, the chapter offers a set of recommendations for developing an action agenda. A market for civic net-working will emerge when the following three requirements are sufficiently met to spark a critical mass:

- growth in consumer demand for useful and beneficial information products and services that address local community needs and civic life;
- a regulatory framework that sufficiently promotes new competition and lower prices, while supporting universal service and access;
- the commodification of information infrastructure into low-cost building blocks, from which to create new applications.

What is Civic Networking?

Civic networking is the public use of communication technology for commu-nity economic development, civic participation, and social service delivery. Use of advanced telecommunications, such as the Internet or electronic mail, enlarge the possibilities for civic networking beyond older tools such as newsprint, television, radio, and telephone. Civic networking emphasises applications. It is neutral with respect to technology, or type of organisation. Such applications address small business development, job training, policy debate and advocacy, preventive health and home care, library services, social service case management, arts and recreation, life-long learning, and other areas. Civic networking is community-based or regional in scope, and focuses on the proper use of appropriate technology. Civic networking applications can be developed and delivered by libraries, community network groups, public access cable centres, corporations, small businesses, government agencies, other types of organisation (whether non-profit, for profit, governmental, or non-governmental), and by individuals.

Creating the Market

There are three large-scale processes in play that together can drive the creation of a civic networking market-place within the emerging global information infrastructure. They are the funding of public service application demonstration projects, telecommunications policy reform, and the commodification of functional network elements, where price is driven towards cost through competition.

When viewed from an historical perspective, there have been two funding phases of telecommunications application demonstrations over the past thirty years. The first phase dealt with satellite technology. The second phase now deals with digital information infrastructure. The first phase took place through the mid 1960s to the late 1970s. The second phase began in 1992 through the initiative of the Clinton/Gore administration in the United States, and is now broadening through European Community (EC) initiatives to the G-7 member nations. Telecommunications regulatory reform finally has been achieved in the U.S., has already happened earlier in the U.K., and is to be adopted throughout the EC by 1998. Such reform has at least some prospect of developing new approaches to universal service.

Advanced information and telecommunications technologies (ICTs) are becoming increasingly more powerful and less expensive. On the other hand, policy and regulatory frameworks world-wide are tending towards liberalisation and open, competitive markets. The logical outcome of these processes is the transformation of advanced ICTs into mere unbundled commodities, the "stuff" of which other things are made.

Application Demonstration Projects

Can government-funded ICT demonstration projects promote consumer market demand for useful and beneficial information products and services that address local community needs and civic life?

A variety of government and privately-funded demonstrations of community and civic applications of telecommunications are underway in the U.S., Canada and the EC. A new era in government- and industry-supported ICT demonstration projects began in 1992 with the inception of the Clinton/Gore administration in the U.S. At the 1995 G-7 conference hosted by the EC, plans were drawn for a set of eleven demonstration projects intended in part to "help create markets for new products and services, where appropriate" (REF). While these initiatives are exciting, an unfortunate by-product is a tendency to imagine that all of this is new. But the past is prologue, and there is a need to recall the historical background of ICT application demonstrations so that we can learn from past efforts (see also chapter 4).

The American National Aeronautics and Space Administration (NASA) operated an Application Technology Satellite (ATS) programme through the mid-1960s and into the mid-1970s, launching a series of geosynchronous satellites through which various public service experiments and demonstrations were funded and tested. Jointly with NASA, the Canadian government undertook a similar Communications Technology Satellite (CTS) program in 1976. Intelsat, the international corporation founded by John F. Kennedy under the auspices of the United Nations to promote satellite communications programs in developing countries, also undertook application demonstration projects. The U.S. Agency for International Development (USAID) operated the Rural Satellite Project during the 1970s and early 1980s to promote public service applications in remote rural areas of developing countries. The NASA-sponsored ATS program no longer exists, neither does CTS, or the Rural Satellite Project.

The ATS programme demonstrated telemedicine in Appalachia, electronic town halls in rural Alaska, and educational television in India. Early experiments in data transmission led directly to the development the TCP/IP protocols that drive the Internet. An ATS project during the 1970s, the Pan-Pacific Education and Communication Experiment by Satellite (PEACESAT) continues to this day, having become a line item within the National Telecommunications and Information Administration (NTIA). The CTS program included remote distance-learning and public safety satellite demonstrations into the far reaches of the Canadian frontier, as well as a number of sponsored projects in developing countries. The USAID Rural Satellite Project undertook an innovative Radio Mathematics Project in Nicaragua before the revolution, and spearheaded development of the Indonesian satellite system that now spreads across a vast archipelago of islands spanning thousands of miles.

The combined initiatives spent great sums during their tenure. However, the passage of time between this earlier wave of demonstration projects and current efforts makes it all too easy to neglect a proper study of these efforts, and the lessons they may have for the present.

The Academy for Educational Development used to maintain a specialist library in Washington, D.C., that served as a repository of reports and papers generated by the wide range of ICT application projects funded across agencies and governments during the mid-1960s to the mid-1980s. That library has now closed, its holdings either broken up and distributed to various researchers across the U.S., or simply disposed of. This makes it difficult for researchers or programme evaluators involved in the new ICT application projects to study the work that went before. During the 1980s to the early 1990s, there was little government or private interest in stimulating public service ICT applications, other than some small efforts such as the Apple Computer, Inc. Community Affairs Program. All that has now changed, yet without much understanding or analysis of the first wave of demonstration projects.

A new American grant programme, called the Telecommunications and Information Infrastructure Assistance Program (TIIAP), made tens of millions of dollars of grants across the country in 1993, leveraging half as much again in matched private investment. Grants supported the planning, demonstration, and sustainable financing of public service applications of the emerging information infrastructure. The grants are awarded to non-profit entities rather than commercial firms, and range from new efforts to provide Internet access in low-income communities, to development of digital archives for museums (see Chapter 11 for a detailed discussion). During the G-7 conference in 1995 hosted by the EC, plans were made to undertake a joint set of eleven application projects coordinated across the G-7 nations. These application demonstrations are to be based upon "information society" principles crafted by the EC, phrased in language that promotes universal service and social equity. The formal process to undertake these projects was finalised during the G-7 Conference on the Information Society held in South Africa in May 1996.

The application areas for the G-7 projects are similar to the application areas funded by TIIAP. Indeed Administration officials from the U.S. have actively helped to shape the G-7 process. The application themes of the G-7 initiative include several of those promoted by TIIAP including on-line government, public safety, and healthcare delivery. The G-7 initiative, unlike TIIAP, makes explicit two additional themes. These are cross-cultural training and education, and the development of global markets for small and medium enterprises. While the TIIAP programme funds many small community-based non-profit organisations, the G-7 initiative favours the funding of larger institutions, and it is still uncertain to what extent those institutions will be non-governmental.

It would be prudent for researchers in government, academia, and public interest communities from all affected nations to take a hard look at the work that went before, to better understand the prospects and problems being generated now. Such vast sums of money can indeed stimulate the creation of new markets - or they can languish instead as old reports in specialist libraries, that eventually close their doors.

Telecommunications Reform and Universal Service

Under-served groups are untapped markets. To encourage growth of new consumer markets, universal service policy should promote the development of beneficial information products and services that address local community needs and civic life. Such policies should be designed to have a levelling effect between information "haves" and "have-nots". They should spur new community economic development and civic participation in both urban and rural areas (Civille 1995).

The 1996 Telecommunications Act in the U.S. and similar policies proposed by the EC, have some promise of crafting new ways of ensuring universal service in a competitive marketplace. The American law creates a new partnership with state governments through a Federal/State Joint Board to redefine universal service and devise new types of financing mechanism (see chapter 10 and 15). In 1995, the EC submitted the last regulatory proposals required to achieve liberalisation of EC-wide telecommunications by 1998. The "information society vision" unveiled at the 1995 G-7 Conference includes language that recognizes a need to ensure that benefits in quality of life, employment, and education and training are evenly distributed.

Any federal framework for universal service should provide maximum flexibility for states (or EC member nations, or Canadian provinces) to develop their own priorities and financing mechanisms. From this, local communities need to be empowered to establish their own criteria, programmes, and services. A significant percentage of funds collected from telecommunications providers for universal service might be best spent as "block grants" in local communities to encourage grass-roots solutions to access and equity in the information society. Experimentation at the local level needs to be strongly encouraged, as this can be the best means to create demand to attract private investment.

A uniform universal service policy blanketing the seven industrial democracies would be unlikely and unwise. However, there are several themes that should be addressed wherever telecommunications policy is being liberalized. Universal service not only needs to ensure access to the infrastructure, but also to ensure that the infrastructure is effectively used for maximum social and economic benefit. Universal service policy should develop means to:

- combine market incentives and individual tax credits to increase computer ownership amongst low-income households, and small or home-based businesses. In the U.S., for example, the Earned Income Tax Credit - already designed to target low- and moderate-income working families with children - could be used to provide one-off credits for the purchase of computers, networked information services, software, and training that could be set to various levels, depending upon family size and household income;
- provide electronic mail services for children and job-seekers. By encouraging broad access to Internet electronic mail, universal service policy can

effectively reduce the costs associated with meeting new people and maintaining relationships, that can lead over time to new employment and education opportunities;

- promote the development of public access network services. The federally-funded TIIAP grants are beginning to demonstrate the utility of various models of access including community networks and computer centres located in libraries, schools, health clinics, and other community-based organisations;
- fund network literacy programmes through adult education programmes, public libraries, and schools. Without the necessary skills to use the National Information Infrastructure, access is meaningless, and competition for jobs will leave the unskilled far behind. Simply acquiring computer skills has become insufficient in the age of the Internet. It has become important to be literate in the use of networked information, and any universal service policy must address this.

Commodification

Developing beneficial information products and services that address local community needs and civic life will require access to various functions and elements within networks, as well as pieces of ICTs. The developers of such applications will use these underlying technology components as building blocks to be combined into useful new forms. Commodification in the form of the unbundling and marketing of network elements and functionality is becoming commonplace. An early example of this is Caller ID, which had previously been used for internal network operations, and was not originally designed as a consumer product.

Personal computers are built from commodity components, i.e., hard-drives, modems, monitors, keyboards, and processors. The popular term "plug and play" speaks directly to commodification. The Internet makes possible a vast range of new applications that combine personalized computer interfaces, like Web browsers, to remote relational databases using telephone networks connected to high-speed data networks. Applications built this way combine elements of different networks and pieces of ICTs.

Much is written about huge new markets for interactive entertainment that will float upon a high-speed information infrastructure. This infrastructure would grow progressively more powerful and cost progressively less. Prices for using the infrastructure would approach cost through unregulated competition. In this scenario, profit margins for telecommunications providers could approach zero, spurring on the same corporations to develop value-added content and information services instead. This prospect is said to explain a momentum towards mergers within the entertainment and telecommunications industries. But this trend also suggests the emergence of other consumer markets as well - beyond entertainment, home shopping, and banking. Soon, wholesale blocks of high-speed network time for international video conferencing will be sold as futures on commodity exchanges, as if they were bushels of corn. How could such a commodity be built into an international civic networking application that connects grade school students together for electronic field trips?

Description of the Total Market

A recent consumer survey suggested that voting in elections was a highly-desired use of networked information services and that "60 percent of respondents expressed a moderate-to-strong interest in being part of public-opinion polls; 57 percent would like to participate in interactive, electronic town-hall meetings with political leaders and other citizens; and 46 percent want to send video or text e-mail to elected representatives " (Pillar 1994).

What is the total global market for beneficial information products and services that address local community needs and civic life? What are the indicators and growth characteristics of a consumer market for civic networking applications? What are the sectors that need to be examined for evidence of such a growing market? For example, the total market for Internet service providers (ISPs) in the United States is estimated at one billion dollars a year annually. What is this figure across the G-7? There are examples of non-profit community networks developing useful community and civic information content using the Web, that small ISPs in the same area also use to attract customers. What is the value of such information content to the consumer base served?

According to the National Public Telecomputing Network, its 53 affiliate systems have almost 380,000 users alone, making them the fourth largest consumer on-line service in the country. If the total number increases as a function of the annual growth rate of the Internet itself, which nearly doubles yearly, this number could be close to five million within three years. What is the value of these services, if most of the subscribers paid a fair price, or if universal service subsidies were available to support the low-income users many of these systems seek to serve?

There are 2,000 cable access centres around the U.S. with operating budgets averaging at about $250,000 a year. Operating costs of community networks have also been estimated in this average range. How much local economic activity would be generated in technology purchases, salaries, and rents if small businesses such as these existed in every municipality across the U.S., Canada, Europe, Australia and New Zealand? It is beyond the scope of this chapter to propose the size of this total market for beneficial information products and services that address community needs and civic life. Such an analysis deserves further attention by researchers.

A Case Study on the Growth of Consumer Demand

While much work remains to be done to describe a total market in these terms, it is clear that its size and scope could be considerable. A small experiment undertaken by the U.S. Federal Trade Commission (FTC) suggests some trends (See Figure 1). The FTC, like many Federal agencies, undertook experimental projects during 1995 to use the Internet to disseminate government information to the public. Indeed, these experiments have more recently taken on the force of law through passage of the Paperwork Reduction Act. The Act requires agencies to establish programmes to disseminate information to the public electronically. The Center for Civic Networking was contracted by the FTC to design, promote, and monitor access to a wide range of consumer-interest brochures. Over 150 brochures were reformatted electronically, topically indexed, and placed on gopher and web sites. The electronic brochures were marketed across the Internet, with special focus given to public library patrons and subscribers to the commercial on-line services. Usage of the materials were monitored over a six-month period.

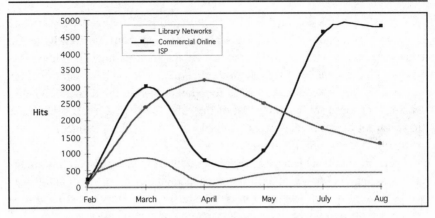

Figure 1: *How Individuals Reach FTC ConsumerLine*

Usage data collected during 1995 showed growing consumer demand for information about credit, automobile purchases, and small business. The data indicated that more public library patrons accessed the brochures than did subscribers of commercial on-line services for several months. This trend changed sharply when some of the major providers - Prodigy and America OnLine - began to offer their subscribers tools to browse the World Wide Web in the Spring and early Summer of 1996.

A recent consumer survey indicated that the poorest Americans - those in households earning less than $15,000 a year - are the most interested in acquiring independent consumer product information on automobile and health insurance, eyeglasses, and prescription drugs. Upper-income consumers are less concerned. Lower-income individuals spend a higher proportion of their income on such needs than upper-income individuals do, and thus want better-informed purchasing decisions (Mogelonsky 1994). Data from the FTC experiment would seem to support the findings of this survey. Implications are two-fold. First, the data appear to suggest that low- and moderate-income consumers - often those who cannot afford home computers - will visit public libraries to seek information to inform their purchasing needs. Secondly, general demand grows even greater when such access becomes available through commercial on-line services such as Prodigy and America OnLine - affordable to millions of consumers.

Towards an Action Agenda

There are relationships between investments in ICT applications, policies that broaden deployment in use, and the creation of new markets and economies. It is in the manner these forces are shaped that good social and economic outcomes result.

An action agenda that can foster good social and economic outcomes of the emerging global information infrastructure by building new consumer markets should:

- involve actors from all affected countries in either a coalition or association framework that currently does not exist. The purpose of this effort might be to promote, in a cross-sectoral and non-partisan manner, the creation of a global consumer market for beneficial information products and services that address local community needs and civic life. Such a coalition or association would need to effectively address both policy and practice, at both strategic and tactical levels;
- research the first phase of telecommunications application demonstration projects such as the ATS and CTS experiments, the Rural Satellite Project, Intelsat demonstration projects, and others. Such research should be able to generate insights from past experience that would be helpful to current efforts. Of particular interest might be research into older evaluation models, surveys of user constituencies, descriptions of unexpected consequences, and the characteristics of projects that survived to become sustainable programmes or new organisations;
- describe the total market for civic networking applications in all affected countries. A cross-sectoral analysis needs to be undertaken that examines such sectors as library information services, public information programmes by governments, Internet service providers, community networks, public access television, and others;
- price certain types of highly-scalable information products and services that address community needs and civic life. Types of scalable service might deal with voting and campaign contributions of public officials, digital maps of neighbourhood crime activity and police response, personal privacy software, network literacy training, home care for the elderly and disabled, or Internet marketing cooperatives for small businesses;

- create a clearing house for best practice, policy, pricing, and marketing models. Such a clearing house would hold information about local projects that demonstrate promise for scalability and sustainability, policy frameworks that have been proposed or adopted, pricing structures for services, and marketing approaches to promote such services.

This paper has attempted to present evidence of an emergent international consumer market for new information products and services that address local community needs and civic life. However, this market for civic networking applications is not likely to simply emerge of itself. It needs to be actively promoted across the G-7 countries and the developing nations.

The strategist looks at changing the regulatory environment so that telecommunications development can occur. The tactician starts from what applications are available and what s/he would like to see happen with them. Proponents of civic networking must balance not only a strategic overview and a tactical agenda, but maintain an international perspective to "think globally and act locally."

References

Civille, R. (1995), The Internet and the Poor. In: Kahin, B. and Keller, J. (eds.): Public Access to the Internet (Cambridge, MA: MIT Press).

Mogelonsky, M. (1994), Poor and Unschooled, but a Smart Shopper. American Demographics. July.

Pillar, Ch. (1994), Consumers Want More Than TV Overload from the Information Superhighway, but Will They Get It? (MacWorld). September.

17. The Information Superhighway and the Less Developed Regions/Smaller Entities: Implications for Policy in the EU

Paschal Preston

Introduction

The current debates over the information superhighway, and the National (and Global) Information Infrastructures (NII and GII, respectively) raise sets of important issues for less developed economies and regions, and smaller entities. In my reading of the relevant policy documents, many of these issues have been neglected or - if recognized - have been treated as relatively marginal concerns.

This chapter highlights the importance of these regional issues, with a particular focus on the European Union (EU) policy context. It addresses certain fundamental flaws in current EU strategies from the perspective of issues related to the less developed economies and regions in Europe. The first section examines some similarities and differences in USA and EU institutional strategies for the superhighway; the next considers features of the EU's regional policies in relation to the superhighway strategy. The following two sections address some of the macro-economic, and then micro-economic, implications of the superhighway for less developed economies and regions. The next examines some of the strategic issues posed by "convergence" trends, and the implications of current EU strategies for the content components of the electronic communications sector and the related matters of political and cultural diversity. The final section addresses aspects of universal service provision, as well as demand and "consumption gap" issues with particular reference to the less developed regions.

This chapter adopts a critical perspective on superhighway initiatives within the EU, and examines some of their underlying assumptions and contradictions. It discusses specific strategy considerations which are neglected at present. It is recommended that they should occupy a more central place within current policy debates, especially in the EU context. For reasons stated below, I focus discussion on the specific implications of superhighway strategies for regional development, and spatial cohesion within the EU.

Differences and Similarities between EU and USA Contexts

In the case of the "regional problem", and questions of geographical patterns of uneven socio-economic development, we are not concerned with any absolute or physical forms of space. Rather, we are primarily concerned with political-economic and, indeed, cultural dimensions of what Lefebvre (1974) has defined as a constructed "social space". Thus, it is important to flag a number of important institutional differences (as well as similarities) between the USA and EU contexts at the outset. These raise some important considerations about the status, meaning, and characteristics of the "social space" of their respective superhighway strategies.

First, we must stress that there are major differences between the USA and the EU in terms of their fundamental status as economic and, especially, political and socio-cultural entities. These differences have implications for the discussion of similarities and differences in superhighway strategies. For example, the USA is a long-established and fully-integrated Federal state system. The EU can best be characterized as a collection of previously separate nation states. Less than 40 years ago, the original six embarked upon a project of economic integration (in many ways similar to the more recently-launched NAFTA project on the other side of the Atlantic), and they have sought to deepen the process of economic, political, regulatory, and - to a lesser extent - social integration in much more recent times.

As such, the current state of construction of the EU as a cohesive and integrated political-economic entity and "social space" is best defined as at the very tentative, emergent, or embryonic stage (Preston 1996). This means, for example, that distinctive national and regional identities, affiliations, and sentiments are much more important, salient, and influential within the EU, compared to the USA (Corcoran and Preston 1995).

Second, these considerations mean that any comparative approach to superhighway (or other) policies must take full account of fundamental differences between the status, autonomy, and relative powers of central allocative authority and resources of the EU (with respect to its Member States), and of the Federal US government (with respect to its state authorities).

Third, it is only in the past 7-10 years that the EU Commission has sought to shift the location of key decision-making for public policy in the electronic communications arena, from national capitals to Brussels. This was prompted and actively supported by certain economic and political interests external to the Commission. But the Commission itself was partly motivated by a sort of "social-engineering" mission; one reflecting the perception that a unified approach to electronic communications would help cement the project of increased political, economic, and socio-cultural integration in the EU. However, this conception is one that was - and is - resisted by many other interests and groups within the EU.

Fourth, in relation to strategic and convergent superhighway policy considerations, it is important to note that the Commission was most successful in shifting the locus of public policy-making from national capitals to Brussels only in the case of telecommunications proper. Such a shift has been less complete in the neighbouring fields of television and film. Certainly, the EU has developed some new powers, policies, and institutions in these more "cultural" areas over the past decade. But national political and cultural sensitivities have meant that individual member states have ceded less of their powers and responsibilities in these areas. As I indicate below, this has important strategic implications for the analysis of the "convergence" and cultural aspects of the superhighway in relation to the smaller economies and less developed regions within the EU.

Fifth, we are not simply dealing with differences in formal, political, or legal structures. In addition, national and regional political and cultural identities continue to play a much greater role in Western Europe than is the case in the USA. In many respects, (despite its much reported internal racial cleavages and other tensions), the USA - in terms of collective self-image - is a much more integrated economic, political, and cultural unit than the EU. This is as true for the purposes of research analysis as it is for social and political action.

Sixth, I wish to stress that giving due recognition to the embryonic status of the EU as an integrated political-economic and social space does not necessarily imply a rejection of the project of increasing European integration - nor of the potential role of the superhighway in furthering such aims. Indeed, it merely underlines the possibility, and importance, of attempts to construct a distinctive approach and coherent action plan for Europe's way to the information society.

One major justification for the increasing economic and political integration of the member states of the EU is that there is a distinctive European inheritance of political values and social goals and orientations. In certain historical and comparative perspectives, it is possible to identify some distinctive values and orientations which have been shared by (many) national social systems within Europe - since the nineteenth century if not since the Enlightenment (Preston 1995c, 1995d)

In general, despite the common experience of capitalist industrialisation and urbanisation, there are certain institutional and other traditions which render many European societies quite distinct and different from others - such as the USA. One frequently noted theme has been the development of a welfare state system, and other distinctive institutional changes, which are perceived to be closely linked to social democracy within Western Europe. These dimensions of a European approach include forms of citizenship rights, collective forms of consumerism, and consumption rights which differ markedly from the relatively weak notions of citizenship and individualized forms of consumerism which have been typical of U.S. developments since the late nineteenth century.

Yet, ironically, existing EU strategies for the superhighway do not really reflect any such distinctive European traditions or characteristics. Indeed on examination of key policy documents, it appears that EU and USA strategies for the superhighway are more marked by their similarities than by any differences (Preston and Lorente 1995; Preston 1995b, 1995c).

Regional Cohesion, Regional Policy, and "Europe's Way to the Information Society"

The evolving process of the widening and deepening of European economic and political integration has been accompanied by a growing role of EU-level regional policy concerns and actions. The 1957 Treaty of Rome made reference to regional disparities, and indicated the desirability of reducing regional differences to ensure a harmonious pattern of development within the early conception of European economic co-operation. In 1973, the accession of new member countries was followed by the setting up of the European Regional Development Fund (ERDF). The ERDF was the first EU initiative explicitly designed as a vehicle for regional policy, but it aimed to merely lend support to the regional policies of member states.

In the second half of the 1980s, however, the incorporation of Spain, Greece, and Portugal into membership and the single European market (SEM) initiative both served to position regional development issues more centrally within the EU policy agenda. Early analyses had paid little attention to the likely regional impacts of the SEM, but critics pointed out that increasing concentration and intensified competition on a European scale may not produce equal benefits all round - and that the less developed member states and the more peripheral regions could be relative losers. The Maastricht Treaty requires the EU to reduce regional development disparities, and to improve social and economic cohesion throughout the EU (Dignan 1995).

Concerns about the regional impacts of the SEM led to the expansion of the structural funds, designed to promote the development of the lagging economies and regions. This represented a significant shift in the EU's responsibility for regional policy matters, and implied the acceptance of a possible link between the process of increasing integration and the problem of regional disparities in per capita GDP - often defined as "cohesion" in Eurospeak. The regional question, for the EU, is often seen to lie in the possibility that the process of integration may itself provoke increased disparities between peripheral and core regions - and any such gaps may pose a threat to the further integration of the EU. For some commentators, the project of increasing EU economic integration points to 'a fundamental tension between the processes of widening and deepening' (Dignan 1995: 4).

So what are the implications of the EU's superhighway project for future spatial patterns of development and cohesion within the EU? Here, of course, we are not seeking to address any autonomous impacts or effects of new information and communication technologies (ICTs) and infrastructures. Rather we are concerned with the whole ensemble of EU political initiatives and policy actions for the overall electronic communication services sector, and the orientations of the key private sector actors which are currently shaping the development, diffusion, and application of the various technologies and networks underpinning the superhighway.

We should note that the Bangemann Report (CEC 1994c) pays very little specific attention to the issues of regional development and cohesion (Bianchi 1996). This is not a trivial point as it represents the EU's master-document, and key reference point, for policy initiatives related to the superhighway and the electronic communication sector more generally. Its few explicit references to regional questions are couched in rather utopian terms, and point to a one-way flow of benefits for the less developed economies and regions. They refer to the positive impacts of the superhighway in reducing the costs and barriers of peripherality.

A similar failure to address the fundamentally new kinds of uneven regional development challenges emerging within the EU, can be found in other related policy documents such as the Green Paper on the Audiovisual Sector (CEC 1994b). It is also evident in the pace, direction, and content of the EU's core policies for restructuring the telecommunications services sector (Preston 1995a). This tendency to neglect the scale, and importance, of uneven spatial development within the EU must be noted as fundamental in its nature and its implications. It is fully in keeping with the rather smug assumptions about the universal, national, and regional distribution of benefits which marked the early analyses of the SEM in the 1980s.

For sure the issues of regional disparities and cohesion are not totally denied within EU policy initiatives. They are at least recognized and addressed (however inadequately) in, for example, the 1994 White Paper (CEC 1994a). But the point here is that, as a general rule, issues of uneven regional development and cohesion are either neglected, or treated as relatively marginal, within the core EU strategy documents relating to the electronic communication sector (as elsewhere).

Here there are some similarities with the treatment of social inequality within these same EU policy documents. In this case, social exclusion and polarisation is conceived as a relatively minor threat that is linked to lack of access to some particular set of technologies or skills. The widespread existence of poverty and increasing social inequalities within the EU are not only neglected, but implicitly denied, by such conceptions (Eurostat 1994). Both social and spatial inequalities are viewed as relatively minor issues which merely require some specific ameliorating research and policy initiative - conceived as a technical adjustment to the (assumed) overall benign impacts of existing policy strategies. The possibility that any such inequalities might be related to the core tenets and assumptions of those strategies is simply not on the agenda; it is beyond the bounds of legitimate consideration.

It is in this light that we can now begin to identify and evaluate some of the strategic implications of the EU's electronic communication sector policies for the lagging regions and smaller economies. And it is in this light that one can address the spate of more specialized (or marginalized) EU policy initiatives focused on the implications of new ICTs for national and regional disparities, as well as related research or consultancy documents (e.g., CEC 1995b; 1995c; 1995d).

Macro-Economic and Industrial Development Issues

So what are the major implications of the EU's superhighway and information society initiatives for future patterns of regional cohesion, and the development prospects of the smaller and weaker economies within the EU? At the macro-economic level, a key question is whether the superhighway will tend to widen or reduce the disparities in wealth or income between regions? This topic has been more widely recognized than others, at least within the EU.

On the whole, the recent literature paints a favourable picture, one which stresses the potential benefits of the superhighway for all regions. One common theme stresses its benefits in terms of providing peripherally-located firms - especially those in the service sector - with more ready access to core markets. It is frequently suggested that new ICTs, combined with neo-liberal regulatory policies, offer radical opportunities for a reduction or diminution in regional disparities. The emphasis in on the one-way flow to economic actors within the less developed regions, even if it recognized that these benefits do not automatically flow to all regions and localities (CEC 1995b, 1995c). We can also identify a parallel argument which stresses that, even if regional disparities do not radically diminish, less favoured regions (LFRs) will at least benefit from the "rising tide that lifts all boats" impact of the new ICTs and infrastructures.

Ultimately, the predominantly optimistic tone of EU approaches to these questions seem to rest on rather heroic assumptions about the benign distributional impacts of new ICTs and/or market-driven approaches to regional development (CEC 1994c).

There is little doubt that the diffusion of advanced ICTs in the context of current economic and policy strategies will expand the parameters of "space-time distanciation" within the EU (Giddens 1995). It will serve to deepen the scale and intensity of economic integration and divisions of labour within the EU. In particular, it will serve to concentrate ownership and control, and increase the tradability of information service industries across EU regions.

But it is quite another matter to claim, or assume, that such economic and spatial restructuring will be neutral with respect to the existing unequal pattern of economic and social space within the EU. Here I wish to reject claims that new ICTs, in tandem with neo-liberal policies, are bringing about fundamental shifts of economic power and opportunities in favour of the less developed EU economies - claims such as that "power is shifting to a range of competing suppliers, to specific user groups, to policy makers, and to local and regional communities themselves" (CEC 1995c: 4). Rather the evidence points to increasing concentration and centralisation of economic power as the dominant trend across the majority of sectors within the EU.

Such assumptions are based on idealised images of the nature and extent of market competition in most industrial sectors. They neglect the reality of increasingly oligopolistic market structures, and other barriers to the operation of the hidden hand of market regulation. As with the early analyses of the impacts of the SEM, they neglect the practical force of economies of scale and scope attaching to the large oligopoly firms. They fail to recognize the unequal playing fields of most economic sectors for small and medium-sized firms operating out of the smaller and less developed economies, or the implications of vast regional disparities in innovation potential (e.g., R&D indicators).

In some of the relevant EU documents it is fully acknowledged that new ICTs are neither a panacea, nor a singular solution, to the development problems of the lagging economies (e.g., CEC 1995c: 5; NEXUS 1994). But in many cases, the optimistic scenarios for the development prospects of the less developed economies ultimately rely on the old, but born-again, "magic multiplier" model of ICT investments.

Indeed much like earlier approaches to regional policy planning within the EU, they rely on unrealistic assumptions about the benefits of infrastructural investments (Dignan 1995); the only difference is that now the emphasis is on the dynamic impacts of convergent and broadband electronic communication infrastructures. Overall, the EU's superhighway initiatives, combined with the dominant trends of economic and political change, will tend to amplify the macro-economic fluctuations and disparities of development across space. Such disparities have always been a feature of the spatial structure of capitalist development in Europe. But the economistic dimensions, and emergent status, of the EU as an integrated political and social space means that these (amplified) tendencies towards regional disparities in per capita GDP and incomes, are unlikely to be ameliorated by the kinds of internal fiscal and monetary transfers which were possible at the level of the nation state (Dignan 1995). Yet again, current debates surrounding the pace and direction of EU policies for the superhighway and the electronic communications sector fail to address and interrogate these strategic macro-economic issues.

Thus the conclusion here is that these challenges, and the goal of cohesion and minimising regional disparities, must be accorded much greater importance at the core of public policy goals within the EU. They must become a central rather than marginal feature in the policy debates over the construction of a more integrated Europe. A more realistic and critical approach is called for. This must recognize a continuing and important role for creative regional development policies at the EU and national state levels, as well as local and regional levels. And just as importantly, the regional cohesion dimension must play a greater role in shaping a more co-ordinated approach in other areas of public policy within the EU (e.g., in the areas of telecommunications regulation; industrial and procurement policies; education and research policies; military policies etc).

Micro-Economic Impacts: the Information Economy and the Communications Sector

Let us now turn to consider some of the micro-economic implications of the EU's superhighway strategy for the future economic development of the electronic communication services sector within the less favoured regions. An important feature in this respect is that current EU information infrastructure policies are likely to result not only in a smaller core telecommunications sector in the less favoured regions, but also one that is more open to external control. The most likely impact of current policy approaches will be a diminution of the direct employment and innovation/wealth creation opportunities, in the immediate future, within (most of) the LFRs and smaller economies of the EU (Preston 1995a)

Policy debates both at the EU level and within the less developed EU economies have yet to fully address the strategic issues that this poses. So far, there has been little debate or research focused on the potentially negative strategic impacts of diminished regional/local control over electronic communications networks and services. These challenges are the result of the rapid pace of the EU's liberalisation programme - whose major impact may be (partial) privatisation, rather than the introduction of competition per se - and the peculiar features of competition which prevail in the telecoms sector. The negative impacts of such externalisation of control on future national/regional innovation potential in the expanding downstream ICT applications and products markets, has not been fully addressed at either national or EU levels.

There are other strategic policy issues concerning the economic role of the telecommunications services sector within the less developed economies which have not been adequately recognized in shaping the direction and pace of EU policies over the recent past. For one thing, there are very distinct and significant problems concerning the viability and feasibility of infrastructure duplication and ONP/ONA approaches in the case of the less developed economies - whatever about their potential benefits in wealthier core regions (Preston 1995a). For another, there is little sign in this sector that the new regime of competing suppliers offering competing technologies is producing much by way of new employment opportunities, as promised by the advocates of reform (e.g., EU and OECD policy documents). Indeed, in the case of Ireland and other less developed economies within the EU, the experience in the recent past, and for the immediate future, is a massive reduction in such employment opportunities. There has been (and continues to be) a major shake-out in the number of jobs available in what was previously one of the most secure and highly-paid employment sectors of those local economies. The knock-on effects of the loss of such employment and income on the local economy have yet to be addressed by either EU or most national policy-makers.

If the EU's superhighway and information society initiatives are to deliver any of their shiny-new economic and social benefits within the less developed regions, then core elements of current policy approaches for the electronic communications sector must be urgently evaluated and reshaped, or reversed. Otherwise, regional disparities are likely to increase rather than decrease, at least with respect to the distribution of jobs, and to wealth creation which is directly related to the core telecommunications services sector and emergent downstream activities. Currently, most of these policies share the assumption that new ICTs, combined with market forces, will automatically ensure a rosy future for the electronic communications sector in most LFRs or peripheral economies. This view neglects the historical evidence on the tendencies towards skewed locational and distributional impacts associated with major new technology innovations in the past, especially those based in the (precursor) information and communication sectors (Hall and Preston 1988).

The Cultural and Political Implications of Convergence for Less Favoured Regions

The much-touted tendencies towards convergence of communication technologies and modes directly pose new challenges for the cultural component of the superhighway and, indeed, the political communications dimension (see Chapter 12 for a detailed discussion of the latter). The implications for both the cultural and the political dimensions of the public sphere must be considered more directly than in common in most current debates.

One important point of difference between the EU and the USA relates to the convergence and content dimensions of superhighway policy debates. The US-based media and communication industries have long enjoyed a dominant position in the most globalized sub-sectors or markets (e.g., cinematic films and TV programmes or packaged computer software products). Partly because of specific economic characteristics of such informational products (together with distributional as well as technological monopolies), these sectors are increasingly marked by highly oligopolistic structures at the global level.

One important implication is that the invisible hand of the market is not particularly effective in this sector -at least from a European perspective, or that of actors based in a small society or less developed region. Thus any EU strategy relying primarily on a market-driven approach (as celebrated by the EU's Bangemann Report) is one that is doomed to failure as regards these particular dimensions of the information infrastructure strategy and goals (Preston 1995a; 1995d).

Another implication is that there will be a much more complex interplay of interests related to the convergence of telecommunications and broadcasting in Europe as compared to the USA. There are some common tensions over policy between specific economic and industrial interests in both the USA and EU. But in the case of the various political institutions and state bureaucracies within the EU, there are - and will continue to be - important additional tensions. There are conflicts between the policy orientations of individual member states, as well as between them and central EU bodies, concerning both the direction and location of decision-making related to the content and convergence dimensions of the superhighway.

Many of these tensions arise from the very specific policy status of the EU in relation to its constituent member states. The latter remain the most important focus (or "containers") of very specific cultural identities and political collectivities, based on distinctive national traditions and value-systems. The nation-state remains the crucial locational focus for (horizontal) political identity formation and cultural mobilisation within contemporary Europe, notwithstanding the existence of other minority cultures and political identities (e.g., stateless nations). Thus, despite the increasing integration of markets (private sector production, distribution, and exchange relations) the EU does not represent anything remotely approaching an integrated social space, at the level of political and cultural relations.

Secondly, the clearly expanding role of electronic communications infrastructures for all forms of economic, political, and cultural exchanges, combined with the (relatively slow) tendencies towards a convergence of technologies and modes, raises specific problems of regional cultural and social

development within the EU. Unlike the USA case, many of the LFRs corre-
spond to the locale of distinct national political collectivities and cultural identities (e.g., Ireland, Greece, Portugal, Austria) or two or more such cultural
collectivities (e.g., Belgium). At the very least, this consideration would seem
to imply that the EU's approach to the convergence and content aspects of the
superhighway project must be especially attentive to the protection, and promotion, of cultural and political diversity (compared to that of the U.S. government, for example).

These two considerations represent particular examples of key differences
between the EU and U.S. superhighway policy contexts noted at the start of
this chapter. Yet one looks in vain for unique or distinctive features of the
direction and content of the EU's strategy which take adequate account of
these fundamental peculiarities or policy challenges.

Neither the Green Paper on the audio-visual sector (CEC 1994b), nor the
White Paper (CEC 1994a), nor the Bangemann Report to which the White
Paper is explicitly linked (CEC 1994c), address the strategic issues. For example, they fail to examine the important challenges to the maintenance of
cultural and political diversity which are posed by the inherent market-driven
tendencies towards oligopoly within the (content and carrier) communication
services industries. Nor do they address the externalisation of ownership and
control of these services, or the weakening of traditional national regulatory
controls - both of which tendencies are directly promoted by the EU's push
for the privatisation, commodification, and liberalisation of the sector.

It should be pointed out that these flaws in the EU strategy for the electronic communications sector do not reflect any primarily technology-
determined logics or outcomes. Rather they directly result from a crude form
of economism underpinning EU strategy. This not only idealises the scope
for, and benefits of, competition and market-driven allocation of resources. It
also denies the diverse forms of public sector support for, and existing scale
of, emerging technological innovations and applications, and the potential of
national and EU-level initiatives to reshape these along alternative - and more
socially and culturally progressive - paths of development.

As regards matters of cultural and political pluralism in relation to electronic and other audio-visual communication content services, the EU's strategy lacks coherence. It is fundamentally flawed in terms of both industrial
and cultural policy criteria. These flaws have particularly acute implications

for the future patterns of cultural and political diversity, especially in the case of the smaller and less developed nations and regions.

Universal Service and "Consumption Gap" Issues

There are also some very particular policy challenges related to the funding, maintenance, and provision of universal service within the electronic communications services sector, when regional economic disparities (e.g., innovation potential and per capita income) are taken into account. In both the USA and the EU, the real challenge is not only one of redefining universal service to take account of technological change. It also requires a consideration of the role of basic electronic communications - especially the Plain Old Telephone System (POTS) - for all forms of social and economic exchanges, and how basic access to such an increasingly important resource can be made available to all of the population, irrespective of economic status.

Within the EU, there are marked regional differences in access to POTs which need to be addressed as a matter of urgency. There is the additional challenge of linking universal access/service policies to the goals of cohesion.

A related concern is the relative lack of demand for new ICTs. The "consumption gap" problem is one that has received insufficient attention in EU policy documents related to the superhighway, and it not clear the matter is much different in the USA. Indeed, the problem of the continuing large gap between the availability of various new ICTs on the one hand, and households' reluctance to adopt and use them on the other, has posed a challenge to manufacturers and policy-makers for many years now.

The consumption gap issue is a structural problem that reaches beyond suppliers' pursuit of "the killer application", and is linked to long-run change in average consumption norms. It is an issue which has been largely neglected in recent EU policy initiatives. For example, this is evident in the Bangemann Report which seems to simply dismiss the demand problem as one of the cost of leased lines (CEC 1994c). It is also evident in the case of the EU's current R&D programme (4th Framework) where - despite the rhetoric on users and applications - we can still detect a strong technology supply approach to expenditure and research priorities .

It must be stressed that the consumption gap problem is a very real and significant challenge which is rarely addressed by many influential political and economic figures promoting visions of the superhighway and the information society. The problem is certainly much more challenging than that of the relative cost of leased lines in Europe as compared with the USA. It requires serious socio-economic analysis of the restructuring of consumption norms and practices as they relate to the diffusion and adoption of major new technology systems. Despite the huge funds expended on superhighway projects on both sides of the Atlantic, very few dollars or ECUs have been expended on this kind of research issue.

It should be noted that the consumption gap problem takes on a particularly acute form in case of less favoured regions, and that dimension of the problem has not yet been adequately addressed in EU policy debates. With lower per capita spending power, the consumption gap problem is clearly more marked in the LFRs than in the more prosperous ones. Combined with relatively low levels of technological skills and capacity in the less favoured regions, there is a real danger of a vicious circle of regional disparity and polarisation, especially if demand for superhighway-based products does begin to eventually grow in core regions. Here, too, the limits of the market-driven approach become only too readily apparent. Only new and comprehensive public policies can begin to recognize and address this problem.

Some Conclusions and Implications

This chapter has raised some fundamental criticisms of the likely impacts and implications of current superhighway strategies (and their underlying assumptions), for the future economic, cultural, and political development of less developed economies and regions. It has done so with particular reference to the EU, which was largely unavoidable given the EU's important differences from the USA discussed in the second section of the chapter.In contrast to the generally optimistic images of the impacts of advanced communication infrastructures and networks on regional development posed by the EU's policy and research documents, this chapter has emphasised many of the threats and challenges facing the less developed economies. The foregoing analysis suggests that a radical revision is required in the overall direction and content of current EU strategies for the electronic communications sector, if the goal of regional and social cohesion is to be realized.

Postscript

This article has adopted a fundamentally critical view of the European Commission's approach to regional and social cohesion with a view to stressing some of the ingredients required for a more viable and progressive strategy for 'Europe's Way to the Information Society'. It has echoed some of the most frequent criticisms of the thinking underlying the 'Bangemann Report' , including its rather technocratic and economistic vision as well as its failure to address the important cultural and social roles of the content industries.

That is not to suggest that these issues have been totally neglected within recent EC policy documents related to the information society project. For example, the recent report by the High Level Group of Experts has at least recognised that there is a need for "a fundamental rethinking of 'regional cohesion' policies within the framework of the emerging IS'" and that "although connectivity is becoming a precondition for economic growth in all regions, the sheer existence of the information super-highway does not guarantee development" (CEC, 1996a: 43). This report also recognised that "a multicultural vision of Europe could be supported within the IS" (CEC, 1996a: 66). This suggested that one key challenge for national policy actors (i.e. those concerned with both economic and cultural issues) is to ensure that this 'could be' is consistently translated into a 'will be' --in line with the interests of the indigenous information content and media industries in the peripheral regions and smaller economies.

The more recent developments and debates concerning the 'social dimensions' and 'cohesion' aspects of the EU's 'information society' project suggest to this author that there is a growing need for academic researchers (given their traditional role as sort of 'public intellectuals') to propose a more radical and challenging agenda for innovation strategies related to the adoption and application of new ICTs within the EU regions. This would include considerations of new regional development policies to match the challenges of the emerging new social and economic space of the information economy, and the adoption of new policies for the cohesive development of the media/content and multimedia sectors.

This appears to be all the more pressing in the light of the recent publication of the EC's 'Green Paper' on social aspects of the information society project (CEC, 1996b). Compared to earlier discussion documents, such as the interim report of the High Level Group of Expert (CEC, 1996a) , this document is a major disappointment in terms of its role as a key map to the social dimensions of 'Europe's Way to the Information Society'. Published in the fall of 1996, this 'People First' document was much criticised at the colloquium accompanying its launch (CEC, 1996c). Referring to its rather narrow and determinist technocratic vision, one critic suggested that the Green Paper should really be entitled 'technology first' to better reflect its actual content and analysis. The document was criticised for its failure to advance an adequate social vision or overall strategy in line with general European social, regional and communication policy traditions and for its failure to provide an official response to many of the criticisms which were directed at the Bangemann report.

In relation to regional cohesion and disparities, its overwhelming emphasis is on the distance shrinking benefits of new ICTs, and the assumed benefits of the combination of further liberalisation and new technologies. It also stresses the need for infrastructural development and related education and training policies. However whilst it briefly notes that "liberalisation will not automatically bring .... benefits to all regions of the Community" , the overwhelming stress of the document falls on the opportunities to 'make the best of the new regulatory framework' (CEC, 1996b: 22). It advances a number of worthy and wordy ideals ('the information society should be about people and it should be used for people and by people'). But it fails to engage directly with many of the structural problems underlying regional and social inequalities identified earlier in this paper. The is also a marked absence of specific sections dealing with the issues of media and content diversity or the cultural dimensions of multimedia, the Internet/WWW and other new ICTs. There are many silences and absences in the Commission's Green concerning the significant challenges posed by structural obstacles to successful innovation and industrial strategies in the mature media and new communication industries for the majority of EU member states and regions--many of which are directly linked to the current regulatory regime.

The launch of the Green Paper was accompanied by invitations to participate in debate over the future direction of the socio-economic, regional and indeed cultural dimensions of 'Europe's Way to the Information Society' . Now I do not wish to overestimate the role and influence of academic researchers or other 'public intellectuals' in relation to the processes of EU policy formation in this field (or to ignore the force of the many critiques of 'the democratic deficits' involved in these processes). But these considerations suggest the need for a fundamental 'paradigm shift' in terms of the boundaries and contours of a specific European 'information society' project and related regional and media content policy approaches and initiatives. If the promised popular benefits of the new ICTs (heralded for well over a decade now) for all regions and social groups are to be realised, this paradigm shift needs to occur sooner rather than later.

The issues considered immediately above suggest an urgent need to widen the rather conservative parameters of contemporary official policy approaches/debates concerning the socio-economic, spatial and cultural implications of new ICTs across the EU member states and regions (including those related to the development of multimedia and other content industries). A key irony to be stressed here is the striking dissonance between the strident claims about the radical or revolutionary characteristics or 'impacts' of new ICTs on the one hand, and the ultra-conservative discourses and actions dominating the official policy agenda in Europe and elsewhere, on the other hand.

These considerations suggest the need for a radical re-orientation of boundaries of contemporary policy debates in Europe in order to address strategic questions such as:

a) The scope/prospects for a shift towards new types of consumption norms and institutional innovations similar to those which occurred at the time of the 'first communications technology revolution' ; for example, improve living standards and expanded leisure time (expanded time and money budgets) for the majority of consumers and citizens across the EU regions and member states;

b) The scope of comprehensive approaches which can address both the industrial and cultural dimensions of (new and mature) media/content industries and related policy goals in tandem; these should exploit the many complementarities between socio-cultural policy goals and the employment/economic growth potential of the new multimedia and the established content industries;

c) The new possibilities afforded by the increasingly integrated EU economic and industrial policy contexts for progressive social and cultural policy innovations, including new definitions of work and non-work , guaranteed minimum incomes etc (which would be much less tenable within a fragmented national or regional policy making context)

References

Bianchi, A. (1996), Can Local economic systems in the less favoured regions face the pressures and opportunities of the Information Society? Paper to the Academic Network on European Telecommunications workshop. (Paris) Feb. 2-3.

CEC (1994a), Growth, Competitiveness and Employment: The Challenges and Ways Forward into the 21st Century, White Paper (Luxembourg: EU).

CEC (1994b), Strategy Options to Strengthen the European Programme Industry in the Context of the Audiovisual Policy of the European Union: Green Paper" (Brussels: CEC: COM(94) 96 Final; 06.04.1994).

CEC (1994c), Europe and the Global Information Society: Recommendations to the European Council Report by Members of the High-Level Group on the Information Society ('Bangemann Report'). (Brussels (26 May, 1994): CEC).

CEC (1994d), Proposals for Council Decisions concerning the specific Programmes implementing the fourth European Community Framework Programme 1994-1998 (Brussels: CEC COM(94) 68).

CEC (1995a), Europe's way to the Information Society. An action plan. Communication from the Commission to the Council and the European Parliament and to the Economic and Social Committee and the Committee of Regions. Document obtained through Internet.

CEC/DGXIII (1995b), Telematics Applications for Urban and rural Areas (Brussels: CEC:DGXIII-C2). [Pph].

CEC/DGXIII (1995c), (Promoting Local and Regional Development Using Telematics Brussels: CEC:DGXIII-C2).

CEC (1995d), An Assessment of the Social and Economic Cohesion Aspects of the Development of the Information Society in Europe. Three volume study commissioned by DG XIII.A.7 and DG XVI. Conducted by Nexus, CCS & CURDS.

CEC (1996a), Building the European Information Society for Us All: First Reflections of the High Level Group of Experts Brussels: CEC (Directorate General for Employment, Industrial Relations and Social Affairs).

CEC (1996b), People First: Living and Working in the European Information Society. (Luxembourg: Bulletin of the European Union) Supplement 3/96.

CEC (1996c), People First: Report on the Dublin Colloquium, Dublin Castle, 30 Sept. - 1 Oct. 1996. (Brussels: DGV).

CEC (Information Society Forum) (1996d), Networks for People and their Communities: First Annual Report to the EC from the Information Society Forum. (Final rev. 5/7/96).

Committee of the Regions (1994), Opinion on the communication ... on trans-European data communication networks between administrations. Official Journal of the European Communities EJC C 217/32 (6.8.94).

Communication Workers Union (1994), The Future of the Telecommunications Industry in Ireland: A Submission on Behalf of the Staff of Telecom Eireann (Dublin: CWU).

Corcoran, F. and Preston, P. (eds.) (1995), Democracy and Communication in the New Europe: Change and Continuity in East and West (Creskill New Jersey: Hampton Press Inc.).

Dignan, T. (1995), Regional disparities and regional policy in the European Union. In: Oxford Review of Economic Policy 11, Summer 1995.

Eurostat (1994), Poverty Statistics in the Late 1980s. (Luxembourg: CEC).

Forbairt (1995), Telecommunications, Employment and Growth: Report of the Telecommunications Industry Task Force (Dublin: Forbairt).

Giddens, A. (1991), Modernity and Self-Identity: Self and Society in the Late Modern Age. (Cambridge: Polity Press).

Grisold, A. and Preston, P. (1995), Unpacking the Concept of Competition in Media Policy Making: The Case of Ireland and Austria. In: Corcoran, F. and Preston, P. (eds.), Democracy and Communication in the New Europe: Change and Continuity in East and West (Creskill NJ, USA: Hampton Press Inc).

Hall, P. and Preston, P. (1988), The Carrier Wave (London: Unwin Hyman).

Lefebvre, H. (1974), The Production of Space [Engl. Transl. 1991] (Oxford: Blackwell).

NEXUS ET AL (1994), Telematics and Regional Development: A review of the research literature (EU ACCORDE Project, Deliverable 1, May 1994) [mimeo].

OECD (1991), Report on the Kiruna Seminar on the Regional Impact of Advanced Telecommunications Services (Report of Working Party No. 6 Regional Development Policies) (Paris: OECD) (mimeo).

OECD (1994a), The Benefits of Telecommunication Infrastructure Competition (Paris: OECD; Restricted Doc) (Working Party on Telecom. and Info. Services; DSTI/iccp/tisp(93) 13/REV1).

Preston, P. and Lorente, S. (1995), Competing Visions of Information Superhighways: Implications for Users. Presentation to PICT International Conference on "Social and Economic Implications of New Information and Communication Technologies", Queen Elizabeth II Conf. Centre, London, 10-12 May 1995.

Preston, P. (1994), The EU's Approach to the Information Superhighway/Society: An Irish and Small Country Perspective. Presentation to the ANET workshop on "Competing Visions of the Information Superhighway", Copenhagen, 16-17 Dec. 1994.

Preston, P. (1995a), Competition in the telecoms infrastructure: implications for the peripheral regions and small countries in Europe. In Preston, P. and Blackman, C. (eds) Telecommunications Policy Vol. 19, No. 4, pp. 253-272. (Special issue on "Competition and telecommunications infrastructure in the peripheral regions and smaller economies of Europe").

Preston, P. (1995b), Comparing Policy Initiatives and Perspectives on the ISH, NII and GII. Paper presented at the International Communications Association, Pre-conference Workshop "Perspectives on National and Global Information Infrastructures". Albuquerque, New Mexico, 25 May, 1995.

Preston, P. (1995c), Information for Citizens & Citizenship. Paper to EC DGXIII workshop on Information and Citizenship, Luxembourg, 17 October, 1995.

Preston, P. (1995d), Contrasting National and International Approaches to the 'Information Superhighway' and the 'Information Society'. Invited presentation at EIPSN workshop on "Policy Issues in Creating the European Information Society", European Commission, Luxembourg, 6 July 1995.

Preston, P. (1995e), The Adoption of New Communication Technologies: Historical Trends and Statistical Issues. Invited presentation at COST 248 Workshop on "The Future European Telecom User", Bad Honnef, Germany, April, 26-27, 1995.

Preston, P. (1996), Technology, Space and Cohesion: Ireland and Europe´s Way to the Information Society, in: Telematics and Informatics, Vol. 13, No 2/3, pp. 123-140.

Venturelli, S. (1995), Liberal Fundamentalism on the Information Superhighway: The Paradox of Competition Policy int the EU and US Regulatory Debate. Paper to IAMCR European Conference Conf. "Communication Beyond the Nation State", June 27-30, Portoroz, Slovenia.

18. The Social Shaping of Information and Communications Technologies

Robin Williams

Introduction

This chapter draws upon the body of research into the social shaping of technology (SST), and in particular of Information and Communications Technologies (ICT), in order to gain a better understanding of the kinds of process that may shape the future emergence and development of the new Multimedia based products and services expected to arise with the emerging Information Superhighways.

The first part of the chapter introduces the idea of the social shaping of technology (SST) showing the origins of the social shaping perspective in studies which showed how a range of social and economic, as well as narrowly 'technical' factors, patterned the development and use of technologies. In reviewing the rich understanding of the process of technological change offered by SST research, it highlights some contradictory tendencies surrounding the interplay between technological dynamism and entrenchment, and the engagement between technology supply and use. These are reflected in features of contemporary technology, in particular in the growing importance of industry and public standards, and the increasingly configurational character of technologies as assemblages of standard and customised components.

The second part of the chapter examines how SST improves our understanding of the development and adoption of ICT. It starts by examining some of the social and economic processes that have historically shaped the overall structure and architecture of ICTs. It then goes on to review research into social shaping processes in the application of ICT encompassing the design and use, examining separately industrial applications of IT and ICTs in everyday life. Finally it presents a model of innovation in multimedia, to provide a framework for analysing the future emergence of Multimedia and related technologies.

Part 1: The Social Shaping of Technology (SST)

The Origins of the Social Shaping Perspective

The 'social shaping perspective' arises from the recent shift in social and economic research on technology to explore and analyse both the content of technologies and the detailed processes of innovation (MacKenzie & Wajcman 1985, Bijker & Law 1992). SST is conceived as a 'broad church' encompassing a variety of scholars, with differing concerns and intellectual traditions, including for example, industrial sociology, evolutionary economics, economic history, sociology of science (Williams & Edge 1996). SST stands in contrast to post-Enlightenment traditions which, by treating 'technology' as if it was separate from 'society' and not amenable to social explanation and analysis, limited the scope of inquiry to monitoring its 'social impacts' - i.e. the social adjustments it saw as being required by 'technological progress'. SST emerged through a critique of the 'technological determinism' inherent in this tradition, with its presumptions that particular paths of technological change were both inevitable (perhaps reflecting an inner technical logic or economic rationality) and required particular kinds of 'social' change. Instead SST studies show that technology is a social product, patterned by the conditions of its creation and use. At every stage in both the generation and implementation of new technologies a variety of technical options are available. Which option is selected cannot be reduced to simple 'technical' considerations, but is shaped by a range of broader social, economic, cultural and political factors.

The concept that there are 'choices' (though not necessarily conscious choices) in the design of artefacts and technological systems is thus central to SST.[1] Different technological routes are available, potentially leading to dif-

---

1   There is however considerable debate between the various intellectual traditions within SST about the character and conceptualisation of such choices. See Pickering (1992) and Williams and Edge (1996) for a further discussion of this point.

ferent outcomes in terms of the form of technology: the content of technological artefacts and practices. Significantly, these choices could have differing implications for society and for particular social groups. SST thus goes beyond traditional approaches, merely concerned with assessing the 'social impacts' of technology, to examine what shapes the technology which is having these 'impacts', and the way in which these impacts are achieved (MacKenzie and Wajcman 1985). In this way SST broadens the policy agenda; it allows people to get inside science and technology, offering the prospects of moving beyond defensive and reactive responses to technology, towards a more pro-active role.

Further, SST offered a more realistic understanding of the process of technological change than the mainstream 'technocratic' approaches which had inherited from Post-Enlightenment traditions a concept of technological progress that did not seek to problematise technological innovation. These views were not well-equipped to deal with the experiences of technology, which have been seen as increasingly problematic, particularly since the 1970s, on at least two fronts. First is the experience of unintended and undesired consequences of technology (for example health and environmental hazards). Second, the growing pace and salience of technological change has drawn attention to the difficulty of achieving successful technological innovation - and the realisation that the traditional approach of supporting technological supply was not, by itself, sufficient to achieve technological advance, let alone its application to achieve improvements in economic performance and social well-being. In contrast to the certainties held out by images of social and technological progress, technological change was revealed by a growing body of SST research as a highly uncertain and unpredictable process.

The Process of Technological Change

SST approaches attempt to grasp the complexity of the socio-economic processes involved in technological innovation. SST criticised the presumption of 'linear models' of innovation that technology supply would generate solutions that corresponded to user requirements, that could then be simply diffused through the market to fulfill society's needs. In contrast SST has shown that identifying, let alone meeting, current and emerging demand for technologies can be difficult. In particular, social needs, and the means by which they may be fulfilled, are not fixed entities, but evolve, partly in the face of new technical capabilities. These problems are particularly acute in relation to radical innovation (as opposed to the incremental enhancement of existing devices with well-established uses), since the potential uses and usefulness of an emerging technology are often not well understood by suppliers let alone by potential users.

However innovation is not restricted to technology supply - but continues through its implementation, consumption and use. Fleck (1988a) coined the term 'innofusion' to highlight the important innovative effort as (industrial automation) suppliers and users struggle to get supplier offerings to work in their particular circumstances. In this process, user needs and requirements are discovered and technologies are further innovated. Other SST writers have developed broadly homologous concepts to stress the active and innovative characteristics of the processes of consumption and use of technologies in other settings - and in particular their domestication within the household (Silverstone 1991).

The importance of innovation around the application and use of technologies is one of the reasons why the potential uses and utility of a technology often cannot be fully understood at the outset of a programme of innovation. We have only limited ability to anticipate the development of technological capacities and, more importantly, to pre-conceive future applications/uses. For perhaps the biggest uncertainties here surround the responses of the user and the evolution of 'social needs' . The future uses and utility of a new application may not at first be self-evident (as we show below, for example, in relation to the telephone). This is because of the difficulty of anticipating the outcome of the protracted learning processes involving suppliers and users alike as technologies are applied and used.

Consideration of (intermediate and final) users, in turn, draws our attention to the range of players involved in innovation, with their different relationships to the technology and varying commitments in terms of past experience and expertise. These players - including technical specialists from supplier organisations, suppliers of complementary as well as competing products, consultants, policymakers, existing and potential users - may have widely differing understandings of technology and its utility (Pinch and Bijker, 1984). SST emphasises the negotiability of technologies - in the sense that artefacts typically emerge through a complex process of action and interaction between these heterogeneous players, rather than being determined by any one player.

These considerations draw our attention to potential problems of communication and collaboration between these different players. Technological development often involves the combination of diverse bodies of expertise - knowledge of different technical fields, as well as expertise in non-technical areas such as marketing, finance. In this context there is considerable scope for failures of communication between groups. Indeed the 'bounded rationality' (Simon 1982) inherent in such situations may result in satisficing behaviour, as groups draw upon imperfect representations of others' abilities to contribute to problem solving. Difficulties, for example, in ensuring the flows of information between various expert, managerial and other groups, with their differing perspectives and knowledge bases, potentially become more difficult as technological products become more complex and draw upon more extensive bodies of technical and business knowledge (Fincham et al. 1995). Particular problems concern how to match technical specialists' understanding of technical possibilities with non-specialist users with their understanding of the application domain.

The complexity of these interactions is one of the reasons why the development and application of technology involves deep uncertainties. Technological innovations often fail altogether; they usually develop far slower than suppliers and promoters predict and may follow rather different trajectories than was initially anticipated.

Two aspects of these social processes in technological innovation are of particular interest to SST. The first concerns processes by which technologies become stabilised, or may become destabilised, reflected in the interplay between entrenchment or dynamism of technological innovation. The second surrounds the tensions that may arise in matching the generic potential of new technologies to current and emerging user requirements. We discuss these in turn, below, reviewing some concepts that have been advanced to capture these features. The rest of this part of the paper explores how these contradictory pressures, for example between globalisation and standardisation, and the enormous dynamism of technological innovation today are reflected in some distinctive features of contemporary technologies - viz. the increasingly 'configurational' character of technologies and the growing role of 'interoperability standards'.

The Dynamism and Entrenchment of Technology

A certain stability is a necessary and important feature of technology - for example we want to be sure that certain technical components will perform reliably, and continue to do so under a range of circumstances. On the other hand such rigidity can be counter-productive, where for example, technological design becomes fixed and embodies features that do not prove attractive to potential users. This entrenchment of technology arises in part because technologies develop cumulatively, utilising, where appropriate, the knowledge base and the social and technical infrastructure of existing technologies. An important aspect of the success of the modern technological project is the way it has been able to build upon earlier achievements. This underpins the gradual improvements in performance of technologies as technological knowledge is refined and developed, and is a major source of (to use economic terminology) the increasing returns from established technological options as a result of 'sunk investment'. This is one important way in which the results of earlier technological choices constrain later technological decision-making. These 'path dependencies' can result in 'lock-in' to established solutions and standards, even where these technologies are no longer optimal (David 1975, Arthur 1989, Cowan 1992). Well-known examples of this are the QWERTY keyboard and railway gauges.

At the same time, SST draws our attention to the turbulence of innovation processes; to the range of actors bearing upon the design and use of artefacts and their diverse and changing requirements and commitments to technologies. Innovation processes involve an interplay between sets of forces favouring entrenchment and favouring dynamism.

Entrenching factors are not just economic, but include, importantly, shared perceptions and expectations of a technology. Alignment of perception is an important step in innovation. For example, engineers must project visions of a technology and its capabilities to enroll the support of other players if they are to obtain the technical and human resources needed to create it. Developing such alliances of players - the socio-technical constituencies (Molina 1989) needed to create new technologies - may involve establishing consensus around particular technological concepts and options. The extension of such consensus to include the range of suppliers, consumers of an artefact and other relevant social groups presages technological 'closure' and the stabilisation of technological artefacts (Pinch and Bijker 1984). However, alignments that are premature or embody particular presumptions or visions of a technology can focus attention too narrowly on particular technological paths in a way that can prove disastrous if circumstances and perceived user requirements change (an example is the recently abandoned $150 million investment in the EFTPoS UK pilot for Electronic Funds Transfer at Point of Sale [Howells and Hine 1993]). This is just one example of how inflexible development contexts may result in inflexible technological designs (Collingridge 1992).

Technological dynamism is, in part, underpinned by the development of new technological knowledges. However supply-push is only one of a range of factors and actors in innovation (otherwise technological development would indeed be a more predictable, linear process, with the main shaping force being the principles embedded in the technology). In particular, technological offering have to be fitted to the current and emerging requirements of existing and future users, as already noted. User responses may be an entrenching factor in innovation - as common perceptions and understandings emerge. However, technologies, once implemented, may in turn provide the basis for further innovation. Suppliers may identify new applications for their offerings, or may seek to adapt them to make them suitable for newly identified groups of users. Users, importantly, may find new, innovative ways of using artefacts that may take a technology in directions not anticipated by its originators. This is particularly noticeable in the area of ICT, as we see below.

So we find that technological innovation is subject to two contradictory tendencies. On the one hand, we identify processes forces that will tend to stabilise technologies, by aligning expectations, and reducing the uncertainties and costs of established models. On the other hand, the dynamics of the development both of new technological opportunities and of user requirements - new problems thrown up by societal changes, and the articulation of new ways of linking those problems with technical possibilities - may open up new application possibilities, and undermine existing solutions, reversing the trend to stabilisation (Brady et al. 1992). An important influence here concerns the dynamics of particular product markets. Economic pressures may favour established approaches, in a context of positive returns on past investment and economies of scale. Standardisation of technology has played an important role - yielding substantial economic benefits for various players:

bigger markets and greater profits for suppliers and important price advantages for consumers who can share development costs (which may be very high with high-technology, knowledge intensive products). In this way, some technical artefacts may become stabilised and standardised. They may be made available to the user through the market as 'black-boxed' solutions, as 'commodities' with well-established attributes. However, competitive considerations may also counteract this. Once new markets have been established this will attract new entrants to compete with established suppliers, who in turn may seek to differentiate their offerings and retain their existing customer base through technological leadership. And users may seek to gain 'competitive advantage' by adopting these new offerings. So here again we find a complex interplay between standardisation and commodification - consolidating and undermining technological entrenchment over time.

The scope for standardisation and commodification partly reflects market structure, but is equally a function of the kinds of knowledge deployed, both of technologies and of the user domain, and their distribution between supplier and user firms (Fleck 1995), and the extent to which this knowledge remains local and contingent or can be appropriated and centralised. For example, the creation of 'black-boxed' technical solutions, implies that substantial parts of the knowledge required to create it and used it can be appropriated and incorporated into a generic solution (which can therefore be sold and used in a variety of settings). An important element of this may involve reducing the knowledge needed by the local user to apply and use the technology (either because the technology is simple to operate or because the principles of its operation are widely understood - a consideration which may encourage designers of new products to seek to mimic the look and feel of established artefacts). However, as von Hippel (1990) has pointed out, some problems are 'sticky' - hard to separate from the context in which they arise - and can only be handled on the basis of local knowledge and experience - limiting the scope for central supply of such black-boxed solutions, and requiring closer collaboration between supplier and user.

The Engagement between Supply and Use

SST has become increasingly concerned to explore the engagement between supplier offerings and user requirements as new technologies are applied and used, and as new product markets are constructed. We can also distinguish a range of different circumstances in terms of the relationships between suppliers and users. We will explore two extremes on this range by contrasting industrial process technologies and consumer goods sold on a mass market basis for use in the home. These represent very different contexts for engagement between suppliers and users.

Thus supplier-user communication might be relatively straightforward in relation to industrial technologies, where there are direct links between supplier and consumer and where both supplier and consumer share relatively high levels of technical skills as well as presumptions about the values associated with technology. In practice, however, attempts to implement industrial technologies often prove difficult. Supplier and user often find themselves in an unplanned process of joint development in the struggle get novel technologies to work under actual conditions of use. Fleck's (1988a) concept of 'innofusion' seeks to capture the kind of 'learning by struggling' which is involved. Implementation provides a test ground, where suppliers learn about user requirements, and both parties learn about the utility of (and problems in using) technological products. It is an important, though often overlooked, site of innovation, yielding knowledge that can inform further innovations. The importance of such supplier-user interactions has been demonstrated in a range of ICTs, including robotics (Fleck 1988a), computer systems in the finance service sector (Fincham et al. 1995) and computer-aided production management systems in manufacturing (Clark & Newell 1993, Webster & Williams 1993).

Supplier-user relations, conversely, can be expected to be much more problematic in the case with mass-produced consumer goods, where users are highly dispersed and localised, and there is little scope for direct engagement between suppliers and users, and where engineer's have little understanding of the user and the use setting (for example in relation to domestic technologies). Since the supplier does not have direct links with all its customers (customers who, in the case of radical new products, do not even exist yet) the supplier must find some way of modeling user requirements. The consumer may be represented 'by proxy' - for example, through market research on panels of potential customers or through discussions with intermediate users (e.g. retailers of the goods and services being produced). The supplier is forced to play a major role in prefiguring, or indeed constructing, the customer and the market (Collinson 1993). This remains a rather difficult and uncertain process for many suppliers - particularly where the technologies are consumed in the private sphere of the household (Silverstone 1991).

It may also be necessary to enroll a range of other actors, including users, and, on occasions, competing suppliers and suppliers of complementary products (Collinson 1993), to participate in developing markets - as for example in the case of new biotechnology-based products (Green 1992, Walsh 1993). Where there is no existing market for a new technology, "the 'market' may have to be created to go with the product" if suppliers are to realise its 'commercial potential' (Green 1990:165). A key constraint concerns the need to diffuse the knowledge required to understand the utility of new products, and how to use them.

The lack of direct links with the supplier in relation to mass-produced goods equally poses problems for the final consumer, who may have little opportunity to influence their design and development, other than the `veto power' to adopt or not (Cockburn 1993). However, the presumption that, even in such situations, consumers are wholly passive recipients of the meanings inscribed in the artefact, has come under increasing criticism within SST (Sørensen 1994). As we see below in relation to ICTs in everyday life, diverse consumers develop their own understandings of the artefact and its uses. (Pinch and Bijker 1984, Sørensen and Berg 1992, Akrich 1992). Indeed, consumers have shown remarkable inventiveness in sidestepping presumptions about the use of artefacts inscribed within technological design, and adapting technologies to their own purposes. This may contribute to new understandings of the significance of a technology - as the case of the 'reinvention' of the telephone as a social (rather than a business) communication tool shows (Fischer 1992). In this sense, even in relation to actors who have no power to affect technological design, closure is never final.

Features of Contemporary Technology

This brings us back to some of the implications of SST's analysis of the process of innovation for our understanding of the character of contemporary technologies as the condensates of these complex 'sociotechnical' processes. First is the concept that complex technologies are configurations of heterogeneous technical and social components rather than finished systemic solutions. Second concerns the increasing importance of standards as a feature of certain current innovation processes characterised by rapid technological dynamism amongst a wide array of players. These point to changes in the relationship between 'technology' and 'society'.

Technologies as Configurations

The concept of configurational technology was articulated as part of the critique of received ideas about technological innovation which overemphasised the role of technology supply. As already noted, these ideas involved a stereotypical view that technologies were created as 'systems': internally coherent, finished solutions that matched user demand. Some technologies are of course available in this way - in particular standardised component technologies such as microprocessors, personal computers. Applications of technology with well-delimited functions (e.g. word-processor packages can also be acquired as packaged solutions. However, this is less feasible when we come to more complex applications of technology which must be more closely 'configured' to the requirements of the particular user - for example company-wide internal computer systems which must support a wide range of activities, can rarely be obtained in the form of standard solutions. Instead, firms must 'customise' solutions to fit their particular structure, working methods and requirements. They may be forced to select, and link together, a variety of standard components from different suppliers. The result is a particular configuration - a complex array of standardised and customised automation elements. Moreover, no single supplier has the knowledge needed to design and install such complex configurational technologies. Instead, this knowledge is distributed amongst a range of suppliers (of different technological components) and a range of groups within the firm. Configurations are highly specific to the individual firms in which they are adopted - and local knowledge of the firm, its markets, its production and administration processes, its information practices, and so on, are at a premium (Fleck 1993).

The concept of configurational technology emphasises the uniqueness of particular settings in which technologies are applied. It points to the tension between the need to cater for specific user situations and the advantages of

adopting cheap standardised solutions. In particular it suggests ways of re-
solving these through a 'pick-and-mix' strategy, drawing upon cheap standardised components, and combining a particular selection of these, with a
modicum of customisation, into a specific assemblage configured to the specific purposes concerned.

Standards

An increasingly important feature of current technological changes - particularly in the area of ICT, is that technologies are becoming so complex and
intricate that no single player controls development of an entire technological
field. For example suppliers cannot produce complete technologies from
scratch but must instead make offerings which incorporate or are incorporated
within the offerings of a range of other players. This is partly a result of the
increasing linkages between technologies, and partly reflects the dynamism
and turbulence of a system under which innovation proceeds on many fronts
'in parallel'. In this setting, standards for interoperability between different
technologies have particular importance. This relates both to de jure standards
arising from open, public standard setting processes and the de facto industrial standards which emerge from the choices and commercial strategies of
players in the supply chain.

   The importance of standards partly rests upon the distinctive economics of
many contemporary technologies - technological products that are knowledge
intensive, and that exhibit strong network externalities. The huge Research
and Development costs of new high technology products, are offset by massive potential economies of scale given the relatively low costs of their reproduction - in a market that is increasingly operating at the global level. Economies of scale bring great uncertainties for developers: huge losses for those
that fail and potentially enormous returns for successful products. Suppliers
are increasingly drawn to collaborate in development to share these costs and
reduce the risks. Economists have drawn attention to increasing returns to
past investment and network externalities (the situation in which the value of a
product increases with the number of other users - the telephone is an obvious
example) which mean that a technology may not be attractive until a certain
level of usage is achieved and perhaps will not be viable unless its promoters
are able to convince sufficient numbers of potential customers and co-

suppliers that this represents the way forwards (Williams 1995). This is particularly relevant where there are competing products embodying different standards or technological solutions - for example the VHS-Betamax competition for domestic Video Cassette Recorders. Confidence that a product will not become obsolete is important for both customers and producers of complementary products (Swann 1990).

The emergence of industry standard products (black-boxed solutions) 'creates' markets, offering cheaper products and a greater choice of suppliers for consumers. This creates an incentive for suppliers to collaborate in creating larger and more stable markets. Increasingly, firms are coming together, with competitors and suppliers of complementary products, to agree standards for emerging technologies (Cowan 1992, Collinson 1993). Future technologies/markets are being pre-constructed in a virtual space constituted by the collective activities of players around standards for the interconnection between products! As we see later, such standards have been critical in the development of technologies such as the Internet and multimedia.

These developments, though primarily concerned with the commercial shaping of technologies, also have consequences for their broader social implications. For we can see, in the creation of inter-operability standards, and the spread of configurational technologies a shift in supply strategies from the creation of products designed as complete solutions dedicated to particular uses, towards multipurpose products that can be combined with others and adapted for a range of purposes. In contrast to early SST analyses, for example Noble's (1979) study of automatic machine tools, which emphasised how the particular objectives of those controlling the design and development of technologies became embodied in new artefacts, the effect of these developments is to divorce the design process for particular artefacts (and especially component artefacts) from the particular social contexts and priorities of their origination, in order to open them up to the widest possible market. This creates increasing distance between technological design and its social application. The fluidity of this situation suggests that it is not helpful to look for the social implications of a technology at the level of specific artefacts (eg particular components, or even the integrated artefact given the potential range of configurations available for the same function), but rather at how they are inserted into broader systems of technology and social practice.

These observations apply with particular relevance to information and communications technologies, and it is to these that we now turn.

Part 2: Understanding the Development and Adoption of Information and Communication Technology

The installation of Information Superhighways, coupled with advances in processing power and usability of information technology, have led to widespread expectations of the rapid adoption of a new cluster of technologies under the rubric of multimedia. Applications based upon these technologies are, moreover, expected to be widely diffused in many areas of working and social life, and to have profound social and economic implications. In short, these technologies are expected to underpin the transition to an information society. However, beyond this global vision, there is little certainty about the kinds of applications that can be expected to emerge.

How can we assess the prospects and societal implications of these new technologies? Experience with these technologies is extremely limited. Initial applications may, anyway, be far from typical of future offerings. Much contemporary discussion is based upon visions of future offerings - which are predominantly technology driven visions, and informed by supplier perspectives. The lessons from earlier technologies suggest that these visions may be deeply misleading.

The past can provide us with important insights into the future (Bruce 1988, Dutton 1995). In the history of ICTs a number of general issues and problems recur - though they may be resolved differently in different periods and contexts, and have shaped technological development. These include the following:

i) Local and Global: how to reconcile the specificity of the social contexts of application and use of ICT with the claims to universality of ICT. This bears centrally upon the promises held out of the ready availability of powerful ICT solutions, particularly given the enormous price advantages of mass-produced standard offerings.

ii) Formalisation and ambiguity: ICTs have their roots in formal and mathematical models and representations. Early commercial applications of IT focused on routine and simplified information processing activities, such as payroll and account-keeping. These could readily be described in mathematical terms, converted to algorithms and implemented in software. Difficulties arise in attempts to apply ICTs to human communication and decision-making processes involving complex judgments and interpretation in contexts that are typically characterised by ambiguity and uncertainty and that are inherently more difficult to describe in formal mathematical terms.

iii) Expectation and experience: The creation of expectations about the performance and utility of future technologies is a pre-requisite for attracting investment. Similarly, supplier product announcements, or 'vapourware' may be a means of shaping the behavior of competitors and collaborators. However expectations must not become too far removed from emerging capabilities. Technical specialists have tended to underestimate the complexity of application areas, and the consequent difficulties of applying ICTs, which has contributed to the repeated experience that ICTs fail to meet the expectations generated by technology-driven visions.

iv) Interpreting artefacts and user requirements: while technology driven views typically takes the utility of the artefact for granted - assuming that new functionalities offered will somehow match user requirements. However, users do not have determinate pre-existing 'requirements'; requirements are constructed - built upon earlier templates and evolving with use of new artefacts. This is one of the reasons why various players (suppliers and current and future intermediate and final users) may have quite different perceptions of artefacts and their utility.

v) Suppliers and users: matching supplier offerings to user need can thus prove problematic, particularly with novel technologies where there are few established models of the application or its use. The relationship between suppliers and users may be particularly difficult given the uneven distribution between them of technical and other pertinent knowledges (for example of the application domain). This is reflected, for example in the 'difficulties in communication' frequently experienced between technical specialist suppliers and non-expert users.

We can now explore these processes through a review of research into social and economic factors shaping the development and use of ICT. First we examine the historical shaping of the core ICT technologies and their overall structure and architecture. We then explore the industrial application of ICT in the workplace, which has been the subject of extensive research, before going on to examine the more limited body of research into technologies used in everyday life: specifically communication technologies and technologies in the home. There are important differences between shaping processes across these different settings of innovation, and it may be misleading to draw direct comparisons. This does not prevent us from drawing important and enlightening parallels between social shaping processes in these contexts. Moreover, current technologies more readily span the two settings and blur the distinction between work and leisure and between public and private life. The final part of this chapter draws together these findings to present a model of these emerging multimedia technologies and present a few concluding suggestions about its future development.

Shaping the Overall Structure and Architecture of ICTs

First, a general observation: the very structure and architecture of contemporary information technology is itself a product of historical processes of social and economic shaping. The idea of the computer had been prefigured by von Neumann's theoretical exposition of the idea of computability in which he envisaged a universal calculating and symbolic processing engine that could be applied to the full range of human activities. However there was no clear idea of how this would be achieved.

At the outset there was little separation between the actors and institutions responsible for the supply and use of electronic data processing. The first computers were built by the very people who used them. The subsequent history of computing has been characterised by its segmentation into different technical elements, and the differentiation of their supply, starting with the separation between hardware and software.[2] Software itself has become hierarchically segmented between Utilities: such as operating systems or programming languages, which are closely related to the functionality of computer machines and Applications Solutions, such as accounting and payroll

---

2   As Pelaez (1990) has pointed out, the creation of the software market was itself a direct consequence of a political action. Regulatory intervention to prevent IBM from bundling together software with its hardware sales created the basis for the establishment of an independent software supply sector.

systems which concern the use of computers for example in organisations including industry specific applications such as electronic funds transfer systems in banking (OECD 1985). This segmentation reflects the creation and differentiation of a specialised supply sector. It also marks out a degree of autonomy between the development of different components of the technological system, whereby interaction between each set of components is restricted, for example by stabilising the interfaces between components. This can be seen as reflecting a strategy for managing the growing complexity of the IT infrastructure; a process of 'black-boxing': stabilising certain elements while segmenting the knowledge involved in their development and use (Fincham et al. 1995).

These developments both made possible and reflect a process of differentiation in the industrial sectors engaged in the supply of computing technologies. So whereas industrial users of automatic data processing machines, such as Prudential Assurance and Lyons, were heavily involved in the construction of the earliest commercial computers (Campbell-Kelly 1989) and in the creation of the first operating systems (Friedman 1989), today these technologies are developed almost exclusively by specialised IT suppliers (Brady et al. 1992).

This highlights two further observations about innovation in ICT. The first concerns the important contribution made by the users of computing to innovations and the ways these may be taken up in future technology supply and ultimately become sedimented in core technologies. This continues today - the most famous recent example being the development by CERN scientists of the ideas that underpinned the World Wide Web. Second, it highlights an important dynamic of innovation, involving the separation of component technologies from particular contexts of use. In other words, elements of technologies have become increasingly standardised and independent from applications. This is readily demonstrated in relation to hardware. The first computing machines were 'hard-wired' - dedicated to particular applications, such as code breaking and calculating missile trajectories. In those days, before the introduction of stored programmes, reprogramming involved physical reconfiguration and switching of machines. Even with stored programming there were still particular machines for particular commercial (and military) computing purposes - until IBM launched its 360 series as a family of machines with the prospect of portability of programmes and data from one machine to the next, which heralded an era of cheaper mass-produced machines and underpinned the growth in commercial computing. Standard operating systems and languages were designed to allow portability of software between different manufacturers' computers. This process has continued until today, for example, core technologies such as microprocessors are produced for genuinely global markets, to be incorporated into a plethora of ICT products.

An important driving force for these developments has been the powerful economic advantages of mass producing standardised products, as much or more than the vision of universal technical solutions. The economics of certain IT 'globalised' products such as microprocessors and computer operating systems involves huge R&D costs of new products, coupled with massive potential economies of scale. This bring great uncertainties: huge losses for those that fail and potentially enormous returns for those that prevail. These, coupled with the pace of innovation in IT, and the need to maintain interoperability between the offerings of different players, have profoundly shaped the development of ICT. The market for a component technology is effectively defined by the installed base of complementary products (for example software that can run on a particular computer's operating system). This provides enormous incentives for the development of industry standards (for example the IBM personal computer). Competitive strategies of 'architectural technology' have emerged, notably in the microprocessor industry, where some elements of a product remain constant through several different generations (Morris and Ferguson 1993). This allows producers to innovate their products without abandoning their existing markets and provides some guarantee of compatibility over several product generations for consumers and producers of complementary products. Attempts to launch radical new microprocessor designs, such as the Japanese TRON project, have often been unsuccessful, given the widespread diffusion of Intel and Motorola's CISC (complex instruction set computing) architectures. However, new RISC (reduced instruction set computing) architectures have emerged, involving an 'open' alliance of suppliers and users, that have begun to challenge the market dominance of CISC. This commercial strategy is reflected in the very design of their products for example by offering open access to codes to enable interoperability, and incorporating the ability for users of existing CISC products to run their current software (Molina 1992, 1994).

So we find that ICT developments is profoundly shaped by the commercial strategies of the supply side-players seeking to create and maximise their share of a globalised market. These battles are often around the creation of industry standards. Such 'standards wars' started in relation to hardware (microprocessors; computer architectures), but today are increasingly operating in the area of software - in terms of operating systems and applications programmes (i.e. at the human computer interface). Similar commercial strategies have been played out - for example in the area of spreadsheet packages, some suppliers seeking to exploit the proprietary advantages of their products, and others pursuing a more collaborative strategy, notably Lotus 1-2-3 which was offered as an open platform on which other applications could be mounted (Swann & Lamaison 1989, Swann 1990). Today much attention is directed towards the anticipated battle between proprietary Microsoft and 'open' Java operating systems and principles for the next generation of applications on the Internet.

These interactions between global (technologies, markets) and local (user contexts) are often played out in relation to software. Software represents the critical layer in IT systems - it forms the interface between the 'universal' calculating engine of the computer, and the wide range of social activities to which IT is applied. For IT systems to be useful, they must, to some extent, model and replicate parts of social and organisational activity. Human beings are adept at dealing with problems of communication, pattern recognition and decision-making in contexts of ambiguity and uncertainty - contexts which have proved difficult, if not impossible, to formalise and appropriate within software systems. Moreover, it is through software that the purposes of an IT application become realised; software is designed to achieve particular purposes; its design embodies particular values and social relationships. The various social groups involved in or affected by IT may have different objectives and priorities. Software is thus a potential site of conflict and controversy (Dunlop and Kling 1991, Quintas 1993). This is particularly evident in relation to the complex integrated software systems being developed to support the activities of large organisations.

There has at the same time been an important recent shift in the design and supply of software involving the development of packaged software tools - such as spreadsheets - which can be adapted by the user to a wide range of purposes. Some of the most successful applications in communications technologies, such as electronic mail or latterly desk-top video-conferencing, are in the form of media, that offer little constraint on the content to be exchanged and that can thus be applied in a wide variety of contexts. So we find a dichotomy in software development strategies between on the one hand attempts to designing more of 'society' (and specific contexts of use) into the software and on the other, attempts to design 'society' (and specific contexts of use) out of the artefact.

We can show how these conflicting pressures, between maximising the extent to which software matches particular social settings or maximising market size in the case of strategies for the supply the industrial software applications - displayed graphically in Figure 1 below (Procter and Williams 1996). This shows at the one extreme, custom software designed around the needs of a particular user and, at the other, discrete applications (e.g. spreadsheet or word processing software) that are supplied as cheap commodified solutions to an increasingly globalised market. The former is expensive, but offers solutions that are well-matched to local needs; the latter offers very cheap solutions to particular tasks.

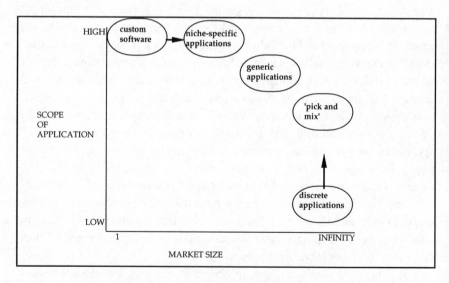

Figure 1: *Volume Variety Characteristics of Packaged Software Solutions*
(from Procter and Williams 1996)

Between these extremes we find the emergence of niche-specific applications, geared towards organisation with broadly similar settings and activities (e.g. credit-card processing); or generic applications designed to be adapted by the user to meet a variety of particular circumstances (e.g. production control and scheduling systems) (Fincham et al 1995, Webster and Williams 1993). One other strategy is becoming increasingly influential in contemporary ICT applications. With the emergence of inter-operability standards, it becomes possible to select a range of standard components (hardware and software - e.g. personal computers, network management software, database technologies) and to knit them together in conjunction with customised components into a particular configuration that matches the particular circumstances of use. Configurational technologies offer a much cheaper way to meet the particular needs of a complex organisation than fully customised solutions. Complex ICT systems today are increasingly taking on these 'configurational' characteristics. Indeed, given the enormous cost advantages of standard hardware and software components, few developers would build a new system entirely from scratch.

The Social Shaping of Industrial Applications of ICT

It is in the workplace that information and communication technologies first became widely adopted. We have much more experience and understanding of processes of social shaping of workplace technologies than in other parts of our life. The workplace is in addition an almost public arena - certainly one that has been extensively studied by industrial sociology and organisation theorists. The industrial context therefore provides a convenient place to begin exploring the social shaping processes that surround the application of ICT

Research into the social shaping of industrial applications of ICT has addressed the design/ development of systems; examining the various players involved, their concepts of the technology and their objectives for organisational change. It further highlights the fit, or lack of fit, between these design presumptions and the actual circumstances and requirement of use. Research into the implementation of these systems has revealed complex social processes, which may frustrate or modify these initial goals and conceptions of the technology. This shows how ICT applications emerge through an iteration between supply and use (innofusion) - in which the point of implementation is a critical laboratory in which supplier offerings are tested and further innovated in the struggle to get them to work under the particular circumstances of the user organisation (Fleck 1994).

Whereas most early applications of IT were discrete technologies applied to specific or closely-related functions, there is now a shift towards integrated technologies which link together increasingly diverse activities (for example, of design, administration and production). Discrete applications tend to automate well-defined functions, and can thus be standardised and readily obtained through the market place; they typically involve a single supplier and a single department/group of workers within the organisation. Integrated applications, when applied to internally intricate and diverse activities in manufacture, can rarely be put together by a single supplier as a 'packaged solution'. Instead, suppliers must select a range of components, and link them together in a network. This will involve some customisation to allow different components to operate together (insofar as interfaces are not yet standardised). Moreover, since standard technological offerings operating at the level of the whole organisation are unlikely to fit the precise requirements, structures and operating practices of any individual firm, this will require more extensive customisation (Fleck 1988b). The development of inter-organisational systems has rather different characteristics - as it requires a range of different organisations to reach agreement about the exchange of information.

Discrete Applications

Research into the implementation of 'discrete' technologies has uncovered a wide range of factors shaping the design of industrial technologies and associated forms of work organisation. These factors include the economic and political objectives of suppliers and managers in user companies, the occupational strategies of different groups in the user firm, their skills and negotiating strength, and specific features of the tasks being automated. As well as the immediate features of the labour process, the broader context, including the industrial relations system, and national culture, have all been shown to be important.

Research has shown that the introduction of discrete IT systems into the factory or the office brings about no single pattern of work organisation.

Though these technologies may have been designed around templates of existing jobs/tasks, coupled with specific objectives for social and organisational change - not only economic objectives, but also political conceptions of how jobs could be redesigned, in practice, these expectations have only been partially fulfilled (Fleck et al. 1990, Webster 1990). The radical improvements promised by a range of technologies have often not materialised. Their implementation involves a typically painful learning process that has, to date, been repeated for each new technical offering as it emerges (Senker 1987). User firms and suppliers have consistently underestimated the difficulty of implementing new technologies, and the need to invest in developing the organisation, training, and so on.

In the late 1970s, a rationalising model of technology prevailed: new technology was seen as a way of bringing the economics of mass production and 'Taylorist' work organisation to small and medium-sized batch methods, which had hitherto been largely exempted. In the 1980s, faced with popular perceptions of 'the Japanese challenge', new models of firm behaviour were articulated. Technologies began to be promoted and assessed on the basis of flexibility rather than just productivity. Initially, the priority was flexibility at the point of production, through, for example, programmable equipment. More recently, with the emergence of integrated applications, attention has shifted to the level of the firm and its strategic responsiveness to its environment (Zuboff 1988, DTI/PA Consultants 1990).

Integrated Applications

The socio-technical constituencies involved in the emergence of integrated IT systems tend to be more complex and diverse than with discrete technologies. Many suppliers may be involved, together with a range of members from different departments within the user organisation, with distinctive sets of interests, working practices and types of expertise. Clearly, the development of integrated information technologies is even more fluid than that of discrete technologies.

Integrated systems tend to be directed towards the overall performance of the organisation, rather than the conduct of particular tasks. Ideas about how integrated technologies will proceed are closely paralleled by concepts of industrial organisation (Clark & Staunton 1989; Webster & Williams 1993).

For example, in the financial services sector, integrated databases and new methods of service delivery based on IT were seen as allowing banks and building societies to become 'financial supermarkets' (Fincham et al. 1995). Similarly the concept of 'Computer-Integrated Manufacturing' (CIM), in which the diverse kinds of information involved in manufacturing are centralised on an integrated database, had an organisational correlate in emerging notions of the 'flexible firm', which has close linkages between its sales, marketing, design and production functions, as well as with its suppliers and customers (Fleck 1988b). Production and Inventory Control Systems (PICS) were projected as a stepping-stone towards this vision of CIM. This coincided with a growing emphasis on the success of organisational practices of Japanese firms - 'just-in-time' (JIT) - which also stressed flexibility of production, but through rather different means. These changing concepts of good industrial practice influenced the development of CIM technologies: JIT modules and other elements were added to PICS software systems. Packaged systems were promoted as a 'technical fix' to the problems of UK manufacturing organisations. However the initial supplier offerings often had their roots in large US corporations manufacturing complex assemblages and with very formalised information and decision procedures. The requirements of this software was far removed from the haphazard data collection and idiosyncratic planning practices of many of the UK firms who tried to adopt them. Initial implementations often proved unsuccessful (Clark and Newell 1993, Fleck 1993, Webster and Williams 1993).

Integrated IT systems are complex configurations of technical and organisational elements, which must be customised to the conditions into which they are introduced. Though integrated technologies were promoted alongside a vision of the transformation of organisations, in practice it was the former which was more immediately changed. Users were forced to reconfigure these technologies to suit their own particular local circumstances. This process threw up technical and organisational innovations, some of which could be applied elsewhere (Fleck 1994). So although expectations of dramatic improvements in organisational performance were not immediately fulfilled, despite substantial levels of investment (Freeman 1988), this 'innofusion' process may provide the basis for further technological and organisational development.

Inter-organisational Networks

Attention has shifted towards the development of IT networks that link different organisations ('Inter-Organisational Network/Systems' - IONS). The constituencies underpinning the development of IONS have a very different structure to those in company-level computerisation, where the user organisation ultimately retains control over the interface between the various components and the overall system operation, and has a direct contractual relationship with all the players (e.g. external suppliers). With IONS, the number of organisations linked to the network may be very large - indeed, notionally infinite. Organisations may thus be affected by the actions of others in the network with which they have no immediate contact. It is therefore essential to develop and agree standards for interfaces and protocols for data exchange to maintain the integrity and functioning of such networks. Organisations need to cooperate to agree these standards.

The first IONS thus emerged where relatively homogenous, and closely aligned groups of players were trading together intensively - for example Electronic Data Interchange (EDI) in the UK retail sector. This oligopolistic industry was also able to exploit the product/producer identification systems already established for bar-coding. Existing cheque clearing system similarly provided an informational template for the development of 'Electronic Funds Transfer At Point of Sale' (EFTPoS) (Kubicek and Seeger 1992, Williams 1995). Once established, these networks tend to grow, due to powerful network externalities - whereby their value to each player increases with the number of players using the system. The cost and inconvenience of catering for multiple, proprietary system has motivated the search for open systems.[3] There has been considerable success in agreeing protocols for transmitting data between different kinds of machines. It has proved more difficult to agree the content of messages, as these relate to the aims and practices of organisations that vary substantially between firms, industries and nations.

IONS, like the other organisational technologies we have reviewed, were conceived as enabling radical organisational change, by allowing firms to

---

3 Another factor has been public policy which saw EDI as a means of improving trading efficiency. In particular, the European Commission has been significant player in the search for global EDI standards - seeing in these a technological correlate of its vision of a single European market - to ensure that incompatible national EDI standards did not constitute a barrier to international trade.

change their strategic relationships with other players in the supply chain, securing competitive advantage, changing power relationships or even by-passing other players altogether. However the immediate need for competing firms to collaborate in agreeing the information to be exchanged has meant that many IONS reproduce existing commercial relationships, or change them only incrementally (Spinardi et al. 1996). Similarly, electronic markets, which could have dramatic affects on competition within a sector, have often been designed to provide 'a level playing field', that balanced the interests of existing players while preventing any one player gaining undue control. There is a complex interplay between collaboration and competition. This has, for example, shaped the design of EFTPoS systems (Kubicek and Seeger 1992, Howells & Hine 1993).

Today, attention is beginning to focus upon the emerging 'Information Superhighway' and in particular, the Internet. Although many 'social' and 'technical' problems must still be resolved concerning issues of access, security, reliability, usability, intellectual property rights etc., these developments are expected to have enormous implications for business (Dutton et al. 1994, Kahin & Keller 1995). This may have important consequences for the development of business applications. Many firms are using the Internet standards as the basis for their own internal systems - Intranets. A plethora of new offerings are coming on stream, including technologies such as Desk-Top Video-Conferencing (DTVC) and Computer-Supported Cooperative Work tools. Their design for end-user configuration and their adoption of open industry standards means that they can be flexibly adopted - including by business users with only modest technical knowledge. This suggests a very different kind of development process than that used for conventional ICT systems (Procter and Williams 1996). In addition, the features of these systems suggest that they may have profound importance for business activities. On the one hand their provision of relatively open communication facilities may make them more amenable tools for conducting business activities than earlier ICTs. For example, if DTVC is able to create communication that has the same characteristics as a face-to-face meeting ('virtual presence'), it may indeed facilitate the kinds of spatial restructuring of activities (for example teleworking) which have to date only happened to a limited degree with conventional ICT systems. Perhaps most importantly, the Internet opens up IONS to a much wider range of providers and customers, bringing business communication and services to a host of other firms and into the home.

ICTs in Everyday Life

The widespread societal application of ICTs started in the workplace. This has some distinctive features: the organisation provides a semi-public forum for innovation, with opportunities for direct engagement between organisational users and its suppliers.

As the price of microelectronic-based goods has fallen suppliers have sought to exploit the huge market of domestic consumers. Supplier-user relations are very different with mass consumer products and services - such as telematics technologies and ICT in the home - since the supplier does not have direct links with all its customers. The consumer may be represented `by proxy' - for example, through market research on panels of potential customers. However, the supplier has to take a major role in prefiguring, or indeed constructing, the customer and the market (Collinson 1993). This remains a rather difficult and uncertain process for many suppliers - particularly where the technologies are consumed in the private sphere of the household (Silverstone 1991).

Telematics Technologies

It is in the area of mass communication products/telematics that we have some of the clearest evidence about the centrality of user responses in shaping not only the differential success of new products, but the very conception of these products. Perhaps the most striking example is the telephone, which was originally conceived and promoted as a business communication tool for conveying price information to farmers, but which was re-invented by people in rural areas, particularly women, as a medium for social communication (Fischer 1992).

The markedly uneven success of telematics products and services (such electronic mail, videotex and fax) points to some of the complexities surrounding the design and uptake of technologies (van Rijn and Williams 1988). Success of new telematics services does not simply reflect their functionality and price, but also the extent to which they are compatible with the skills, understandings and habitual practices of potential users (Miles 1990, Thomas & Miles 1990). Network externalities are particularly important here - and a technology may not be attractive to a potential user if sufficient numbers of other users cannot be convinced to sign up - as in the case of videophones (Dutton 1995). This may explain the uneven success of technologies such as videotex, which have been strongly promoted over the last two decades, but which in most countries dramatically failed to fulfill the predicted rates of uptake (Bruce 1988, Thomas & Miles 1990, Schneider 1991, Christoffersen and Bouwman 1992). There are important, and enlightening exceptions - in particular the case of Minitel in France. Here France Telecom created circumstances favourable to the diffusion of the technology, and to social learning in innovating new services. This included making terminals available to large numbers of domestic consumers at low cost, and creating a framework for service suppliers to operate (including provision for charging for services through the customer's phone bill). As a result a huge range of information services could be made available - many of which proved commercially viable.

The history of facsimile technology also represents an extremely interesting case. 'Fax' was first conceived as early as 1843 and the first commercial launch was in 1865. However, this and successive attempts to develop the technology did not meet with success (though there were viable niche applications - for example in the technology used by newspapers to transmit photographic etc. images to remote offices). Fax did not take-off until the last decade, when its explosive growth was attributed to the success of Japanese suppliers in 'manufacturing a superior machine' that was cheap and designed into an easy-to-use package (Coopersmith 1993: 48). Only then was fax technology close enough to the requirements of everyday business and domestic members for them to be enrolled as consumers.

Significantly, the fax, and the other most widely spread telematics application, electronic mail, are both genuine media, making few presumptions about the kinds of communication they support. In this sense they parallel the tool-based approach which proved so successful in personal computing.

IT in the Home

The consumption of IT in the home remains a largely private sphere, with only weak, and predominantly indirect linkages between supplier and user (Cawson et al. 1995). A relatively small group of researchers has been addressing the development and adoption of ICTs for use in the home, including videotext, the home computer and home automation products e.g. the smart house (Silverstone and Hirsch 1992, Cawson et al 1995, Berg and Aune 1994). This work highlights the complexity of the household as a focus of innovation. Domestic users (and refusers) are not homogeneous; their responses are differentiated by gender, generation and class, and shaped in the complex social dynamics (or 'moral economy') of the family (Silverstone and Morley 1990, Silverstone 1991).

Given the paucity of links between designers and potential users, designers have often relied primarily upon their own experience and expertise; starting from their understanding of technological opportunities and imagining how these might be taken up in their own households - which may be far from typical (Cawson et al 1995). This may cause problems in the acceptability of ICT offerings. Perhaps the most obvious example today is the 'baroque' design of most contemporary video cassette recorders - which the vast majority of consumers find very difficult to use. Similarly, suppliers' lack of understanding of 'the housewife' as a possible user, and of 'her' needs, means that technologies in the area of the smart house reflect technology-push rather than user-need; they have not really addressed the realities of domestic labour and have had little appeal to many customers (Berg 1994b). This may be one reason why the adoption of domestic IT has often fallen far short of expectations (Thomas and Miles 1990).

The case of the home computer provides an illustration of how technologies are appropriated by domestic users (Silverstone and Hirsch 1992). The evolution of this technology became subject to a web of competing conceptions articulated by various players: government, suppliers, parents, children. Though initially promoted as a means of carrying out various 'useful' activities (word-processing, household accounts, and in particular as a support for educational programmes), this was largely subverted by consumers in the family. In particular boys, though possibly pressurising their parents to acquire a computer for educational reasons, were really interested in using them for playing computer games. Indeed their enormous interest in computer-games has shaped the evolution of home computers, leading to the creation of a specialised market for these products (Haddon 1992).

The final consumer may have little opportunity to engage upon the design and development of mass-produced goods, such as domestic ICTs (Cockburn 1993). However, even in this setting it is important to acknowledge the scope for these actors to articulate their own representations of technologies and uses which may differ from those articulated by technology suppliers (Sørensen and Berg 1992, Akrich 1992, Cockburn 1993). Where products are embraced by households, consumption continues to be an active process, involving decisions to purchase the technology and appropriate it within the household - in terms of where it is located and how it is incorporated within family routines (Silverstone and Morley 1990). Although the designer may seek to prefigure the user - and thus implicitly to constrain the ways in which the product is used - the final user still retains flexibility in the meanings they attribute to technologies, and in choices about the artefact will be appropriated. This often involves innovation by the consumer - using technology in ways not anticipated by the designer (Berg 1994a).

A Model of Innovation in Multimedia

The Future of Multimedia - the Importance of Social Learning

Multimedia refers literally and most generically to the facility to present information in a variety of media (for example, voice, and graphics as well as text) through a single integrated channel. Today it is used more specifically to refer to the expected convergence[4] of information and communication and broadcasting technologies, involving the installation of high-speed broadband communications networks, coupled with advances in processing power and usability of information technology, enabling the storage, processing and transmission of large volumes of digitised information creates the scope to

---

4   We should however treat claims about convergence with some caution. There is doubt as to the extent to which industries and product markets will indeed converge. (Fransman 1996). Concepts of convergence have gained currency at several stages in the history of ICT - underpinning the imputed 'Information Technology Revolution' (combining telecommunications and computing [see Forester 1985]) and the subsequent emergence of Information and Communications Technology (Dutton 1995).

handle graphics (static and animated) and sound as well as text. Multimedia thus does not refer to a particular technology, but to a cluster of innovations. Their ability to make information technology systems easier and more engaging to use underpin expectations of the rapid adoption of a new cluster of technologies under the rubric of multimedia, and the further expectation that applications based upon these converging technologies will rapidly become widely adopted in many areas of working and social life, and have profound social and economic implications.

Equally, the key aspect of Multimedia does not reside in any particular technical feature, but in the increased control and choices it offers for processing information. In this, two features are salient - interactivity between the user and the product or other users (for networked products) and 'multimedia-ness' - the scope to present data through more vivid forms than simple text (i.e. voice, graphics, moving images). There are a variety of alternative technical paths for delivering essentially the same kind of functionality, and there is little certainty at this stage about which technical routes will eventually succeed.

The development of multimedia is surrounded by enormous uncertainties. Whilst continued progress can be expected in the performance of the generic technical components (e.g. increasing information processing power) there is much less agreement about how these will be configured into delivery systems and about which applications will succeed..

Though significant technical obstacles remain (e.g. regarding the reliability and security of transactions across the Internet) perhaps the most profound uncertainties surround the social uptake and use of the new products and services. This is an area where we have very little direct experience or relevant knowledge. Indeed one of the key features of 'the multimedia revolution' to date is that it has primarily been driven by the perspectives of suppliers of equipment and services, informed largely by their expectations of what might be technically feasible. There is remarkably little evidence concerning the nature and extent of user demand. This may not be surprising insofar as few exemplars of these future services have been created to date - so there is little possibility to assess their attractiveness to the user. Most of the multimedia applications that have emerged to date are markedly conservative innovations - often simply on-line replicas of existing products and services. This represents a very rational strategy by suppliers seeking to minimise uncertainty, drawing on their existing expertise and links with existing customers. However, as we show below, the experience of earlier generations of technology suggests that the main products and services that eventually prevail in the future information society may well be far removed from the embryonic offerings available today. It is extremely difficult for suppliers to assess what user requirements will emerge - and supplier mis-perceptions have led to market failure of a number of new offerings. Suppliers of new products and services are forced to operate in a context of only limited information and considerable uncertainty about 'the user' and 'their needs' and how they might be satisfied by multimedia. Moreover 'users' and 'user needs' are not pre-existing and static entities, but emerge and evolve through an interaction between supplier offerings and user responses. In some ways, the supplier can be said to 'construct the user' - or rather to seek so to do. The key questions about the future of multimedia thus concern the engagement between supplier and user.

If multimedia is to become widespread, we suggest that an important feature of its evolution will be a highly distributed process - that we describe as social learning - involving a range of suppliers, promoters and intermediate and final users (Procter and Williams 1996). There has been some recognition of the importance of such social learning processes in the proliferation of social experiments, pilot projects and commercial trials of multimedia and related technologies (for example interactive-TV).

Multimedia as Configurational Technology

The concept of configurational technology is also highly relevant to understanding these developments. In particular it provides a schema for understanding how contradictory requirements are reconciled - in particular the tensions between global technological development and its local appropriation, and how supplier offerings may be matched to local user requirements. Like other rapidly changing complex technologies, multimedia is heterogeneous, combining offerings from a range of different suppliers to meet particular requirements, affording considerable flexibility in development, implementation and use. The concept of technological configurations can be applied at two levels:

i) to highlight the way that a range of component technologies (fibroptic cable, microprocessors, software tools) are assembled into particular configurations in terms of delivery systems (for example public kiosks, interactive TV or networked personal computers taking these systems into the home);

ii) to show how these delivery systems are themselves configured to the purposes of the particular networked multimedia applications that run upon them (for example teleshopping, on-line newspapers, games, interactive TV services). This is summarised in figure 2 below (Collinson 1996).

APPLICATIONS	Specific configurations - services, applications and products, within particular sectors and contexts	video-on demand tele-shopping CD-I education packages video-conferencing electronic cash-cards
DELIVERY SYSTEMS	Combinations of technologies for storage, display, delivery, distribution	CD-ROMs, PDAs Interactive-TV/set top boxes The Internet and services
COMPONENTS	basic building blocks that can be combined to enable product and system development	microprocessors, video standards ISDN bandwidth screen resolution software tools compression techniques
	definition	examples

Figure 2: *The Three Layer Model of Innovation in Multimedia (adapted from Collinson 1996)*

The importance of this schema is in charting the complexity of the innovation process underpinning the emerging information infrastructure. In particular, it opens up for examination the level of autonomy between the different levels. It suggests that certain components can be used in a variety of different platforms and applications, and can be put together in different ways with different social and technical characteristics and implications.

In terms of the influence of the user and social learning processes on multimedia the key social shaping processes concern the development and implementation of applications and their attendant delivery systems. It is here that the most salient societal choices about the character of the information superhighways and the applications running upon them will be made. For example some kinds of delivery system will be closely dedicated to particular kinds of application (for example, an interactive television terminal) - while others will provide a more open platform on which a range of networked services can be mounted (for example a personal computer linked to the Internet). These choices about the flexibility of the delivery system will therefore have important social implications - concerning the types of applications that the mass of users will readily be able to access, and the range of roles that these consumers will have. For example, will they mainly be passive consumers of informational products (on a broadcasting model) or will they be able to engage in more interactive uses, or will they even be information producers in their own right. This range of scenarios encompasses very different images of the character of the future 'Information Society'.

The significance of these processes are heightened by 'path dependencies', which are particularly pronounced with network technologies like multimedia. A number of application areas are likely to be the 'key drivers', bringing networked multimedia products into the home and workplace, and establishing models for other products and services, which may in turn constrain the kind of further applications that can be mounted upon them. The first widespread application will involve enormous sunk investments, by suppliers and users. This could be an important influence upon the shape of multimedia and its societal implications in the medium term, particularly if it leads to the widespread implementation of delivery systems and devices that are dedicated around the requirements of those specific applications (e.g. video-on-demand) rather than offering more flexible configurations (e.g. networked PCs). Public policy could be an important influence - particularly in relation to regulatory etc. requirements for the use of open standards and interoperability between services - though this will also be affected by the strategies of commercial providers and the balance they adopt between collaboration and the competitive pursuit of closed, proprietary solutions.

Conclusion

The future of multimedia is still open. Today a new generation of products and services are being envisaged around the development of 'multimedia' technologies (Collinson 1993, Cawson et al. 1995) and the 'information superhighways' that could bring digitised video and sound, as well as text messages, into the home. A plethora of products are being launched for the workplace (Procter and Williams 1996). Central and local government are investing in developments - particularly in relation to education. Huge markets are anticipated for new products that are interactive, easier to use, and more engaging. However, as this review has shown there is little understanding of what the products that will eventually prevail will look like (Dutton et al. 1994, Kahin & Keller 1995).

Though choices being made today may constrain future developments, there are enormous uncertainties - reflected for example in the formation and reformation of industrial alliances by some of the largest strategic players in the field. Experiences from earlier technologies are important. They point to the dangers of extrapolating from supplier-driven perspectives - particularly at a time when there is very little understanding of user requirements. Two particular lessons may perhaps be paramount:

i) the first concerns the need to maintain flexibility in our adoption of these new technologies. Let us take the example of telecommunications networks and standards. It is clearly desirable to avoid technological closure around incompatible systems, that might result in 'stove piping' in telecommunications networks (Spacek 1995). We could pursue open standards where these are established, or gateways between proprietary systems. However the search for universal, open standards has its dangers - as is shown in the case of EDI standards. It can be slow and result in unworkable, over-engineered solutions. Public policies can lead to premature closure around standards which become outmoded (for example Minitel in France may constitute an obstacle to adopting the new features offered by Internet standards. This suggests the need to consider migration paths, to allow upgrading of systems to be compatible with emerging standards;

ii) the second concerns the importance of user responses to successful innovation. Despite the huge amount of energy devoted by suppliers, promoters and media popularisers of multimedia-based products and services, there is remarkably little evidence about the nature and strength of user demand. The long awaited 'killer application' that will herald the multimedia revolution still somehow eludes. Many of the first round services launched (e.g. interactive TV) are only on the margins of commercial viability. Successful applications will doubtless emerge. In the meantime public and commercial promoters have recognised the need to develop better understanding of existing and nascent requirements of potential consumers/users of their offerings. They have even looked to social science and to social experiments to provide this information.

Social shaping of technology research can offer important insights here. It can also point to the need for continued scepticism. For example, we still do not know how best to match user requirements to the new technical possibilities - whether the biggest contribution will come from building more societal knowledge into the design of new applications - or whether to design generic offerings, and let final users learn how to adapt supplier offerings to their purposes.

References

Akrich, M. (1992), Beyond Social Construction of Technology: The Shaping of People and Things in the Innovation Process (Chapter 9, pp. 173 -190, Dierkes and Hoffmann (eds.) op. cit.).

Arthur, W. B. (1989), Competing Technologies, Increasing Returns and Lock-in by Historical Events (The Economics Journal Vol. 99, March, pp. 116-131).

Berg, A. (1994a), Technological Flexibility: Bringing Gender into Technology (or is it the other way around)? Chapter 5, pp. 94 - 110 in Cockburn, Cynthia and Furst-Dilic, Ruza (eds.) op. cit..

Berg, A (1994b), A Gendered Socio-technical Construction: the Smart House Chapter 9 pp. 165 - 180, in Cockburn, Cynthia and Furst-Dilic, Ruza (eds.) op. cit.

Berg, A and Aune, M. (eds.) (1994), Domestic Technology and Everyday Life - Mutual Shaping Processes, COST A4 Vol. 1, Social Sciences, European Commission Directorate-General Sciences Research and Development, Luxembourg: Office for Official Publications of the European Communities.

Bijker, W. and Law, J. (eds.) (1992), Shaping Technology/Building Society: Studies in Socio-technical Change (Cambridge/MA, London: MIT Press).

Brady, T., Tierney, M. and Williams, R. (1992), The Commodification of Industry Applications Software (Industrial and Corporate Change, Vol. 1 No. 3 pp. 489-514).

Bruce, M. (1988), Home Interactive Telematics - Technology with a History, in van Rijn, F. and Williams, R. (eds.) Concerning Home Telematics (Amsterdam: North-Holland, pp. 83-93).

Campbell-Kelly, M. (1989), ICL: A Business and Technical History (Oxford: Oxford University Press).

Cawson, A., Haddon L. and Miles, I. (1995), The Shape of Things to Consume: Delivering IT into the Home (Aldershot, Avebury).

Christoffersen, M. and Bouwman, H (eds.) (1992), Relaunching Videotexm (Dordrecht: Kluwer).

Clark, P. and Staunton, N. (1989), Innovation in Technology and Organization (London: Routledge).

Clark, P. and Newell, S. (1993), Societal Embedding of Production and Inventory Control Systems: American and Japanese Influences on Adaptive Implementation in Britain (International Journal of Human Factors in Manufacturing, Vol. 3, No. 3, pp. 69-81).

Cockburn, C. (1993), Feminism/Constructivism in Technology Studies: Notes on Genealogy and Recent Developments (Paper to Workshop on European Theoretical Perspectives on New Technology: Feminism Constructivism and Utility Brunel University, September 1993).

Cockburn, C. and Furst-Dilic, R (eds.) (1994), Bringing Technology Home: Gender and Technology in a Changing Europe (Milton Keynes: Open University Press).

Collingridge, D (1992), The Management of Scale: Big Organizations, Big Decisions, Big Mistakes (London/NY: Routledge).

Collinson, S. (1993), Managing Product Innovation at Sony: the Development of the Data Discman (Technology Analysis and Strategic Management, Vol.. 5, No. 3, pp. 285-306).

Collinson, S. et al. (1996), Forecasting and Assessment of Multimedia in Europe 2010+, Final Report to European Commission, (Edinburgh: University of Edinburgh).

Coopersmith, J. (1993), Facsimile's False Starts (IEEE Spectrum, February, pp. 46-49).

Cowan, R. (1992), High Technology and the Economics of Standardization (Chap. 14, pp. 279-300 in Dierkes and Hoffmann (1992), op. cit.).

David, P. (1975), Technical Choice, Innovation and Economic Growth: Essays on American and British Experience in the Nineteenth Century (Cambridge: Cambridge University Press).

Dierkes, M. and Hoffmann, U. (eds.)(1992), New Technology and the Outset: Social Forces in the Shaping of Technological Innovations (Frankfurt/NY: Campus/Westview).

DTI/PA Consultants Group (1990), Manufacturing into the 1990s (London, HMSO).

Dunlop, C. and Kling, R. (eds.) (1991), Computerization and Controversy : Value Conflicts and Social Choices (Boston : Academic Press).

Dutton, W., Bloomler, J., Garnham, N., Mansell, R., Cornford, J. and Peltu, M. (1994), The Information Superhighway: Britain's Response, (Policy Research Paper, No. 29, Programme on Information and Communications Technologies, Economic and Social Research Council).

Dutton, W. (1995), Driving into the Future of Telecommunications? Check the Rear View Mirror, Chap. 5. pp. 79 - 102, in Emmott, S.J. (ed,) Information Superhighways : Multimedia Users and Futures (London: Academic Press).

Fincham, R., Fleck, J., Procter, R., Scarbrough, H., Tierney, M. and Williams, R. (1995), Expertise and Innovation: Information Strategies in the Financial Services Sector (Oxford: Oxford University Press/Clarendon).

Fischer, C. (1992), America Calling. A Social History of the Telephone to 1940 (Berkeley: University of California Press).

Fleck, J. (1988a), Innofusion or Diffusation? The Nature of Technological Development in Robotics (Edinburgh PICT Working Paper No. 7, Edinburgh University).

Fleck, J. (1988b), The Development of Information Integration: Beyond CIM? (Edinburgh PICT Working Paper No. 9, Edinburgh University). A digest of this paper, prepared for the Department of Trade and Industry, is available as Information-Integration and Industry (PICT Policy Research Paper No. 16, Economic and Social Research Council, Oxford, 1991).

Fleck, J. (1993), Configurations : Crystallizing Contingency (International Journal of Human Factors in Manufacturing, Vol. 3, No. 1, p.15-36).

Fleck, J. (1994), Learning by Trying: the Implementation of Configurational Technology (Research Policy, Vol. 23, pp. 637 -652).

Fleck, J. (1995), Configurations and Standardization, pp. 38 - 65 in Esser, J., Fleischmann, G., and Heimer T. (eds), Soziale und Okonomische Konflicte in Standardisierungsprozessen (Frankfurt: Campus Verlag).

Fleck, J., Webster, J., and Williams, R. (1990), The Dynamics of IT Implementation: a Reassessment of Paradigms and Trajectories of Development, (Futures, Vol. 22, pp. 618-40).

Forester, T. (1985), The Information Technology Revolution (Oxford: Blackwell).

Fransman, M. (1996), Information Regarding the Information Superhighway and Interpretive Ambiguity (IEEE Communications Magazine July 1996, pp. 76 - 80).

Freeman, C. (1988), The Factory of the Future: the Productivity Paradox, Japanese Just-In-Time and Information Technology (PICT Policy Research Paper No. 3, London: Economic and Social Research Council, Programme on Information and Communications Technologies).

Friedman, A. and Cornford, D. (1989), Computer Systems Development: History Organisation and Implementation (Chichester: John Wiley & Sons).

Haddon, L. (1992), Explaining ICT Consumption: The Case of the Home Computer (Chap. 5, pp. 82 - 96 in Silverstone and Hirsch (eds.) (1992)).

Howells, J. and Hine, J. (eds.) (1993), Innovative Banking: Competition and the Management of a New Networks Technology (London/NY: Routledge).

Kahin, B. and Keller, J. (eds.) (1995), Public Access to the Internet (Cambridge MA/London: MIT Press).

Kubicek, H. and Seeger, P. (1992), The Negotiation of Data Standards: a Comparative Analysis of EAN- and EFTPOS-Systems (Chap 15, pp. 351 - 374 in Dierkes and Hoffmann (eds.) (1992)).

MacKenzie, D. and Wajcman, J. (eds.) (1985), The Social Shaping of Technology: How the Refrigerator Got Its Hum (Milton Keynes, Open University Press).

Miles, I. (1990), Home Telematics: Information Technology and the Transformation of Everyday Life (London: Frances Pinter).

Molina, A. (1989), The Social Basis of the Microelectronics Revolution (Edinburgh: Edinburgh University Press).

Molina, A. (1992), Competitive Strategies in the Microprocessor Industry : the Case of an Emerging versus an Established Technology (International Journal of Technology Management, 7, 6/7/8 [Special issue on the Strategic Management of Information and Telecommunication Technology], p.589-614).

Molina, A. (1994), Understanding the Emergence of a Large-scale European Initiative in Technology (Science and Public Policy 21, 1, p. 31 - 41).

Morris, C. R. and Ferguson, C. H. (1992), How Architecture Wins Technology Wars (Harvard Business Review Vol. 71, No. 2, pp. 86 - 96).

Noble, D. (1979), Social Choice in Machine Design: the Case of Automatically Controlled Machine Tools, pp. 18-50, in Zimbalist, A. (ed.), Case Studies on the Labour Process (New York: Monthly Review Press).

OECD (1985), Software: an Emerging Industry (Paris: Organisation of Economic Cooperation and Development).

Pelaez, E. (1990), What Shapes Software Development? (Edinburgh PICT Working Paper No. 10, Edinburgh University).

Pickering, A. (ed.) (1992), Science as Practice and Culture (Chicago: University of Chicago Press).

Pinch, T. & Bijker, W. (1984), The Social Construction of Facts and Artefacts: Or How the Sociology of Science and the Sociology of Technology might Benefit Each Other (Social Studies of Science, Vol. 14, No. 3 (August), pp. 399-441).

Procter, R. N. and Williams, R. (1996), Beyond Design: Social Learning and Computer-Supported Cooperative Work: Some Lessons from Innovation Studies, Chap. 26, pp. 445 - 464, in Shapiro, D., Tauber, M. and Traunmueller, R. (eds), (1996), The Design of Computer-Supported Cooperative Work and Groupware Systems (Amsterdam: North Holland, 1996).

Quintas, P. (ed.) (1993), Social Dimensions of Systems Engineering: People, Processes, Policies and Software Development (NY/London: Ellis Horwood).

Schneider, V. et al., (1991), The Dynamics of Videotex Development in Britain, France and Germany: A Cross-national Comparison (European Journal of Communication Vol. 6 No. 2, June 1991).

Senker, P. (1987), Towards the Automatic Factory?: the Need for Training (Bedford, IFS).

Silverstone, R. (1991), Beneath the Bottom Line: Households and Information and Communication Technologies in an Age of the Consumer (PICT Policy Research Papers No. 17, Swindon: Economic and Social Research Council).

Silverstone, R. and Morley, D. (1990), Families and Their Technologies: Two Ethnographic Portraits, pp. 74-83, in Putnam, T. and Newton, C. (eds.), Household Choices (London: Futures Publications).

Silverstone, R. and Hirsch, E. (eds.) (1992), Consuming Technologies : Media and Information in Domestic Spaces (London: Routledge).

Simon, H. (1982), Models of Bounded Rationality (2 volumes) (Cambridge, Mass.: MIT Press).

Sørensen, K. H. (1994), Adieu Adorno: The Moral Emancipation of Consumers (pp. 157 - 169 in Berg and Aune (eds.) op. cit.).

Sørensen, K. H. and Berg, A. (eds.) (1992), Technologies and Everyday Life: Trajectories and Transformations, Proceedings from a Workshop in Trondheim, May 28-29 1990, Report No. 5 (Oslo: Norwegian Research Council for Science and the Humanities).

Spacek, T. (1995), How Much Interoperability? (Chapter 4 in this volume).

Spinardi, G., Graham, I. and Williams, R. (1996), EDI and Business Process Re-enginering Why the Two Don't Go Together (New Technology, Work and Employment, March 1996 Vol. 11, no 1, pp. 16 - 27).

Swann, P. (1990), Standards and the Growth of a Software Network, pp. 383-93, in Berg, J. L. and Schumny, H. (eds.) An Analysis of the Information Technology Standardization Process (Amsterdam: Elsevier Science/North-Holland).

Swann, P. and Lamaison, H. (1989), The Growth of an IT Network: a Case Study of Personal Computer Applications Software (Discussion Papers in Economics, No. 8807, Brunel University).

Thomas, G. and Miles, I. (1990), Telematics in Transition (London: Longman).

von Hippel (1990), The Impact of "Sticky Data" on Innovation and Problem Solving, Sloan School of Management Working Paper, 3147-90-BPS (Cambridge, Mass.: MIT Press).

van Rijn, F. and Williams, R. (eds.) (1988), Concerning Home Telematics (Amsterdam: North-Holland).

Walsh, V. (1993), Demand, Public Markets and Innovation in Biotechnology (Science and Public Policy Vol. 20, No. 3, pp. 138-156).

Webster, J. (1990), Office Automation: the Labour Process and Women's Work in Britain (Hemel Hempstead: Harvester Wheatsheaf).

Webster, J. and Williams, R. (1993), Mismatch and Tension: Standard Packages and Non-standard Users , Chapter 9, pp. 179 - 196, in P. Quintas (ed.), (1993).

Williams, R. (ed.) (1995), The Social Shaping of Inter-organisational IT Systems and Electronic Data Interchange COST A4 Vol. 3, Social Sciences, European Commission Directorate-General Sciences Research and Development, Luxembourg: Office for Official Publications of the European Communities.

Williams, R. and Edge, D. (1996), The Social Shaping of Technology, Research Policy, Vol.25, pp.865-99

Zuboff, S. (1988), In the Age of the Smart Machine : the Future of Work and Power (Oxford: Heinemann).

19. Different Roads to the Information Society? Comparing U.S. and European Approaches from a Public Policy Perspective

Volker Schneider

Introduction

Since the late '70s, the information and communications sectors in the industrialized world have been subject to increasing political intervention. In the context of declining employment in traditional sectors, it is hoped that the rise of communications and information industries - telematics - will spur new business activities and create new jobs. The growing importance of these industries is accompanied by a vision that telematics will transform the old social order of the industrial era; the new "information society" is a development goal supported by many governments through a variety of policy instruments.

Different countries vary in their commitment to supporting the sunrise sectors, however. It is no coincidence that the strongest political support for telematics has come from countries like Japan and France. Both have engaged in the most pronounced socio-political discourse on the information age. In Japan, this discourse emerged as early as the late '60s; In France, a decade later, it was stimulated by the Nora and Minc report.[1] In both countries, government policy on telematics is explicitly neo-mercantilist. This stands in contrast to countries like the USA, Germany, and the U.K., where political intervention in the area has been less pronounced. In these latter countries, governments have restricted themselves to improving supply conditions in the private sector. By the '80s, the European Community (EC) instigated a series

---

1 For Japanese developments, see Ito (1980); the French report on societal informatization is was published by Nora and Minc (1978).

of policy initiatives for promoting relevant R&D in European firms, and for opening up the telecommunications markets of its member states (Schneider et al. 1994).

Since the early '90s, a new wave of policy measures is swamping the telematic sectors in North America and Europe. The focus has shifted from political intervention into meso-industrial development, to the initiation of large scale infrastructural projects at the intersectoral level. The new wave was triggered by the U.S. government in 1993, with the launching of its National Information Infrastructure (NII) Initiative. In the following year, the European Union (EU) established its action plan *Europe's way to the Information Society*. Both policy initiatives address similar problems, aim at similar goals, and adopt similar strategies. However, there are important policy differences between the two which require analysis.

Taking a comparative public perspective based on an actor-centered institutionalist perspective (Mayntz and Scharpf 1995, Scharpf 1997), this chapter discusses the major similarities and differences between the American and European approaches, with respect to agenda-building and programme formulation. It then explains these differences in terms of what separates the two structural and institutional policy contexts.

The Social Shaping of Technology Development from a Comparative Public Policy Perspective

During the past decade much social and political research has focused on understanding technological development, i.e., the identification of factors which shape innovative technical artifacts and systems. In contrast to concepts in which technologies just emerge as a function of changes in technological opportunity structures, a growing literature emphasises the importance of social factors in technology development.

It is important to note that the suggestion that technical artifacts are socially constructed does not only mean that technology is man-made - such a proposition would hardly be provocative. Rather, there are more intriguing arguments stating that technical artifacts are not only manifestations of natural laws and rule systems, implemented by human agents, but socio-technical configurations that are inherently shaped by social interests and their related dynamics. Some sociologists of science and technology even assert that everything in a technology can be interpreted in terms of its social relations.[2] Such a radical constructivist perspective over-stretches the theoretical problematic: technology is constructed by social subjects, but not all elements in the construction set can be manipulated by human action. While technical decisions are made by human actors embedded in social institutions, they are also constrained by the rules of the physical world.

In a large technical system, social action and social relations do not belong to the environment of the technology (i.e., a technical artifact, or a network of artifacts) but are integrated components which contribute to the overall performance of the system (Mayntz and Hughes 1988). Individual actors, organizations, institutions, networks of resource exchange, individual artifacts, and interconnected machines - all are components of a complex, heterogeneous, and hybrid web. For engineering scientists it may be sufficient to compress these disparate social elements in a global "remainder". In the social and political sciences, however, distinguishing between the different levels and pillars of the social fabric is our "core business" (Schneider 1993).

What is meant by explaining the genesis and evolution of a large technical infrastructure - such as the information superhighway - from a comparative public policy perspective? The study of its social shaping is, on the one hand, concerned with the process of public policy-making involving the whole machinery of political decision-making. On the other, it uses an inductive explanation strategy in which differences in the explanandum are essentially explained by differences in the explanans. However, such a comparative explanation in the narrow sense cannot be applied to all research problems. In situations where few cases can be observed, this mode of explanation cannot operate in statistical terms (e.g., controlled variation, and search for degrees of variance explained by one or several variables) but can only be made more or less plausible on narrative grounds.

A first question in a public policy perspective is why a technological project does not remain solely with technologists or business firms, but becomes a matter of public policy and state decision-making. One explanation goes that some societal problems become a political matter when market-guided economic activities fail to provide an autonomous and self-regulated solution to a

---

2   For instance, Latour holds that machines are "alliances between brains, microbes, electrons and fuels" (Latour 1987 p.128) and technical systems are seen as "actor networks".

particular social need. In the case of technological infrastructures, many arguments are advanced as to why pure market activities are unable to mobilize resources, or coordinate the whole endeavour (see Denkhaus and Schneider 1997).

One of those market failures is a minimal size problem: some infrastructures (e.g., the telephone network) are lumpy or indivisible, in the sense that they cannot be incrementally set up, but only perform efficiently beyond a certain minimum size. It only becomes attractive for users to join such a system, (with a given price for network access) when a critical mass of other users are already connected.[3] Partly (but not exclusively) because of this size problem, infrastructural investments often involve extremely high financial risks which private entrepreneurs are usually not inclined to carry. The argument for public provision of infrastructures is an old one, used by Adam Smith in the 18th century.

There are other arguments for a public provision of infrastructures such as the inapplicability of the exclusion principle to such investments; their status as generalized essentials; their creation of positive externalities; or the myopia of consumers, which will not be discussed at length in this context.

In contrast to such an economic perspective, in which the market is treated as the natural state of society and the "mother of all problem-solving", there are approaches which emphasise other societal subsystems, or partial rationalities, which shape political intervention in this arena. In such a macro sociological perspective, non-economic governance mechanisms have the status of "devices of last resort", only applied to redeem the failures that are produced by market coordination. In contrast, these are relatively autonomous subsystems existing in their own right, which create their own rationale for political intervention into society. State intervention into technological developments may be purely politically-motivated, e.g., in a political culture which expects government action, or in a party system where different parties or candidates out-bid each other in proposals for state intervention.

While market failure and non-economic governance theories are generally based on structural arguments, there are also theories which explain government intervention in terms of the core interests of elites, classes, or other

---

3   For a discussion and application of the critical mass concept see also Hohn and Schneider (1991).

power groups which capture and instrumentalize the state apparatus to achieve their goals.

Given the variety of reasons for public intervention into the development of technological systems, the process of public policy-making may be analytically differentiated into, on the one hand, its constituent phases and its actor systems and decision arenas, and, on the other, the typical instruments that are applied by government to respond to the policy topic in question.

Policy analysis generally distinguishes between agenda-building, programme formulation, and implementation. The notion of an actor system points to the (inter-relationships of) different groups and organizations that are involved in a policy topic. The arena concept relates to the institutional landscapes and battle grounds where policy decisions are selected. Policy instruments, finally, are usually classified into the categories of money (applied mainly in (re)distributive policy); norms and regulations (used in regulative and legislative policy); ideas and visions (applied in persuasive or ideational policy); and organizational or institutional arrangements (used in coordinative policy-making).

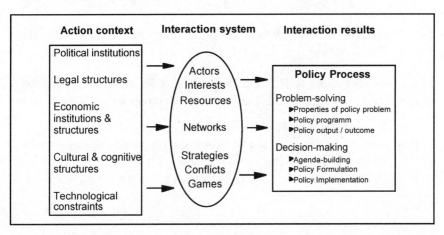

Figure 1: *An institutionalist and actor-centered framework for policy analysis*

A further distinction separates the situational dimension (i.e., alliances, tactics, strategies, games, and constellations) of the policy action systems, from its structural and institutional setting. Public policy-making is usually not only situationally-determined but is also embedded in more stable and enduring environments which frame policy opportunities and restrictions. The different levels and sequences of this analytical schema are presented in Figure 1, adapted from Schneider and Mayntz (1995). This model clarifies how technologies are shaped by non-technical factors. If social factors had no explanatory power, the technological pool and its opportunity structures would completely determine the shaping process.

A further relevant distinction in policy analysis is the differentiation between policy output and policy outcome. Are we discussing the policy output in terms of the public action programme which addresses the policy goal, or the final policy outcome, i.e. the transformation of the programme into reality including its second order effects? In the case of the unfolding of information society initiatives, policy outcomes are not yet available to us. It will be some years before the superhighway materializes in concrete arrays of networks and service applications, or becomes a living reality for its users. Nevertheless, the very planning activities and the mobilization of financial subsidies for pilot applications have triggered great expectations.

Scrutinizing the Policy Process: Similarities and Differences in Public Intervention into High-Tech Development

In the following sections, U.S. and European policies for advanced telematic infrastructures will be treated as (varying) policy outputs with respect to:

- their different pathways to the policy agenda; and,
- their process characteristics and programme formulation outputs, including the establishment of advisory bodies and task forces, the support of field trials and pilot projects, and the initiation and sponsoring of legislation.

Problem Perception and Agenda-Building

In both Europe and the U.S., public intervention into telematics has a long history. In both, telecommunications (a major component of the telematics field) has been an established policy domain since the beginning of this century. In European telecommunications in general, national governments were directly responsible for network construction and services operation, through specialized administrative departments or public corporations. In contrast, the U.S. government was only indirectly involved, through regulatory policy via independent agencies in this sector. Technology development, network construction, and service operation was undertaken by AT&T - a private company enjoying a quasi-monopoly - and a number of smaller independent private operators.

During the '70s and '80s - when the telecommunications and information sectors started to converge, and telematics grew in economic importance - this sector received increased attention from trade and industrial policy-makers. Telecommunications in both the U.S. and the U.K. became a prime target for deregulation and liberalization measures. At the same time, impressed by Japan's industrial modernization, the EC also identified telematics as a key to global competitiveness[4]. As computing and telecommunications increasingly became infrastructural essentials for most other economic activity, they also gained increasing relevance for competition, trade, industrial, and media policy-making[5]. Thus, analysing the agenda-building on superhighway issues demands a broad perspective in which telecommunications is nested in a number of other policy fields creating a complex "ecology of policy games" (Dutton 1992).

Although Europe and the U.S. enjoy roughly equal technological capacities, the politics of agenda-setting in the two superhighway initiatives reveal some significant differences between them. With respect to how the superhighway issue was politicized and the topic advanced to a high priority amongst governmental actors, the U.S. is a case of a primarily domestic policy determination. In contrast, the European initiative was clearly shaped at the level of transnational relations, and primarily has to be understood as a reaction to the pressures and constraints of global competition.

The U.S. NII initiative emerged in 1992/1993, and was conditioned by a combination of special features of the U.S. political system, with a presidential campaign starting in the context of a broad public discussion on an infrastructural crisis[6]. An important peculiarity of U.S. presidential campaigns is

---

4 For the historical process of EC intervention into the telecommunications sector, see Schneider et al. (1994), and for a current overview see Curwen (1995).

5 A structural analysis of the telecommunications domain in Germany and an evaluation of its growing importance over the last decades is presented in Schneider and Werle (1991).

6 An overview of the discussion on infrastructures is offered by Gramlich (1994).

that they usually concentrate on very few topics: the NII quickly advanced on the policy agenda because the Clinton team used it as a key bullet point in their election campaign. They were running as New Democrats who stood for strong government leadership in industrial and technological development, and contrasted sharply with the laissez-faire approach of the Reagan and Bush era. The presence of Senator Al Gore on the team - an expert on telecommunications issues who had been advocating the construction of an information highway for years - signalled that the NII had a high priority for the incoming Clinton administration (Drake 1995).

When Clinton was elected in late 1992, the topic shifted to the arena of government policy, and by February 1993, the NII found official expression for the first time in *Technology for America's Economic Growth. A New Direction to build Economic Strength* (Clinton and Gore 1993). In May 1993, a newly-established Council for Competitiveness (COC) presented a document entitled *Vision for a 21st Century* (COC 1993). In September 1993, this lead to the proposal of *The National Information Infrastructure: Agenda for Action* (Infrastructure Task Force 1993). In the same year, a specialized Information Infrastructure Task Force (IITF) was formed, and a Telecommunications Policy Roundtable (TPR) was established to bring together the major interests concerned.

In contrast to this exclusively domestic policy process in the U.S., the EU initiative should be conceived as the result of global policy diffusion. In essence, it is an adoption and response to the U.S. initiatives and to similar objectives pursued by Japan[7]. Notwithstanding these global origins, however, the European initiative is by no means a simple policy replication of the American process. It was adapted to the specific European policy problem context, a context involving the EU-level as well as the national level of different EU member countries.

The EC superhighway policy is often reduced to the Bangemann Report (Bangemann 1994), without appreciating it within the broader frame of EC telecommunications policy-making, and the Internal Market programme in general. Since 1986, the EC has launched a series of R&D projects and liberalization measures for telecommunications. Of particular importance here is

---

7   The Japanese way toward the information society is described in Latzer (1995). For a
    description of further national initiatives especially in - but not restricted to - Europe,
    see Vedel (1997).

the RACE (Research on Advanced Communication in Europe) programme, by which the research efforts of European firms were funnelled to develop and produce advanced information and telecommunications technologies (ICTs) that are competitive in global markets (Grande and Häusler 1994). In contrast to the general EU policy tendency to promote market integration - also called "negative integration" (Scharpf 1995) - the coordination of common R&D projects, the building of European network infrastructures, and the promotion of European computer networks, have always been seen as important elements of "positive" European integration.

Against this background, the EC initiative may be seen as the logical consequence, and simple continuity, of traditional European research, competition, and industrial policy initiatives. An interesting anomaly to this continuity thesis, however, is that the promotion of integrated broadband networks has not received much support from national network operators since the late '80s. This resistance has less to do with the opposition of critical groups to integrated digital communications than with a concern with over-capacity and the high financial risks associated with giant investments. Operators such as the German Bundespost - having tenaciously promoted a B-ISDN (Broadband Integrated Services Digital Network) during the '80s - became rather prudent in the early '90s.

Interestingly, as soon as the NII had conquered the U.S. government agenda and all began talking about the superhighway to come, European scruples about infrastructural overcapacities were forgotten. The EU policy of promoting the construction of Trans European Broadband Networks (TEBN) suddenly had the support of its member countries. Echoing old European fears, U.S. and Japanese deregulation and liberalization policies dramatized how Europe might be economically colonized. Once it was realized that the Americans were making the "big leap" towards the information society, the fear emerged, this time round, that they would gain complete global control of converging multimedia sectors.[8]

As other chapters in this volume have noted, a key event in this process was the White Paper on *Growth, Competitiveness and Employment - The*

---

8 At least in France such interpretations florished: "L'importance politique et industrielle du projet de "Global Information Infrastructure" proposé par Al Gore ne fait aucun doute: l'objectif américain est très clairement le controle du plus grand nombre possible des maillon mondiaux de la nouvelle chaine numérique de la communication." (Théry 1994)

Challenges and Ways Forward into the 21st Century, commissioned by Jacques Delors in December 1993 (Commission of the European Communities 1993). It highlighted the move towards the information society as a key strategy to promote economic growth and employment; the construction of information networks, and European networks in the transport and energy sectors, were to be of prime importance. Subsequently a group of senior industrialists, coordinated by Commissioner Martin Bangemann, was established to report to the next European Council meeting in Corfu. The resulting Bangemann Report - *Europe and the Global Information Society - Recommendations to the European Council* - was published in May 1994 (Bangemann 1994). It proposed liberalization measures, arguing that the best support for the growth of information networks and services would be open and competitive markets.

At the request of the European Council in Corfu in June, the Commission prepared an Action Plan containing a set of policies and actions directed toward revising the regulatory framework to support a fully liberalized institutional environment; promoting pilot projects for the development of networks, applications, and new services in a list of key areas; and reflecting social and cultural aspects of the information society (Commission of the European Communities 1994). Working groups of senior industrial leaders were established to define the practical implementation of these projects, which would be marketed through the Information Society Project Office (ISPO) created in December 1994 for that purpose.

Finally, it should not be forgotten that the fourth R&D framework programme for the period 1994-1999 was also launched during this period. It specified three programmes directly concerned with accelerating the launching of the information society: information technologies, telematics applications, and advanced communication technologies and systems (Commission of the European Communities 1993a).

Policy Programme Formulation

The next stage of analysis refers to similarities and differences in policy formulation. It is useful to distinguish between process characteristics and content features.

With respect to the process, we find a number of similarities: both procedures begin with expert reports and White Papers which are finally transformed into Action Plans (in the U.S., the Agenda for Action; in the EU, the
Action Plan discussed above. Based on the latter, specific tasks are distributed to either the relevant administrative units or coordination committees. In
both cases, advisory boards or discussion forums have been created to channel contributions from broader socio-political interest groups.

There are also some important differences between the two processes. One
is that the U.S. process is more participatory, open, and transparent than its
EU counterpart. The three main arenas of policy-making in the U.S. are the
Clinton Administration, Congress, and the FCC (Federal Communications
Commission). Initiation, promotion, and planning occur in the White House
and the relevant administrative departments, especially in the NTIA (National
Telecommunications and Information Administration) within the Department
of Commerce. Legislative policy-making is done in Congress, and the set-up
of regulations in the FCC. All these sites are highly transparent to the general
public; a plurality of interests may gain access through, for example, hearings.

Of special importance here is institutionalized representation in the NII Advisory Council. The relationship between the contending political forces is
highly competitive. This means that legislative proposals, each sponsored by
different Congressmen and supported by varying extra-parliamentarian alliances, often compete directly (Abernathy 1994, Drake 1995). The process is
characterized by serious lobbying. In the selling of the superhighway, the
stakes were high. For example, the special interest donations to congressional
committees with power over deregulation and communications were as high
as donations in the health reform initiative (Abernathy 1994). A compromise
bill was finally found in late 1995, passed House and Senate again, and came
into force in February 1996, thus profoundly rewriting the 1934 Communications Act[9] (see Chapter 10 in this volume for a detailed discussion).

With respect to the planning of concrete applications for the superhighway,
the Clinton Administration maintained contact with public interest groups and
other non-profit organizations, seeking to counterbalance the tremendous
lobbying activities of corporate interests. In addition, the whole process was

---

9   The legislative process of the Telecommunications Act of 1996 is documented in detail
    in the Internet at URL: http://www.bell.com/.

closely observed by the mass media, giving American superhighway politics a high degree of transparency.

In contrast, the EU programme has been shaped with considerably less openness. It was formulated primarily through expert committees, almost exclusively composed of bureaucrats and industrial corporate interests. In contrast to the U.S. process, public interest groups representing non-commercial social interests were virtually irrelevant. Only later was representation broadened and formalized with the setting-up of the European Information Society Forum. Compared to its American counterparts, this forum is extremely large and represents too many non-aligned interest groups at once (whether territorial, functional, or cultural). From a decision perspective it is clearly a forum and not a council, where decisions are prepared and bargained for. In this respect the "real" decisions are made in much smaller, restricted, and more specialized committees.

In the current political science literature there is a general consensus that the major decision arenas in EU policy-making are the councils and committees surrounding the Commission, and the Council with its Committee of Permanent Representatives (COREPER). As a rule, policies are debated and coordinated in advance so that, in most cases, the Council merely rubber-stamps the compromises already agreed by the relevant expert committees sponsored by the Commission (van Schendelen 1993). This does not mean that pre-arranged compromises between policy experts and technocrats always survive at the Council level; for thorny issues, pre-bargaining often proves impossible. However, as a general rule, policies are largely agreed in advance, so that in the final phase of decision-making at the Council level there is no direct competition between different policy proposals. This differs profoundly from legislation in the U.S. Congress.

Besides these process variations, there are also similarities and differences with respect to the content of the programmes. At a rather abstract level, the American and European policy initiatives have very similar goals: both are directed towards creating new markets, increasing productivity, and reducing coordination costs. Both also coincide in the diagnosis that advanced industrial societies are about to become information societies. To eliminate existing legal restrictions during the transition, both programmes aim at further deregulation and liberalization of broadcasting and telecommunications. In the

EU, we find a long list of directives aimed at achieving this goal[10], e.g., the directive on full competition in telecommunications (96/19/EC). As mentioned earlier, the U.S. has recently enacted the most significant rewriting of telecommunications and broadcasting law since 1934.

Besides these similarities, however, there are important differences in the contents of the two programmes. The U.S. programme - inspired by Al Gore's technological optimism - is highly visionary. It encompasses a social and political vision, as much as an economic perspective. The NII initiative emphasises the potential of ICTs to solve social problems (e.g., to augment democratic control, to broaden access to information, and to support educational activities). The EU initiative has a much more commercial character. In the EU technocratic perspective, the information society consists of a basic physical network, generic services (e-mail, databases etc.), and applications such as telework, telebanking, and telemedicine. However, this commercial and technocratic vision is no surprise. It is not political and cultural integration which cements the EU, but economic and technological cooperation. As a "union", the EU is still in its infancy (see Chapter 17 for a discussion).

Related to this conceptual difference, there seems to be a reverse relationship between visionary and symbolic content, and real money spending. As a detailed comparison of the U.S. and EU programmes show, public financial investments in the U.S. cover only a fraction of the huge public spending within the EU (Lobet-Maris and d'Udekem-Gevers 1995, and see Chapter 11 of this volume). EU measures are backed by a large bundle of financial subventions to telematic industries, in conformity with the EU's general distributive policies towards agriculture and R&D.

A further difference is that public, or semi-public, infrastructural projects - Trans-European ISDN or IBC networks, for instance - play a bigger role in Europe than in the U.S., despite the latter's concern with their "infrastructural crisis". In the American context, the role of government is more or less reduced to promoting and coordinating private investments, and regulating negative externalities.

The universal service idea applied to advanced computer networks - the concern that the cleavage between information "haves" and "have-nots" could be widening - seems to be weightier in the American than in the European

---

10 A complete listing of EU directives since the mid '80s in telecommunications and broadcasting is given at the Internet URL: http://www.ispo.cec.be/infosoc/back.html.

context. Universal service has been an established goal of U.S. telecommunications policy since the beginning of the century; the U.S. was the first to achieve real universal services in traditional telephony in the '60s, when, in some European capitals, the telephone was still considered to be a luxury. With the Clinton/Gore initiative this concept has been extended from telephony to telematics. Although universal service also features in EU documents, it was a late arrival on the agenda and is largely restricted to traditional telecommunications, excluding computer networking (see Chapter 14 for a detailed discussion).

To summarize, the U.S. and EU share similar - but not identical - goals in their information society policies. Each deploys quite distinct "policy mixtures": persuasive and regulative policy instruments dominate in the U.S., whereas a mix of regulative and distributive policies for the superhighway characterise the EU.

Explaining the Differences

Policy differences can be explained by contextual variations such as different technological environments; cultural or ideological differences related to specific attitudes toward new technologies; different economic contexts and industry structures; different political institutional structures; and, not least, different situational interests and actor constellations.

Technological Pools and Environments

Despite the great similarity in European and American R&D capacities in telematics, there is a large gap between them in terms of the social application and implementation of telematic networks and services. To a large extent, this is connected to the liberalization gap between the two continents. In Europe, access to computer networks via telecommunication lines was liberalized only a few years ago, whereas, in the U.S., the liberalization of modems and enhanced telecommunications networks was effected in the early '70s. A multitude of networks and on-line services have flourished on the other side of the Atlantic, but not in Europe.

Therefore, when the superhighway topic made the agenda, the diffusion and usage of high-speed transmission capacities and sophisticated computer networking in the U.S. was far in advance of Europe. Certainly, there are European countries with extensive cable networks, and high penetration rates of on-line service connections, e.g., France with Télétel, and Germany with its great number of ISDN connections. However, the penetration of an integrated computer network infrastructure - such as the Internet - into European telematic activities is still embryonic.

Cultural and Ideological Structures

We find a major difference between the dominant technological ideology of both areas. The American populace are, in general, more optimistic about the capacity of technology to solve social problems. In Europe, by contrast, the prevailing belief (in some quarters, at least) is that technology creates more problems than it solves. The European tendency toward technological pessimism correlates with left-wing party preferences, whereas in the U.S., both conservatives and liberals (e.g., the now forgotten "Atari democrats") take a more positive stance towards telematics, and towards more problematic technologies such as genetic engineering. In the U.S., enthusiasm for telematics is often combined with a Jeffersonian democratic vision; the Internet is sometimes presented as a paradigm case for democratic communication structures. In Europe (especially in countries with long social democratic traditions, such as Germany, the Netherlands, and Denmark) left-wing parties and trade unions generally emphasise the darker implications of new technologies. Potentially negative effects of telematics on civil liberties (the "Orwell syndrome") or "technology as a job-killer" dominate public discourse much more than the positive opportunities which ICTs can bring. Europe's downbeat cultural heritage contrasts with the optimism about, and enthusiasm for, technological advancement that flourishes in American politico-technocratic circles.

Economic and Industrial Structures

Major historical variations also exist between the industrial structures and institutional arrangements of the telecommunications and electronic mass media sectors. In the U.S., there is a rather homogenous industrial space characterized by strong - but pluralist - computer, telecommunications, and media sectors. In contrast, despite major advances in European integration within the last decade, Europe's industrial and commercial space is rather heterogeneous, and in some areas is still characterized by segmented monopolies.

The U.S. is strong in all key components of telematics and multimedia, and - despite some level of concentration - specific sectors are still rather pluralistically patterned. In the late '70s and early '80s, massive deregulation, and the subsequent AT&T divestiture, transformed the former monopoly in telecommunications into pluralist market structures. The personal computer (PC) and network revolution did the same in computing. Europe's industrial structures in the relevant sectors differ amongst themselves, revealing significant structural asymmetries. There are strong telecommunications industries in France and Germany; some major computer suppliers in Germany and Italy; a consumer electronic giant in the Netherlands; and a media giant in Germany. Within the different telematic sectors, there is less plurality than in the USA. The weakness of the computer industry together with the general strength of the telecommunications sector in Europe, may explain Europe's vehement emphasis on the promotion of "hardware prone" Trans-European Telecommunications Networks (ISDN and IBC) in contrast to the rather "software prone" innovations in computer networking.

Political Institutional Structures and Policy Styles

The two political structures are difficult to compare, since the U.S. is a 200-year old political system, whereas the EU polity is just emerging. Both political systems are divided, in the sense that there is no single centre of political power (Laver and Shepsle 1991). However, there are huge differences between the American combination of presidentialism, parliamentarism, and federalism and the more complex European decision-making system. In the U.S., there is strong national government with a potentially high degree of political leadership (presidentialism); a strong but divided (and often paralyzed) parliament; a pluralistic interest group system; and a high degree of regulatory delegation to independent regulatory agencies. Despite these internal divisions (often positively labelled as "checks and balances"), the U.S. system enables more consistent national policy initiatives to be pursued than is the case in the EU.

Despite its strong and relatively cohesive techno-bureaucracy (the Commission), the EU government (i.e., its Council of Ministers) is still comparatively weak in terms of "capacities of collective political action" (Ronit and Schneider 1995). A major reason for this is that decision-making at EU level is based on a mixture of unanimity and qualified majority-voting. Thus, EU policy initiatives always represent compromise. They always tend toward the lowest denominator which, for instance, aims to reconcile the fire of French neo-mercantilism with the water of British neo-liberalism[11]. In addition, political sovereignty between the EU and its member states is divided in such a way that the individual nation state has the final say. While the EU has important legal powers to establish effective regulatory and legal frameworks, the detail is supplied at the level of each member state. This gives room for rather different national strategies and approaches to be pursued in the EU. For instance compare German developments - where even some federal states such as Bavaria, Baden-Wurttemberg, or Brandenburg have their own specific "information society" or "multimedia" policies - with related developments in France, where Télétel and Minitel completely dominate the on-line sector.

A further difference concerns policy style with regard to planning and regulation. In general, the U.S. is more pragmatic and incrementalist in its regulatory design, and is much less planning-oriented then Europe. American regulators do not like to design big regulatory frameworks at the outset, when nobody can really judge what will actually happen in practice. Shaped by its cultural heritage of a rationalist tradition, continental Europe - and, to some degree, Britain too - is much more prone to pre-planning.

With respect to specific patterns of policy-making (i.e., which actors are typically constellated, and which arenas typically receive political attention) both the U.S. and the EU are predominantly pluralist. Both systems involve a large number of actors and interests in their policy processes. Europe's system, however, is more asymmetric than its American counterpart. In Europe, industrial interests enjoy much stronger leverage than do labour and consumer interests. Corporate interest representation is generally supported (in the form of corporate pluralism) in the EU. A related specificity of EU politics is that different interests do not compete openly, but tend to pre-bargain for solu-

---

11 This conflict characterizes EU telecommunications policy-making since its inception (see Schneider et al. 1994).

tions. In contrast, the American policy approach typically involves open competition, often based on adversarial relations between the contending forces. In the U.S. Congress, it is common for a number of similar bills to compete openly during the legislation process. This leads to a market-like process where rhetorical and symbolic elements play a much bigger role than in Europe.

Policies within the EU, in contrast, tend to be bargained on at an early stage of the policy cycle by policy networks which contain relatively few actors. Here, the communications infrastructure of the galaxy of committees is very important. The major actors - besides the EC Commission - are the still-monopolist national telecommunications operators and the telecommunications industry, partly represented by national and European associations, and partly by big European firms directly. Public interest groups and associations of telecommunications and media users have completely peripheral positions in the EU policy arena. These specific EU institutional structures lead to a much lower degree of transparency than those in the U.S. policy arena. Specific U.S. legislation, such as the Freedom of Information Act and the Sunshine Act, ensure that Americans have broad access to information about all relevant policy processes.

Despite the many shortfalls of the EU system of policy-making as a democratic process, the fact that EU policy decisions are usually pre-bargained by the most relevant actors leads to fewer implementation problems in Europe. When agenda setting and programme formulation are evaluated from this perspective, the American NII policy initiatives seem a great deal more uncertain than the EU's with respect to their final policy outcomes. Short-term political and economic change - such as a budget crisis, new electoral majorities, or the election of a new president - may change the American scenery completely.

References

Abernathy, J. (1994), 'Highway Robbery: Selling the Net', PC World, May 1994, 56-66.

Bangemann, Martin et al. (1994), Europe and the global information society. Recommendations to the European Council (Brussels), May 26, 1994. <http://www.ispo.cec.be/infosoc/backg/bangeman.html>

Clinton, W. J. and Gore, A. Jr. (1993), Technology for America's Economic Growth. A New Direction to Build Economic Strength (Washington, D.C.: U.S. Government Printing Office), February 22, 1993. See also <http://www.usgs.gov/public/nii/tech-posit.html>.

Cohen, E. (1992), Le Colbertisme "high tech". Economie des télécoms et du grand projet (Paris: Hachette).

Council on Competitiveness (1993), Vision for a 21st Century Information Infrastructure (Washington, D.C.: COC).

Curwen, P. (1995), 'Telecommunications Policy in the European Union: Developing the Information Superhighway', Journal of Common Market Studies 33, 3: 331-360.

Denkhaus, I. and Schneider, V. (1997), The Privatization of Infrastructures in Germany. In: Lane, Jan-Erik (ed.), Public Sector Reform. Only Deregulation, Privatization and Marketization? (London: Sage, forthcoming).

Drake, W. (1995), 'The National Information Infrastructure Debate: Issues, Interests, and the Congressional Process', in Drake, W. (1995) (ed.), The New Information Infrastructure. Strategies for U.S. Policy (New York: The Twentieth Century Fund Press).

Dutton, W. H. (1992), 'The Ecology of Games in Telecommunications Policy', in Sapolsky, Harvey M. et al. (1992) (eds.), The Telecommunications Revolution (London: Routledge), 65-88.

Feick, J. (1992), 'Comparing comparative policy studies - A path toward integration', Journal of Public Policy, 12(3): 257-285.

Gramlich, E. M. (1994), 'Infrastructure Investment: A Review Essay', Journal of Economic Literature, 32: 1176-96.

Grande, E., and Häusler, J. (1994), Industrieforschung und Forschungspolitik: Staatliche Steuerungspotentiale in der Informationstechnik, (Frankfurt/M.: Campus).

Hohn, H.-W. and Schneider, V. (1991), 'Path-Dependency and Critical Mass in the Development of Research and Technology', Science and Public Policy, 18: 111-122.

Infrastructure Task Force (1993), The National Information Infrastructure: Agenda for Action, Information (Washington, D.C.), September 15, 1993. <Http://www.usgs.gov/public/nii/NII-Agenda-for-Action.html>

Ito, Y. (1980), 'The "Johoka Shakai" Approach to the study of communication in Japan', Keio Communication Review, 1: 13-40.

Latour, B. (1987), Science in Action. How to Follow Scientists and Engineers through Society. Cambridge, (Harvard University Press).

Latzer, M. (1995), 'Japanese Information Infrastructure initiatives', Telecommunications Policy, 19: 515-529.

Laver, M. and Shepsle, K. A. (1991), 'Divided Government : America is Not Exceptional', Governance, 4: 250-269.

Lobet-Maris, C. and d' Udekem-Gevers, M. (1995), 'Comparative and structured analysis of pilot applications promoted by the U.S. and the EU'. Paper presented at the International Conference "The Social Shaping of Information Highways - Comparing the NII and the EU Action Plan", Bremen, 5.-7. October 1995.

Mayntz, R. and Hughes, Th. P. (1998) (eds.), The Development of Large Technical Systems (Frankfurt a. M.: Campus).

Mayntz, R. and Scharpf, F. (1995) (eds.): Gesellschaftliche Selbstregelung und politische Steuerung (Frankfurt a. M.: Campus).

Mayntz, R. and Schneider, V. (1988), 'The Dynamics of System Development in a Comparative Perspective: Interactive Videotex in Germany, France and Britain', in Mayntz, R., and Hughes, T. P. (1988) (eds.), The Development of Large Technical Systems (Frankfurt/M.: Campus), 263-298.

Nora, S. and Minc, A. (1978), L'Informatisation de la Société (Paris: La Documentation Française).

Ronit, K. and Schneider, V. (1995), 'Organisierte Interessen in nationalen und supranationalen Politökologien: Ein Vergleich der G7-Länder mit der Europäischen Union', Paper presented at the Workshop "Verbände in vergleichender Perspektive" (Berlin, 17.-18. November).

Scharpf, F. (1995), Negative and Positive Integration in the Political Economy of European Welfare States (Florenz: EUI) (Jean Monnet Chair Papers #28).

Scharpf, F. (1997), Games Real Actors Play: The Tools of Actor-Centered Institutionalism (Boulder, CO: Westview Press, forthcoming).

Schendelen, M.P.C.M. van (1993) (ed.), National Public and Private EC Lobbying (Dartmouth: Aldershot).

Schneider, V. and Mayntz, R. (1995), 'Akteurzentrierter Institutionalismus in der Technikforschung. Fragestellungen und Erklärungsansätze', in Jahrbuch Technik und Gesellschaft, 107-130.

Schneider, V. (1991), 'The Governance of Large Technical Systems: The Case of Telecommunications', in La Porte, T. R. (1991) (ed.), Responding to Large Technical Systems: Control or Anticipation (Dordrecht: Kluwer), 18-40.

Schneider, V. (1993), Games and Networks in Large Technical Systems: The Case of Videotex, in Scharpf, F. (1993) (ed.), Games in Hierarchies and Networks (Frankfurt: Campus), 251-286.

Schneider, V., Dang Nguyen, G. and Werle, R. (1994), 'Corporate Actor Networks in European Policy-Making: Harmonizing Telecommunications Policy', Journal of Common Market Studies, 32: 473-498.

Schneider, V. and Werle, R. (1991), 'Policy Networks in the German Telecommunications Domain', in Marin, B., and Mayntz, R. (1991) (eds.), Policy Networks. Empirical Evidence and Theoretical Considerations (Frankfurt a.M.: Campus), 97-136.

Théry, Gérard (1994), Les autoroutes de l'information. Rapport au Premier ministre, (Paris: La documentation franÁaise).

Vedel Thierry (1997), Les politiques des autoroutes de l,information en Europe.: convergences et écologies des jeux. In: Revue politiques et management public (forthcoming).

List of Contributors

V.J.J.M. Bekkers, Associate Professor of Public Administration at Tilburg University, the Netherlands.

Michel Berne, Institut National des Télécommunications in Evry, France.

Andrew Blau, Director, Communications Policy and Practice, Benton Foundation, Washington, D.C.

Herbert Burkert, senior researcher at the Gesellschaft für Mathematik und Datenverarbeitung, Sankt Augustin, Germany.

Richard Civille, Director of the Center for Civic Networking, Washington, D.C., U.S.A.

Tarja Cronberg, Regional Council of North Karelia, Joensuu, Finland.

William J. Drake, Associate Director of the Communication, Culture and Technology Program at Georgetown University in Washington, D.C.

William H. Dutton, Professor of Communication and Public Administration at the Annenberg School for Communication at the University of Southern California, Los Angeles, U.S.A.

Louisa Gosling, Researcher in the Political Science Department of the European University Institute in Florence (Italy). Until October 1996, she worked as a telecommunications expert in DG IV of the European Commission.

Marcel Haag, European Commission, General Directorate IV, Brussels, Belgium.

Thomas A. Kalil, Senior Director to the White House National Economic Council, Washington, D.C., with responsibility for science, technology and telecommunications.

Hans J. Kleinsteuber, Professor for Political Science at the University of Hamburg, Germany.

Herbert Kubicek, Professor of Applied Computer Science, University of Bremen, Germany.

Claire Lobet-Maris, Professor at the Institut d'Informatique, Cellule Interfacultaire de Technology Assessment, Namur, Belgium.

James McConnaughey, National Telecommunications and Information Administration, U.S. Department of Commerce, Washington, D.C., U.S.A.

Michael Niebel, European Commission, ISPO, Brussels, Belgium.

Paschal Preston, Director COMTEC, Dublin City University, Dublin, Ireland.

Volker Schneider, Professor for Political Science at the University of Konstanz, Germany.

Thomas R. Spacek, Bellcore, Morristown, N.J., U.S.A.

Marie d'Udekem-Gevers, Institut d'Informatique, Cellule Interfacultaire de Technology Assessment, Namur, Belgium.

Robin Williams, Research Centre for Social Sciences, University of Edinburgh, Edinburgh, Great Britain.

List of Abbreviations and Acronyms

AFL-CIO	American Federation of Labor - Congress of Industrial Organizations
AFTEL	Association Francaise de Télématique
APEC	Asia-Pacific Economic Cooperation
ARD	Arbeitsgemeinschaft der öffentlich-rechtlichen Rundfunkanstalten der Bundesrepublik Deutschland
ARPA	Advanced Research Projects Agency
ATM	Asynchronous Transfer Mode
ATP	Advanced Technology Programme
ATS	Application Technology Satellite (programme)
ATV	Advanced Television
AT&T	American Telephone and Telegraph Corporation
BBC	British Broadcasting Corporation
B-ISDN	Broadband Integrated Services Digital Network
BMFT	Bundesministerium für Forschung und Technologie (Ministry for Research and Technology)
BMWi	Bundesministerium für Wirtschaft (Ministry for Economic Affairs)
BOCs	Bell Operating Companies
BT	British Telecom
BTX	Bildschirmtext
CAD	Computer Aided Design
CATV	Community Antenna Television System
CBS	Columbia Broadcasting System

CCETT	Centre Commun d'Études de Télédiffusion et Télécommunications
CCITT	Comité Consultatif International Télégraphique et Téléphonique
CDU	Christlich-Demokratische Union
CEC	Commission of the European Communities
CLT	Compagnie Luxembourgoise de Télédiffusion
CNC	Computer Numerical Control
CNET	Centre National d'Études des Télécommunications
COREPER	Committee of Permanent Representatives
COST	Cooperation on Scientific and Technical Research
CSPP	Computer Systems Policy Project
CST	Conseil Superieur de la Télématique
CSTB	Computer Science and Telecommunications Board
CSU	Christlich-Soziale Union
CTA	Comité de la Télématique Anonyme
CTA	Constructive Technology Assessment
CTS	Communications Technology Satellite (programme)
DBP	Deutsche Bundespost
DBS	Digital Broadcasting Satellite
DG	Direction Générale
DGT	Direction Générale des Télécommunications
DSF	Deutsches Sport Fernsehen (German Sports Channel)
DSR	Digital Satellite Radio
DSS	Digital Satellite System
DVB	Digital Video Broadcasting
DTH	Direct to Home
EC	European Communities
ERDF	European Regional Development Fund
EU	European Union
FCC	Federal Communications Commission
FDP	Freiheitlich-Demokratische Partei
FTC	Federal Trade Commission

FTTC	Fibre to the Curb
FTTH	Fibre to the Home
GATT	General Agreement on Tariffs and Trade
GDP	Gross Domestic Product
GII	Global Information Infrastructure
GIS	Global Information Society
GTE	General Telephone Company
HDTV	High Definition Television
Hi-OVIS	Highly Interactive Optical Visual Information System
HPCC	High Performance Computing and Communications Initiative
IBC	Integrated Broadband Communications
IBM	International Business Machines Corporation
ICTs	Information and Communication Technologies
IECs	Inter-Exchange Carriers
IITF	Information Infrastructure Task Force
IP	Internet Protocol
ISDN	Integrated Services Digital Network
ISH	Information Superhighway
ISPs	Internet Service Providers
ISPO	Information Society Project Office
ITs	Information Technologies
ITU	International Telecommunication Union
LAN	Local Area Network
LECs	Local Exchange Carriers
LFRs	Less Favoured Regions
MIT	Massachussetts Institute of Technology
MMBG	Multimedia-Betriebsgesellschaft
MPEG	Moving Pictures Expert Group (Standard for Video Compression)
MSG	Media Service GmbH
MTV	Music Television

NAFTA   North Atlantic Free Trade Area
NASA   National Aeronautics and Space Administration
NII   National Information Infrastructure
NSFNET   National Science Foundation Network
NTIA   National Telecommunications and Information Administration
NTT   Nippon Telegraph and Telephone

OECD   Organization for Economic Cooperation and Development
ONA   Open Network Access
ONP   Open Network Provision
OSTC   (Belgian) Federal Office for Scientific, Technical and Cultural
            Affairs
OVS   Open Video Systems

PAL   Phase Alteration Line (Color TV Standard)
PC   Personal Computer
PCS   Personal Communication Service
PEACESAT   Pan-Pacific Education and Communication Experiment by
            Satellite
PEG   Public, Educational, and Governmental (programmes)
PEN   Public Electronic Network
PMS   Picturephone Meeting Service
POTS   Plain Old Telephone System
PTO   Post and Telecommunications Operator
PTT   Post, Telegraph, Telephone
PUC   Public Utility Commission

RACE   Research and Development in Advanced Communication
            Technology in Europe
RBOCS   Regional Bell Operating Companies
R & D   Research and Development
RTL   Radio Television Luxembourg

SCT   Service de Calcul par Téléphone
SEM   Single European Market
SES   Société Européene des Satellites S.A.

SPD	Sozialdemokratische Partei Deutschlands
SST	Social Shaping of Technology

TAP	Telematics Application Programme
TCP/IP	Transmission Control Protocol/Internet Protocol
TEBN	Trans European Broadband Networks
TIIAP	Telecommunications and Information Infrastructure Assistance Programme
TMU	(Danish) Intergovernmental Committee on Information Technology
TPC	Telecommunications Policy Committee (of IITF)
TPR	Telecommunications Policy Roundtable
TVR	Télétel Vitesse Rapide

UFA	Universum Film AG
UK	United Kingdom
USA	United States of America
USAID	U.S. Agency for International Development
USF	Universal Service Fund
USWG	Universal Service Working Group (of IITF)

VoD	Video on Demand

WAN	Wide Area Network
WIPO	World Intellectual Property Organization
WTO	World Trade Organization
WWW	World Wide Web

ZDF	Zweites Deutsches Fernsehen

Index